FOREWORD

by IAN KNIGHT

It will shortly be 125 years since the last sh~~~
Drift, and if anything public interest in that battle is greater than ever. The same
element of desperate courage against overwhelming odds which made the story the
subject of numerous dramatic newspaper illustrations at the time continues to exert
a powerful fascination today. In a very real sense, the men who defended Rorke's
Drift were popular heroes from the very beginning, cheered on occasion through the
streets, and the subject of a high degree of media interest throughout their lives – as
the many accounts from press sources, included in this book, testify. In more recent
times, the feature-film Zulu (1964) has drawn on the folk mythology of Rorke's
Drift, recasting the story in a new and even more potent form for a new age.

In the light of this extraordinary fascination, it is all too easy to lose sight of the
individual experiences of the men who took part in the battle. Our appreciation of
courage after the fact can all to easily lead us to suppose that the defenders of
Rorke's Drift were essentially extraordinary men, the equivalent, perhaps, of some
Victorian 'special services' unit, hand-picked for the task of holding a remote
outpost against an anticipated attack. Yet nothing can be further than the truth. Prior
to the extraordinary events of 22 January 1879, Rorke's Drift was not considered a
particularly important spot; it was merely one of a number of garrisons and supply
depots on the lines of communication of the British columns invading Zululand. No
more than cursory thought had been given to the need to defend it – and even that
had not been put into action before the battle began. There were no great generals or
dashing commanders at Rorke's Drift – on the British side, at least. The most senior
officer was no more than a lieutenant. Nor were B Company, 2nd Battalion, 24th
(2nd Warwickshire) Regiment – who made up the bulk of the defenders – selected
as a garrison by anything more than the luck of routine duties. They were not tough,
battle-scarred veterans; most were young short-service soldiers who had received
their baptism of fire only a few months before on the Eastern Cape Frontier. Had the
battle taken place a day or two later, it is possible B Company might no longer have
been at Rorke's Drift – they might have been replaced, or at the very least reinforced,
by one of the companies who, even on the 22nd, were preparing to march forward
from Helpmekaar. Indeed, if the Zulu response to the British invasion been different
at this early stage of the war, it might even have been some different garrison at some
different outpost upon whom the fury descended, and whose voices would now be
heard through this book.

Nor, in a very real sense, was Rorke's Drift a battle of great strategic consequence.
Despite a widespread belief at the time that its defence prevented a Zulu invasion of
the colony of Natal, this was never in fact likely. The Zulu forces who attacked
Rorke's Drift were not in a position to mount anything other than a limited border
raid, nor does the evidence suggest that they ever intended to do so.

In this book Alan Baynham Jones and Lee Stevenson have accumulated a remarkably comprehensive range of first-hand accounts from British troops who fought at Rorke's Drift, ranging from official and semi-official reports to press interviews and obituaries. Many of the latter are gleaned from regional papers, where the veterans of Rorke's Drift later lived, and died. As one who has returned to the subject of Rorke's Drift several times myself, I stand in awe of their diligence and tenacity in seeking them out. Sadly, they are not matched in either quantity or depth by accounts from Zulu sources, although of course the perspective of the attackers is of equal importance to that of the defenders. Nonetheless, we have tried to add some insights into the way this battle – so celebrated among the British – was regarded in a very different light by the Zulu. In its way, it took as much courage to run up repeatedly to the British barricades, through a curtain of rifle-fire and bayonet thrusts, as it did to stand behind them, although in this battle, more than many, the memory is largely that of the victors.

It is through the words of the defenders – recorded according to the abilities of the individual concerned, often incomplete, sometimes clouded by slips in memory – that one here gains the most vivid insight into the experience and responses of the men who fought at Rorke's Drift. It was fashionable in Victorian times to underplay emotional issues, and it is clear that the defenders of Rorke's Drift were only rarely asked their feelings about the battle. Yet those responses can still be discerned through the stilted and sometimes reticent prose of the day – the sense of desperation, of determination, anger and fear, and finally of the horror of protracted close-quarter killing, which clearly left many survivors afflicted with Post Traumatic Stress Disorder in an age when emotional wounds went entirely untreated.

And that is ultimately what makes Rorke's Drift seem so remarkable, even after the passage of more than a century, when the causes of the Anglo-Zulu War and the uncomfortable implications for the Zulu people are largely forgotten by the wider world, and bloodier, more decisive engagements are remembered only by a handful of enthusiasts.

It is the story of a random cross-section of the Victorian Army, trapped by chance in a momentous and terrifying event outside their control.

It is the story of very ordinary soldiers, caught up in very extraordinary events – and who rose to the challenge.

Ian Knight
Chichester, West Sussex
November 2003

RORKE'S DRIFT
By Those Who Were There

by Alan Baynham Jones and Lee Stevenson

"...probably no more desperate and brilliant defence of a post has ever been chronicled among the gallant deeds of British soldiers than the defence of Rorke's Drift..."

Lt Charles Ernest Commeline,
5th (Field) Company, Royal Engineers, 1879

With a Foreword by IAN KNIGHT

Published by Lee Stevenson Publishing
Brighton, East Sussex

Published by

Lee Stevenson Publishing
80 Hollingbury Park Avenue
Brighton
East Sussex
BN1 7JF

ISBN 0-9541963-1-7

Printed in the UK by

RPM Print & Design
2-3 Spur Road
Quarry Lane
Chichester
West Sussex
PO19 8PR

...Yet master, you'll believe it, I
Was proud the other day -
I didn't first receive it - I
Was in the field away,
A minding of the cattle - when
'Twas told to every one
That Jones's boy in battle had
The cross for valour won.

T'was he that held the gateway, as
The sick were moved away,
Firm planted in the straight way, as
A lion stands at bay.
The savages were many, and
His comrades were but two,
But sturdy chaps as any, and
They found them work to do.

The sun set on them fighting, and
Before he rose again,
The black men and the white men both
Had many brave men slain.
But daylight came at last, and then
The foe was forced to yield,
And scarce a hundred Englishmen
Were masters of the field

They stood by one another there,
Distinction there was none;
They all of them were brothers there,
And Britons everyone -
The proudest title man can bear,
However great he be;
And one the greatest only share
With common folk like me

Extract from "A Country Fellow," by a poet identified simply as
"R.C. 1879"

CONTENTS

INTRODUCTION

Although some 125 years have passed since the end of the Anglo-Zulu War of 1879, the defence of Rorke's Drift remains arguably the most well known of all the military actions fought during the hey-day of the British Empire.

Indeed continuing interest and the seemingly ever growing demand into the Anglo-Zulu campaign and the defence of Rorke's Drift in particular, has seen a constant flow of new books, television documentaries, and more recently a web site devoted to this one specific military action. Whilst there is nothing wrong with that, and we personally as 'enthusiasts' are most keen to foster further genuine historical research in the subject, we feel that the actual original version of the events of January 22nd–23rd, 1879, as told by those men who were actually present at Rorke's Drift, is in danger of being lost and diluted by the growing tendency for 'modern day' analysis and the trend for comparison of 'modern day' 21st Century perspectives to late Victorian values and attitudes. This compilation therefore is merely a selection from our files of, stories, accounts and information about the battle and the participants at Rorke's Drift, be they defender or attacker, which we feel captures the true picture but told from their own perspective.

Our own individual interests in the battle actually spans well over thirty years. During that time we have amassed a considerable collection of material pertaining to the battle itself, and, to a larger extent, the lives of the individual 'defenders,' (of which it is our intention to deal with in a separate volume in due course).

It is noted that a number of the accounts included in this book have already been used in previous published works, many of which are listed in the bibliography. However, we have discovered upon going back to the actual original document that many of the modern versions differ considerably from what was first recorded. As a result therefore, and wherever possible, we have tried to restore to their full original content a number of the altered, and or, abridged accounts which have previously been published and of which, it would appear, have subsequently become accepted as wholly accurate.

The accounts by the 'defenders' fall into three main categories; firstly, those official statements made at the behest of some higher authority, i.e., the 1880 account by John Chard produced by him at the specific request of Queen Victoria, or James Reynolds' official report compiled for the Director General of the Army Medical Department. The second batch, the personal letters of the defenders themselves written to loved ones and friends in the days, weeks and even months after the battle, offer an invaluable insight into the minds of these men in the immediate aftermath of the disaster at Isandlwana and the slaughter of their friends and comrades, but also of their own miraculous survival against quite overwhelming odds at Rorke's Drift. The third selection offers more in-depth and refined accounts. These were written, for the most part, many years after the battle when perhaps the passage of time had allowed space for reflection and for a far greater appreciation of what they had actually experienced back in 1879. Whilst it might be argued that an old soldier might tell any fanciful story for a pint in the pub, there is no easy way of knowing that his version of events is as a result anymore false or fanciful to that of a man whose story is told in a magazine as the 'real' version of events. In fact there are contradictions and inaccuracies found in nearly all of the accounts. It should also not be forgotten that a soldier's immediate perception and subsequent description of a battle, especially one as close and intimate as occurred at Rorke's Drift, is often limited pretty much to those events which took part in front of his own eyes. The publication of successive stories by defender's could therefore easily have some influence over the next man's version of events, and in some cases the influence of these earlier accounts can be clearly seen. Not that this in any way detracts from the truthfulness of the next man's story. In many cases these men had probably been telling the same story unaltered for years and years in the local pub or as a means of entertainment for enthralled grandchildren, largely unaware that anyone else would be at all interested in their story from a long forgotten war.

Any book on the defence of Rorke's Drift remains wholly unbalanced without the inclusion of the perspective of 'the attackers', the Zulu. In compiling this book it became immediately apparent that where Zulu accounts do exist, they were often brief or anecdotal, and were, for the most part, compiled by British officers or officials from statements taken from Zulu prisoners or from old men many years after the war was over. It was clear that simply listing what is known of the Zulu side of the battle would not present a sufficiently clear or balanced picture of their participation at "kwaJim." With that in mind we were most pleased to enlist the help of Ian Knight, arguably the leading authority on the Anglo-Zulu War, who kindly offered his assistance in writing a detailed explanation of the battle based on contemporary Zulu accounts and reports of their view of the battle.

A further chapter deals with the numerous contemporary reports given in the British press, which relate specifically to the defence of Rorke's Drift, and which, in our opinion, offer a real view of the battle as it was received by the public at the time. From the initial confused reports of a great disaster occurring to the British troops at 'Rorke's Drift', subsequently corrected to 'Isandula' or Isandhlwana, to the first full accounts of the defence, and countless snippets and 'private correspondence' from interested parties to the final reports detailing the arrival home of the Heroes of Rorke's Drift.

Where ever possible we have tried to reproduce the accounts as they were first recorded. We have not attempted to alter, punctuate, or omit anything including discrepancies in the spellings, i.e., 'Isandula' for Isandlwana, etc., from the original format.

Alan Baynham Jones & Lee Stevenson
November 2003

ACKNOWLEDGEMENTS

We would like to take this opportunity thank everyone who has offered us assistance over the years, although we hope they will forgive us as the demands of space will prevent us from mentioning everyone. However we would like to thank the following for their material assistance with the production of this book in particular. Ian Knight, for his excellent Foreword and for tackling the subject of Zulu participation, and their subsequent accounts of the battle of Rorke's Drift in such a concise and detailed manner with, "Finished up at Jim's; The Zulu view of Rorke's Drift." We are also most grateful to Ian for granting us access to his extensive library and archive of material on the Anglo-Zulu War; Major Martin Everett, curator of the South Wales Borderers Regimental Museum, for granting us both access and permission to reproduce numerous records from the regimental archives at Brecon, also a special thank you to Celia Green, for her kindness and continuing assistance with our research; Ron Sheeley, for the free use of his photographs; Those nice gentlemen of The Keynsham Light Horse namely; Ian Woodason, Tim Day, Rai England, for their willingness to share information and for the fine job they are doing in locating the graves of the participants of the Anglo-Zulu campaign; The curator and staff of the Soldiers of Gloucestershire Museum, with a special mention going to Manny Schneider. Lt. Col Ian Bennett for granting us permission to reproduce W.A. Dunne's account of the battle from his "Eyewitness in Zululand," and for his help in tracing the letters of Francis Attwood, D.C.M.; Miss Pamela Clark, Registrar, and the staff, at the Royal Archives at Windsor Castle, The British Newspaper Library at Colindale, and the staff of Newport Public Library.

A special thank you to the descendants of the garrison of Rorke's Drift, of which there are perhaps too many to mention by name here, who have been most courteous in allowing us to delve into their family histories over the years. However we would like to extend our especial thanks to the following for their contributions and support with this book, Mrs Cecilia Cheetham, Mrs Kathleen Mysberg, Mrs Rose Morgan and family, Roger Lane for allowing us to quote once again from his father's recollections of Sergt. HE Gallagher, Bill Jones and family, Mrs Rena Mills and family, Mr D. Mason, the family of the late Mr Edwin Ewart, the Prothero family and many more.

In South Africa, we are most grateful for the continued assistance and friendship of Ron Lock, battlefield guide and author; and to our researcher, Mrs Pam Barnes for the excellent job she has done, and continues to do collecting and collating information from the numerous sources at her disposal in Kwa-Zulu Natal and elsewhere; Mrs Bobby Eldridge, archivist at the Killie Campbell Africana Library for her help in locating sources for Zulu accounts of the battle; Diana Madden, archivist of the Brenthurst Library, Johannesburg; the staff of the Kwa-Zulu Natal Archives Depot, Pietermaritzburg, the staff of the Natal Museum, Pietermaritzburg, and the staff of the South African Library, Capetown.

A special mention to Jonathon Harry, and the staff at R.P.M. for their excellent work in the production of this book and to Ian Tyrrell for his excellent cover design.

Finally to our respective families, Irene and Pauline and the children, our thanks for their patience, and perseverance with our continuing fascination/obsession with a 125 year old battle and all the inherent problems that have been created as a result.

CHAPTER 1: THE V.C. WINNERS

Lieutenant John Rouse Merriott Chard, 5th (Field) Company, Royal Engineers

His first official report on the defence of Rorke's Drift: [WO32/7737, The National Archives, (Public Record Office, hereafter P.R.O.), London]. The sections in **BOLD** *appear in the original in Chard's handwriting.*

Rorkes Drift
25th January 1879

Sir,

I have the honour to report that on the 22nd. inst I was left in command at Rorkes Drift by Major Spalding, who went to Helpmakaar to hurry on the Compy. 24th Regt ordered to protect the ponts. -

About 3.15 p.m. on that day, I was at the ponts when two men came riding from Zulu-land at a galop, and shouted to be taken across the river. -

I was informed by one of them, Lieut. Adendorff of Lonsdales Regt (who remained to assist in the defence) of the disaster at Isandhlwana Camp, and that the Zulus were advancing on Rorke's Drift -

The other a Carabineer rode off to take the news to Helpmakaar. -

Almost immediately I received a message from Lieut. Bromhead, commg. the Company 24th Regt at the Camp near the Commt. Stores, asking me to come up at once. -

I gave the order to inspan, strike tents, put all stores &c into the wagon, and at once rode up to the Commt. Store and found that a note had been received from the Third Column to state that the enemy were advancing in force against our post, which we were to strengthen and hold at all costs. -

Lieut. Bromhead was most actively employed in loopholing & barricading the store building and hospital and connecting the defence of the two buildings by walls of mealie bags and two wagons that were on the ground. -

I held a hurried consultation with him and with, Mr Dalton of the Commt. (who was actively superintending the work of defence, and whom I cannot sufficiently thank for his most valuable services) entirely approving of the arrangements made. I went round the position and then rode down to the ponts and brought up the guard of 1 Sergt. + 6 men, wagon &c -

I desire here to mention the offer of the pont man Daniells and Sergt. Milne 3rd Buffs to moor the ponts in the middle of the stream and defend them from their decks with a few men. -

We arrived at the post about 3.30 p.m. Shortly after an officer of Durnford's Horse arrived and asked for orders. I requested him to send a detachment to observe the drifts and ponts to throw out outposts in the direction of the enemy, and check his advance as much as possible, falling back upon the post when forced to retire & assist in its defence. -

I requested Lieut. Bromhead to post his men, and having seen his and every man at his post, the work once more went on.

About 4.20 p.m. the sound of firing was heard behind the hill to our South. The officer of Durnfords returned, reporting the enemy close upon us, and that his men would not obey his orders, but were going off to Helpmakaar, and I saw them apparently about 100 in number going off in that direction. -

About the same time Captain Stephenson's detachment of Natal Native Contingent, left us, as did that officer himself.

I saw that our line of defence was too extended for the small number of men now left us and at once commenced a retrenchment of biscuit boxes. -

We had not completed a wall two boxes high, when about 4.30 p.m. 500 or 600 of the enemy came in sight around the hill to our South and advanced at a run against the South wall. They were met by a well sustained fire, but notwithstanding their heavy loss continued the advance to within 50 yards of the wall, when they met with such a heavy fire from the wall & cross-fire from the store, that they were checked, but taking advantage of the cover afforded by the cook-house, ovens &c kept up a heavy fire. -

The greater number however, without stopping moved to the left around the hospital and made a rush at our N.W. wall of mealie bags, but after a short but desperate struggle were driven back with heavy loss into the bush around the work.

The main body of the enemy were close behind and had lined the ledge of rock and caves overlooking us about 400 yards to our South from where they kept up a constant fire and advancing somewhat more to their left than the first attack, occupied the garden, hollow road & bush in great force.

Taking advantage of the bush which we had not time to cut down, the enemy were able to advance under cover close to our wall, and in this part soon held one side of the wall, while we held the other. -

A series of desperate assaults was made extending from the hospital along the wall as far as the bush reached, but each was most splendidly met and repulsed by our men with the bayonet. Corpl. Schiess N.N.C. greatly distinguishing himself by his conspicuous gallantry. -

The fire from the rocks behind us, though badly directed, took us completely in reverse and was so heavy that we had suffered very severely, and about 6 p.m. were forced to retire behind the retrenchment of biscuit boxes. -

All this time the enemy had been attempting to force the hospital and shortly after set fire to its roof -

The Garrison of the hospital defended it room by room, bringing out all the sick who could be moved before they retired -

Privates Williams, **Hook, R. Jones** and **W.** Jones 24th Regt. being the last men to leave, holding the doorway with the bayonet, their own ammunition being expended. From the want of interior communication and the burning of the house it was impossible to save all. With most heartfelt sorrow I regret we could not save these poor fellows from their terrible fate.

Seeing the hospital burning and the desperate attempts of the enemy to fire the roof of the stores, we converted two mealie bag heaps, into a sort of redoubt which gave a second line of fire all round, Asst. Commy. Dunne working hard at this though much exposed, and rendering valuable assistance. -

As darkness came on we were completely surrounded and after several attempts had been gallantly repulsed were eventually forced to retire to the middle and then inner wall of the Krall on our East. The position we then had we retained throughout. -

A desultory fire was kept up all night and several assaults were attempted and repulsed; the vigour of the attack continuing until after midnight, our men firing with the greatest coolness did not waste a single shot; the light afforded by the burning hospital being of great help to us. -

About 4 a.m. 23rd inst. the firing ceased and at daybreak the enemy were out of sight over the hill to the South West. We patrolled the ground collecting the arms of the dead Zulus, and strengthened our defences as much as possible.

We were removing the thatch from the roof of the stores when about 7 am a large body of the enemy appeared on the hills to the SW. -

I sent a friendly Kaffir, who had come in shortly before, with a note to the Officer Commanding at Helpmakaar asking for help. -

About 8 am the third column appeared in sight, the enemy who had been gradually advancing, falling back as they approached I consider the enemy who attacked us to have numbered about 3,000 (three thousand).

We killed about 350 (three hundred & fifty).

Of the steadiness and gallant behaviour of the whole garrison I cannot speak too highly

I wish especially to bring to your notice the conduct of

Lieut Bromhead 2/24th Regt and the splendid behaviour of his Company B 2/24th

Surgeon Reynolds AMD, in his constant attention to the wounded under fire where they fell

Acting Commt. Officer Dalton to whose energy much of our defences were due, and who was severely wounded while gallantly assisting in the defence

Asst. Commy. Dunne

Acting store keeper Byrne (Killed)

Col. Sergt. Bourne, 2/24th

Sergt. Williams 2/24th (wounded dangerously since dead)

Sergt. Windridge 2/24th

Corpl. Schiess 2/3 Natal Native Contgt (wounded)

1395 Private Williams 2/24th	**Private Hook 2/24th**
593 Private **W.** Jones 2/24th	**716 Private Jones 2/24th**
Private McMahon A.H.C.	**Private Roy 1/24th**

The following return shows the number present at Rorke's Drift 22nd Jany. 1879:

	Officers	NCO Men	Sick Officers	Sick Men	Total
Staff		1			1
Royal Artillery	1			3	4
Royal Engineers	1	1			2
3rd Buffs		1			1
1/24th Regt.		6		5	11
2/24th Regt.	1	81		17	99
90th Lt. Infantry				1	1
Commt. & Transport Dept.	3	1			4
A.M.D.	1	3			4
Chaplain	1				1
Natal Mounted Police				3	3
Natal Native Contgt.	1			6	7
Ferryman		1			1
	8	96	0	35	139

The following is a list of the killed

Sergt. Maxfield   2/24th Regt.
Pte   Scanlon   "   "
"   Haydon   "   "
"   Adams   "   "
"   Cole   "   "
"   Fagan   "   "
"   Chick   "   "
1398 Pte Williams 2/24th Regt.
Pte   Nicolls   1/24   Regt
"   Horrigan   1/24   "
"   Jenkins   1/24   "
Mr Byrne Commt. Dept.
Trooper Hunter N.M. Police
"   Anderson N.N.C.
1 Pte (Native)   "

Total 15
12 wounded * of whom two have since died
viz, Sergt. Williams, 2/24th Regt.
Private Beckett,   1/24th   "
Making a total killed of 17
* List already forwarded by Medical Officer

Herewith is appended a plan of the buildings showing our lines of defence
The points of the compass referred to in this report are as shown in sketch approximately magnetic

I have the honor to be
Your obedient servant
John R.M. Chard
Lieut., R.E.

To Col Glyn, CB.,
Comg 3rd Column.

"The Brighton Examiner," March 18th, 1879

The Defence of Rorke's Drift

Lieutenant Chard's report of the defence at Rorke's Drift is the most cheering document which has, up to this moment, arrived from South Africa. The numerous friends of Lord Chelmsford have been defending him on the score of his many undoubted virtues and excellencies, which only fail when he is in chief command. Lord Chelmsford has given another proof of the nobility of his character in the few lines prefixed to Lieutenant Chard's report. There is no sign of a pretty mind in the hearty praise which the defeated general grants to the victorious lieutenants. He extols the readiness which took advantage of every scrap of cover, and made a sketchy but sufficient breastwork out of mealie bags. If Lord Chelmsford continues to command her Majesty's forces in Zululand he will doubtless take a lesson from Lieutenants Chard and Bromhead. The businesslike and careful report of Lieutenant Chard is in strong contrast to the melancholy narrative of Isandula. There is here no hesitation, no haziness. Lieutenant Chard observed all that passed with the watchfulness of a dispassionate looker-on. When Lord Chelmsford's forces were seen on the other side, the Zulus withdrew, and Chard's task was over. He and Bromhead has saved the colony, and had shown the forethought, coolness, determination, and courage of true commanders. We now know the perils which the desertion of their native contingent added to the situation. We see that they had but an hour in which to fortify their post, and that while panic was busy on every side. Their achievement, and that of their men, will never be forgotten in English history.

"The Natal Colonist," May 17th, 1879

Rumoured Death Of Major Chard, R.E.

We were sorry to hear a rumour in town yesterday, based evidently on pretty liable authority, that Major Chard, R.E., had died at Helpmakaar of fever. It is quite unnecessary to remind our readers who Major Chard is. If it should transpire that the statement is correct, another very sad incident has to be added to the many melancholy events connected to the war.

An unidentified 'rival' Natal newspaper, c. May 1879

Major Chard, R.E.

The *Colonist* on Saturday, stated it was sorry to hear, on good authority, that Major Chard, one of the heroes of Rorke's Drift was dead. The report, we are glad to say, was quite unfounded, and was brought to us on Friday. We found however, on enquiry at the proper quarters, that there was no foundation for it. Major Chard is in hospital, and is, we are glad to hear, recovering from the attack of fever, from which he has recently been suffering.

"The Natal Colonist," May 22nd, 1879

Major Chard, V.C.

It is with very great pleasure that we are able to contradict the report of the death of this valiant soldier, to which we reluctantly gave currency, although, only as a report, not a fact, as amiable contemporaries assert. We are glad to state that he is now reported nearly well, and will shortly resume his duties. such men can be ill spared.

"The Times," October 18th, 1879

Major Chard, V.C., and Surgeon-Major Reynolds, V.C.

Last evening Major Chard, V.C., and Surgeon-Major Reynolds, V.C., were entertained at dinner by the Wanderers' Club, Pall-mall, 'in recognition of their splendid defence of Rorke's Drift.' There was nothing formal about the proceedings, which were altogether of a social and friendly character. Lord Headley was in the chair, and had the guests of the evening on his right and left. Among the company, which numbered about a hundred, were Major-General Sir Hastings Doyle, Colonel Hope, V.C., Colonel Bousfield, M.P., Major-General Raines, C.B., Sir F. Perkins, M.P., Colonel J. Ward, Colonel E. Galt, Dr. Swettenham, Captain W. Oughton Giles, Mr. W. Jameson, Mr. P. Penn-Gaskell, Captain Jameson, Mr. C. Armstrong, and Mr. C.W.E. Pineo, secretary.

After the usual loyal toasts,

The CHAIRMAN proposed 'The Army, Navy, and Auxiliary Forces.'

Sir HASTINGS DOYLE, in returning thanks for the Army, remarked that he had spent 21 long years serving with the gallant 24th Regiment (Cheers.)

Mr. Armstrong responded for the Navy, and Captain W.O. Giles and Colonel Bousfield for the Auxiliary Forces.

The CHAIRMAN, in proposing the toast of the evening, said he believed he was within the mark in stating that at Rorke's Drift 120 or 130 men rendered a good account of something like three or four thousand enemies. (Cheers.) At all events, four or five hundred bodies were found on the field next morning. He felt it would be impossible for any eloquence to exaggerate the services which those men rendered to the State; but he was sure that all who heard him were too well aware of the important effects to the British Army and the whole Empire from their gallant services to need any words of his to describe them. (Cheers.)

Major Chard, who on rising to return the thanks was received with loud cheers, said he was sure that none of those who had taken part in the defence of Rorke's Drift ever realized the great interest taken in them by the people of England. since he landed a few days ago he had travelled from one end of the kingdom to the other, and had everywhere met a kind reception and a hearty welcome, which showed what people thought of what they did that day. (Cheers.) But he always felt that those who did honour to him did honour to those who took part in that defence, and he was always sorry that he was receiving it alone. (Cheers.) It was a pleasure now to receive hospitality in company with one who had acted so gallantly at the time as Surgeon-Major Reynolds (hear, hear); but it was unnecessary for him to say any more of his gallant friend. The gallant officer on his right (Sir Hastings Doyle) had alluded to his connexion with the 24th Regiment, and had paid him a very high compliment. Proud as that gallant officer was to have served with that regiment, it would be ever a pride and pleasure to himself to have been associated with Major Bromhead and the other gallant lads of that regiment. (Loud cheers.) In conclusion he thanked them most heartily for the kind way in which they had spoken of him, and for the splendid entertainment they had given him. (Loud cheers.)

Three hearty cheers were here given for Major Bromhead and the 24th Regiment.

Surgeon-Major Reynolds, who on rising was also received with enthusiasm, said he thanked them very much for the cordial way in which his health had been proposed and received. It was very gratifying to him to have found on his return to this country that his own club should have taken such an interest in the conduct of one of its members when far away, and above all that it should have given him such a welcome. (Cheers.) The genial greeting which he had received in a telegram before he left the ship made him very proud. During the time he had been abroad, now about six years, he had met with some hardships and privations, but he had never looked back with the smallest regret to any of them, because he believed they had done much to earn for him the good wishes and good opinions of such friends as he saw around him that night. (Cheers.) He felt he had been very lucky in having had an opportunity of doing his duty in circumstances of difficulty and danger, and he was glad that his friends who were present tonight though he had done his duty. (Cheers.)

"The Western Daily Mercury," November 17th, 1879
[Chard is speaking on the occasion of the presentation of a sword of honour in Plymouth.]

"...I cannot but feel grateful to those brave fellows to whose devoted gallantry I owe the fact of my being here to-day...You all know how they behaved and how, one and all, they proved themselves ready to sacrifice their lives if necessary for their Queen and their country...I read in the paper as I came down to-day how Bromhead and myself had a tankard of ale together on the morrow of the affair of Rorke's

Drift...The story is very true, except the point about the tankard as there were none of those about there...But we did have a bottle of beer together, and you may imagine that we congratulated ourselves heartily on having come out safely from that business..."

"...Those Zulus were an enemy that it was some credit to us to have defeated. Their bravery and courage could not have been excelled, and their military organisation and their discipline might have given a lesson to more civilised nations. Cruel and savage as they were, the Zulus were, however, a gallant enemy, and I cannot understand for one moment how Englishmen could ever have been brought to believe the reports that appeared and the stories that were circulated of cruelties perpetrated, or, at all events, permitted, by British officers. I don't think it necessary for me to say they were false - it appears to me that they carried denial on the face..."

"The Royal Engineers Journal," December 1st, 1879, [reporting further details of Chard's speech at the same occasion].

"...And if, war does happen, and a time of danger and difficulty may arise, and the odds may appear against us, I pray to God that men like Bromhead, Dalton and Reynolds, and the rest of the brave fellows who were with us at Rorke's Drift may be with me on that occasion..."

An account of the defence of Rorke's Drift, compiled at the personal request of H.M. Queen Victoria. Submitted to the Queen at Windsor Castle, February 21st, 1880. The subheadings shown in **Bold** *are actually written in the margin of the original document: [The Royal Archives, Windsor. Appears by kind permission of H.M. Queen Elizabeth II].*

RORKE'S DRIFT

Start from Durban
Early in January 1879, shortly after the arrival of the 5th Compy., Royal Engineers, at Durban, an order came from Lord Chelmsford directing that an officer and a few good men of the R.E., with mining implements, etc., should join the 3rd Column as soon as possible.

I was consequently sent on in advance of the company, with a light mule wagon, containing the necessary tools, etc., and in which the men could also ride on level ground; with a Corporal, three Sappers and one Driver, my batman, who rode one, and looked after my horses.

The wagon was driven by a Cape black man, with a Natal Kaffir lad as vorlooper.

Bad Roads
The roads were so bad, that in spite of all our exertions, our progress was slow, and although we got a fresh team at PieterMaritzburg, we did not reach Rorke's Drift until the morning of the 19th Jany. 1879.

Arrive at Rorke's Drift
The 3rd Column was encamped on the other side (left bank) of the river Buffalo, and the wagons were still crossing the Ponts.

I pitched my two tents on the right (Natal) bank of the river, near the Ponts, and close to the store accummulated there for keeping them in repair.

3rd Column leave Rorke's Drift
On the 20th Jany., the 3rd Column broke up its camp on the Buffalo River and marched to Isandhlwana, where it encamped, and the same evening, or following morning,

Durnford arrives at Rorke's Drift
Colonel Durnford's force arrived and took up its camp near where the 3rd Column had been.

Ponts
There were two large Ponts at the river, one of which only was in working order, and my sappers were during this time working at the other, which was nearly finished, to get it also in working order.

Sappers ordered to Isandhlwana
Late in the evening of the 21st Jany. I received an order from the 3rd Column to say that the men of the R.E., who had lately arrived, were to proceed to the camp at Isandhlwana at once.

I had received no orders concerning myself.

I reported this to Major Spalding, who was now in command at Rorke's Drift, and also pointed out to him that the sappers leaving, there were no means at my disposal for putting the Ponts in working order, or keeping them so.

Major Spalding had also received no orders respecting me, except that I was to select a suitable position protecting the Ponts, for Capt. Rainforth's Compy. 1/24th to entrench itself.

I consequently asked, and obtained permission from Major Spalding to go to the camp at Isandhlwana and see the orders. -

Take sappers to Isandhlwana
On the morning of the 22nd January, I put the corpl and 3 sappers in the empty wagon, with their field kits, etc., to take them to the camp of the 3rd Column; and also rode out myself. -

The road was very heavy in some places, and the wagon went slowly; so I rode on in advance, arrived at the Isandhlwana camp,

Arrive at Isandhlwana
went to the Head Quarter tent, and got a copy of the orders as affecting me, & found that I was to keep the Ponts &c. in working order, & also the road between

Helpmakaar and Rorke's Drift and the orders also particularly stated that my duties lay on the <u>right</u> bank of the river Buffalo.

A N.C.O. of the 24th Regt. lent me a field glass, which was a very good one, and I also looked with my own,

See the Enemy

and could see the enemy moving on the distant hills, and apparently in great force. Large numbers of them moving to my left, until the lion hill of Isandhlwana, on my left as I looked at them, hid them from my view. The idea struck me that they might be moving in the direction between the camp and Rorke's Drift, and prevent my getting back, and also that they might be going to make a dash at the ponts.

Meet Durnford

Seeing what my duties were, I left the camp, and a quarter of a mile, or less, out of it, met Col. Durnford R.E., riding at the head of his mounted men. -

I told him what I had seen, and took some orders, and a message all along his line, at his request. -

At the foot of the hill, I met my men in the wagon and made them get out, and walk up the hill with Durnford's men. -

Return to Rorke's Drift

I brought the wagon back with me to Rorke's Drift, where on arrival I found the following order had been issued. The copy below was given me, & preserved from the fact of its being in my pocket during the fight.

COPY

Camp Rorke's Drift
22nd Jany. 1879

Camp Morning Orders

1. The force under Lt Col Durnford, R.E., having departed, a Guard of 6 privates and 1 NCO will, be furnished by the detachment 2/24th Regt. on the Ponts.
A Guard of 50 armed natives will likewise be furnished by Capt. Stevenson's detachment at the same spot. - The Ponts will be invariably drawn over to the Natal side at night.
This duty will cease on the arrival of Capt. Rainforth's Company, 1/24th Regt.

2. In accordance with Para 19 Regulations for Field Forces in South Africa, Capt. Rainforth's Company, 1/24th Regt., will entrench itself on the spot assigned to it by Column Orders per. - dated -

(sd). H. Spalding, Major,
Commanding.

The Guard as detailed was over the Ponts. -
Capt. Rainforth's company had not arrived. -

Report to Spalding

I went at once to Major Spalding on arrival, told him what I had seen, and pointed out to him that in the event of an attack on the Ponts, it would be impossible with 7 men (not counting the natives) to make an effective defence. -
(According to the orders, Capt. Rainforths compy. should have been already at Rorke's Drift.) Major Spalding told me he was going over to Helpmakaar, and would see about getting it down at once. -
Just as I was about to ride away he said to me
"Which of you is senior, you or Bromhead"?
I said, "I dont know"
He went back into his tent and looked at an Army list, and coming back, said -

Left in commd by Spalding

"I see you are senior, so you will be in charge, although, of course, nothing will happen, and I shall be back again this evening early."
I then went down to my tent by the river, had some lunch comfortably, and was writing a letter home, when my attention was called to two horsemen galopping towards us from the direction of Isandhlwana. -

2 Fugitives from Isandhlwana arrive

From their gesticulations, and their shouts, when they were near enough to be heard, we saw that something was the matter, and on taking them over the river, one of them, Lieut. Adendorff of Lonsdale's

Lt Adendorff N.N.C.

Regiment Natal Native Contingent, asking if I was an officer, jumped off his horse, took me on one side, and told me, that the camp was in the hands of the Zulus, and the army destroyed; that scarcely a man had got away to tell the tale, and that probably Lord Chelmsford and the rest of the column had shared the same fate. -
His companion, a Carbineer, confirmed his story. -
He was naturally very excited, and I am afraid I did not, at first, quite believe him, and intimated that he probably had not remained to see what did occur.
I had the saddle put on my horse, and while I was talking to Lieut. Adendorff,

message from Bromhead

a messenger arrived from Lieut. Bromhead, who was with his Company at his little camp near the Commt. Stores, to ask me to come up at once. -
I gave the order to inspan the wagon, and put all the stores, tents, &c., we could into it. I posted the sergt. and six men on the high ground over the Ponts, behind a natural wall of rocks, forming a strong position from which there was a good view over the

river & ground in front, with orders to wait until I came or sent for them. - The guard of natives had left some time before and had not been relieved. -
I gallopped up at once to the

Ride up to Rorke's Drift
Commissariat Stores and found that a pencil note had been sent from the 3rd Column by Capt. Allan Gardner to state that the enemy were advancing

News of Enemy Advancing
in force against our post. -

Work commenced
Lieut. Bromhead had, with the assistance of Mr Dalton, Dr Reynolds and the other officers present, commenced barricading; and loopholing the Store building and the Missionary's house, which was used as a Hospital, and connecting the defence of the two buildings by walls of mealie bags, and two wagons that were on the ground.

Native Contingent
The Native Contingent, under their officer, Capt. Stephenson, were working hard at this with our own men, and the walls were rapidly progressing.

Letter sent by Bromhead to O.C. Helpmakaar
A letter describing what had happened had been sent by Bromhead by two men of the Mounted Infantry, who had arrived fugitives from Isandhlwana to the Officer Commanding at Helpmakaar. -
These two men crossed the river at Fugitives Drift, with some others, and as they have since reported to me, came to give notice of what had happened, to us at Rorkes Drift, of their own accord, and without orders from anyone. -

Consult with Bromhead & Dalton
I held a consultation with Lieut. Bromhead, and with Mr Dalton, whose energy, intelligence and gallantry were of the greatest service to us, and whom, as I said in my report at the time, and I am sure Bromhead would unite with me in saying again now, I cannot sufficiently thank for his valuable services. -
I went round the position with them and then rode down to the Ponts where I found everything ready for a start, ponts in midstream, hawsers & cables sunk &c. -

Daniells and Sergt. Milne 3rd Buffs
It was at this time that the Pontman Daniells, and Sergeant Milne, 3rd Buffs, who had been employed for some time in getting the ponts in order, & working them under Lieut. MacDowell, RE (killed at Isandhlwana), offered to defend the Ponts, moored in the middle of the river, from their decks with a few men. -

Sergt. Williams 24th
Sergeant Williams 24th and his little guard were quite ready to join them. -

Arrive at Commt. Store
We arrived at the Commissariat Store about 3.30 p.m.

Some of Durnford's Horse arrive
Shortly afterwards an officer of Durnford's Horse reported his arrival from Isandhlwana, and I requested him to observe the movements, and check the advance, of the enemy as much as possible until forced to fall back. -
I saw each man at his post, and then the work went on again. -

Fugitives
Several fugitives from the camp arrived, and tried to impress upon us the madness of an attempt to defend the place. -
Who they were I do not know, but it is scarcely necessary for me to say that there were no officers of HM Army among them. -
They stopped the work very much - it being impossible to prevent the men getting around them in little groups to hear their story. -
They proved the truth of their belief in what they said, by leaving us to our fate, and in the state of mind they were in, I think our little garrison was as well without them.

Lt. Adendorff
As far as I know, but one of the fugitives remained with us - Lieut. Adendorff, whom I have before mentioned. -
He remained to assist in the defence, and from a loophole in the store building, flanking the wall and Hospital, his rifle did good service. -

Sergt. Windridge 24th Regt.
There were several casks of rum in the Store building, and I gave strict orders to Sergt. Windridge, 24th Regt., who was in charge (acting as issuer of Commt stores to the troops), that the spirit was not to be touched, the man posted nearest it was to be considered on guard over it, and after giving fair warning, was to shoot without altercation anyone who attempted to force his post, and Sergt. Windridge being there was to see this carried out. -
Sergt. Windridge showed great intelligence and energy in arranging the stores for the defence of the Commt. store, forming loopholes, &c. -

Rev. Geo. Smith
The Revd. George Smith, Vicar of Estcourt, Natal and acting Army Chaplain, went for a walk (before the news of the disaster reached us) to the top of the Oscarberg, the hill behind Rorke's Drift. -

Mr Witt

Mr. Witt, the missionary, went with him, or met him there. They went to see what could be seen in the direction of the Isandhlwana camp. -

Smith

He saw the force of the enemy which attacked us at Rorke's Drift, cross the river in three bodies -and after snuff-taking, and other ceremonies, advance in our direction. - He had been watching them for a long time with interest, and thought they were our own Native Contingent. -

There were two mounted men leading them, and he did not realise that they were the enemy until they were near enough for him to see that these two men also had black faces. -

He came running down the hill, and was agreeably surprised to find that we were getting ready for the enemy. Mr. Witt, whose wife and family were in a lonely house not very far off, rode off, taking with him a sick officer, who was very ill in the hospital and only just able to ride. -

Mr. Smith, however, although he might well have left, elected to remain with us, and during the attack did good service in supplying the men with ammunition. -

Sound of Firing

About 4.20 p.m. the sound of firing was heard behind the Oscarberg. -

The officer of Durnford's returned reporting the enemy close upon us, and that his men would not obey his orders but were going off to Helpmakaar,

Durnford's Horse leave

and I saw them, about 100 in number, going off in that direction. -

I have seen these same men behave so well since that I have spoken with several of their conduct - and they all said, as their excuse, that Durnford was killed, and it was no use. -

Native Contingent Desert

About the same time Capt. Stephenson's detachment of Natal Native Contingent left us - probably most fortunately for us.-

I am sorry to say that their Officer, who had been doing good service in getting his men to work, also deserted us. -

We seemed very few, now all these people had gone, and I saw that our line of defence was too extended,

Retrenchment made

and at once commenced a retrenchment of biscuit boxes, so as to get a place we could fall back upon if we could not hold the whole. -

Private Hitch 24th

Private Hitch 24th was on top of the thatch roof of the Commt. Store keeping a look-out. -

He was severely wounded early in the evening, but notwithstanding,

Corpl Allen 24th

with Corpl Allen 24th who was also wounded, continued to do good service, and they both when incapacitated by their wounds from using their rifles, still continued under fire serving their comrades with ammunition. -

Attack commenced 4.30 p.m.

We had not completed a wall two boxes high when, about 4.30 p.m., Hitch cried out that the enemy was in sight, and we saw them, apparently 500 or 600 in number, come around the hill to our south (the Oscarberg) and advance at a run against our south wall. -

We opened fire on them, between five & six hundred yards, at first a little wild, but only for a shot or two, a chief on horseback

Private Dunbar 24th

was dropped by Private Dunbar 24th, the men were quite steady, and the Zulus began to fall very thick. -

However it did not seem to stop them at all, although they took advantage of the cover and ran stooping with their faces near the ground. It seemed as if nothing would stop them, and they rushed on in spite of their heavy loss to within 50 yards of the wall, when they were taken in flank

Zulus checked

by the fire from the end wall of the store building, and met with such a heavy direct fire from the mealie wall, and the Hospital at the same time, that they were checked as if by magic. -

They occupied the Cook house ovens, banks and other cover, but the greater number, without stopping, moved to their left around the Hospital, and made a rush at the end of the Hospital,

1st Assault

and at our N.W. line of mealie bags. -

There was a short but desperate struggle during which Mr. Dalton shot a Zulu who was in the act of assegaing a corpl. of the Army Hospital Corps, the muzzle of whose rifle he had seized, and with Lieut. Bromhead and many of the men behaved with great gallantry. -

The Zulus forced us back from that part of the wall immediately in front of the Hospital, but after suffering very severely in the struggle were driven back into the bush around our position. -

Main body of Enemy
The main body of the enemy were close behind the first force which appeared, and had lined the ledge of rocks and caves in the Oscarberg overlooking us, and, about three or four hundred yards to our south, from where they kept up a constant fire. - Advancing somewhat more to their left than the first attack, they occupied the garden, hollow road, and bush in great force. -
The bush grew close to our wall & we had not time to cut it down -
The enemy were thus able to advance under cover close to our wall, and in this part soon held one side of the wall, while we held the other.-

Series of Assaults
A series of desperate assaults was made, on the Hospital, and extending from the Hospital, as far as the bush reached; but each was most splendidly met and repulsed by our men, with the bayonet. Each time as the attack was repulsed by us, the Zulus close to us, seemed to vanish in the bush, those some little distance off, keeping up a fire all the time. -
Then, as if moved by a single impulse, they rose up in the bush as thick as possible, rushing madly up to the wall (some of them being already close to it), seizing, where they could, the muzzles of our men's rifles, or their bayonets, and attempting to use their assegais and to get over, the wall. -
A rapid rattle of fire from our rifles, stabs with the bayonet, and in a few moments the Zulus were driven back, disappearing in the bush as before, and keeping up their fire. - A brief interval, and the attack would be again made, and repulsed in the same manner. -
Over and over again this happened, our men behaving with the greatest coolness and gallantry.-
It is impossible for one individual to see all, but I particularly myself noticed the behaviour of Col. Sergt. Bourne 24th, Sergt. Williams 24th, Corpl. Scheiss N.N.C., Corpl. Lyons 24th, Private McMahon A.H.C., Privates Roy, Deacon, Bush, Cole, Jenkins 24th, and many others.-
Our fire at the time of these rushes of the Zulus was very rapid - Mr. Dalton dropping a man each time he fired his rifle, while Bromhead and myself used our revolvers. - The fire from the rocks and caves on the hill behind us

Fire from Oscarberg takes us in reverse
was kept up all this time and took us completely in reverse, and although very badly directed, many shots came among us and caused us some loss - and at about 6.00 p.m.

Enemy extends his attack
the enemy extending their attack further to their left, I feared seriously would get in over our wall behind the biscuit boxes. -
I ran back with 2 or 3 men to this part of the wall and was immediately joined by Bromhead with 2 or 3 more. The enemy stuck to this assault most tenaciously, and

on their repulse; and retiring into the bush, I called all the men inside our retrenchment - and the enemy immediately occupied the wall we had abandoned and used it as a breastwork to fire over. -

Mr Byrne killed

Mr. Byrne, acting Commissariat Officer, & who had behaved with great coolness and gallantry, was killed instantaneously shortly before this, by a bullet through the head, just after he had given a drink of water to a wounded man of the N.N.C.

Enemy fire and Break into Hospl.

All this time the enemy had been attempting to force the Hospital and had at length set fire to its roof and got in at the far end. - I had tried to impress upon the men in the Hospital the necessity for making a communication right through the building - unfortunately this was not done. -

Probably at the time the men could not see the necessity, and doubtless also there was no time to do it. - Without in the least detracting from the gallant fellows who defended the Hospital, and I hope I shall not be misunderstood in saying so - I have always regretted, as I did then, the absence of my four poor sappers, who had only left that morning for Isandhlwana and arrived there just to be killed. -

The gallant Defence of the Hospital

The garrison of the hospital defended it with the greatest gallantry, room by room, bringing out all the sick that could be moved, and breaking through some of the partitions while the Zulus were in the building with them. -

Private Williams, Hook, R. Jones, W. Jones 24th

Privates Williams, Hook, R. Jones & W Jones being the last to leave and holding the doorways with the bayonet their ammunition being expended. -

Private Williams' bayonet was wrenched off his rifle by a Zulu, but with the other men he still managed with the muzzle of his rifle to keep the enemy at bay. -

Reynolds

Surgeon Reynolds carried his arms full of ammunition to the Hospital, a bullet striking his helmet as he did so. -

But we were too busily engaged outside to be able to do much, and with the Hospital on fire, and no free communication, nothing could have saved it. -

Sergt. Maxfield killed

Sergeant Maxfield 24th might have been saved, but he was delirious with fever, refused to move and resisted the attempts to move him. -

He was assegaied before our men's eyes. -

Seeing the Hospital burning, and the attempts of the enemy to fire the roof of the Store (one man was shot, I believe by Lt Adendorff, who had a light almost touching the thatch),

Redoubt of Mealie Bags

we converted two large heaps of mealie bags into a sort of redoubt, which gave a second line of fire all around, and formed a strong position to hold, and rally round, in case the store building had to be abandoned, or the enemy broke through elsewhere. -

Dunne

Asst. Commy Dunne worked hard at this; from his height, being a tall man, he was much exposed, in addition to the fact that the heaps were high above our walls, and that most of the Zulu bullets went high. -

Trooper Hunter N.M.P. Killed

Trooper Hunter, Natal Mounted Police, escaping from the Hospital, stood still for a moment hesitating which way to go, dazed by the glare of the burning Hospital, and the firing that was going on all around. - He was assegaied before our eyes, the Zulu who killed him immediately afterwards falling. -

Dalton severely wounded

While firing from behind the biscuit boxes, Dalton, who had been using his rifle with deadly effect, and by his quickness and coolness had been the means of saving many men's lives, was shot through the body. -

I was standing near him at the time, and he handed me his rifle so coolly that I had no idea until afterwards of how severely he was wounded. - He waited quite quietly for me to take the cartridges he had left out of his pockets. -

We put him inside our mealie sack redoubt, building it up around him. -

Good shooting of Pte. Dunbar 24th

About this time I noticed Private Dunbar 24th make some splendid shooting, seven or eight Zulus falling on the ledge of rocks in the Oscarberg to as many consecutive shots by him. -

Corpl Lyons 24th

I saw Corpl. Lyons hit by a bullet which lodged in his spine, and fall between an opening we had left in the wall of biscuit boxes. I thought he was killed, but looking up he said,

"Oh, Sir! you are not going to leave me here like a dog?" - We pulled him in and laid him down behind the boxes - where he was immediately looked to by Reynolds.

Corpl Scammle N.N.C.

Corpl. Scammle of the Natal Native Contingent, who was badly wounded through the shoulder, staggered our under fire again, from the Store building where he had been put, and gave me all his cartridges, which in his wounded state he could not use. -

Pte Jenkins 24th

While I was intently watching to get a fair shot at a Zulu who appeared to be firing rather well, Private Jenkins, 24th, saying look out Sir, gave my head a duck down just as a bullet whizzed over it. - He had noticed a Zulu who was quite near in another direction, taking a deliberate aim at me. -

For all the man could have known, the shot might have been directed at himself. -

I mention these facts to show how well the men behaved and how loyally worked together. -

Corpl Schiess N.N.C.

Corpl. Scheiss, Natal Native Contingent, who was a patient in Hospital, with a wound in the foot, which caused him great pain, behaved with the greatest coolness and gallantry throughout the attack, and at this time creeping out a short distance along the wall we had abandoned, and slowly raising himself, to get a shot at some of the enemy who had been particularly annoying, his hat was blown off by a shot from a Zulu the other side of the wall. -

He immediately jumped up, bayonetted the Zulu and shot a second, and bayonetted a third who came to their assistance, and then returned to his place. -

Darkness

As darkness came on we were completely surrounded. The Zulus wrecking the camp of the company 24th and my wagon which had been left outside, in spite of the efforts of my batman, Driver Robson (the only man of the Royal Engineers with us), who had directed his particular attention to keeping the Zulus off this wagon in which were, as he described it, "Our things." -

They also attacked the East end of our position, and after being several times repulsed, eventually got into the kraal,

Enemy drive us out of Kraal

which was strongly built with high walls, and drove us to the middle, and then to the inner wall of the kraal - the enemy occupying the middle wall as we abandoned it. - This wall was too high for them to use it effectively to fire over, and a Zulu no sooner showed his head over it than he was dropped, being so close that it was impossible to miss him. -

Troops from Helpmakaar

Shortly before this, some of the men said they saw the red-coats coming on the Helpmakaar road. -

The rumour passed quickly round - I could see nothing of the sort myself, but several men said they could. -

A cheer was raised, and the enemy seemed to pause, to know what it meant -

But there was no answer to it, and darkness came on -

It is very strange that this report should have arisen amongst us, for the two companies 24th from Helpmakaar, did come down to the foot of the hill, but not, I believe, in sight of us. -

They marched back to Helpmakaar on the report of Rorkes Drift having fallen. -

After the first onslaught, the most formidable of the enemy's attacks was just before we retired behind our line of biscuit boxes, and for a short time after it, - when they had gained great confidence by their success on the Hospital. -

Although they kept their positions behind the walls we had abandoned, and kept up a heavy fire from all sides until about 12 o'clock, they did not actually charge up in a body to get over our wall after about 9 or 10 o'clock. -

After this time it became very dark, although the Hospital roof was still burning - it was impossible from below to see what was going on, and Bromhead and myself getting up on the mealy sack redoubt, kept an anxious watch on all sides. -

Enemy in force all around

The enemy were now in strong force all around us, and every now and then a confused shout of "Usutu" from many voices, seemed to show that they were going to attack from one side and immediately the same thing would happen on the other, leaving us in doubt as to where they meant to attack. -

Fire slackens

About midnight or a little after the fire slackened, and after that, although they kept us constantly on the alert, by feigning, as before, to come on at different points, the fire was of a desultory character. - Our men were careful, and only fired when they could see a fair chance. The flame of the burning hospital was now getting low, and as pieces of the roof fell, or hitherto unburnt parts of the thatch ignited, the flames would blaze up illuminating our helmets & faces. - a few shots from the Zulus, replied to by our men - again silence, broken only by the same thing repeatedly happening. -

This sort of thing went on until about 4 a.m. and we were anxiously waiting for day break and the renewal of the attack, which their comparative, and at length complete silence, led us to expect. -

Daybreak

But at daybreak the enemy were out of sight, over the hill to our South West. -

A plucky Zulu

One Zulu had remained in the kraal and fired a shot among us (without doing any damage) as we stood up on the walls, and ran off in the direction of the River - although many shots were fired at him as he ran, I am glad to say the plucky fellow got off. -

patrol around

Taking care not to be surprised by any ruse of the enemy, we patrolled the ground around the place, collecting the arms, and ammunition, of the dead Zulus. -

Curious Wounds
Some of the bullet wounds were very curious.

One man's head was split open, exactly as if done with an axe. -

Another had been hit just between the eyes, the bullet carrying away the whole of the back of his head leaving his face perfect, as though it were a mask, only disfigured by the small hole made by the bullet passing through. -

One of the wretches we found, one hand grasping a bench that had been dragged from the Hospital, and sustained thus in the position we found him in, while in the other hand, he still clutched the. knife with which he had mutilated one our poor fellows, over whom he was still leaning. -

Strengthen the Defences.
We increased the strength of our defences as much as possible, strengthening and raising our walls, putting sacks on the biscuit boxes, &c, and were removing the thatch from the roof of the Commt. Store, to avoid being burnt out in case of another attack,

Enemy re-appear
when at about 7 A.M., a large body of the enemy, (I believe the same who had attacked us), appeared on the hills to the South West. -

I thought at the time that they were going to attack us, but from what I now know from Zulus, and also of the number we put hors de combat, I do not think so. -

I think that they came up on the high ground to observe Lord Chelmsford's advance; for from there they could see the Column, long before it came in sight of us. -

Friendly Kaffir sent to Helpmakaar
A frightened & fugitive Kaffir came in shortly before, and I sent for Daniells, the Pontman, who could speak Zulu a little, to interview him. -

Daniells had armed himself with Spalding's sword, which he flourished in so wild and eccentric a manner that the poor wretch thought his last hour was come. -

He professed to be friendly and to have escaped from Isandhlwana, and I sent him with a note to the Officer Commanding at Helpmakaar, explaining our situation, and asking for help; for now, although the men were in excellent spirits, and each man had a good supply of ammunition in his pouches or pockets, we had only about a box and a half left besides, and at this time we had no definite knowledge of what had happened, and I myself did not know that the part of the Column with Lord Chelmsford had taken any part in the action at Isandhlwana, or whether on the Camp being taken he had fallen back on Helpmakaar. -

The enemy remained on the hill, and still more of them appeared, when about 8 A.M.

3rd Column appears
the Column came in sight, and the enemy disappeared again. - There were a great many of our Native Levies with the column, and the number of red coats seemed so few that at first we had grave doubts that the force approaching was the enemy. - We

improvised a flag, and our signals were soon replied to from the Column. -
The mounted men crossed the Drift and galloped up to us, headed by Major Cecil
Russell and Lieut. Walsh, and were received by us with a hearty cheer. -

Lord Chelmsford arrives
Lord Chelmsford, with his staff, shortly after rode up, and thanked us all with much
emotion for the defence we had made. -
The column arrived, crossing by the Ponts, and we then had a busy time in making
a strong position for the night. -
I was glad to seize an opportunity to wash my face in a muddy puddle, in company
with Private Bush 24th; whose face was covered with blood from a wound in the
nose caused by the bullet which had passed through & killed Private Cole 24th. -
With the politeness of a soldier, he lent me his towell, or, rather a very dirty half of
one, before using it himself, & I was very glad to accept it. -

A bottle of beer with Bromhead
In wrecking the stores in my wagon, the Zulus had brought to light a forgotten bottle
of beer, and Bromhead & I drank it with mutual congratulations on having come
safely out of so much danger. -

My wagon driver's escape
My wagon driver, a cape (coloured) man, lost his courage on hearing the first firing
around the hill. - He let loose his mules and retreated concealing himself in one of
the caves of the Oscarberg. -
He saw the Zulus run by him and, to his horror, some of them entered the cave he
was in, and lying down commenced firing at us. -
The poor wretch was crouching in the darkness; in the far depths of the cave, afraid
to speak or move, and our bullets came into the cave, actually killing one of the
Zulus. - He did not know from whom he was in the most danger - friends or foes, -
and came down in the morning looking more dead than alive. -
The mules were recovered; they were quietly grazing by the riverside. -

My vorlooper's escape
On my journey homewards, on arriving at the railway station, Durban, I asked a
porter to get me some Kaffirs to carry my baggage to the Hotel. - He sent several,
and the first to come running up was my vorlooper boy who had taken me up to
Rorke's Drift. - He stopped short and looked very frightened, and I believe at first
thought he saw my ghost. -
I seized him to prevent his running away, and when he saw that I was flesh and
blood, he became reassured. - He said he thought I had been killed, and upon my
asking him how he thought I got away. He said (the solution of the mystery just
striking him),
"I know, you rode away on the other horse" -

As far as I could learn and according to his own story, - the boy had taken the horse I rode up from the river to the Commt. stores, and, wild with terror, had ridden it to PieterMaritzburg without stopping, where he gave it over to the Transport people - But having no certificate to say who he was, they took the horse from him and would not give him any employment. -

Escapes from the Hospital
During the fight there were some very narrow escapes from the burning Hospital.

Private Waters 24th
Private Waters, 24th Regt. told me, that he secreted himself in a cupboard, in the room he was defending, and from it shot several Zulus inside the Hospital. - He was wounded in the arm, and remained in the cupboard until the heat and smoke were so great that they threatened to suffocate him. - Wrapping himself in a cloak, or skirt of a dress, he found in the cupboard, he rushed out into the darkness, and made his way into the Cookhouse. - the Zulus were occupying this, and firing at us from the wall nearest us. -

It was too late to retreat, so he crept softly to the fireplace and, standing up in the chimney, blacked his face and hands with the soot. - He remained there until the Zulus left. -

He was very nearly shot in coming out, one of our men at the wall raising his rifle to do so at the sight of his black face and strange costume - but Waters cried out just in time to save himself. -

He produced the bullet that wounded him, with pardonable pride, and was very amusing in his admiring description of Dr Reynold's skill in extracting it. -

Gunner Howard, R.A.
Gunner Howard, R.A. ran out of the burning hospital, through the enemy, and lay down on the upper side of the wall in front of our N Parapet. - The bodies of several horses that were killed early in the evening were lying here, and concealed by these, by Zulu bodies & the low grass and bushes, he remained unseen with the Zulus all around him until they left in the morning. -

Private Beckett 24th
Private Beckett, 24th Regt. escaped from the hospital in the same direction - he was badly wounded with assegais in running through the enemy. -

He managed to get away and conceal himself in the ditch of the Garden - where we found him next morning. -

The poor fellow was so weak from loss of blood that he could not walk, and he died shortly afterwards. -

Mealie bag walls replaced
Our mealie-bag walls were afterwards replaced by loopholed walls of stone, the

work making rapid progress upon the arrival of half the 5th Company R.E. with Lieut. Porter. As soon as the sappers arrived, we put a fence around, and a rough wood cross over, the graves of our poor men who were killed.

Monument to the dead
This was afterwards replaced by a neat stone monument & inscription, by the 24th, who remained to garrison the place. -
I have already, in my report, said, how gallantly all behaved, from Lieutenant Bromhead downwards, and I also mentioned those whom I had particularly noticed to have distinguished themselves. -

Number of Enemy killed
On the day following, we buried 351 bodies of the enemy in graves not far from the Commt Buildings - many bodies were since discovered and buried, and when I was sick at Ladysmith one of our Sergeants, who came down there invalided from Rorke's Drift, where he had been employed in the construction of Fort Melvill - told me that many Zulu bodies were found in the caves and among the rocks, a long distance from the Mission house, when getting stone for that fort. -
As, in my report, I underestimated the number we killed - so I believe I also underestimated the number of the enemy that attacked us - and from what I have since learnt I believe the Zulus must have numbered at least 4,000. -
As the Revd. Geo. Smith said in a short account he wrote to a Natal Paper -
"Whatever signs of approval may be conferred upon the defenders of Rorkes Drift, from high quarters, they will never cease to remember the kind and heartfelt expressions of gratitude which have fallen both from the columns of the Colonial Press and from so many of the Natal Colonists themselves"
And to this may I add that they will ever remember with heartfelt gratitude the signs of approval that have been conferred upon them by their Sovereign and by the People and Press of England.

JOHN R.M. CHARD
Captain & Bt Major, RE
January 1880 -

Surgeon James Henry Reynolds, M.B., Army Medical Department.

Extract from "The Army Medical Department Annual Report," Appendix V for 1878: [courtesy the Curator, Army Medical Services Museum, Aldershot]

REPORT OF THE DEFENCE OF "RORKE'S DRIFT"

On January the 22nd at about 12.30 p.m. we were surprised at Rorke's Drift by hearing big guns in our neighbourhood, and almost immediately I commenced climbing up the hill of Oscarberg in company with the Missionary Met, and Mr Smith, Army Chaplain. We expected to get a view of what was happening, but on looking across the Buffalo River from the top we discovered that Isandlana Mountain (five miles away) shut from our view the scene of action. The reports of three more guns were distinctly audible after we completed the ascent, there being, I should say, a quarter of an hour's interval between each of them.

At 1.30 a large body of natives marched over the slopes of Isandlana in our direction, their purpose evidently being to examine ravines and ruined kraals for hiding fugitives.

These men we took for our own Native Contingent. Soon afterwards appeared four horsemen on the Natal side of the river galloping in the direction of our post, one of them was a regular soldier, and feeling they might possibly be messengers for additional medical assistance I hurried down to the hospital and got there as they rode up. They looked awfully scared and I was at once startled to find one of them riding Surgeon Major Shepard's pony. They shouted frantically, "The camp at Isandlana has been taken by the enemy and all our men in it massacred, that no power could stand against the enormous number of Zulus, and the only chance for us all was by immediate flight."

Lieutenant Bromhead, Acting Commissary Dalton, and myself forthwith consulted together, Lieutenant Chard not having as yet joined us from the pontoon, and we quickly decided that with barricades well placed around our present position a stand could best be made where we were.

In other words, removing the sick and wounded would have been embarrassing to our movement, and desertion of them was never thought of.

Just at this period Mr. Dalton's energies were invaluable. Without the smallest delay, which would have been so fatal for us, he called upon the men (all eager for doing) to carry the mealie sacks here and there for defences, and it was charming to find in a short time how comparatively protected we had made ourselves. Lieutenant Chard arrived as this work was in progress and gave many useful orders as regards the lines of defence. He approved also of the hospital being taken in, and between the hospital orderlies, convalescent patients (8 or 10) and myself, we loopholed the building and made a continuation of the commissariat defences round it. The hospital however, occupied a wretched position having a garden and shrubbery close by, which afterwards proved so favourable to the enemy, but comparing our prospects with that of the Isandlana affair we felt that the mealie barriers might afford us a moderately fair chance. The patients I must mention were retained in the hospital although situated at our weak end, as every part of the commissariat house was crowded with stores, and we did not consider either building would be taken unless with the fall of the whole place.

When our plans of temporary defence were nearly completed, I was relieved by seeing Mr. Met, and Mr. Smith safely inside the laager. They had just then returned from the hill where they remained up to a late moment continuing to believe the natives I before alluded to were our men, instead of which they were the very Zulus who fought against us later on at Rorke's Drift. Mr. Smith was at this time looking for his horse and told me afterwards he should have to remain as his Kafir groom had bolted, and apparently taken with him the horse.

Mr. Met, was making preparations to ride away.

About 3.30 p.m. the enemy made their first appearance in a large crowd on the hospital side of our post, coming on in skirmishing order at a slow slinging run. We opened fire on them from the hospital at 600 yards, and although the bullets ploughed through their midst and knocked over many there was no check or alteration made in their approach. They seemed quite regardless of the danger, and what struck me as most strange they had no war cry, nor did they at this time fire a single shot in return.

As they got nearer they became more scattered, but the large bulk of them rushed for the hospital and the garden in front of it. My attention being altogether directed for a while to these points I cannot state with authority whether the Zulus whom I shortly afterwards saw in a large number on the opposite or north side of our fort got there by extending this body or if they came independently from the other direction, thereby carrying out their reputed mode of attack in a bull's horn fashion.

However it was, we found ourselves quickly surrounded by the enemy with their strong force holding the garden and shrubbery. From all sides, but especially the latter places, they poured on us a continuous fire, to which our men replied as quickly as they could reload their rifles; again and again the Zulus pressed forward, and retreated until at last they forced themselves so daringly and in such numbers as to climb over the mealie sacks in front of the hospital, and drove the defenders from there behind an entrenchment of biscuit boxes, hastily formed with much judgement and forethought by Lieutenant Chard, R.E. I discovered afterwards that this officer when planning our defences reckoned on the assistance of the Basutos who deserted at the last moment.

It followed from this that our men at first had to be distributed over so large an area in proportion to our numbers as dangerously to weaken any one point and render it unequal to repel a determined rush, I am convinced but for this entrenchment our fort could not have held out five minutes longer.

A heavy fire from behind it was resumed with renewed confidence and with little confusion or delay, checking successfully the natives, and permitting a semi flank fire from another part of the laager to play on them destructively. At this time too the loopholes in the hospital were made great use of, so that the combined fire had the desired effect of keeping the Zulus at bay. It was, however only temporary as after a short respite they came on again with redoubled vigour. Some of them gained the hospital verandah and there got hand to hand with our men defending the doors. Once they were driven back from here, to find shelter again in the garden, but others soon pressed forward in their stead, and having occupied the verandah in larger numbers than before pushed their way into the hospital where confusion on our side naturally followed. Everyone tried to escape as best he could, and owing to the rooms not communicating with one another the difficulties were insurmountable.

Private Hook, 2/24th Regiment, who was acting hospital cook, and Private Connolly, 2/24th Regiment, a patient in hospital, made their way into the open at the back of the hospital, by breaking a hole in the wall with a pickaxe and then climbing over the sacks into the curtailed laager. Most of the patients escaped through the small window looking into what may be styled the neutral ground. Those who madly tried to get off by leaving the front of the hospital were all killed with the exception of Gunner Howard. He gained with most extra ordinary luck a detached rear without being noticed by the enemy, and after dusk, the Zulus still close about him, he left this retreat to hide himself in the long grass 400 or 500 yards away. He did not rejoin us until daylight the following morning when it was no longer dangerous to move about.

Private Hunter, Natal Mounted Police, was the only one killed of those who made an escape through the small window. He was shot dead while crossing over to the biscuit boxes after his exit through the window, by a fire from the enemy behind mealie sacks.

The only men killed in the hospital, were three, excluding a Kafir under treatment for a compound fracture of femur. Their names were Sergeant Maxfield, Private Jenkins, both unable to assist in their escape (being debilitated by fever), and Private Adams, who was well able to move about but could not be persuaded to leave his temporary refuge in a small room, and face the danger of an attempt at escape to the laager. During this partial success of the enemy, very heavy firing was being made on our fort from all sides, and it was in this period we lost a large majority of our killed and wounded. The engagement continued more or less until about 7 o'clock p.m. and then when we were beginning to consider our situation rather hopeless the fire from our opponents appreciably slackened giving us some time for reflection. Lieutenant Chard here again shined in resource. Anticipating the Zulus making one more united dash for the fort and possibly gaining an entrance, he converted an immense stack of mealies standing in the middle of our enclosure and originally cone fashioned, into a comparatively safe place for a last retreat. I would explain that the top of the cone was removed and a number of sacks taken out from the heart of what remained, forming a sheltered space, sufficient to accommodate about 40 men, and in a position to make good shooting. Mr. Dunne, Commissariat officer, assisted in this work. Just as it was completed smoke from the hospital appeared and shortly burst into flames. The light given by it, however, proved advantageous to us *(it being now nightfall)*, a matter which the Zulus themselves must have recognised, as no further attack was made from that quarter. During the whole night following desultory firing was carried on by the enemy, and several feigned attacks were made, with much shouting of their war cry, but nothing of a continued or determined effort was again attempted by them. About 6 o'clock a.m. we found, after careful reconnoitring, that all the Zulus, with exception of a couple of stragglers, had left our immediate vicinity, and soon afterwards a large body of men were seen at a distance in Zululand marching towards us. For a long time, and even after redcoats were distinguished through our field glasses, we believed them to be the enemy, some of them dressed in the kits of those who had fallen at Isandlana. Indeed we could not think otherwise, as the Basuto officer who escaped with his men from Isandlana and retreated on our post the day before reported that the General's party had been broken up into small lots, each trying to get back into the Colony by any route.

Not until the mounted infantry, forming an advanced party, crossed the Buffalo drift, about a quarter of a mile off, were we convinced of our relief. Then we raised a white flag *(for they were not certain of us either, seeing the hospital still smoking)*, and gave three cheers, really feeling that it was all right for us.

I do not think it possible that men could have behaved better than did the 2/24th and the Army Hospital Corps *(three)*, who were particularly forward during the whole attack, as well as odds and ends of other regiments who happened to be present at Rorke's Drift on the occasion. It would be difficult to pick out the heroes from our garrison, but Corporal Schiess of the Natal Native Contingent *(a Swede by birth)* came under my notice as the most deserving of praise and recommendation.

Extract from "The V.C.," (a magazine), c. 1903.

HOW V.C.'S ARE WON.
A TALE OF RORKE'S DRIFT. Told By Its Last V.C.

This spare, well-dressed gentleman, with silver hair, spectacles, and soft modulated voice, who smokes his cigarette at the club, and discusses the topics of the town with a pleasant relish for life, stood in a ring of mealie sacks by the Buffalo River on the scorching afternoon of January the 22nd 1879, and helped to unlock the many fingered black hand that had suddenly crept round the mountain and clutched at the flag of England.

Lieutenant Colonel J. H. Reynolds, V.C., was in those days a man of thirty-five, an Army doctor of Irish birth, a man with many years knowledge of Africa at his back - a knowledge which proved of great avail when the black hand came round the mountain.

"Tell me," I asked him, "the story as you remember it" There are many people, be it known, who consider that the tale has not yet been told with completeness; in any case, it is a story that will never grow tedious with the telling.

"I remember," he said, smiling, "my feeling of disappointment when Lord Chelmsford marched away with his army, and left me with about a hundred other men to sit still and bite the bullet of inactivity at Rorke's Drift. There was to be no fighting for us, no doctoring for me: the army moved away to gain glory, and we sat down in what Lord Halsbury would call a sort of a base, to envy the other chaps their chances!

But the dust had hardly cleared away from behind the heels of Chelmsford's force when we heard in the distance the booming of big guns. 'If we can't fight,' said I, 'at least we can look on - and off we went, clambering up the hill called Oscarberg to get a view of the battle. However, when we arrived on the top and looked across the Buffalo River, we discovered - to our indignation with Nature! - that the

Isandlana mountain - five miles away completely cut off the view. The firing we had heard, I must tell you, began at 12.30, and it was an hour after that we saw a body of native troops scrambling about on Isandlana. We took them for our own Native contingent and wondered how the other side was fairing. In the midst of our wonderment three horsemen appeared in the distance riding for dear life. I thought they might be coming for some medical aid, and hurried down old Oscarberg to meet them. I was thinking of my chances of going forward to join our victorious army.

But their tale wore a whiter face. The British force at Isandlana had been wiped away, like a speck from a piece of paper: crushed, beaten, destroyed, massacred by an overwhelming force of Zulus. We must fly for our lives - as quick as we could. I consulted with Bromhead (Chard had not then joined us from the pontoon) and an ex Colour-Sergeant, Dalton by name. The result of this conference was the determination to barricade ourselves with mealie sacks and to await the impi from Isandlana. It was here that Dalton proved something of a god in our ramshackle car. The Colour Sergeant returned to him in a minute, and he was here, there and everywhere, quietly getting the men to put their backs into the work, The mind of that man was the working of destiny. Now I must tell you we built a fairly big laager to permit of the friendly Basutos joining us; but when they came and found that to fight with the white man meant fighting to the death shut up with no means of escape Not for this child! said Master Basuto, and wishing us the best of good luck trotted away to the safety of the open.

Bromhead, at this point, certainly saved the situation by cutting the laager in half by means of biscuit tins. But for that we should have been smashed to pieces - not a doubt of it. He saw the wisdom of concentrating our defence in the nick of time, and accomplished it. But this traverse meant leaving the hospital, with my thirty five patients, outside our laager. So I and a few orderlies set about loopholing and rendering it as strong as we could. We had to leave the patients there, for every part of the commissariat house was crowded with stores.

At 3.30 p.m. a swarm of Zulus came round the crook of the mountain at a slow, slinging trot, spreading themselves out in skirmishing order, and made straight at us, an innumerable swarm of blacks. They came in perfect silence - no war-whoops, no dancing, no shouting, and holding their fire. Striking looking figures, of great physical beauty, the Martini in one hand, the assegai slung across the back - fresh from the massacre of Isandlana, running in perfect silence to wipe out the little body of left-behinds at Rorke's Drift

At six hundred yards we opened fire on them from the hospital, and I must confess we were a little put to it by the impotence of our volley. On they came at the same slow, slinging trot, their heads forward, their arms outspread, their bodies poised in a sort of aim at our mealie circus, and all in a dead silence. Here and there a black body doubled up, and went writhing and bouncing into the dust; but the great host came steadily on, spreading out spreading out - spreading out till they seemed like a giant pair of nut-crackers opening round the little nut of Rorke's Drift. It was nasty, really nasty, the inevitability of that silent closing in upon us.

Well, the main body got to the hospital, and seized on that position, with its cover of garden and shrubbery, to pour in upon us a galling fire. It was a frightful oversight - the leaving of that garden and shrubbery. Heavens! they rained lead on us at the distance of a cricket pitch or two. We could only withdraw our forces from the hospital into the smaller laager behind the biscuit-tins. One patient refused to run the short distance - persuasion, everything was vain; he preferred rather to stay there and be butchered than to face the ordeal of that brief run. Another patient it was impossible to remove, and we had to leave him there to be killed. Ah! poor fellow! And sometimes, thinking it over, I cannot help feeling that I might somehow or another have devised escape for him. I cannot help feeling it. But it's hard to think coolly in a rush of that kind.

The rest us just a story of sticking to it. We stood up face to face, white men and black, and blazed at each other till nightfall. They broke in upon us, and we drove them out. They hammered at us, and we struck the hammer up. And then God sent the night and the flag was still flying. We expected another attack, and Chard constructed a cone-shaped stack of mealies in the middle of our laager for a last stand; But the Zulus set fire to the hospital, lighted themselves up for us in lurid flames against the darkness, and we poured in death upon them with a rush that swept them away. Desultory firing was continued throughout the night, but no big rushing attack; and in the morning - they were gone!"

"And how did you win your Cross?"

"Oh ! I carried ammunition to the hospital!"

"During the attack?"

"Yes."

"That must have been rather nasty."

"It wasn't nice. But - well it's just a sense of responsibility, that's all one had to do it, it was one's duty, and a bullet through my helmet was my only wound!"

And he sits in his club thinking of some possible plan whereby he might have saved that single life in the hospital.

Extract from "The British Medical Journal," March 19th, 1932.
A statement made by Mr. Walter G. Spencer, based on his recollections of conversations between himself and Surgeon Lt. Col. James Henry Reynolds, V.C.

Whilst Colonel Reynolds was in charge of the Pimlico Clothing Department he frequently sent workers to Westminster Hospital for treatment and later he came to me about his health, the last time at the beginning of 1929. Then a cancer, for which grave operation would previously have been called for, disappeared in about ten days under radium. Colonel Reynolds was thus able to walk at the head of the V.C.'s at the Thanksgiving Ceremony, and to be present at the dinner in the House of Lords. Our conversations often returned to Rorke's Drift, and from the notes I jotted down I have picked out a few of his reminiscences which I have not noticed in print. There were 36 patients in the hospital, most in different stages of typhoid fever. No preparations had been made for the defence of the station. Reynolds was the senior officer, having been already six years in South Africa; Bromhead and Chard were young subalterns, just out from England; Dalton was an Army non-com, who had rejoined, and had had experience in the methods of defence employed by the Boers, and when fugitives from Isandhlwana reached Rorke's Drift it was first proposed to evacuate the station, but Reynolds declared that to be impossible. Even if the convoy could cross the river the ascent of the opposite bank was so long and steep that the Zulus would certainly catch it up. It was Dalton who arranged the defence with mealie bags. When the Zulus came into view there appeared horsemen in scarlet, and the cry was that the cavalry were returning, but Reynolds pointed out that the riders were not rising in their saddles, but sat the horses as did natives. Coming nearer, the Zulu impi drew up and ceremoniously took snuff, heralding a charge to the uttermost. A few Zulus got into the garden and into the hospital before two patients in bed could be got within the laager; a third lost his head, took a wrong turning, and was also killed. The remaining 33 cases were saved and survived the subsequent stench.

A letter written by JRM Chard in response to a request from Surgeon General J.A. Woolfryes for corroboration of Reynolds' actions at Rorke's Drift. (see also Dalton's statement): [WO138/3, The National Archives, (P.R.O.), London]

The P.M.O.
S. Africa
Ladysmith
6th April 1879

Sir,
With reference to your letter and statement of Mr Dalton (returned herewith) -
I have the honor to state that I did not myself witness the occurrence described by Mr Dalton, - With regard to Mr Dalton 's remarks as to Surgeon Reynolds' activity and energy in helping in the work of defence I can corroborate them entirely. -
The wounded were not able to be removed there being no men spare for that purpose - Surgeon Reynolds without the slightest hesitation attended to these men performing the necessary operations and placing them under as good cover as could be got, where they fell. -
In my official report of the action at Rorke's Drift on the 22 23rd Jany last - I brought Surgeon Reynolds name to the particular notice of his Excellency the Lieut General Commanding for his constant attention to the wounded under fire -
I have the honor to be Sir
Your most obedient servant
John R.M. Chard.
Lt. R.E.

Public Presentation of the Victoria Cross to Two Officers of the 1-24th Regiment

A special parade of all the troops there encamped was held at Pinetown at 8 a.m. on Tuesday, August 26th. The 17th Lancers, the 1-24th, the 3rd Buffs, and the depot battalions (numbering all told, upwards of 2000 men) were present. Colonel Glyn having called upon Surgeon-Major Reynolds and Lieutenant Browne, both of the 1-24th regiment to step forward, announced, that by special permission, he had been deputed to present to each of them the decoration - of which any man might well be proud - of the Victoria Cross. To Dr. Reynolds it was awarded for bravery during the defence of Rorke's Drift; and to Lieutenant Browne for heroic conduct in saving the life of one of the mounted infantry under his command at Zlobane. The Colonel then dismounted from his horse and pinned the ribbon and cross upon the breast of each of the recipients; and with evident emotion he congratulated them, and trusted that they might for many years be spared to enjoy the high honour that they had won. The band of the 3rd Buffs performed and many residents and visitors were present at the interesting ceremony. Amongst the visitors was the Rev. George Smith, the chaplain formerly to Colonel Glyn's column, and latterly to the second division. Mr. Smith, as is well known, took an active part in the defence of Rorke's Drift, rendered good service to the wounded and dying, and performed the last offices of the church over the slain upon the battle field of Ulundi.

We have seen how a brave doctor has been well and properly rewarded; how a V.C. has been added to his well merited promotion, whilst the College in which he was trained have conferred upon him two of its highest degrees.

With the clergyman above referred to how different matters stand. We see no expression of Royal favour - in the shape of an order of merit; no sign of approbation on the part of high dignitaries in ecclesiastical or academical quarters!

With reference to the letter of the Aboriginal Protection Society to The Times, and quoted in our issue of August 26th, our readers may be glad to learn that when Cetywayo's messengers, Umfunzi and Nkisimane, arrived in Lord Chelmsford's camp near Emtonjaneni, the Rev. George Smith, the chaplain to the second division, volunteered to accompany them to the King's kraal. The General thanked Mr. Smith for his offer, but did not deem it advisable to run the risk of complicating matters.

We note this to show that there was "a gentleman of character and position" on the spot, who was ready and willing to perform the services so ostentatiously proffered and advertised by Mr. Chesson's correspondent.

Acting Assistant Commissary James Langley Dalton, Army Commissariat Department

Dalton's letter to Surgeon General J.A. Woolfryes testifying to the actions of Surgeon Reynolds at Rorke's Drift: [WO138/3 The National Archives, (P.R.O.), London]

Deputy Surgeon General,

Agreeably to your request, I beg to make the following statement with reference to the part taken by Surgeon Reynolds A.M.D. On the afternoon of the 22nd January last when intelligence of the disaster at Isandhlwana reached Rorkes Drift it was resolved by Lieut. Bromhead, in conversation with Surgeon Reynolds and myself, to hold the Post at all costs and we at once set about connecting the Hospital and Commst. Store by means of two breast works of mealie bags. Surgeon Reynolds was most energetic in causing the Hospital to be barricaded and loopholed in anticipation of the threatened attack, both in voice and jesture encouraged the men to hasten the completion of the work.

On the repulse of the first attack the defenders of the Hospital ran short of ammunition and shouted loudly for more. All the other officers and men being hotly engaged, Surgeon Reynolds (who was with the main body behind the Retrenchment of biscuit boxes) instantly volunteered to convey the ammunition, and filling his folded arms and pockets with as many cartridges as he could carry he ran from behind the entrenchment of biscuit boxes across the intervening space, a distance of about 25 yards, and swept by the enemy's cross fire to the Hospital, receiving a bullet through his helmet in the crossing. Having succeeded in supplying the defenders of the Hospital with the ammunition he returned at once across the same exposed space to attend to the wounded.

PMBurg 28th March 1879
J.L. Dalton
A.A.C.

A letter written by JRM Chard in response to a request from Commissary General E. Strickland for corroboration of Dalton's bravery prior to a recommendation for a V.C. being made: [WO32/7386, The National Archives, (P.R.O.), London]

To Sir Edward Strickland K.C.B

Durban
20th Augt 1879

My dear Sir Edward,

I had endeavoured in my report of the attack on Rorke's Drift 22 - 23 Jany 1879, to express my admiration of Mr Daltons conduct on that occasion, and my sense of the great importance of the service rendered by him - but I have very much pleasure in writing as you request the following short account of his services as noticed by myself. -

- It was in a very great degree owing to the exertions of Mr Dalton that we were enabled to put the place in so short a time in the state of defence which, imperfect as it was was undoubtedly the means of our repulsing the Zulu attack. -

- When the fugitives from Isandhlwana passed by with their terrible news & expressions of the madness of an attempt at defence, Mr Dalton's calm treatment of their remarks and his example of cool determination were of the greatest service in inspiring our little garrison with confidence. -

He was amongst the foremost of those who received the first attack at the corner of the Hospital, where the deadliness of his fire did great service, and the mad rush of the Zulus met its first check, and where by his cool courage he saved the life of a man of the Army Hospl. Corps, shooting the Zulu who having seized the muzzle of the man's rifle, was in the act of assegaing him. -

Throughout the attack he was ever present, using his rifle with deadly effect, making sure of each man & picking off those who were annoying us with their fire, or who coming on to the attack were on the point of causing us some loss. After shooting one of these & while his rifle was empty he was seriously wounded by a shot through the body. He handed me his rifle & spoke so calmly that although I saw he was disabled I had no idea until afterwards of the severity of his wound. - For all through the night although he must have been suffering intense pain he still continued to give the same example of cool courage.

Believe me
Dear Sir Edward
very faithfully yours
[signed] John R. M. Chard
Capt & Bt. Maj R.E.

"The Natal Witness," October 16th, 1879, page 3

The Arrival of the 2-24th

The spectators in Church Street could not make out why one company of the noble 24th suddenly raised a deafening cheer on coming to the Club House.

The fact was that B Company, the gallant defenders of Rorke's Drift, under Major Bromhead, V.C., had recognised among the spectators Assistant Commissary Dalton, one of the leaders in that night.

May we ask why Mr. Dalton, who originated the defences at Rorke's Drift, and who was wounded while gallantly leading a portion of the men, has not yet received the Victoria Cross?

Military Notes

...Assistant-Commissary Dalton, whose gallant behaviour at the defence of Rorke's Drift, will be remembered by all, is at present staying in this city during his convalescence. It is to be hoped that his exertions on that memorable occasion will not be forgotten when he is able to resume his duties...

"The Illustrated London News," c. November 1879

Sub-Assistant Commissary Dalton, V.C.

Along with Major Chard, Major Gonville Bromhead, and Surgeon Reynolds, the name of Mr. James Langley Dalton, Sub-Assistant Commissary, will be remembered for the heroic defence of Rorke's Drift, with a hundred men against three thousand, throughout the night of Jan. 22, after the disastrous affair at Isandhlwana. The *Gazette* a fortnight ago recorded that her Majesty the Queen has bestowed the Victoria Cross upon 'this officer to whose energy much of the defence of the place was due.' It is officially stated, more particularly, that 'he actively superintended the work of defence, and was amongst the foremost of those who received the first attack at the corner of the hospital, where the deadliness of his fire did great execution, and the mad rush of the Zulus met its first check, and where by his cool courage he saved the life of a man of the Army Hospital Corps by shooting the Zulu, who, having seized the muzzle of the man's rifle, was in the act of assegaing him.' Mr Dalton was severely wounded during the contest, 'but still continued to give the same example of cool courage.' This testimonial of 'conspicuous gallantry,' as the official writer calls it, is equal to any praise of that kind earned by officers or soldiers in the late campaign. Mr Dalton, we are informed, entered the service in 1849, as a private soldier in the 85th Regiment, in which he served twelve years, till he volunteered to the Commissariat Staff Corps. He completed his term of twenty-one years, and was pensioned as a first-class staff-sergeant. He was granted the medal for long service and good conduct before his discharge. On leaving the army he settled in Natal, but on the outbreak of the war, he applied for employment in the Commissariat, in which he was given a temporary appointment as Acting Assistant Commissary. He was employed in the duties of that office at the Rorke's Drift depot, when the Zulus attacked the post, and he then performed the acts of 'conspicuous gallantry' above described. He has since received a commission in the Commissariat and Transport Department as Sub-Assistant Commissary...

"The Times," March 17th, 1880

Court Circular
Windsor Castle, March 16

...Assistant-Commissary James Langley Dalton, V.C., arrived at the Castle to-day, and had the honour of an interview with the Queen.

James L. Dalton, V.C.

"Years following years, steal something every day
At last they steal us from ourselves away."
With much regret we have to chronicle to-day the death of Mr. J.L. Dalton, V.C., a gentleman who has played an important part in comparatively recent South African history. Deceased, who was 53 years of age, served for some considerable time with the 85th Regiment, and had military experience in many parts of the Empire. After retiring from the Army, he resided for a time in Port Elizabeth, but in the early part of 1879 again resumed service with the expedition against the Zulus. On the night of the 22nd January, when at Rorke's Drift, the enemy in great force attacked a small party of men stationed there. On the occasion deceased exhibited conspicuous bravery, and materially assisted in repulsing the Zulus, and it has always been maintained, averted a serious disaster to the Colony of Natal. His services were rewarded by the presentation of the Victoria Cross and the offer of a commission in the Army. The Cross was presented at Fort Napier, Maritzburg by General Clifford, C.B., amid surroundings well calculated to make it impressive to participators and spectators alike. Mr. Dalton went to England, but shortly afterwards resigned his officer's commission and retired into private life. During the Egyptian campaign, however, he had further service as a volunteer, and obtained the rank of Captain. Subsequently he returned to South Africa, and, until recently, was engaged in gold mining affairs in the Transvaal. About three weeks ago he came to Port Elizabeth and stayed with his old comrade in arms, Mr. Williams, of the Grosvenor Hotel. He exhibited few signs of illness, and, until Friday seemed in fairly good health. On that day, however, he kept his room, and seems to have expired suddenly in bed about seven o'clock in the evening. The matter was reported to the Resident Magistrate and the District Surgeon, and an enquiry will be held to-day.

The remains were interred yesterday afternoon in the Catholic Cemetery, the Rev. Father Kelly officiating at the grave. It was anticipated by many people that deceased would have had a military funeral, but the affair was a very quiet one. Major Dears, Dr. Ensor, Mr. James Lyons, Mr. Gleeson, and a number of others, who, we imagine, respected the character of deceased, followed the body to its last resting place. Had it been the fate of deceased to die in some town where he was thoroughly known the memory of Mr. Dalton would have been honoured in a different fashion.

However, it is not every brave soldier who meets a soldier's death or receives a soldier's burial. The country he secured will probably soon forget him - as she has nearly forgotten others who lie in the hills and valleys of the Crimea, on Spanish Sierras, on arid Indian plains, in the wilds of Ashantee, in Zululand, in Egypt. Nineteenth century life seems to permit few opportunities of cultivating either a heroic or an extra patriotic spirit, but he has few of the characteristics of the Anglo Saxon who will not accord to the memory of brave men a tribute of generous praise.

Yesterday the little burying ground in Russell Road received the remains of as brave a soldier as ever wore Her Majesty's uniform.

Corporal F. C. Schiess, Natal Native Contingent

A letter written by JRM Chard to Lord Chelmsford: [WO32/7390 The National Archives (P.R.O.), London]

Beaconsfield Club
Marlborough Gate
S.W.
22nd October 1879.

Sir,
I have the honor in accordance with instructions from the Field Marshal Commanding in Chief, to forward for your approval this my application for the decoration of the Victoria Cross on behalf of Corporal Schiess late Natal Native Contingent in recognition of his gallant conduct on the 22nd - 23rd Jany. last at Rorkes Drift.

This man who had been wounded in the attack on Sirayo's Kraal a few days before, was a patient at Rorkes Drift on the 22nd Jany. 1879 - and in spite of his wound (in the foot) he particularly attracted my notice by his activity & devoted gallantry throughout the defence Amongst many acts of his I may mention one I myself witnessed - After we had retired to our inner line of defence. The Zulus occupied the wall of mealie bags we had abandoned. Corporal Schiess without any order, crept out along this wall a few feet, to dislodge one in particular of the enemy who was shooting better than usual; on his raising himself to get a shot, the Zulu who was close to him the other side of the wall, fired knocking off his hat. Corpl. Schiess immediately jumped on the wall, & bayonetted the Zulu, & in less time than I take to write it, shot a second and bayonetted a third & then came back to the cover of the inner defence again.

I have the honor to be Sir
Your obedient servant
John R.M. Chard
Capt & Bt. Maj., R.E.

To Major Genl. Lord Chelmsford, G.C.B.

Military Secretary
Forwarded for the very favourable consideration of His Royal Highness the Field Marshal commanding in chief -
Chelmsford
L.G.
Bath 25 October 1879

The Victoria Cross
Presentation In Maritzburg

There have been few, if any interesting sights than that witnessed in our Market Square on Tuesday afternoon, when Her Majesty's High Commissioner, a strong muster of Her Majesty's Army, and a large concourse of Her Majesty's subjects assembled to do honour to a hitherto obscure Swiss irregular soldier - Corporal Schiess - late of the Natal Native Contingent. On that night, famous now in history and song, when a handful of British soldiers withstood, as the beetling cliffs of their island home withstand the shocks of the angry seas, the successive assaults of several thousand Zulus behind their 'flimsy parapet', as Sir Garnet called it, at Rorke's Drift, Corporal Schiess the hero of Tuesday afternoon displayed the most distinguished bravery, and richly merited that cherished trophy of the soldier, the cross given by the gracious Victoria 'for valour.'...

...His Excellency Sir Garnet Wolseley with his staff, and accompanied by His Excellency Sir Henry Bulwer and Mr Haden, rode on to the ground. Taking up his position at the base, His Excellency, the General called Corporal Schiess to his side. The hero, who had been chaperoned by his later gallant Commandant, was modestly attired in the well-known Lonsdale uniform, in which he did his great service, and looked not a little abashed as, the cynosure of all eyes, he stepped to the front...

...His Excellency Sir Garnet Wolseley then addressed Corporal Schiess as follows;- 'Corporal Schiess, I have very great pleasure, in obedience to Her Majesty's commands, in conferring upon you to-day this Victoria Cross, and in doing so, as Her Majesty's representative, in this public manner. This is, as you are well aware, the highest distinction that any soldier or sailor in Her Majesty's service can aspire to, and I am very glad to have this opportunity afforded me to give you this cross in the presence of so many members of the colonial community as an evidence of how anxious Her Majesty is to reward valour and merit, not only in her regular army, but also in the ranks of her colonial troops as well. The extract which has been read from the London Gazette describes very accurately the deed for which you are to receive this cross, but I wish to call the special attention of the soldiers to the deed, especially to two distinguishing points which distinguish it in a remarkable manner. First is the fact that you were suffering from a wound previously received, and which many men of a less brave temperament would have been inclined to use as an excuse for remaining in idleness and not taking part in the defence which was made on that occasion. A second and still more remarkable fact is that this deed of valour for which you are now to be decorated was one not of mere passive defence at a loophole, or standing behind a wall where you had been posted; but you went out - sallied out - from that place, and in a most gallant manner, and in front of your defence - the defence of that flimsy parapet on which you had to rely for your lives

- distinguished yourself in the manner described.

These circumstances enhance the great pleasure I have on the present occasion in giving you this cross in the name of Her Majesty the Queen..."

The Victoria Cross
After The Ceremony

...Later on Scheiss' health was drunk by a large party at the Royal Hotel where Col. Lonsdale in a neat speech complimented his former companion-in-arms, and follower, upon his meritorious conduct and on the distinguished ovation of which he had been the subject. In the course of his remarks the gallant Colonel said, 'I myself feel the honour that has been done to Schiess today perhaps more than he does, and I am in a better position than the public to estimate the importance of the varied military services of which the part he took in the glorious defence of Rorke's Drift has been but the crown and the completion. Corporal Scheiss was not only a member of my own corps, but had previously during five and a half years faithfully and honourably served the flag of France. He has been but two and a half years in South Africa, but during that time he has succeeded in distinguishing himself in very many battles in the arduous campaigns against the Kafirs in the Cape Colony. If I could wish anything further for him, it would be that he should again find himself in similar scenes of danger to those in which he has reaped so much distinction..."

"The Natal Witness," Friday, February 6th, 1885

Death of a Zulu War V.C.

It may be remembered that Corporal Scheiss V.C., was sent Home from this by the troopship *Serapis*. Word has now been received of the poor fellow's death. It is thus chronicled in the Portsmouth *Times*:-

"Corporal Scheiss served as a volunteer during the last Zulu war, and was present in several engagements, including Rorke's Drift, where he showed conspicuous gallantry, and was awarded the Victoria Cross.

At the close of the war he returned to Natal, where for some time he existed in a state of absolute want. At the time of the arrival of the *Serapis* his abject condition led the inhabitants to raise a sum by subscription to pay for his rations for the voyage home. He was taken on board, but his long exposure told on him, and about the 14th December he died on board."

"The Natal Witness," November 2nd, 1899

Personalia

Corpl. F. Schiess, Natal Native Forces, was at Rorke's Drift in January 1879. P.G. Crow asks where he is now.

"The Natal Witness," November 4th, 1899

Personalia

A correspondent writes that he remembers reading years ago, both in the '*Witness*' and the '*Advertiser*' of Corpl. Scheiss (of Rorke's Drift fame) dying in India destitute.

"The Natal Witness," November 6th, 1899

Personalia

A correspondent writes:- I see information is asked of the whereabouts of the late Corpl. Schiess. Immediately after the Zulu War he joined the Telegraph Service as linesman and was stationed at Durban. He left after being decorated with the V.C. He went through the Basuto War later, and returned to Durban invalided and destitute. He was (if memory serves me correctly) sent to England in one of H.M. transports, and died either in Netley or Haslar Hospitals. The Hon. Mr. Jameson was, I think the means of his being sent Home. I have a good photo given me by Schiess. Should anyone care for a copy I will get it retaken.

Lieutenant Gonville Bromhead, 'B' Company, 2nd/24th Foot

His official letter of recommendation for the award of the Victoria Cross to members of the 2nd/24th: [WO32/7390 The National Archives, (P.R.O.), London]

From/Lieut. Gonville Bromhead 2/24th Regt:
To/The Officer Commanding 2/24th Regiment:

Rorke's Drift
15th February 1879

Sir,
I beg to bring to your notice the names of the following men belonging to my Company who especially distinguished themselves during the attack by the Zulus on this Post on the 22nd & 23rd January last; & whose conduct on this occasion came under my personal cognisance.
No. 1395 Private John Williams was posted by me together with Private Joseph Williams & Private William Horrigan 1/24th Regt. in a further room of the Hospital. They held it for more than an hour, so long as they had a round of ammunition left, when, as communication was for the time cut off, the Zulus were enabled to advance & burst open the door. They dragged out Private Joseph Williams & two of the patients by the arms, and assagaied them. Whilst the Zulus were occupied with the slaughter of these unfortunate men, a lull took place, during which Private John Williams - who with two patients were then only men left alive in this ward - succeeded in knocking a hole in the partition, & in taking the two patients with him into the next ward, where he found

No.1373 Private Henry Hook. These two men together, one man working whilst the other fought & held the enemy at bay with his bayonet, broke through three more partitions, & were thus enabled to bring eight patients through a small window into our inner line of defence.

In another ward, facing the hill, I had placed

No.593 Private William Jones &

No. 716 Private Robert Jones: They defended their post to the last, until six out of the seven patients it contained had been removed. The seventh, Sergeant Maxfield, 2/24th Regt: was delirious from fever. Although they had previously dressed him, they were unable to induce him to move. When Private Robert Jones returned to endeavour to carry him away, he found him being stabbed by the Zulus as he lay on his bed -

No. 1240 Corporal William Allen &

No. 1362 Private Frederick Hitch, must also be mentioned. It was chiefly due to their courageous conduct that communication with the Hospital was kept up at all. Holding together at all costs a most dangerous post, raked in reverse by the enemy's fire from the hill, they were both severely wounded, but their determined conduct enabled the patients to be withdrawn from the Hospital, & when incapacitated by their wounds from fighting themselves, they continued, as soon as their wounds had been dressed, to serve out ammunition to their comrades during the night. -

I have the honour to be Sir

Your most obedient servant

G. Bromhead

Lieut. 2/24th Regt.

Commanding B. Company 2/24th Regt.

A private letter written to Lieutenant Godwin-Austen, 2nd/24th Foot. [Appears courtesy of the South Wales Borderers Regtl. Museum, Brecon, Acc. No. 1984.61]

Rorkes Drift
19th Feb. 1879

My Dear Austin,

I can't tell you how grieved I was to hear on the return of the Column on the 23rd of January that your brother had been left in that fateful camp. He had been attached to B. Co. at Greytown, and we got on so jolly together that he told me he should ask the Col. to let him stay with the Company, but I am sorry to say it was not to be.

The night before the Column crossed the River it came out in orders that B Company were to remain here and your Brother was sent back to G Company and Griffiths who was Company Officer as usual was posted to the Company. Your Brother who was knocked up from over work at the ponts where he had been working day & night, to get the troops across the River had to go sick, but still he march with the Column. I have not got over the dreadful .... we received yet, in fact can hardly believe it. We had an awful night of it here as you may fancy. We heard the Camp had been taken, and were also afraid that the Column had received a heavy blow, and the Zulus came at us in such force & with such fierce pluck. I thought we should never pull through it, but the Company behaved splendidly and as our ammunition held out and we held them back till daylight. We were on the Natal side of the Buffalo but can do nothing as far as I can see, till we are fitted up again. I hope they are going to send us out some more troops or you wont see many of us again. The Zulus are so strong we stand a poor chance against them, as it is we expect to be attacked any day. I hope the wound is better, and that you do not suffer from it. Yours sincerely,

G. Bromhead.

An extract from a private letter written to his sister, date unknown. [Appears courtesy of the South Wales Borderers Regtl. Museum, Brecon, Acc. No. D87.72]

...I fear you will be very anxious about me as no doubt we are rather in a fix. I am getting over the excitement of the fight and the sickness and fury at our loss. It is not so much the poor fellows being killed as the way the savages treat them. Having been left alone we have built a mud fort, which I think we ought to hold against any amount of Zulus, till we get help from England...

...I send you a paper with the report of the fight and the remarks of the General on the behaviour of my company which are flattering. If the Government gives all the steps of the poor fellows killed I shall most probably get my company into the 1st Battalion who are to go home directly after the war is finished...

...I have not got over the wonder of there being one of us left. God was very good to us in giving us a little time to get up a defence, or the black fellows would have taken us by surprise, which they will find hard to do now...

"The Times," April 30th, 1879

A Close Call for Lieutenant Bromhead

The following extract from the letter of an officer with the column under Lord Chelmsford who arrived at Rorke's Drift on the morning of January 23rd, will still be read with interest;-

"From the distance we saw the hospital in flames and thought all was over. The mounted men rode up carefully and were greeted with cheers by the little garrison. When Lord Chelmsford rode up Bromhead came out alone to make his report, and was received most enthusiastically by what was left of Lord Chelmsford's column. The men never stop their yarns about him, and we are full of admiration at the coolness, forethought, pluck, and determination which he showed. With hardly a man to spare, he still posted two men in the Commissariat rum stores to prevent any from helping themselves. During every lull in the attack he sallied out, disarmed the dead Zulus, and destroyed their weapons. In the middle of the night he went out with one man to see for himself how the reserve ammunition was holding out. Cautiously striking a match, to count the boxes, the Zulus saw it and fired; the lantern was smashed and the man killed."

"The Irish Times," March 5th, 1879

...The world rings with the fame of Gonville Bromhead, of the 24th, who with his brother officers, Chard, Adendorf, Dunne and Reynolds, and the men under his command, certainly deserves all the praise that has been lavished on the magnificent pluck displayed under circumstances that might have daunted a Homeric hero. To such a soldier the nation owes the highest honours, and we have no doubt Government will not be tardy in recognising the gallantry which shines so brightly as to lighten in some measure the shadow of gloom which fell upon our troops at Isandula. It is said that Bromhead, for his wondrous feat, has been promoted to the position of captain in his regiment, and has also obtained his brevet majority; but it appears to be the universal opinion that full justice will not have been done, and the nation will not have discharged the indebtedness to him, unless a V.C. and C.B. shall be also conferred upon him. He is the youngest son of the late Major Sir Edmund de Gonville Bromhead, Bart, of Thurlby Hall, Lincolnshire, and it is gratifying to us in this country to know that Irish blood flows largely in the veins of the young hero, who is a near relative of our resident magistrate, the Hon. Martin Jos. Ffrench. Gonville Bromhead's elder brother - Major Charles Bromhead - was in England with the depot of his regiment when Lord Chelmsford's telegraphic despatches arrived, and the moment the gallant Major heard the war's dread news he obtained leave, and, warrior that he is, he rushed at once for the front, and, without waiting for the drafts, sailed in the first available vessel for the seat of war...

"The Natal Witness," c. 1879

Victoria Cross presented to Major Bromhead

...At half past eight we had a parade of all the troops in garrison, consisting of the 2-24th, the three squadrons of Dragoons, and the detachment of Royal Artillery with two guns, were drawn up in front of our headquarters, in three sides of a square; and then the General attended by his staff and many other officers rode on to the ground. General Colley then called out Brevet-Major Bromhead and Private Jones, who both came forward from the ranks; a letter from the Secretary of State for War to the General Commanding in South Africa was then read, and afterwards extracts from the London Gazette, giving the acts for which the Victoria Cross was to be presented.

Sir G. Wolesley having had the much-prized honours handed to him by Colonel Degacher, said:

"Colonel Degacher and men of the 2-24th - The extracts just read describe very fully two acts for which her Majesty the Queen has been pleased to order these two crosses to be awarded. The decoration is the highest one that a soldier can obtain, and is naturally highly prized in consequence. It is worn at the present time by many brave officers and men in our army; but none for better services to the State than those for which it is given today, in gallantly defending Rorke's Drift against overwhelming numbers of savages; the defence, I believe, is only an instance of what British soldiers can do when properly handled and led. That fight will always be remembered with pride by every British regiment, as well as by the 2-24th; and when so thought of I feel sure that the names of the two who now obtain the cross will be associated with it in the regimental annals, together with those other brave men who have also obtained the cross..."

The General then pinned the crosses on their left breasts and wished them a long life, and many opportunities of gaining other medals...

Extract from an unidentified Lincolnshire newspaper, c. 1880, which covered Bromhead's triumphant return to the city of Lincoln, c. June 24th, 1880

Public Reception of and Presentation to Major Bromhead, V.C, at Lincoln.

...Major Bromhead, who was received with loud and prolonged cheering, said;-
"Mr Mayor and citizens of the ancient city of Lincoln. I beg to thank you very much for the kind and flattering address you have presented me this day, and also for the magnificent sword, which, I assure you, will remain in my family as heirlooms for ever. I feel great difficulty in adequately expressing to you my deep sense of the kindness with which I have been received since my return from Zululand, but I may tell you that nothing has given me greater satisfaction that the splendid reception I have met with this day, especially as, since my boyhood, since I left Thurlby, I have been rather a stranger, and personally unknown in these parts. I am not vain enough to take this flattering reception to myself. I beg to thank you on behalf of Major Chard, Surgeon-Major Reynolds, Mr Dalton, Mr Dunn, the Rev. Mr. Smith, and those stalwart men who were with us on the night of the 22nd January 1879, the greater part of whom, I am proud to say, I still retain in the Company which I have the honour to command. I beg again to thank you for the grand reception you have given me."...

"The Times," May 19th, 1880

Court Circular
Windsor Castle, May 18

...The Earl of Beaconsfield, K.G., Lord Rowston, C.B., Sir Theodore Martin, K.C.B., and Lady Martin and Major Gonville Bromhead, V.C, (24th Regiment), arrived at the Castle yesterday...
...Her Majesty's dinner party included...Major Gonville Bromhead, V.C....

"The Natal Witness," February 14th, 1891

Death of Major Bromhead

The death is announced at Allahabad of Major Gonville Bromhead, V.C., of Rorke's Drift fame.

"The Prompter," c. 1891

The Death of Major Bromhead

at Allahabad deprives England of one of her most skilful and most valiant soldiers, a born leader of men. It is fitting that Gonville Bromhead's and Chard's heroic defence of the little farmhouse at Rorke's Drift, during the most critical juncture of the Zulu War of 1879, should be recalled when the lamentable news of this gallant officer's early death is fresh. This famous feat of arms, which will ever redound to the credit of the British Army, is commemorated by a page Illustration of Rorke's Drift, in a corner of which is inserted a portrait of the late Major (then Lieutenant) Bromhead. At once will all who followed with breathless interest the story of the Zulu War in the pages of the Penny Illustrated remember the sturdy stand Bromhead and Chard, with but a handful of British soldiers, made all night against the fierce Zulu host, emboldened by Cetewayo's victory at Isandhlwana. Fighting tooth and nail, they kept the thousands of Zulus at bay; and they 'held the fort' till succour came, as is delineated in the P.I.P. Illustration. It is sorrowful news indeed, that Major Bromhead, gallant scion of a fighting family, and a son of whom Lincolnshire and all England is proud, lies dead in India. We mourn for a true hero.

2-24/1240 Corporal William Wilson Allan, 'B' Company, 2nd/24th Foot

A private letter written to his wife.

Helpmakaar, 4th February 1879,

My Dear Wife,
I am able to write this myself, so you will see that I am getting the better of my wound, more rapidly than could be expected. We got here (that is the sick and wounded) on the 26th of January, and have been waiting an ambulance to convey us down the country, which is expected every day. My arm is mending quickly, though I am sorry I cannot say the same for the other wounded men, who appear to be making no progress towards recovery. We are in a strongly entrenched fort here, with two companies of the 1/24th, three of the 2/24th, detachment of the 13th, part of a company of the Royal Engineers, and a battery of Artillery. Smith is still at Rorke's Drift, where the whole of the regiment and part of the 1/24th are assembled. Everything is quiet, and we don't expect any fighting till the arrival of troops from home. My dear wife, I trust you will feel too thankful to God for having preserved

my life, to fret over what might have been a great deal worse. I feel very thankful to God for leaving me in the land of the living. Give my respects to your relatives and love to yourself and the children, from your loving husband.
William

"The Times," October 27th, 1879

Naval and Military Intelligence.

...The blue-jackets forming the Naval Brigade in the Zulu war, and the men of the 1st Battalion 24th Regiment, were entertained at Portsmouth, by the inhabitants, on Saturday. The guests included 330 men of the Shah, 31 men of the Active, 158 men of the 24th Regiment, and a number of invalids from Netley Hospital, consisting of three from the 80th Foot, 55 from the 99th, seven from the 57th, two from the 13th, 14 from the 91st, five from the 3d Buffs, five from the 3d Battalion 60th Rifles, one from the 24th, six from the 90th, and a Royal Engineer. No commissioned officers were present.

The proceedings, which were held at the Portland Hall, and lasted from 12 until 4 o'clock, were of a hearty and free-and-easy character, the men being encouraged to enjoy themselves with songs, &c., instead of being wearied with long speeches. After dinner the Mayor proposed 'The Queen,' and alluded to the womanly interest which Her Majesty took in the welfare of her soldiers and sailors, and to her having proceeded from Osborne to Netley for the purpose of showing her sympathy with the wounded from the war, and of pinning the Victoria Cross upon the breast of Private Hitch. Hitch was, unfortunately, not present, but Corporal Allan, who had earned the decoration was, and he would have had the cross that day had it not happened that, while the cross had been forwarded to South Africa, Allan himself had been sent to England. Three cheers were given for Allan...

"The Monmouthshire Beacon," Saturday, March 15th, 1890

DEATH OF SERGEANT INSTRUCTOR ALLAN, V.C.

Much regret was felt in the Town on Wednesday, and especially amongst the Volunteers when it became known that Sergeant Instructor W.W. Allan had succumbed to a complicated attack supervening on influenza. Three years and a half ago he succeeded Sergt. Prendergast as Instructor to the local C. Co., 4th Volunteer Batt, S.W.B. He came here with a good reputation as one who had won the much-coveted Victoria Cross at the famous engagement of Rorke's Drift, and he has always been popular amongst the Volunteers and respected by the townspeople generally. The influenza epidemic, which attacked so many people last month, was the originating cause of Sergeant Allan's illness. He was laid up first six weeks ago, partially recovered from the influenza, and then suffered a relapse, a complication of disorders setting in, and although having the advantage of the Co. Surgeon. Mr. T.G. Prosser and his assistant, Mr. Groves, the patient gradually got weaker and died early on Wednesday morning, aged 46. He leaves a widow and seven young children, for whom much sympathy is felt, they being almost wholly unprovided for.

Deceased joined the Army when young and served with the 2nd Batt. of the 24th Regiment for about 25 years. He was in India for 13 years of the early part of his military service, and in February, 1878, sailed with his Regiment on board the *Himalaya*, which took out reinforcements for the Cape of Good Hope, where the campaign against the Kaffirs had taken a serious turn. Everyone recollects the terrible disaster which overtook the 1st and 2nd Battalions of the gallant 24th Regiment at Isandhlwana mountain on the 20th of January, 1879, and the memorable defence of Rorke's Drift which followed. The latter stands out as one of the grandest achievements in the annals of the British Army. It was for his brave conduct on this occasion that Sergeant (then Corporal) Allan obtained the V.C., in historical records of the 2nd Batt. 24th Regiment, a vivid account is given of the defence of the hospital and other buildings at Rorke's Drift, and referring to the part played by Corporal W. Allan and Pte. J. Hitch, the author says;- "It was chiefly due to the courageous conduct of these men that communications with the hospital was kept up at all, holding together, at all costs, a most dangerous post, raked in reverse by the enemy's fire from the hill, they were both severely wounded, but their determined conduct enabled the patients to be withdrawn from the hospital. When incapacitated by their wounds from fighting, they continued as soon as their wounds had been dressed, to serve out ammunition to their comrades during the night." Private Hook, a Monmouth man, was associated with those who helped hold the enemy at bay, and subsequently received the Victoria Cross, while still at the Drift, from Sir Garnet Wolseley, who had taken over from Lord Chelmsford. Sergt. Allan received his Cross from the hands of the Queen herself, while lying in Netley Hospital.

The remains of the late Sergeant Instructor will be interred at the cemetery on Monday with full military honours. The cortege will leave the Volunteer Drill Hall at 2.30pm.

"The Monmouthshire Beacon," March 22nd, 1890

MILITARY FUNERAL.

The remains of Sergeant Instructor W.W. Allan V.C., whose death we recorded last week, were interred at the Monmouth Cemetery with full military honours on Monday afternoon. The towns-people turned out in large numbers to witness the obsequies and Monnow Street and Agincourt Square were thronged with spectators, the fact of the deceased being a Victoria Cross man, and one of the gallant Rorke's Drift defenders, creating an unusual amount of interest in the sad affair. At 2.30 the cortege left the drill hall in the following order: A firing party composed of members of the local C. Company of Volunteers, to which the late non-commissioned officer was instructor, under Colour Sergeant W. Gardiner and carrying their arms reversed; the band of the R.M.E.M. conducted by Sergeant G. Renecle, playing the Dead March; the coffin, borne on a hand bier, and surmounted by the Union Jack, deceased's accoutrements and wreaths of flowers; Sergeant Instructors Jamieson (Abergavenny), Reardon (Blaenavon), Donoghue (Pontypool) and Kelly (Usk) acting as pall bearers; two mourning coaches containing the widow and other relatives of the deceased; a few private mourners, the members of C Company 4th Volunteer Battalion SWB, Volunteer representatives from Newport, Usk, Coleford, Pontypool, Abergavenny, Chepstow, & c., and the permanent staff of the R.M.E.M., the rear being brought up by Surgeon T.G. Prosser, Lieutenant C.C. Powell, and Captain and Adjutant Birch, along the whole of the route the horses in the first coach gave a great deal of trouble, plunging and rearing constantly, much to the danger of those in front, and but for the promptitude and exertions of several onlookers there would probably have been a serious accident.

Shutters were up and blinds drawn at nearly every shop and private residence and every mark of respect shown for the memory of the deceased. The Vicar (Rev. Wentworth Watson) conducted the funeral service, at the conclusion of which the usual three volleys were fired over the grave. The troops then returned to the drill hall and were dismissed.

A portrait and short biography of the deceased appeared in Monday's Daily Graphic. As will be seen from our advertising columns, an effort is to be made to place the widow and family in a Position which will relieve then from want, and we trust the appeal will meet with a good response. Sergt. Allan never boasted of the conduct which gained him the Victoria Cross, but all who remember the wonderfully plucky defence made by the Rorke's Drift garrison against overwhelming odds, can appreciate the spirit of bravery which must have animated ever man who took part therein, and it should never be said that when the occasion arises Englishmen do not know how to recognise such deeds of "derring do".

25B/1362 Private Frederick Hitch, 'B' Company, 2nd/24th Foot

"The Cambrian," June 13th, 1879

The Massacre At Rorke's Drift
(Narrative By Survivors)

Private Hitch and Waters and Corporal Lyons, who took part in the memorable defence of Rorke's Drift, have reached Netley Hospital, and have furnished the following interesting narratives to our Southampton correspondent. Frederick Hitch states:-

I am a private in the 2nd-24th, and left England about sixteen months ago, and was engaged in the Cape Colony under Lord Chelmsford. On the threatened Zulu outbreak my regiment was ordered to Natal, and we went up in one of the coast mail steamers. The first news I had of what had happened at Isandhlwana was when one of the mounted infantry, named Evans, came galloping up to the mission house, and said that a part of the camp across the river had been destroyed by the Zulus, that two guns had been taken as well as all the ammunition, and that the enemy was advancing in force to attack Rorke's Drift. This was about three o'clock in the afternoon. I was ordered by Lieutenant Bromhead to mount the roof of the stores to watch for the Zulus.

I went up immediately, being the only man up there, and in about five minutes I saw an advanced guard of the enemy coming over the brow of a hill on our right front. Every man in Rorke's Drift set to work piling up the mealie bags, and had soon finished. The big mob of the enemy soon came up, extending from the right, and the column appeared to me, as I watched them from the roof of the house, to be about a mile and a half in length. They were then just beyond gunshot, but were perfectly quiet. They then made a right wheel, and the extreme right moved into the caves on the adjoining hill, and as I was about the only man they could see, being on the roof, they took a pot shot at me but missed. I reported the movements to my comrades below, and fired three shots, these being the first that was fired at the Zulus at Rorke's Drift; the enemy made a yell and came at the little front with a rush, and I then got down and took my position with the rest of the company, on the right front, Mr Bromhead being close to me. The sun was just beginning to set at the time the Zulus came up close to the front, and after they had taken the hospital and was burning it Lieutenant Bromhead and three privates, with Colour-sergeant Bourne, kept the position in the right front, in order to keep the enemy from getting a line of fire at the men of the 24th, who were firing to the front from behind a pile of biscuit boxes. I was here for about an hour, being all the time between three cross-fires. I saw one of my comrades - Private Nichols - killed; he was shot through the head, his brains being scattered all about us. He had up to his death been doing good service with his rifle. Another corporal - Sheath, of the Natal Contingent, was shot on my left. I myself kept shooting into a good mob of the enemy, who were very quiet in all they did. About a quarter to seven I was shot from the left, the ball striking me under the right shoulder blade and came out through the shoulder. I knew at the time that the ball had passed right through me. I fell down, and Mr Bromhead said, 'Mate are you hit' and I said 'Yes.' I had not had time to form an opinion as to whether the Zulus would take the fort or not. My only wish was - as I believe was that of every other man - to fight as hard as I could, and I did it until I was wounded. I crept to the rear, and with the assistance of Private Deakin, tied up my wound as well as I could by tearing off the sleeve of a greatcoat for the purpose. I then knocked about as well as I could, serving the others with ammunition until I became exhausted from loss of blood and fell down unconscious. I did not come to until the morning, just as peep of day, and I then found myself in a stable. The Zulus, meanwhile, had retired, but were again advancing to attack us, and they saw the General and his column coming, and again retired. I was sent down to Durban, but did not reach there until the end of April, the journey down being rather rough. I was under medical care at Durban, and was sent home in the Tamar.

A private testimonial written by G Bromhead: [Hitch scrapbook]

I have much pleasure in testifying to the excellent character borne by F. Hitch V.C. whilst serving in the 2/24th Regt. He served under my command in the Kaffir War 1878, and subsequently in the Zulu War and was present with his Company at the Defence of Rorke's Drift. I found him a clean, sober & hardworking man, and in the defence of Rorke's Drift he so distinguished himself by his personal gallantry that he was awarded the Victoria Cross which was graciously presented to him by Her Majesty in person.
In this engagement he was severely wounded and rendered unfit for active service as a soldier
Gonville Bromhead
Major 2/24th Regt.
Pinetown - Natal
November 1879

His own hand written letter: [Hitch scrapbook. A second version of this letter exists at the South Wales Borderers Regtl. Museum, Brecon, Acc. No. 1996.37, the first page of which is reproduced on the front cover]

As I have been asked many times to give my Illustration of Rorkes Drift I cannot say it is A Pleasure for me to do so and to think Back on that treable night of the 22 Jan 1879 it Was about 3.30 o clock noon that We heard of that fatal Disaster of Isandhlwana I was Cooking the tea for the company I tryed to get it Done before the zulus attacked the little Post Rorkes Drift Which I managed taken the tea and My rifle and ammunition and four kettles tea I just got in to the fort When Bromhead asked me to try and get on to the top of the house I at once mounted it as soon as I got on the top I Could see that Zulus had got as near to us as they Could Without us seeing them I told Mr Bromhead that they were at the other side of the rise and was extending for attacked Mr. Bromhead asked me how many I thought there were I told him that I thought numbered from 4, to, 6000. A. voice from be low is that all we Can mnage that lot very well for a few seconds this were Diffrent opinion I staid on the House watching the Blak mass Extending into there fighting line the same time a number of them creaping a long under the Rocks and took up cover in the caves, and keep trying to dismount me from the top of the House there Direction was good but there allevation bad a few minutes later one appeared on the Top of the Mountain from the other side he Could see us in the Largher plain Enough to Count us I put myself in a Laying position but my shot fell short of him he than moved steadely to the right and signelled with his arm the main body at once begune to advance I told Mr Bromhead that they would be all round us in a very short time he at once told the Company to take up there post the Enmey making a right wheel, they attacd us in shap of a bullocks horns and in a few minuts was all round us I found as they got close to the Largur I was out of the fighting so I slid down the thatch roof, droping into the Largur fixting my bainet as I run across the largur taking up my Possition on a open space which we had not time to compleat the Deadly work now Commenced

The zulus pushing right up to the porch it was not untill the bainet was freely used that they flinched the least bit had the zulus taken the bainet as freely as they took the bullets we could not have stood more than fifteen minuts - they pushed on right up to us and not only got up to the Largur but got in with us, but they seemed to have a great dread of the bainet which stood to us from beging to end, during that strugle there was a fine big zulu see me shoot his mait down he sprang forward droping his Rifel and asegis, ceesing hold of the muzle of my Rifel with his left hand and he right hand hold of the bainet thinking to disarme me he pulled and tryed hard to get the Rifel from me but I had a ferm hold of the small of the butt of my rifel with my left hand

My Cartridges on the Top of the meely bags which enabled me to load my rifel and shot the poor reatch

Wilest holding on to his grasp, for some few moments they droped back into the Garden which served a great proction for them had it not been for the Garden and dead wall they could not haved prolonged the Engagement for thirteen houres as they did, there next object was to get possition of the <u>Hospittal</u> which they did by setting fire to it, The greatest Task was in getting the Sick and Wounded out of the <u>Hospittal</u>, which the zulus had bursted open the doors and killed them in there beds Wilest doing this I noticed it was with great difficalty they were keep back.

They keeping up a heavy fire from front and rear from which we suffered very much it was than about when Mr dalton was shot and Mr Dunn, Mr dolton was very activ up till he was Wounded, we had to fall back to the Second line of Defence and when the Zulus took position of the Hospittal, Bromhead & myself & five others took up the Position on the right of the second line of Defence, which we were exposed to three Cross fires, Bromhead took the center, and was the only one that did not get Wounded, there was four <u>killed</u> and two Wounded myselfe was the last of the six one shot Bromhead & myself had it to our twoselves about an <u>hour</u> & a half, Bromhead using his Rifel & revolver with deadly aime Bromhead keep telling the men not to waist one round, About this time we was pressed very much Bromhead was using his revolver with deadly aime, they seemed determined to move Bromhead & myself, we were so buissey that one had got inside and was in the act of assygien Bromhead Bromhead not knowing he was I there, I put my rifel on him knowing at the same time it was empty, Instead of him deliving the assygie which no doubt would have been faitle, he dodge down and hoped out of the Largur Again this was just before they tryed to fire the other building they seemed to me as, if they made up there minds to take <u>Rorkes</u> drift with this rush They rushed up madley not with standing the heavy loss they had all ready suffered it was in this struggle that I was shot, they pressed us very hard several of them mounting the Barracade, I knew this one had got his rifel presented at me but at the same time I had got my hands full in front and I was at the present when he shot me through my right Shoulder blaid and passed through my Shoulder which splintered the Shoulder bone very much, as I have had in all 38 pieces of broaken bone taken from my Shoulder I tryed to keep my feet, but Could not, He could have assygide me had not Bromhead shot him with his revolver Bromhead seemed sorry when he saw me down Bleading so Freely, saying Mate I am very sorry to see you down I was not down not more than a few minuets striped in my shirtsleves with my waistbelt on and Fleas straps I put my wounded arm under my waist belt I was able to make another stand Getting Bromheads revolver and with his assistance in loading it I managed very well with it at this time we were fighting by the ade from the burning Hospital, which was much to our advantage, Bromhead at this time was keeping a strict eye on the ammunision and telling the men not to waist one round as we were getting short, I was serving out ammunision myself when I became thurstey and faint I got worse, a Chum tore out the linnin out of Mr dunn's coat and tied it round my Shoulder, I got so thirsty that I could not do much in fact we were all Exhausted and the ammunision was beging to be Counted, Deacken, a Comerade said to me as I was leaning back against the buicust Boxes, Fred when it Comes to the last shill I shoot you I Declyned no they have very near done for me and they Can finish me right out, when it Come to the Last I dont rember not much after that when I came to myself again Lord Chamford had realived us of our task, Bromhead brought his Lordship to me and his Lordship spoak very kindley to me and the Dr. dressed my wound Bromhead was my Principal, visiter and nurse while I was at the <u>drift.</u>

Finish
Frederick Hitch, V.C. Late 2nd 24th Regt.

Extract from "Chums," (a magazine), March 11th, 1908

FIGHTING FOR EMPIRE
The Story Of Private Hitch, V.C.

For the first time Private Hitch relates his story of the gallant defence of Rorke's Drift, one of the most stirring and heroic fights of the Zulu War of 1879. At the time of Rorke's Drift, Private Hitch was twenty-four years of age, and was serving with the 2nd Battalion of the South Wales Borderers. 'B' Company of his regiment had been left to guard a depot and hospital, which had been established at a Mission Station a few hundred yards from a river crossing known as Rorke's Drift.

"We did not expect any fighting that day, and were occupied in our usual duties, little thinking that a horde of Zulus - the pick of the Zulu Army, in fact - were marching on us, determined to kill every man at our little post.

About one o'clock two men galloped to the Drift, bringing the news that the Zulus had annihilated our force at Isandhlwana, and that they were now marching on to attack our post at Rorke's Drift. Lieutenant Bromhead, who was in charge of the post, and Commissioner Dalton at once held a conference. The position was a difficult one: our little force only consisted of a handful of men, whilst the approaching Zulus, mad with success, must have numbered at least four thousand. And many of them, moreover, were armed. At first it was thought the better part of valour to desert the post, but fortunately this decision was altered. We were to defend the post, and hold it at all costs.

With us were four hundred friendly natives, and these men we at once set to work carrying mealie (corn) bags and boxes of stores, which we placed in position as barricades, making an enclosure or laager of which the mission house, used as a hospital, and some out-buildings formed a part. Just before the barricades had been completed the friendly niggers began to funk it, and as soon as they found out that the Zulus were really coming down upon us in great force they commenced to sneak away. We tried to rally them, but it was of no use. Then their captain went after them with the intention of bringing them back; but he disappeared too. Just to show these back gentleman what we thought of their conduct, some of us, including myself, sent a few shots after them, which brought down dead one of their white non-commissioned officers.

While the men were still barricading the place, Lieutenant Bromhead asked me to climb to the top of a building, which I believe had been used as a church, and keep a look-out for the enemy. Having got to the top of the building I could plainly see the Zulus forming up just over the brow of a hill.

"They are ready to attack, sir," I called out to Lieutenant Bromhead, "and I think there are about four thousand of them."

A little fellow named Morris, who heard me, remarked:

"Oh, if that's all there are, we can manage that lot all right!"

Presently I saw a Zulu, evidently one of their chiefs, who was standing on the summit of a hill, gave the signal by extending his arms, and immediately the whole force commenced to advance on us. They seemed to work on a pivot, the pivot being only about three hundred yards distant, when the final advance began; so that, in order to attack us on all sides at once, the other end of their line had come on at a tremendous pace.

My position on the housetop was a pretty good target for them, but none of their shots hit me. As soon as I saw them on the move, I dropped down into the laager and fixed my bayonet. I was only just in time, which will give you some idea of the rapidity of their movements.

On they came with a rush. With one had the warriors held their shields, and in the other hand they carried their deadly assegais. A few were armed with rifles, just taken from the poor fellows whom they had annihilated at Isandlwana.

We volleyed into the mass as they advanced, but there was little hesitation. Our bullets accounted for many, but there were hundreds to fill their places. They still came on right up to the barricades, and were only turned by the good cold steel of our bayonets, for which they had far more respect than for bullets.

Then it was load and fire and bayonet just as fast as we could. The niggers would retire and come on again in rushes, each rush being announced by a short war cry. This war cry, by the way, was very useful to us: we knew what to expect. Even when darkness came upon us they continued to use their war shout, which was not altogether wise on their part, because it at once put us on the alert. However, we didn't complain on that score.

Fortunately those of the Zulus who had rifles knew very little about their weapons or how to use them. Their shots appeared to go either much too high or too low. I suppose they did not understand the sighting. Had there been a few marksmen amongst them I fear myself and many more would have gone under at Rorke's Drift. Soon it was discovered that it was impossible to defend the laager which we had made, so Major Chard gave an order to make a second line of barricades, inside the outer one. This work was carried out under great difficulties and under heavy fire from a cave close by, where a few Zulus had taken cover. Had the four hundred friendly native troops not bolted, the larger laager would have been none too roomy. This second line of barricades proved a great success, as it meant that we had less ground to cover. There was a certain space of about nine yards where the barricading was uncompleted. It was, of course, the weakest link in the chain, and the Zulus were not long in discovering this fact.

In this position eight of us Bromhead, Nicholls, Fagan, Cole, Dalton, Schiess, Williams, and myself - made a stand, and it was here, I think, that the hardest work was done.

Though the situation was so uncomfortable, there was no bungling. Each man in a businesslike manner singled out the nigger who was nearest him, and dealt out death if he could. In one of these nasty rushes three Zulus were making for me; they seemed to have specially marked me out. The first fellow I shot; the second man I bayoneted; the third man got right into the laager, but he declined to stand up against me. With a leap he jumped over the barricade, and made off.

A few yards from the barricade lay a wounded Zulu. We knew he was there, and that he had only been wounded, and so wanted watching. At the moment we were far too busy with the more active members to find time to put him right out. Presently I saw him, with rifle in hand, taking aim at one of my comrades. It was too late to stop him; he fired, and poor Nicholls fell dead, shot through the head.

I practised a little ruse upon a Zulu at which I had to smile even at the time. This particular Zulu had got through the barricades into the laager, and was in the act of throwing an assegai at Lieutenant Bromhead, whose attention was directed elsewhere. At that moment my rifle was unloaded, and there was no time to reload. I shouted to the Zulu, and brought my rifle up to my shoulder as if to fire. My Zulu soldier didn't wait. With a duck of the head and a mighty leap he bounded over the barricades and made off in a manner worthy of any eminent acrobat.

In one of the many rushes a nigger, who had missed our bullets, came full tilt at me, and seized my bayonet with both his hands. This was quite a new experience for me. There was no time to lose: I had to settle up with him quickly or not at all. For a few seconds we struggled for possession of the rifle; then I managed to point the barrel at his stomach, and fired whilst he still clutched the bayonet. He was a brave fellow. Parson Smith, our chaplain, kept us well supplied with ammunition. Now and then he would ask our men not to swear so much. But the men continued to swear, and fight the harder.

We knew that the poor fellows in the hospital were fighting against great odds for their lives, but we could not see what was going on there. Jones, Williams, Hook and their comrades had kept the enemy off for some time, but now the Zulus had set fire to the roof, which was of thatch, and the patients had to be taken away. In order to reach the laager the patients and their defenders had to cross an undefended space, which was swept by the enemy's bullets. One by one the poor fellows scrambled out of the burning building, and ran the gauntlet. We covered them as much we could, but many of them went under.

When the Zulus set fire to the hospital the other company of the battalion, for which we had been so anxiously waiting, appeared in sight. But they didn't march to our rescue. Seeing the hospital on fire, they came to the conclusion that we had all been annihilated, and with drooping spirits we saw our comrades turn back and retire. It was at this time that the Zulus made one of their most desperate charges, and Rorke's Drift was all but lost. Lieutenant Bromhead encouraged the men.

"Don't lose heart," he called out; "Our men will return as soon as they find we are holding out."

The hospital fire became more fierce. This fire turned out to be our salvation, for as darkness came on it lit up the ground on all sides of the laager, and enabled us to see the Zulus whenever they approached the barricades.

The fighting went on desperately. Rush after rush had been repelled. Of the eight who held the unbarricaded position only two of us were left, Lieutenant Bromhead and myself. Nicholls, Fagan, and Cole were killed, whilst Dalton and Williams were wounded. So Bromhead and I went on together for about an hour, and a rough time we had too. More than once the Zulus got inside the laager, but were beaten back or killed.

We were both very busy with Zulus in front when one of the niggers managed to pass us and get inside. I knew he was there. I was just about to shoot down a Zulu in front, when the Zulu inside shot me through the right shoulder, carrying away the scapula. Turning round quickly, Bromhead at once shot down the man who had wounded me. I got up again, and attempted to use my rifle, but it was no use; my right arm wouldn't work, so I strapped it into my waist belt to keep it out of the way. Then Bromhead gave me his revolver to use, and with this I think I did as much execution as I had done before I was wounded.

Seeing how badly wounded I was, one of my comrades, a man named Deacon, asked me whether he should "put me out" when it came to the finish. He could see that my strength was fast failing, and that if the devils got through I, would be quite unable to strike a blow for myself.

"No, I don't think I want any," I said, I had no desire to have my life ended, but it was kind of my friend Deacon to think of me in this way.

It was about ten o'clock. Four hours I had been bleeding from the wound in my back, and I was getting very faint from loss of blood. I knew that I was losing consciousness, the last of my recollection being that Bromhead still held his post. Then I went down where I had been fighting for seven hours. I was told that later on they dragged me inside the inner laager.

It was not till the next morning that I came to, when I found we had just been relieved by a column under Lord Chelmsford. My chum was one of the relieving force. He, good chap, came and changed my shirt, which was saturated with blood, and did what he could for me.

Later on in the day towards evening Lord Chelmsford himself came to me, and, bending down beside me, said:

"Mr. Bromhead has given me an account of your excellent services. I will recommend you for the V.C., and, if you only survive, you may be sure I will do everything that lies in my power for you."

Extract from "The Daily Telegraph," July 11th, 1910

V.C. Taxi-Driver

The only taxi-driver in London, and possibly in the United Kingdom, possessing the Victoria Cross is Mr Frederick Hitch, of Pond House, Pond-place, Chelsea. Mr. Hitch received the coveted award for an exceptional act of gallantry at the defence of Rorke's Drift on an. 22. 1879. He was serving with the 24th Regiment (South Wales Borderers) and, in company with Private William Allen, who also received the V.C., held open the communication between the hospital and the inner defence, enabling the wounded to be carried across when the Zulus set fire to the thatched building. He was very badly hit by a roughly-made bullet, which inflicted a fearful gash in his shoulder, no less than thirty-six pieces of bone being taken away from the wound. When prevented from firing he served out ammunition during the night. He received the Victoria Cross from Queen Victoria at Netley Hospital on being invalided home.

Mr. Hitch was born in 1856 at New Southgate, and previous to the Zulu War had served through the Kaffir War of 1877-8.

25B/1373 Private Alfred Hook, 'B' Company, 2nd/24th Foot

Extract from a private letter written to his mother in Monmouth which appeared in "The South Wales Weekly Telegram," & "The Daily Telegram," Friday, April 18th, 1879, page 6

...After the enemy had fled from the General's camp, they came across the river here and attacked our commissary stores but fortunately we got an hour's warning and made a fort. By-and-by down they came in thousands - one black mass - so many we did not know where to fire first, they being so many and we were about a hundred all told. But, thank God, after a night of great fighting, we drove them off and we saw the General's forces coming over the hill and that gave us great relief, I can tell you. There were four Monmouth men killed, viz. Sergeant Maxfield (Cinderhill

Street), Private Hopkins (formerly a servant at Gibraltar House, Monmouth and later a policeman stationed at Llanarth), Private Charles (Penalt near Monmouth) and Thomas Bennet (Monnow Street). Sergeant Maxfield was burnt alive in the hospital; the enemy swarmed around and burnt the place before we could save him and, as he was raving mad with fever, he could not save himself. Hopkins and the others were killed in the fight at the General's camp. I had a very narrow escape, for I was in the hospital and when the enemy set fire to it, I had to get out of the window and fight my way through them. - I am now servant to Major Black (his man having been killed) and a nice gentleman he is and I like him very much.

"The Strand Magazine," Vol. 1, January to June 1891

Stories of the Victoria Cross: Told by Those who have Won it
Private Henry Hook

On January 22nd 1879, Private Henry Hook, with his company, under Lieutenant Bromhead, was stationed at Rorke's Drift, to guard the ford and hospital and stores. He thus tells his gallant story:-

Between three and four in the afternoon, when I was engaged preparing the tea for the sick at the out-of-door cooking place, just at the back of the hospital - for I was hospital cook - two mounted men, looking much exhausted, and their horses worn out, rode up to me. One was in his shirt sleeves, and without a hat, with a revolver strapped round his breast; the other had his coat and hat on. They stopped for a few moment and told me that the whole force on the other side of the river had been cut up, and that the Zulus were coming on in great force. They then rode off. I immediately ran to the camp close by and related what I had heard. We were at once fallen in and set to work to strengthen the post by loopholing the windows of the buildings, and to make breastworks of biscuit boxes and mealie bags. About half an hour later the Zulus were seen coming round a hill, and about 1,200 yards off. We were then told off to our posts. I was placed in one of the corner rooms of the hospital.

About this time Captain Stevens and all his men, except one native and two Europeans, non-commissioned officers, deserted us, and went off to Helpmakaar. We were so enraged that we fired several shots at them, one of which dropped a European non-commissioned officer. From my loophole I saw the Zulus approaching in their thousands. They begun to fire, yelling as they did so, when they were 500 or 600 yards off. They came on boldly, taking advantage of anthills and other cover, and we were soon surrounded. More than half of them had muskets or rifles. I began to fire when they were 600 yards distant. I managed to clip several of them, for I had an excellent rifle, and was a "marksman." I recollect particularly on Zulu. He was about 400 yards off, and was running from one anthill to another. As he was running from cover to cover, I fired at him; my bullet caught him in the body, and he made a complete somersault. Another man was lying below an anthill, about

300 yards off popping his head out now and again to fire. I took careful aim, but my bullet went just over his head. I then lowered my sight, and fired again the next time he showed himself. I saw the bullet strike the ground in a direct line, but about ten yards short. I then took a little fuller sight, aimed at the spot where I knew his head would come out, and, when he showed himself, I fired. I did not then see whether he was struck, but he never showed himself again. The next morning, when the fighting was over, I felt curious to know whether I had hit this man, so I went to the spot where I had last seen him. I found him lying dead, with his skull pierced by my bullet.

The Zulus kept drawing closer and closer, and I went on firing, killing several of them. At last they got close up, and set fire to the hospital. There was only one patient in my room with a broken leg, and he was burnt, and I was driven out by the flames, and was unable to save him. At first I had a comrade but he left after a time, and was killed on his way to the inner entrenchment. When driven out of this room, I retired by a partition door into the next room, where there were several patients. For a few minutes I was the only fighting man there. A wounded man of the 24th came to me from another room with a bullet wound in the arm. I tied it up. Then John Williams came in from another room and made a hole in the partition, through which he helped the sick and wounded men. Whilst he was doing this, the Zulus beat in the door, and tried to enter. I stood at the side, and shot and bayoneted several - I could not tell how many, but there were four or five lying dead at my feet. They threw assegais continually, but only one touched me, and that afflicted a scalp wound which I did not think worth reporting; in fact, I did not feel the wound at the time.

One Zulu seized my rifle, and tried to drag it away. Whilst we were tussling I slipped in a cartridge and pulled the trigger - the muzzle was against his breast, and he fell dead. every now and again a Zulu would make a rush to enter - the door would only let in one man at a time - but I bayoneted or shot every one. When all the patients were out except one, who owing to a broken leg could not move, I also went through the hole, dragging the man after me, in doing which I broke his leg again. I then stopped at the hole to guard it, whilst Williams was making a hole through the partition into the next room.

When the patients had been got into the next room I followed, dragging the man with the broken leg after me. I stopped at the hole to guard it whilst Williams was helping the patients through a window into the other defences. I stuck to my particular charge, and dragged him out and helped him into the inner line of defences. I then took my post behind the parapet where three men had been hit just before. One of these was shot in the thick part of the neck, and was calling on me all night to shift from one side to the other. On this side the blaze of the hospital lighted up the ground in front, enabling us to take aim. The Zulus would every quarter of an hour or so get together and make a rush accompanied by yells. We let them get close, and then fired a volley - sometimes two. This would check them and send them back. Then after a time they would rally and come on again. About 3a.m. day began to break, and the Zulus retreated. A party, of which I was one, then volunteered to go across to the hospital, where there was a water cart, and bring it in to the inner enclosure, where there was no water, and the wounded were crying for it. When the sun rose we found the Zulus had disappeared. We then went out to search for our missing comrades. I saw one man kneeling behind the outer defences with his rifle to his shoulder, and resting on the parapet as if he were taking aim; I touched him on the shoulder, asking him why he didn't come inside, but he fell over, and I saw he was dead. I saw several others of our dead ripped open and otherwise mutilated. Going beyond the outer defences I went, as I have said before, whither I had killed the man at whom I had fired three shots from the hospital. Going on a little further I came across a very tall Zulu, bleeding from a wound in the leg; I was passing him by when he made a yell and clutched the butt of my rifle, dragging himself on to his knees. We had a severe struggle which lasted for several seconds, when finding he could not get the rifle from me, he let go with one hand and caught me round the leg, trying to throw me. Whilst he was doing this I got the rifle from him, and drawing back a yard or two, loaded and blew his brains out. I then was fetched back to the fort, and no one was allowed to go out save with other men. Then several of us went out together, and we brought in several wounded Zulus. By this time it was about eight or nine o'clock, and we saw a body coming towards us; at the same time Lord Chelmsford's column came in sight, and the enemy retired.

Lord Chelmsford, soon after he arrived, called me up to enquire about the defence of the hospital. I was busy preparing tea for sick and wounded, and was in my shirt-sleeves, with my braces down. I wanted to put on my coat before appearing in front of the General, but I was told to come along at once, and I felt rather nervous at leaving in such a state, and thought I had committed some offence. When Lord Chelmsford heard my story he praised me and shook me by the hand. The Cross was presented to me on August 3, at Rorke's Drift, by Sir Garnet Wolseley.

Extract from "The V.C.," (a magazine), c. 1904

How V.C.'s Are Won
Private Hook at Rorke's Drift

I was coming out of the British Museum Reading Room when I met him first - a short, broad-shouldered, kindly-looking man in a uniform something between that of a recruiting sergeant and an undertaker's mute. He was handing me back my umbrella in return for a check, when one of the two medals shining on the breast of his dark uniform caught my eye.

"Halloa!" I exclaimed, and my excitement and interest must have been very boyishly in evidence, for the old man smiled at me as I spoke. "Isn't that the Cross you're wearing?"

"Yes, sir."

"And the Zulu medal beside it - Why? you must be Sergeant Hook?"

He smiled again - a pleasant, tired smile. "I'm all that's left of him, sir."

What a difference! This man who handed me my umbrella and called me "sir" was the same who, with blazing rafters overhead and all Hell loose in front, stood fighting single-handed in defence of the wounded and dying on that long-ago day in the little hospital of Rorke's Drift. The story of the fight is well known. I will give Mr. Hook's account of it as near as may be in his own words:-

"I was placed in one of the corner rooms of the hospital, the Zulus kept drawing closer and closer, and I went on firing, killing several of them At last they got close up, and set fire to the hospital. There was only one patient in my room. He had a broken leg and was burnt, poor fellow for while I was shooting the flames became so fierce that I could not save him. At first I had a comrade but he left after a time, and was killed on his way to the inner entrenchments.

"When driven out of this room, I retired by a partition door into the next room, where there were several patients. For a few minutes I was the only fighting man there. A man of the 24th came to me from another room with a bullet wound in the arm. I tied it up. Then John Williams came and made a hole in the partition, through which he helped the sick and wounded men. Whilst he was doing this, the Zulus beat in the door, and tried to enter. I stood at the side and shot and bayoneted several - I could not tell how many, but there were five or six lying at my feet. They threw assegais continually, but only one touched me, and that afflicted a scalp wound which I did not think worth while reporting. In fact, I did not feel the wound at the time. One Zulu seized my rifle and tried to drag it away. Whilst we were tussling I slipped a cartridge in and pulled the trigger - the muzzle was against his breast, and he fell dead. Every now and then a Zulu would make a rush to enter - the door would only let one man in at a time - but I bayoneted or shot every one. When all the patients were out except one - who owing to a broken leg could not move - I went too, dragging him after me, in doing which I again broke his leg again. I then stopped at the hole to guard it whilst Williams was making a hole through the partition into the next room. I stuck to my particular charge, and dragged him out and into the inner line of defence. I then took my post behind the parapet."

J.H.K.A.

"The Monmouthshire Beacon," January 20th, 1905

RORKE'S DRIFT RETOLD

In the February number of the 'Royal Magazine' Sergeant Henry Hook, V.C., re-tells the story of Rorke's Drift, where he won his coveted distinction 'for Valour'. Sergeant Hook is a Gloucestershire man. He was born in 1854, and served five years in the Militia before enlisting in the 24th Regiment, with which he served in the Zulu War. The story of the Zulus' terrible onslaught on the small British detachment at Rorke's Drift is vividly related. It will be remembered that for thirteen hours a handful of Englishmen, outnumbered by at least thirty to one, defended themselves against the furious assaults of Zulu warriors glutted with the victory at Isandhlwana and saved an army, if not a colony, from destruction. Of the defenders 17 were killed and 13 wounded, while of the Zulus 351 were buried and almost as many were left where they had crawled to die. Hook remained at the drift for six months after the fight, and received his decoration there at the hands of Lord Wolseley. He left the army as a private with the V.C. and a yearly pension of £10, his rank of sergeant being the result of twenty years' association with the Volunteer force.

His own account, (edited and transcribed by Mr. Walter Wood.), which appeared in "The Royal Magazine," c. February 1905

Everything was perfectly quiet at Rorke's Drift after the column (Durnford's Force) had left, and every officer and man was going about his business as usual. Not a soul suspected that only a dozen miles away the very men that we had said, "Good-bye" and "Good-luck" to were either dead or standing back to back in a last fierce fight with the Zulus. Our garrison consisted of one Company of the 2nd/24th under Lieutenant Bromhead, and details which brought the total number of us up to 139. Besides these, we had about 300 men of the Natal Native Contingent; but they didn't count, as they bolted in a body when the fight began. We were all knocking about, and I was making tea for the sick, as I was hospital cook at the time.

Suddenly there was a commotion in the camp, and we saw two men galloping towards us from the other side of the river, which was Zululand. Lieutenant Chard of the Engineers was protecting the pont's over the river and as senior officer, was in command of the drift. The pont's were very simple affairs, one of them being supported on big barrels, and the other on boats. Lieutenant Bromhead was in the camp itself. The horsemen shouted and were brought across the river, and then we knew what had happened to our comrades. They had been butchered to a man. That was awful enough news, but worse was to follow, for we were told that Zulus were coming straight on from Isandlwana to attack us. At the same time, a note was received by Lieutenant Bromhead from the column to say that the enemy was coming on and that the post was to be held at all costs.

For some little time we were all stunned, then everything changed from perfect quietness to intense excitement and energy. There was a general feeling that the only safe thing was to retire and try to join the troops at Helpmakaar. The horsemen had said that the Zulus would be up in two or three minutes; but luckily for us they did not show themselves for more than an hour, Lieutenant Chard rushed up from the river, about a quarter of a mile away, and saw Lieutenant Bromhead. Orders were given to strike the camp and make ready to go, and we actually loaded up two wagons. Then Mr. Dalton, of the Commissariat Department, came up and said that if we left the drift every man was certain to be killed. He had formerly been a Sergeant-Major in a line Regiment and was one of the bravest men that ever lived. Lieutenant's Chard and Bromhead held a consultation, short and earnest, and orders were given that we were to get the hospital and storehouse ready for defence, and that we were never to say die or surrender.

Not a minute was lost. Lieutenant Bromhead superintended the loopholing and barricading of the hospital and storehouse, and the making of a connection of the defences between the two buildings with a wall of mealie-bags and wagons. The mealie-bags were good, big, heavy things, weighing about 200 pounds each, and the mealies [Indian corn] were thickly spread about the ground.

The biscuit boxes contained ordinary biscuits. They were big, square wooden boxes, weighing about a hundred-weight each. The meat boxes, too, were very heavy, as they contained tinned meat. They were smaller than the biscuit boxes. While these precautions were being made, Lieutenant Chard went down to the river and brought in the pont guard of a Sergeant and half-a-dozen men, with the wagons and gear. The two officers saw that every soldier was at his post, then we were ready for the Zulus when they cared to come.

They were not long. Just before half past four we heard firing behind the conical hill at the back of the drift, called Oscarberg Hill, and suddenly about five or six hundred Zulus swept around, coming for us at a run. Instantly the native - Kaffirs who had been very useful in making the barricade of wagons, mealie-bags and biscuit boxes around the camp - bolted towards Helpmakaar, and what was worse, their officer and a European Sergeant went with them. To see them deserting like that was too much for some of us, and we fired after them. The Sergeant was struck and killed. Half-a-dozen of us were stationed in the hospital, with orders to hold it and guard the sick. The ends of the building were of stone, the side walls of ordinary bricks, and the inside walls or partitions of sun-dried bricks of mud. These shoddy inside bricks proved our salvation, as you will see. It was a queer little one-storied building, which it is almost impossible to describe; but we were pinned like rates in a hole; because all the doorways except one had been barricaded with mealie-bags, and we had done the same with the windows. The interior was divided by means of partition walls into which were fitted some very slight doors. The patient's beds were simple, rough affairs of boards, raised only about half a foot above the floor. To talk of hospital and beds gives the idea of a big building, but as a matter of fact this hospital was a mere little shed or bungalow, divided up into rooms so small that you could hardly swing a bayonet in them. There were about nine men who could move, but altogether there were about thirty. Most of these, however, could help to defend themselves.

As soon as our Kaffirs bolted, it was seen that the fort as we had first made it was too big to be held, so Lieutenant Chard instantly reduced the space by having a row of biscuit-boxes drawn across the middle, about four feet high. This was our inner entrenchment, and proved very valuable. The Zulus came on at a wild rush, and although many of them were shot down, they got within about fifty yards of our south wall of mealie-bags, biscuit boxes and wagons. They were caught between two fires, that from the hospital and that from the storehouse, and were checked; and gave us many heavy volleys. During the fight they took advantage of every bit of cover there was, anthills, a tract of bush that we had not had time to clear away, a garden or sort of orchard which was near us, and a ledge of rock and some caves (on the Oscarberg) which were only about a hundred yards away. They neglected nothing, while they went on firing, large bodies kept hurling themselves against our slender breastwork.

But it was the hospital they assaulted most fiercely. I had charge with a man that we called "Old King Cole" of a small room with only one patient in it. Cole kept with me for some time after the fight began, then he said he was not going to stay. He went outside and was instantly killed by the Zulus, so that I was left alone with the patient, a native whose leg was broken and who kept crying out "Take my bandage off, so that I can come." But it was impossible to do anything except fight, and I blazed away as hard as I could. By this time I was the only defender of my room. Poor "Old King Cole" was lying dead outside and the helpless patient was crying and groaning near me. The Zulus were swarming around us, and there was an extraordinary rattle as the bullets struck the biscuit boxes, and queer thuds as they plumped into the bags of mealies. Then there was a whiz and rip of the assegais, of which I had experience during the Kaffir Campaign of 1877-8. We had plenty of ammunition, but we were told to save it and so we took careful aim at every shot, and hardly a cartridge was wasted. One of my comrades, Private Dunbar, shot no fewer than nine Zulus one of them being a Chief.

From the very first the enemy tried to rush the hospital, and at last they managed to set fire to the thick grass which formed the roof. This put us in a terrible plight, because it meant that we were either to be massacred or burned alive, or get out of the building. To get out seemed impossible; for if we left the hospital by the only door which had been left open, we should instantly fall into the midst of the Zulus. Besides, there were the helpless sick and wounded, and we could not leave them. My own little room communicated with another by means of a frail door like a bedroom door. Fire and dense choking smoke forced me to get out and go into the other room. It was impossible to take the native patient with me. I had to leave him to an awful fate. But his death was, at any rate, a merciful one. I heard the Zulus asking him questions, and he tried to tear off his bandages and escape.

In the room where I now was there were nine sick men and I alone to look after them for some time, still firing away, with the hospital burning. Suddenly in the thick smoke I saw John Williams, and above the din of battle and the cries of the wounded, I heard him shout, "The Zulus are swarming all over the place. They've dragged Joseph Williams out and killed him," John Williams had held the other room with Private William Horrigan for more than an hour, until they had not a cartridge left. The Zulus then burst in and dragged out Joseph Williams and two of the patients, and assegaied them. It was only because they were so busy with this slaughter that John Williams and two of the patients were able to knock a hole in the partition and get into the room where I was posted. Horrigan was killed. What were we to do? we were pinned like rats in a hole. Already the Zulus were fiercely trying to burst the doorway. The only way of escape was the wall itself, by making a hole big enough for a man to crawl through into an adjoining room, and so on until we got to our inmost entrenchment outside.

Williams worked desperately at the wall with the navvy's pick, which I had been using to make some of the loop-holes with. all this time the Zulus were trying to get into the room. Their assegais kept whizzing towards us, and one struck me in front of the helmet. We were wearing the white tropical helmets then. But the helmet tilted back under the blow and made the spear lose its power so that I escaped with a scalp wound which did not trouble me much then, although it has often caused me illness since. Only one man at a time could get at the door. A big Zulu sprang forward and seized my rifle, but I tore it free and, slipped a cartridge in, I shot him point blank. Time after time the Zulus gripped the muzzle and tried to tear the rifle from my grasp, and time after time I wrenched it back because I had a better grip than they had.

All this time Williams was getting the sick through the hole into the next room, all except one, a soldier of the 24th named Conley, who could not move because of a broken leg. Watching for my chance, I dashed from the doorway and, grabbing Conley I pulled him after me through the hole. His leg got broken again, but there was no help for it. As soon as we left the room the Zulus burst in with furious cries of disappointment and rage.

Now there was a repetition of the work of holding the doorway, except that I had to stand by a hole instead of a door, while Williams picked away at the far wall to make an opening for escape into the next room. There was more desperate and almost hopeless fighting, as it seemed, but most of the poor fellows were got through the hole. Again I had to drag Conley through, a terrific task because he was a very heavy man. We were now all in a little room that gave upon the inner line of defence which had been made. We (Williams and Robert Jones and William Jones and myself) were the last men to leave the hospital, after most of the poor fellows were got through the hole, and the small window and away from the burning building; but it was impossible to save a few of them, and they were butchered. Private's William Jones and Robert Jones during all this time were doing magnificent work in another ward which faced the hill. They kept at it with bullet and bayonet until six of the seven patients had been removed. They would have got the seventh, Sergeant Maxfield, out safely, but he was delirious with fever and, although they managed to dress him, he refused to move. Robert Jones made a last rush to try and get him away like the rest, but when he got back into the room he saw Maxfield was being stabbed by the Zulus as he lay on his bed. Corporal Allen and Private Hitch helped greatly in keeping up communications with the hospital. They were both wounded, but when they could not fight ant longer they served out ammunition to their comrades.

As we got the sick and wounded out they were taken to a verandah in front of the storehouse, and Dr. Reynolds under heavy fire from clouds of assegais, did everything he could for them. All this time, of course, the storehouse was being valiantly defended by the rest of the garrison. When we got into the inner fort, I took my post at a place where two men had been shot. While I was there another man was shot in the neck. I think by a bullet which came through the space between two biscuit boxes that were not quite close together. This was about six o'clock in the evening nearly two hours after the opening shot of the battle had been fired. Every now and then the Zulus would make a rush for it and get in. We had to charge them out. By this time it was dark, and the hospital was all in flames, but this gave us a splendid light to fight by. I believe it was this light that saved us. We could see them coming and they could not rush us and take us by surprise from any point. They could not get us, and so they went away and had ten or fifteen minutes of a war-dance. This roused them up again, and their excitement was so intense that the ground fairly seemed to shake.

Then, when they were goaded to the highest pitch they would hurl themselves at us again. I need hardly say that we were using the Martini, and fine rifles they were too, but we did so much firing that they became hot, and the brass of the cartridges softened, the result being that the barrels got very foul and the cartridge chamber jammed. My own rifle was jammed several times, and I had to work away with the ramrod till I cleared it. We used the old three-sided bayonet, and the long thin blade we called the "lung" bayonet. They were very fine weapons too, but some were very poor in quality, and either twisted or bent badly. Several were like that after the fight; but some terrible thrusts were given, and I saw dead Zulus who had been pinned to the ground by the bayonet going through them.

All this time the sick and wounded were crying for water. We had the water-cart full of water, but it was just by the deserted hospital and we could not hope to get it until the day broke, when the Zulus might begin to lose heart and to stop in their mad rushes. But we could not bear the cries any longer, and three or four of us jumped over the boxes and ran and fetched some water in.

The long night passed and the day broke. Then we looked around us to see what had happened, and there was not a living soul who was not thank full to find that the Zulus had had enough of it and were disappearing over the hill to the south-west. Orders were given to patrol the ground, collect the arms of the dead blacks, and make our position as strong as possible in case of fresh attacks.

One of the first things I did was to go up to the man who was still looking over our breastwork, with his rifle presented to the spot where so many of the Zulus had been. I went up to him, and saw that he did not move, and that he looked very quiet. I went nearer and said "Hello, what are you doing here?" He made no answer, and did not stir. I went still closer, and something in his appearance made me tilt his helmet back, as you sometimes tilt back a hat when you want to look closely into a face. As I did so I saw a bullet-mark in his forehead, and knew that he was dead.

I went away, and was walking up the dry bed of a little stream near the drift with my own rifle in my hand and a bunch of assegais over my left shoulder. When, suddenly I came across an unarmed Zulu lying on the ground, apparently dead but bleeding from the leg. Thinking it strange that a dead man should go on bleeding, and that other Zulus might be about, I resumed my task. Just as I was passing the supposed dead man he seized the butt of my rifle and tried to drag it away. The bunch of assegais rattled to the ground.

The Zulu suddenly released his grasp of the rifle with one hand, and with the other fiercely endeavoured to drag me down. The fight was short and sharp; but it ended by the Zulu being struck in the chest with the butt and knocked to the ground. The rest was quickly over. After that we were not allowed to go on with our task except in two's and three's. When we had done this work we went back to the inner line of defence, sad enough, even the most cheerful of us. We did not know how soon another assault might be made, but we did know that if the Zulus kept on attacking us it was only a question of time before we were cut to pieces, as our comrades a dozen miles away had been destroyed.

The roof of the hospital had fallen in by this time, and only the storehouse was standing. We were ordered to put ropes through the loopholes of the walls of the hospital and pull them down. This we did, and the walls which had already been weakened by our picks, partially collapsed. Then we tore away the thatch from the storehouse so that the Zulus could not, even if they wished, set fire to it, as they had fired the hospital. With the ruins of the walls we strengthened our little fort, and again waited for the Zulus - if they cared to come. But they had finished their attack. We looked about us everywhere for signs of relief, but saw nothing and our hearts sank. Then came an awful time of suspense, two of our men had been on the roof of the storehouse signalling with flags when the Zulus meant to attack us. This gave us time to make ready for them. The signallers were still able to stand above the ground, so that they could be seen at a good distance. We saw their flags going wildly. What was it? Everybody was mad with anxiety to know whether it could be friends to relieve us, or more Zulus to destroy us. We watched the flags flapping, and then learnt that signals were being made in reply. We knew we were safe and that friends were marching up to us.

We broke into roar after roar of cheering, waving red coats and white helmets, and we cheered again and again when, at about six o'clock in the morning, Colonel Russell rode up with some mounted infantry. We saw them come in, and at the same time we saw that the Zulus had once more got ready to sweep around the mountain to attack us. But it was too late and on seeing that we were reinforced they turned silently away, and only their dead and a few wounded were left with us.

There was no time to sit down and mope, and there were sick and wounded as well as the rest to look after. So when the Commander-in-Chief arrived I was back at my cooking in my shirt sleeves, making tea for the sick. A Sergeant ran up and said, "Come as you are, straight away," he ordered, and with my braces hanging about me, I went into the midst of the officers. Lord Chelmsford asked me all about the defence of the hospital, as I was the last to leave the building. An officer took our names, and wrote down what we had done. When the relief had come up the men of the column were sent out to bury the Zulus. There were 351 dead blacks counted, and these were put into two big holes in front of the hospital. The column made the Kaffirs who were with them dig the trenches, but although they dug the holes they positively refused to bury the bodies. There were only a few badly wounded left, as the Zulus had carried off their wounded as they retired. A great many dead were found in a mealie-field not far from the hospital.

As for our own comrades, we buried them. This was done the day after the fight, not far from the place where they fell, and at the foot of the hill. Soon afterwards the cemetery was walled in, and a monument was put in the middle. The lettering was cut on it by a Bandsman named Mellsop, who used bits of broken bayonets as chisels. He drew a capital picture of the fight.

Those who had been killed in action were buried on one side of the cemetery, and those who died of disease on the other side. A curious thing was that a civilian named Byrne, who had taken part in the defence and was killed, was buried outside the cemetery wall. I don't know why, except that he was not a regular soldier.

Extract from "The Bronze Cross," by F. Gordon Roe, London, 1945

Rorke's Drift
A V.C.'s Own Story

...For their splendid work in the defence, Chard and Bromhead, Reynolds and Dalton, Allen, Hitch, Hook, the two Joneses, Williams and Schiess, all receive the Victoria Cross.

Of Hitch, who incidentally had fired the opening shot of the action at Rorke's Drift, it is noted in O'Moore Creagh and Humphris's *The V.C. and D.S.O.* that he was in after years the sufferer by a particularly mean theft. His Cross was stolen from his coat, but by King Edward VII's order was replaced by another. As for Pte. (later Sergeant) Hook, he eventually became an attendant at the British Museum, where, incidentally, my Father met and talked with him. He claimed to be "the only man" of the Rorke's Drift survivors "who got the V.C. on the spot where it had been won." A representative of the since defunct *Daily Graphic* mentioned this in an account of Hook's own story, in the V.C.'s obituary published on March 14th, 1905.

" 'Lord Wolseley gave it to me,' he said, 'on August 3rd, within seven or eight hundred yards of the hospital. . . .' "

" 'The Zulus attacked it, as you know,' continued the V.C., 'and we watched 'em coming nearer and nearer. I was a marksman of my troop, and I dropped some of them. One of them, sheltering himself behind an anthill, I had three shots at. I remember,' said Private Hook reflectively, 'that I went out the next day to see whether I'd hit him the third time. He was lying behind the anthill with a hole in his skull. I'd clipped him...' "

" 'Well, at last they got close up and set fire to the hospital, and we defended it. We had to get through one partition of the hospital after another, as I daresay you know. They were only poor brick partitions, and we had to break holes through two of them.' "

" 'I didn't know. I suppose the attacking Zulus drove you from room to room?' "

" 'That's it. In the second room there were several patients; and for a few minutes I was the only fighting man there. A man of the 24th came to me from another room with a wound in his arm. I tied it up. Then John Williams came in from another room and made a hole in the partition, and we got the sick through that. While he was doing it the Zulus smashed the door open and tried to get in. So I stood at the side of it, and shot at them and bayoneted them as they tried to get in. But they could only get in one at a time, and I killed them as they came in. One Zulu got hold of my rifle and tried to drag it away. But I slipped in a cartridge-the muzzle was against his breast - and so he fell dead. When all the sick were out, [i.e., of that part of the hospital], but one who couldn't move, having a broken leg, I went through the hole too, dragging him after me. I broke his leg again doing that. Then I stood at the other side of that hole, as before, while Williams made another hole into the next room. And so on.' "

" 'Yes,' said the *Daily Graphic.*"

" 'And so at last Williams and I got them all through, * one hole after another, and then through a window into the outer defences.

And there we stopped with the rest during the Zulu attack. They kept making rushes every quarter of an hour or so. But the blaze of the hospital gave us light to take aim by.' "

" 'Yes?' "

" 'And so,' concluded Sergeant Hook - for he was then a Sergeant in the 1st V.B., Royal Fusiliers - 'that's the way it happened...' "

From the thunder and flame of Rorke's Drift to the echoing peace of the British Museum: a fitting pendant.

* As reported, Hook was speaking in general terms. It is stated in the obituary that he "was reluctant to dwell upon his part in the affair" and had to be "pressed for particulars," and consequently this interview cannot be regarded in the light of a considered statement. Actually, some of the sick were killed in or outside the hospital.

Extract from "The Natal Witness," February 4th, 1905

RORKE'S DRIFT HERO
Sergeant Hook's Case
National Neglect
History Revived

The heart of the true Briton swells with pride when stories are recounted of doughty deeds performed in the service of the Empire - deeds which are alas too often overlooked by the Home authorities though rarely forgotten by the humblest claimant to a share in the glorious traditions of the race.

There is no need to turn back the pages of history to the eighteenth century, brilliant though they be with gems of valorous conduct by land and sea, to find thrilling examples of British heroism. The opportunities for displaying extreme heroism have occurred less frequently in more recent decades than in olden times, when fighting was a matter of greater simplicity, and men and mettle played a more important part than wits and machines to-day. For all that, in the hour of trial, the British soldier exhibits the same quiet courage, the same coolness and determination as did his forefathers in days of yore.

No Support

And when the fighting is over, and the fervent patriotism has died away, what does the paternal British Government do for the men who sold their lives dearly for the honour of the nation? Too often it would appear, they shamefully neglect them.

And one experience out of many is the career of Sergt. Hook of the 24th Regiment, who so nobly distinguished himself at Isandhlwana during the fateful Zulu Campaign.

In the "Inter Alia" column of the 'Natal Witness' on Saturday, we drew attention to the circumstances of this case. After the war, Sergeant Hook, on leaving his regiment, was given a position in a menial capacity at the British Museum, which post he has continued to occupy till recently, when, on account of his declining years, he has had to relinquish it.

As he has no other means of subsistence, the 'Natal Witness' has decided to open a subscription list, for which sums of money will be gladly received.

While dealing with the character of the man, we may quote here a letter which was received from Newcastle enclosing a subscription. The writer says;-

Letter of Sympathy

"I have read with great interest your article on "A Stranded Hero" in your issue of the 28th. I have met Sergeant Hook on more than one occasion at the door of the British Museum, where he was employed in an humble capacity, taking charge of umbrellas and walking-sticks which visitors brought with them. I was invariably greeted by our hero with a genial smile and bon homme.

"None of the typical hero about him, just an ordinary looking individual. On one occasion I heard it remarked, 'He doesn't look much of a soldier.' However the fact remains that it was Sergeant Hook who saved the wounded in the hospital at Rorke's Drift from all the fiendish overtures of the Zulus.

"He was a teetotaller at the time, and after the black hordes had been shot down, and the remaining numbers had retired to a safe distance, Hook was asked by the Sergeant if he would take a nip, and replied, 'I think I will after that lot.'

"I would be like to relate one little instance which shows the modesty of the man. I met him at Monmouth, a town in which he is well known, and respected by everyone, and after a little common talk, I asked him to show me his V.C. He had not got it with him, explaining that he did not care to carry it about, as people were so often wanting to view it.

"I am pleased to see that you are open to receive subscriptions on his behalf, and can assure anyone who may subscribe to your list that this is a most deserving case, and one that appeals strongly to all Natalians."...

...We feel sure that all who read it will agree that it is the duty of the British nation, and we in Natal in particular, to see that this man who displayed such conspicuous gallantry in the defence of our land, should be saved from the workhouse, and have his last few years made happy.

Extract from "The Natal Witness," February 13th, 1905

The Hook Fund

On Saturday we closed our list of subscriptions to the fund in aid of Sergeant Hook, V.C., now in reduced circumstances in London. Our thanks are due to those of our readers who so kindly forwarded subscriptions. The total amount received as alreadt acknowledged in the "Witness," was £11. 6s., and this amount was forwarded on Saturday to the Editor of the "African World," Copthall Avenue, London, E.C., to whom those who are still desirous of subscribing are requested to remit direct.

We are pleased to see from the list published in the last issue of that paper to hand on Friday, that a handsome sum is being got together by our contemporary. The amount acknowledged on January 21st was £102. 2s. Many prominent Natalians in London have subscribed, including Sir Albert Hime and Sir William Arbuckle.

Extract from "The Natal Witness," March 15th, 1905

Obituary
Sergt. Hook, V.C.

Gloucester, March 14

Sergeant Hook, V.C., is dead.

25B/716 Private Robert Jones, 'B' Company, 2nd/24th Foot.

"The Strand Magazine," Vol 1., January to June 1891

Stories of the Victoria Cross: Told by Those who have Won it
Private Robert Jones

At the gallant defence of the fort at Rorke's Drift, every man fought like a hero, but some were fortunate enough to attract the particular attention of their superiors. Among these was a private of the 24th Regiment, named Robert Jones, who obtained the Victoria Cross for his conduct on the occasion. His story is as follows:-

On the 22nd January, 1879, the Zulus attacked us, we being only a small band of English soldiers and they in very strong and overwhelming numbers. On commencing fighting, I was one of the soldiers who were in the hospital to protect it. I and another soldier of the name of William Jones were on duty at the back of the hospital, trying to defeat and drive back the rebels, and doing our endeavours to convey the wounded and sick soldiers out through a hole in the wall, so that they might reach safety the small band of men in the square. On retiring from one room into another, after taking a wounded man by the name of Mayer, belonging to the volunteers, to join William Jones, I found a crowd in front of the hospital and coming into the doorway. I said to my companion, 'They are on top of us,' and sprang to one side of the doorway. There we crossed our bayonets, and as fast as they came up to the doorway we bayoneted them, until the doorway was nearly filled with dead and wounded Zulus. In the meanwhile, I had three assegai wounds, two in the right side and one in the left of my body. We did not know of anyone being in the hospital, only the Zulus, and then after a long time of fighting at the door, we made the enemy retire, and then we made our escape out of the building. Just as I got outside, the roof fell in - a complete mass of flames and fire. I had to cross a space of about twenty or thirty yards from the ruins of the hospital to the leagued company where they were keeping the enemy at bay. While I was crossing the front of the square bullets were whishing past me from every direction. When I got in, the enemy came on closer and closer, until they were close to the outer side of our laager, which was made up of boxes of biscuits on sacks of Indian corn. The fighting lasted about thirteen hours, or better. As to my feelings at the time, they were that I was certain that if we did not kill them they would kill us, and after a few minutes fighting I did not mind it more than at the present time; my thought was only to fight as an English soldier ought to for his most gracious Sovereign, Queen Victoria, and for the benefit of old England.

"The Hereford Journal," Saturday, September 10th, 1898

Sad Death Of A Rorke's Drift Hero
Determined Suicide At Peterchurch
The Inquest
Evidence Of The Wife.

On Tuesday some sensation was caused in the Peterchurch district by the suicide of Robert Jones, a farm labourer, in the employ of Major De la Hay. It seems that the deceased, who was a Rorke's Drift hero and had received the Victoria Cross, had not been very well lately. On Tuesday morning he asked for a gun to scare some birds - a practice he often followed - in the garden. He went out, and directly afterwards the gun was discharged. No notice was taken at the time, but one of the maids shortly afterwards made a shocking discovery. Jones was then found to be dead. He had evidently placed the muzzle in his mouth, inflicting terrible injuries, which according to the medical evidence, must have proved fatal instantaneously.

An inquest was held at the Broughton Arms, Peterchurch by the Deputy-Coroner, Mr. T. Hutchinson, on Wednesday, touching the death of Robert Jones, Rose Cottage, Peterchurch.

Elizabeth Jones said she lived at Rose Cottage, Peterchurch, and was the wife of the deceased. He was a farm labourer in the employ of Major De la Hay, and was 40 years old. She last saw her husband alive on Tuesday morning about quarter past seven. He was then in the middle of the orchard going towards the Crossways. He had had two cups of tea, but no food. The last words he said to her were, 'The other sheep is at the Castle.' After that he left her and went off in the direction of his work. About eight o'clock she had a message brought to her that her husband was very ill. Ada Morgan brought the message, and she asked if 'he was dead,' and she said 'No, he is not dead.' Witness asked 'Are you sure?' and she made no answer, but said witness was to prepare a place for him. She asked Mrs. Edwards if she would go down and see what was the matter, and she went and said he was dead. Deceased left in his usual health. She knew of nothing the matter with him. She had no reason for asking Ada Morgan if he was dead, only that she could not believe he was ill. She had never heard him threaten to take his life. On Monday last he was the worse for drink, and she got him home by the policeman's wish. He sold a sheep on Monday unknown to her, and when he came to the house to fetch the sheep he gave her £2 5s. She asked him what it was for, and he said he had sold a sheep. Witness said that it was the same money that he gave for it twelve months ago. She saw he was the worse for drink and asked him to leave the sheep and take the money back to the man, but he went for a halter and put it on the sheep and took it to the fair. She followed him down and gave the money back to the man and had the sheep. She then sold it to Mr. Price for 49s. She waited at the public for the deceased until he came home with her about six o'clock. They had no quarrel about the sheep. He had a good supper and went to bed about twelve o'clock. He was quite well and happy and seemed to be sober before he went to bed. He slept all night and got up about half-past six. He then said 'Good morning,' and that he was very hot. He was very wild, and said he was fit to do anything. She asked him to sit down and she would get him some tea. He insisted on going out, and to prevent him she fastened the front door, he went out at the back. she followed him some distance up the road, and pressed him to come back, and he said, 'You had better go back yourself.' The deceased came back in about half an hour's time. He then seemed all right and said 'Good morning' to Mrs. Edwards. He changed his trousers, shoes and shirt, and drank two cups of tea and then left home. He put his best shoes on. She wondered why he did so, but she did not ask him. He had never done such a thing before. He had been a soldier and served in South Africa. He was at Rorke's Drift, where he was wounded in five places, and he obtained the Victoria Cross. At times he complained of his head. He was wounded close to the eye. He had complained of his head very much this summer. He had also suffered from lumbago and sciatica lately. About three weeks last Saturday he was found in a fit in Major De la hay's garden, and since then he had been different to what he usually was. He went round the grounds when he first started out yesterday. He was a good husband and a kind father.

Louisa Wills said she lived at the Crossway House, and she was a laundrymaid in the employ of Major De la Hay. On Tuesday morning about half-past seven Robert Jones came to the Crossway House. She was having her breakfast. He said 'Good morning' to her and said he wanted the gun. She fetched it, and as he came back he said he was going to shoot a quiest in the celery bed. The conversation took place in the kitchen. They were al having their breakfast. Directly after he went out they heard the gun go off. After finishing breakfast she went out to get some wood. Going from the orchard to the kitchen garden, she opened the door and saw a hat. She went a few steps further and saw a lot of blood, and then she ran away. (The witness fainted and was carried out.)

William Henry De la Hay said he lived at the Crossway House and was a retired major. On Tuesday morning he was summoned by the last witness's screams. He had heard the report of the gun about a quarter of an hour before, and knew by the sound it came from the garden. The deceased was in the habit of using the gun to shoot birds about the garden. He heard from his wife that the servants said Jones had shot himself. Witness dressed himself and went into the garden and found deceased. His hat was in the middle of the path near the garden door and full of brains; his body was lying face downwards and about two feet from the hat on the path. The gun was underneath him. He did not touch the body, but at once sent for the police, and in the meantime his wife had sent the grooms for the doctor. They both arrived and went into the garden together. The last time witness saw deceased alive was on Monday morning, and he thought his manner was peculiar then. As a rule he was a sober man: a small quantity of drink, however affected him.

P.C. Bowen deposed to finding the body.

Dr. McMichael said on Tuesday morning he was called to Crossways and got there about nine o'clock. He went in the garden, found the body, turned it over and examined it. There was a large hole in the back of the roof of the mouth, and the top of the head was blown out. There was no mark of powder on the face, and from the position of the wound the muzzle of the gun must have been put in his mouth and then discharged. The deceased was a big man with long arms, and would have no difficulty in holding the gun in such a position and firing it with his right hand. That was what, in his opinion, took place. He attended the deceased about three weeks ago. It was drink that was the matter with him then. The deceased had a sore throat. He had recently had scarlet fever in the house. He had doctored him at intervals for four years; he had never complained to him about his wounds. Death must have been instantaneous.

The jury returned a verdict of 'Suicide whilst of unsound mind.'

The reminiscences of Mrs Rose Morgan, the only surviving grand-daughter of 25B/716 Private Robert Jones, V.C., 'B' Company 2nd/24th.
November 2003

Whilst I have no direct memory of my grandfather, Robert Jones, sadly he died long before I was born, my memories are of the many stories told to us by my father, who was also called Robert Jones, of Grandfather's heroic deeds at Rorke's Drift and how he won a Victoria Cross.

I remember, when living in my father's house that there were two big pictures on the wall, one of the Defence of Rorke's Drift and the other of Grandfather as well as many photographs of him in old family albums.

I grew up knowing that Grandfather was a very special man. There was a poem written about him in 1879, which is very long and I have a copy at home. In April 1964, I, along with my sister (the late Mrs Wilding nee Jones) were invited to the ABC Cinema in Hereford to see the film "ZULU." It was strange to see a clip of my family history portrayed on film and at the time I said I enjoyed it very much, but I don't think I could sit through it again. It made me very sad to think that my grandfather went through all that.

His medals left the family in the late forties and then in 1950 I heard that they had been auctioned for £150 and I attempted to get them back but the auctioneers refused to give the buyer's name. They have been sold on several times since then. The only time I have ever seen and held the medals was the last time they were up for sale in London.

It was not until about 17 years ago that I heard for the first time about my grandfather's 'suicide.'

I was, along with the rest of my family, devastated. Father had never spoken of it. Since then all sorts of stories and theories have emerged regarding his death and of his last resting place at Peterchurch. Whether or not he did commit suicide, I would like it put on record that at the time of his funeral his coffin was taken over the wall of the churchyard because they simply could not get it through the old "Kissing Gate," (which is long since replaced by a new one), and for no other reason. His headstone, I might add, faces the way it does for one reason, and for one reason only, and that is because my father, Robert Jones' son and heir, wanted people to be able to "read the inscription on the stone of this V.C. Hero" as they walked down the path to the church, and if you take the time to look there are a number of other stones facing the same way as my grandfathers.

I have heard on several occasions that people want the headstone turned around, but I have to say now that the family of Robert Jones most definitely <u>Do Not</u> want it moved or altered in any way and will actively resist any attempt to do so. I do just wish that people would simply let him rest in peace and remember him as the hero he was and not for this one truly tragic event that overtook him in later life.

Finally I would like to say that it was my greatest pleasure when, some 5 years ago, I was introduced to a relative of William Jones, V.C., and also to a relative of the Sgt Maxfield who my grandfather had tried so hard to save from both the fire in the hospital and the Zulus, and even going back in for a second time to try again.

My grandfather, Robert Jones, V.C., was a great British Hero and that's the way we will always remember him.

2-24/593 Private William Jones, 'B' Company 2nd/24th Foot

"The Natal Mercury," Wednesday, June 18th, 1879

...When he (Wm. Jones) came here with his Regiment his wife came with him, but after he had been at the front some time she became dangerously ill, and he obtained leave of absence to come down to attend to her. Jones took a room in a house facing the St. George's Hotel Tap, and there, by working night and day repairing boots and shoes, he managed to earn many comforts for his then dying wife. He was a steady, plodding fellow, but his wife was beyond recovery, and he remained with her until she died. The next day he buried her remains and at once started off to join his Regiment...

"The Times," c. *January 1880*

Court Circular

Osborne, Jan. 14

...The Queen decorated Private William Jones, of the 2d Battalion 24th Regiment, yesterday, with the Victoria Cross for his gallantry at the defence of Rorke's Drift, where he, as hospital orderly, assisted in the removal of the sick from the hospital building while it was being force by the enemy.

"The Strand Magazine," Vol. 1., *January to June 1891*

Stories of the Victoria Cross: Told by Those who have Won it
Private W. Jones

No action in recent warfare is better known than that of the heroic defence of Rorke's Drift. We are here able to give the narratives of two soldiers who gained their Cross for bravery in that day's gallant struggle. Here, first, is Private Jones's account of the affair:-

About half past three o'clock on the afternoon of the 22nd January, 1879, a mounted man came galloping into our little encampment and told us that the Zulus had taken the camp at Isandlwana, and were making their way towards us at Rorke's Drift. We at once set to work, and with such material as we had at hand formed a slight barricade around us; this was formed of sacks of mealies (*Indian corn*), boxes of sea biscuits, &c, of which we had a good supply. We also loopholed the walls of the two buildings. We had scarcely completed our work when the Zulus were down upon us. The hospital being the first building in their line of attack, they surrounded it. Having twenty-three sick men in the rooms, our officer, Lieutenant Bromhead, ordered six men into the hospital, myself being one of the number, to defend and rescue the sick from it. We had scarcely taken our post in the hospital when two out of our number were killed in the front or verandah, leaving four of us to hold the place and get out the sick. This was done by two (viz., Privates Hook and Williams) carrying the sick and passing them into the barricade through a small window, while myself (William Jones) and my comrade (Robert Jones) contended each door at the point of the bayonet, our ammunition being expended. The Zulus, finding they could not force us from the doors, now set fire to the thatched roof. This was the most horrifying time. What with the blood-thirsty yells of the Zulus, the cries of the sick that remained, and the burning thatch falling about our heads, it was sickening. Still we kept them at bay until twenty out of the twenty-three sick men were passed into the barricade under the fire of our own men; the other three sick I have every reason to believe must have wandered back into one of the rooms we had cleared, as they were men suffering from fever at the time. By this time the whole of the hospital was in flames, and we could not stay in it any longer, we had to make our own escape into the barricade, by the window through which the sick had been passed. This we did, thank God, with our lives.

"The Manchester Evening Chronicle," February 9th, 1911

RORKE'S DRIFT.
Survivor's Story of the Fight
A Manchester V.C.
Discovered Wandering in the City
Graphic Narrative.
Heroic Defence by a Handful of Soldiers.

Some twenty years ago Private William Jones, V.C., one of the heroes of Rorke's Drift, was well-known to the public of Manchester and many other big centres in England.

Engaged by the proprietor of Hamilton's Panorama, he appeared nightly, for weeks at a time, at the Free Trade Hall, and thrilled thousands of people with the story of how he won the most-coveted honour that can be gained by a British soldier.

When that employment ceased he vanished from the public eye, and it was only through the announcement in the "Evening Chronicle" yesterday that Manchester people realised they had still living amongst them a hero of that famous fight. The old man is getting very feeble now, and, wandering away from home yesterday, he was unable to give any account of himself, except that he was "William Jones, V.C." A friendly policeman took charge of him, but he was soon traced again by his family, and when an "Evening Chronicle" representative called upon him this morning at his home in Rutland-street, Chorlton-on-Medlock, the war worn veteran was seated comfortably by the fireside.

In conversation with the hero and members of his family, assisted by records carefully preserved, our representative was able to gather up the main threads of the old man's history, and some details of the events which led him to appear before Queen Victoria on January 13, 1880, to have the Victoria Cross pinned on his breast by her Majesty.

Early Years in the Army

Born in 1840, Private William Jones joined the 24th Regiment in 1858, and served in the Mauritius from 1860 to 1865. Four years' service in Burmah followed, and then the 24th were ordered to Madras, where they remained until 1873. After a period at home, Private Jones accompanied his regiment to Cape Colony and was there in 1879, when the memorable campaign against Cetewayo, the Zulu chief, began. His account of the battle of Rorke's Drift is as follows:-

"About half-past three in the afternoon of January 22, 1879, a mounted man galloped into our little encampment at Rorke's Drift, and told us the Zulus had taken the camp at Isandlhwana and were making for us at Rorke's Drift. We at once set to work and barricaded ourselves in with mealie bags, of which we had a good supply, making the barricade flush with the walls of two buildings, which we loopholed. We had scarcely completed our work when the Zulus were upon us, the hospital being the first place they reached. There were 23 sick men in the hospital, and Lieutenant

Broomhead, who was in charge of our small force, ordered six men to be sent into the hospital to defend it.

"I was one of the number, and in addition to defending the building, our duty was to rescue the sick. We had scarcely taken our place in the hospital before two of the six men were killed in front of the building, leaving only four of us to hold the building and get the sick men out. This was done by two men carrying the sick while my comrade, R. Jones, and I kept the doors with our bayonets, all our ammunition being expended.

The Hospital on Fire

"The Zulus, finding they could not force the doors, now set fire to the thatched roof. This was our worst time, for not only had we the enemy to fight, but the fire as well.

"Still we kept them at bay until 20 out of the 23 sick were passed safely out into the barricade. By this time the whole hospital was in flames, and as we could not render any more assistance inside, the three other poor fellows having fallen victims to the Zulus, we had now to make good our own escape. This we were fortunate in being able to do.

"Once inside the barricade we had to assist our comrades in defending it. The Zulus charged us from all quarters through the night, the burning hospital affording us great assistance in tracing them.

"We kept them off until daybreak, when we saw what appeared to us to be a black line winding down the Bashee on the other side of the Buffalo river. For some time we could not tell whether this meant friends or reinforcements for the enemy, but later we could bring the field glasses and the telegraph flags to bear and we discovered it was a British force. We found it was General Lord Chelmsford returning with a portion of the column which he had taken out from the camp at Isandhlwana the day before. The Zulus seem to have known him as soon as we did, for as the troops advanced in one direction they retreated in the opposite, leaving over 500 dead behind them; our total loss being 14 after thirteen hours' fighting.

Figures of the Fight

"The other three men who defended the doors of the hospital with me were Privates Williams, Hook and R. Jones. Only two of the Zulus succeeded in climbing the barricade, which soon became stained with their blood, many of them receiving the fire of the rifles while attempting to wrest them from the hands of the defenders. Our soldiers had fired almost straight downwards, as the Zulus were massed close under the mealie bags.

"I remember seeing between the party bearing the wounded from the hospital and the defenders at the mealie bags, the central group, consisting of Sergeant, [sic], Reynolds, his bull terrier, and a wounded man, the gallant Dalton, who played a prominent part in the defence. Dalton was a man of towering stature, and he had been foremost in the defence, exposing himself fearlessly above the low barricade, and using his rifle with deadly aim, and his bayonet with Herculean strength. He was shot down while in the act of taking aim, and he passed his rifle to another commissariat officer, Mr. Byrne, who was himself shot almost immediately through the head, as he was bringing water to a wounded man of the Natal contingent.

"Dalton's rifle was passed to Lieutenant Chard at the barricade, and a wounded man handed him cartridges. Surgeon Reynolds applied a hasty bandage to Dalton's wound, and he remained to cheer on the defenders.

"Another notable figure I remember seeing there was the Rev. George Smith, the chaplain, who spent his time handing out cartridges to the defenders as well as administering spiritual consolation to the wounded.

"Lieutenant Chard took as active a part in the defence as any of the men, and Lieutenant Bromhead kept an eye on the removal of the sick as well as directing the defenders of the barricade.

"Between the hospital and the commissariat store there was a second line of mealie bags, defended not with the bayonet, but by marksmen, who had the hard task of keeping down the plunging fire of the enemy concealed among the stones, bush, and caves of the Oscarsberg. This was the most dangerous part of the defence, as the ;loss of life showed, though, thanks to the ravines just below, no hand to hand fighting took place here.

"The fire from the mealie bag redoubt, and the biscuit box rampart was very fatal, and the enemy presented a fair mark, thanks to the burning hospital. After midnight the attack of the enemy slackened, but it was a quarter past five the next morning before the last shot was fired. This was at a Zulu who was trying to fire the thatch of the store. It was not until dawn that the Zulus disappeared over the hill.

"I was mentioned in the dispatches sent home by Lieutenant Chard, and after the battle of Ulundi I came back to England, having completed 21 years' service."

Private Jones received his V.C. for his gallant defence of the hospital doors, one of the most notable things ever done by two British soldiers. It was hard hand-to-hand fighting for longer than he likes to think of now.

25B/1395 Private John Williams, (Fielding) 'B' Company, 2nd/24th Foot

"The Victoria Cross Register," [WO98/4, The National Archives, (P.R.O.), London.]

The General Officer Commanding
Gibraltar
13th January 80

Sir,
I have the honour to transmit to you herewith the decoration of the Victoria Cross which The Queen has been pleased to signify Her intention to confer upon Private John Williams, 2nd Battalion 24th Regiment, for his gallant conduct during the recent operations in South Africa, as recorded in the annexed extract of the London Gazette of the 2nd May 1879, and I have received Her Majesty's command to desire that you will take the earliest fitting opportunity after the receipt of this instruction,

of presenting, or causing to be presented, to Private John Williams on his arrival at Gibraltar the accompanying decoration in such a public and formal manner as you may consider best adopted to evince Her Majesty's sense of his courageous conduct on the occasion referred to. -

I have to request that you will transmit to me, as soon as practicable, a report of the proceedings which may be adopted on the occasion of the presentation of the enclosed Cross, and copies of any General Order which may be issued, with a view to the same being recorded in the Registry of the decoration, in accordance with Her Majesty's Warrant of the 29th January 1856. -

I have the honour to be, Sir,

Your obedient servant,

"The Western Mail," January 22nd, 1929

STORY OF RORKE'S DRIFT.
Stirring Tale of Pte. J. Williams, V.C.

Private John Williams is the last survivor of the ten members of the heroic band who were awarded the Victoria Cross for their share in that memorable night's work. For very many years he has lived in Cwmbran, and to-day, in his 71st year, he is living happily with a married daughter at 21, Cocker-avenue.

He has no affectation about him. He is willing to talk about his memorable experience, but all he says is said in a modest vein.

The name under which he won for himself lasting fame is not his real name. That is John Fielding. He took the name of Williams when he enlisted, but, let it be said, there was no reason of shame behind that, and to-day in Cwmbran he is known to everybody as John Fielding.

"I was born at Abergavenny in 1858," he said, "and enlisted on January 22, 1877 - two years to the day before the fight at Rorke's Drift. We got to South Africa in the beginning of 1878, and after remaining at Bailey's Post for some time were sent up country. While there, by the way, Capt. A.G. Godwin-Austen (whose brother was killed at Isandhlwana), was our captain, and Lieut. Bromhead was our lieutenant. We had a brush with the Kaffirs, and Capt. Austin was wounded and went home. He was shot in the loins by a Hottentot who was up a tree. We very soon settled accounts with him. We had him out of that tree like one o'clock. Well, we moved up to Pietermaritzburg, and thence to Rorke's Drift.

"This, of course, was a mission station, and consisted of a few low buildings. The first lot of the regiment crossed on January 11 to the Bashi Valley and soon had an encounter with the Zulus, and then they moved on to Isandhlwana, and you know what happened there. My company was left at Rorke's Drift in charge of the hospital there, as well as the commissariat.

95 AGAINST 3,000.

"We first heard of the great disaster from Col. Groom, who told us about Lieuts. Melvill and Coghill. We had it, too, from the chaplain, the Rev. W. Smith. He is still living, I believe, but in any case I would like to say what a fine man he was, a true hero, who during the night that followed rendered magnificent service.

"I can see it all now as clearly as I saw it on that day. There were 95 of us at that post, and we knew that 3,000 Zulus, flushed with victory and mad for more slaughter, would soon be upon us. We had just time. It was 3.30 in the afternoon when we saw them begin to round the hill, and never did an enemy seem to have an easier prey. We had had no more than time to improvise barricades with biscuit tins and mealie bags, and now they were upon us.

"What did I feel? I don't know that I felt anything more than all the others felt. In his ordinary life a man often contemplates some possibility and feels that he would be unable to face it, but when it happens he does face it. He finds himself up against it, and goes through with it. That is just about what happened to all of us.

"We knew the seriousness of the affair, but we had no time to sit down and think about it. And now there was the Zulus, and there was one watchword for all of us - we must keep the enemy at bay. I heard that many times during the night that followed."

NO TIME TO THINK.

"Besides, when the enemy appeared we had precious little time for thinking. The attack started at 3.30 in the afternoon, and for the next eighteen hours we knew all about it."

Here Pte. John Williams began to show less inclination to talk. One, naturally, wanted him to describe that night of hell and how he helped to save the wounded and the sick. But he would say little more than that it was recorded in the official "Gazette." Therein it is told that -

"Pte. John Williams was posted with Pte. Joseph Williams and Pte. William Horrigan in a distant room of the hospital, which they held for more than an hour, so long as they had a round of ammunition left. As communication was for a time cut off, the Zulus were able to advance and burst open the door. They dragged out Pte. Joseph Williams and two of the patients. and assegaied them. Whilst the Zulus were occupied with the slaughter of these men a lull took place, during which Pte. John Williams with the two patients, who were the only men now left alive in this ward, succeeded in knocking a hole in the partition and taking the two patients into the next ward, where he found Pte. Hook. These two men together, one working while the other fought and kept the enemy at bay with his bayonet, broke through three more partitions, and were thus enabled to bring eight patients through a small window into the near line of defence."

"Yes," proceeded Pte. John Williams, "it was a terrible time. All we were concerned with was to keep the enemy at bay and to save the patients if we could. While they were killing poor Joe Williams and Horrigan I was as busy as I could be knocking that hole in the partition."

All he would add was that when his share in the fighting was ended he had just two rounds of ammunition left...

CHAPTER 2: 1st & 2nd Battalions 24th Foot, (2nd Warwickshire) Regiment

25B/572 Private Thomas Parry, 1st/24th Foot

A letter written to his family which appeared in "The Herefordshire Times," April 12th, 1879

The Massacre of Isundula

Helpmakaar, Feb 14 1879

Dear Father and Mother,

I now take the first opportunity of writing to you that I have had the last week or two. We have been very busy, the few of us that are left of the 1st/24th Regiment, we have had some very hard fighting, and we have had 600 killed altogether belonging to us. The way it was done I will try to tell you. On the morning of the 22nd of January there came into the General's camp a native and told him that the Zulus were about 13 miles away. What did he do but take 1,600 and went out to look for them, he left behind five companies of our regiment to look after the camp, with a lot more natives that he has armed to help us.

He had not gone about ten miles from camp before the Zulus began to show themselves on the top of the hill alongside the camp. It was not long before the fight began, when Col. Durnford, of the RE, came up and took our command.

He wanted our Major to let him have two companies to go out to meet them, but he would not let them go, as he had orders to defend the camp; but in a short time Durnford came back and took them, and sent one company out skirmishing to the right of the camp, about a mile away, and there they fell as they extended not one was seen alive afterwards. The Zulus kept coming on in thousands and they fell in heaps, but that made no difference.

They kept walking over the dead bodies of the others till they got within 50 yards of the few poor fellows that were left. Then the native allies turned round and ran away. Then the butchers began their work. They cut our poor fellows up to pieces. Then they made their way down to Rorke's Drift where I was with a company of the 2nd/24th.

We gave them such a warming there they won't forget for some time to come. They kept coming at us all night, but gave it up as a bad job. We killed 400 of them and lost 10 and 9 wounded. The way I came to be with them down there and not at the camp was that one of my horses got lame and I had to stop with him, or else you would not have heard from me any more. My master got shot and then ripped up. He had my horse shot under him first, then he got some one else's, it was a lucky job for me that his horse got lame. I dare say there is a full account in the papers by this time.

There was a lot of poor fellows from about Wales. The companies that are cut up are the N.A.C.E.F.H. Companies. We had our colours lost, but it was brought into camp two days ago. The two officers that saved it got killed about 200 yards from where we are now. We lost altogether 500 or more rank and file and 15 officers. We expect to have a big fight next Monday. We are about 2,500 strong here and on a fort, but the Zulu King tells that if we don't shift out of his country he will eat us all up. So, dear father and mother, I must conclude with best love, and remain your affectionate son.

Tom.

I forgot Ellen is at home. Give my best love to her and William, Mrs Lewis and Johnny

572 Private Thomas Parry. D/Company 1-24th Regiment. Natal, South Africa.

"The Merthyr Express," April 12th, 1879, page 5

Providential escape of a Merthyr Soldier

This week Mr. Thomas Parry, gardener at the Castle Hotel who had a son in the 24th Regiment at Natal, and had given him up as dead, was over-joyed at the receipt of a letter from the young man reporting himself alive and well, and explaining his providential escape.

He was groom to Colonel Pulleine, whose horse had got lamed, and he took young Parry's horse instead, directing Parry to come along slowly with his own charger. By this exchange Private Parry was delayed on the road so long that he did not reach the camp at all, but was on the march with the lame horse when he met the fugitives, returned to Rorke's Drift, and formed one of the gallant band which repulsed the night attack of the enemy on the evening of the fatal day at Isandula. We hope he will be spared to return to his native country unwounded.

"The Herefordshire Times," April 12th, 1879, page 15

Letter from a Herefordshire man -
Survivor of the 24th Regiment

We have been favoured with the accompanying letter from Private Thomas Parry, who by a mere accident escaped the massacre at Isandlwana, and subsequently fought in the memorable conflict of Rorke's Drift. The gallant soldier is a Herefordshire man, the son of Thomas Parry, now of the Castle Gardens, Merthyr, but formerly of Swainshill Bank, Stretton Sugwas, near Hereford, in which district he is well known. Many of the old friends both of father and son will be glad to hear of the son's escape and prowess, and only too happy to welcome home the soldier when decorated with the Rorke's Drift medal of valour

1-24/1542 Private William John Roy, 1st/24th Foot

An unidentified Dundee newspaper, c. 1879

The Disaster At Rorke's Drift.
Narrative Of A Dundee Soldier.

The following letter from a soldier in the 1st Battalion of the 24th Regiment to his parents in Dundee, may be of interest to our readers at the present time. In his last letter (dated January 20) he bitterly regretted being in hospital, and unable to advance with his regiment on the following day. The letter which is written in pencil, is a follows:-

Dear Father and Mother,

I take the opportunity of writing you a few lines to let you know that I am well, hoping this will find you the same. I am very sorry to inform you that five companies of the 1-24th have been slaughtered, with the whole of the band and staff and one company of the 2-24th with their band and staff. There was only a bandsman escaped. There were about 20,000 Zulus came down on about 600 Europeans, and they slaughtered the lot except two. It happened to be the 1-24th's turn to stay and look after the camp. The General went out along with the column. After he had got about twelve miles away to meet the enemy they came down on the opposite side to which he thought they would, and before he had time to come back, they had taken the camp and slaughtered the lot. Then they came to where we were.

Happily for me, I was in the hospital with a sore throat. There were twelve months supply of rations at this place. There were only 70 men, sick included. When we heard the rapid firing we fortified the Mission Station as well as we could. The hospital was in the missionary's dwellinghouse, and the sick (about 20 of us) manned that, while the company were inside the fortification. We had only about three-quarters of an hour to secure ourselves as well as we could. They came down upon us about three o'clock in the afternoon. To the best of my calculations there were 6000 or 7000 of them. They very nearly overpowered us.

They took the hospital and set fire to it, while I and another old soldier were inside at the back window, and we did not know they had taken it at the front. My rifle got disabled, so I fixed my bayonet and charged out of the house. While we were charging out the old soldier got wounded in the ear. There were about 30 Zulus chasing us, but the men inside the fort shot them before they could harm us. There were four men burned alive in the hospital, they being unable to move with the fever. We kept our position until the morning and then the General came to our assistance. There are only two of us saved belonging to my company. The other man happened to get wounded in the shoulder.

Give my love to all friends.

Good night, for I must go to my post again

"The Times," December 10th, 1879

...Her Majesty decorated, yesterday, at Windsor Castle, several officers and soldiers who had been selected to receive honours in recognition of their services during the recent South African campaign...

...Lance Sergeant William Allen of the 2d. Battalion 24th Regiment, takes the Victoria Cross for bravery at the defence of Rorke's Drift, where he was wounded in the left shoulder, on the night of the 22d of January, in this year, while serving under the command of Lieutenants Chard and Bromhead; and Corporal Roy, who was engaged in the same memorable action, has the distinguished conduct medal for having, while a patient himself in the hospital, broken through the wall and removed, under fire, six of the sick to the laager...

"The Sydney Morning Herald," October 15th, 1887, page 2

Rorke's Drift - A grand Military CONCERT will shortly take place for the benefit of WILLIAM ROY, late Corporal in H.M. 24th Regiment of Foot, one of the heroes of Rorke's Drift. He is now in very sad circumstances, almost blind, and helpless. Particulars in future issue.
T. Brignell, Hon. Sec.

"The Sydney Morning Herald," Friday, October 28th, 1887, page 5

A grand military concert which had been arranged for the benefit of William Roy, late corporal of H.M.'s. 24th Regiment of Foot, who did active duty at the attack on Rorke's Drift, Zululand, but who is now an invalided inmate of a New south Wales benevolent institution, drew together an enthusiastic and fashionable audience at the Exhibition Building, Prince Alfred Park, yesterday evening. The entertainment was under vice-regal and distinguished patronage, and the gathering formed a highly picturesque sight by reason of the varied uniforms and decorations of members of most of the military regiments in Sydney. Here and there were noticeable veterans, naval and military, whose medals and clasps bespoke their participation in events to which the beneficiare of the occasion is known to have been anything but a stranger, and at times enthusiasm rose to no small pitch. The programme was somewhat too long, 26 items having been set down, inclusive of exhibitions of cutlass exercise by the members of the Naval Artillery Brigade, Indian club exercise by Professor Canadell, reel dancing by the pipers of the 5th Regiment, S.R., and a sword dance by the Scottish Rifles...

..It is expected that a net sum of about £120 will be realised.

1-24/447 Private John Waters, 1st/24th Foot

"The Cambrian," June 13th, 1879

**Massacre At Rorke's Drift
(Narrative By Survivors)**

Private Waters tells the following interesting story of his experiences:-

I was special orderly at the hospital at Rorke's Drift, and at this time have seen twenty-one and a quarters years' service. I was in the hospital when Private Evans rode into camp and reported that the Zulus had Massacred the whole column at Isandula. We would hardly believe this at first, but very soon had reason to understand it was only too true. Between half-past four and five, as near as I can remember, the Zulus came over the hill and I saw about fifty of them form a line in skirmishing order, just as British soldiers would do. Their main body was in their rear over the shoulder of the hill. They came about twenty yards, and then opened fire on the hospital. I stopped there firing at the enemy through holes made by other men, and others did the same, but we were not able to prevent the enemy coming right up to the hospital. Some of them came in and set fire to it.

While I was there I took refuge in a cupboard, and Private Beckett, an invalid, came with me. As they were going out I killed many of them, and as I could not stay there long, the place being so suffocating, I put on a black cloak which I had found in the cupboard, and which must have belonged to Mr. Witt, and ran out in the long grass and lay down. The Zulus must have thought I was one of their dead comrades, as they were all round about me, and some trod on me. Beckett had gone out half an hour before me, and he, poor fellow, was assegaied right through his stomach, and went into laager next morning. Dr. Reynolds did all he could to save him, but did not succeed. I got up at daybreak, having expected every minute my life would be taken, and then saw my comrades on the top of the mealie sacks, and I said, 'Thank God, I have got my life.' I had been shot early in the engagement in the shoulder and knee, and here's the bullet, which was taken out next morning by Dr. Reynolds. I knew many poor fellows who fell at Isandula. I saw Private Harrigan killed. Poor Beckett was buried next morning properly. Round the hospital dead Zulus were piled in heaps.

Extract from his army service & discharge papers: [WO97 series, The National Archives, (P.R.O.), London]

...Wounded at Rorke's Drift 22/1/79 - bullet entering outer side of arm 6 inches from point of the shoulder & lodging. It was cut out behind shoulder 12 hours after - distance travelled through fleshy part of arm 4 inches. The joint uninjured & bone uninjured...

He has fair power of motion of the injured arm in all directions, but complains of pain in the track of the wound & shoulder when exerting himself...

2-24/2459 Colour Sergeant Frank Edward Bourne, 'B' Company, 2nd/24th Foot

"The Epsom District Times," Friday, July 29th, 1932

Defence of Rorke's Drift.
The Story Of An Epic Fight
Told At Dorking

The epic story of the fight at Rorke's Drift was told to Dorking Rotarians on Tuesday by one of the defenders, Col. Bourne, who lives in South-street, Dorking. Rorke's Drift was the scene, on January 22nd, 1879, of the most heroic events of the Zulu war. A party of 140 British soldiers, 25 of whom were hospital patients, were attacked by three to four thousand Zulus. At the end of the terrific fight, the little British force had lost 17 killed and nine wounded. And the British soldiers went out the next morning and buried 351 Zulus who had been killed in the fight. Ten Victoria Crosses were awarded among the brave men who defended Rorke's Drift. Only four survivors of the fight are now living.

Col. Bourne was a young Colour-Sergeant - he was nicknamed 'The Kid' - in those days. Before Rorke's Drift, he had spent, as he told the Rotarians, some months in 'chivvying' the Kaffirs in Cape Colony. And then came the Zulu war. Col. Bourne explained graphically the nature of the operations in that war. He told the story of the main British force leaving camp under Lord Chelmsford, and forcing their way through the centre of the horseshoe formation of the Zulu force, but the strong flanks of the horseshoe closed in on the British camp at Isandhlwana, the British loss that day being 21 officers and 655 men killed. Then the Zulus attacked the party who had been left in charge of the hospital and commissariat stores at Rorke's Drift.

Rapidly Prepared Defences

There were 25 men in hospital, and with one civilian, the total of the British at Rorke's Drift was 140, under the command of Lieuts. Chard and Bromhead. When news came of the impending attack, rapid efforts were made to prepare defences with the only materials available - biscuit boxes and sacks of mealie. With these defences, the buildings - principally an old farm house and the hospital, a building of the bungalow type - were connected together. Also a waggon was brought inside the compound. "About 500 of the enemy appeared first," said Col. Bourne, "and by 5 o'clock we were completely surrounded. They made rush after rush, but we kept them at bay. Still they carried on. There was no question of quarter. They asked for none and they gave none. About 7 o'clock, they set fire to the thatched roof of the hospital. That was an advantage to us, because it lit up the countryside. We got most of the patients out of the hospital. I think there was only one Zulu who got into our inner line of defences. He was killed instantly. The Zulus kept us going the whole night. Rush after rush came, but we kept them down. And when daylight broke the next morning they had disappeared."

The Defenders Saved

In that simple language, Col. Bourne described the epic fight which holds an honoured place in the pages of British military history. He went on to tell of the work done quickly to repair the rough defences, and then, he said, they saw a column approaching. "Many of us thought we were in the pincers again," he remarked, but the approaching troops were British, not Zulus. The little garrison at Rorke's Drift was saved. It was possible then to review their position.

"At the beginning of the fight," said Col. Bourne, "each man had 70 rounds of Martini heavy ammunition, and I had 34 boxes of Martin ammunition in reserve. The next morning, when the column joined up, I had only six boxes left. We lost 17 killed and nine wounded. Several men were killed in the hospital. We could not get them out before the fire occurred. Our strength was 140 all hands, but of that number there were only about a hundred fighting men. The Zulu strength, as estimated by Lieut. Chard, was 3,000. Others estimated their strength at 4,000, but I think Chard's estimate was nearer correct. Their loss was 351 killed." The number of the wounded was unknown.

Cockney Humour

Col. Bourne explained that, during the morning after the fight, the men went out to bury the dead Zulus, and the bodies were counted as they were put into the grave. Only one wounded Zulu was found. In connection with that burial of the dead, Col. Bourne told a story typical of the queer humour of the British Tommy - although in those days, the soldier was a 'Redcoat'; he did not become 'Tommy Atkins' until the South African War.

There were, he said, two Cockneys among the men engaged in burying the Zulus. One said to the other, 'George, when I started work I sold newspapers in the Strand. My mother didn't think I had a very good job there. Then I started cleaning boots. Mother didn't like that much better. But she thought I had done well when I got a job as 'Buttons.' Then I joined the Army. Mother liked that, but she never expected me to become sexton to a lot of Christies minstrels.'

"The men at Rorke's Drift behaved splendidly," Col. Bourne said. He described Lieuts. Chard and Bromhead as two single-minded, good-hearted soldiers, and he related that, on the day succeeding the fight, Bromhead wrote a despatch which he (Col. Bourne), had to copy. Not a man's name was mentioned in that despatch. Later, however, it was discovered that Chard was senior, and another despatch was written in which the names were mentioned. Those two officers were so free from selfishness that they did not trouble to discover who of the two was senior.

Rotarian S. Axten, is also an old campaigner, was an appropriate member of the Rotary Club to express thanks to Col. Bourne.

"The Northern Mail," May 17th, 1934

Zulu War Epic
Broadcast By Veteran Survivor

A graphic account of the historic defence of Rorke's Drift during the Zulu War of 1879, one of the finest episodes in British military history, is to be broadcast to-morrow night by Lieut.-Colonel Frank Bourne, a veteran survivor.

Special interest will be given to the talk by reason of the fact that at the Northern Command Tattoo, to be staged from Jul 7 to 14 in the grounds of Ravensworth Castle, Gateshead, the 2nd Battalion the South Wales Borderers will re-enact this famous battle, in which that unit actually took part 55 years ago.

Transcript of his first radio broadcast given in 1934 just prior to the Northern Command Military Tattoo in Gateshead: [compiler's collection]

"I am Lieut. Colonel Bourne and I have been asked to speak on the 'Defence of Rorke's Drift' which took place on the 22nd-23r January 1879 during the Zulu War of that year.

I was Colour Sergeant of B Company 2/24th Regiment which defended the 'Drift', the strength of the Company being one officer and 91 N.C. officers and men, the total strength of this small post was 7 officers and 141 other ranks including one civilian, of this total there were only about 100 fighting men.

During 1878 Cetewayo - the Zulu King - had been frequently warned by the Government to cease raiding the Natal Border and also that he must disband his army of warriors in the case of the latter he showed not the slightest intention of doing so that it became certain that he could only be brought to heel by the invasion of his country and the defeat of his army, therefore in January three Columns under the Command of General Thesiger - later Lord Chelmsford - crossed the Natal Border into Zululand, the third Column, which Genl. Thesiger accompanied, under Colonel Glyn of the 1st Btn 24th Regt. crossed the Buffalo River at Rorke's Drift on the 11th January 79, my company, 'B' 2/24 Regt. being left at that post to guard the Commst. stores, Hospital and pontoons on the Buffalo.

There were two buildings at Rorke's small farm, the larger one with an upper storey was used as the Commst Store, and the smaller actually a bungalow as a temporary hospital, the whole frontage including a stone cattle kraal was about 150 yards and the depth about 50 yards, no attempt had been made in the few days we had been there to connect the two buildings or the stone cattle kraal or put them in a state of defence for I don't think it was ever thought possible by anyone that the Zulus would defeat the Column at Isandhlwana. Well such was the position on the 22nd January, during that morning we distinctly heard firing from the direction of Isandhlwana but not one of us had the slightest idea that before the day was out we might be fighting for our very lives and the safety of the inhabitants of the whole of Natal, up to nearly two o'clock that day our work had gone quite normally but about that time our peace and quiet was knocked on the head by the arrival of two refugees from Zululand telling us that the camp at Isandhlwana had been over run by thousands of Zulus, that our ammunition ...was cut, and that everyone except the few who were mounted and had been able to get away were killed and that a very large body of Zulus were marching on to us. We therefore at once set to work to put the Commissariat stores and hospital into a defensive state by loopholing the walls, and connecting the Commst and hospital by two box (?) wagons, and the front of the hospital with the stone cattle kraal with a line of sacks of Indian corn and oats. Lieut. Gonville Bromhead, our splendid company commander at once sent a message to Lieut Chard R.E. in charge of the pontoons on the Buffalo who immediately came to us, approved of the defence work we had done but thought our defences were too stretched (?) for the number of men available to defend them and suggested a line of biscuit boxes across the centre of our defence, this turned out to be a very wise step for shortly after the attack had developed we were forced to occupy this position and from which we had a perfect line of fire - only about 20 yards - to the front of the hospital where we found the dead next morning were lying four and five deep.

Shortly after 4 o'c, about 500 Zulus appeared from round the 'Oscarsberg' a big hill to our south, they advanced with a rush against our south wall where they were met with such a heavy fire from the Commst store that they were checked but at once took advantage of cover offered by the cookhouse and ovens, a great number without stopping moved to the left round the hospital and made a rush on our North West wall of mealie sacks but after a desperate struggle in which they held on to our bayonets until blown away leaving numbers of dead on the ground. The main body occupied the rocks and cover on the hillside and kept up a steady fire into our defences. Here let me say they were armed with a number of old smooth bore rifles, guns and also several Martini Henry rifles which they had taken from our dead at Isandhlwana and with ammunition from the boxes found on the dead mules at that camp, the mules having bolted when the camp was attacked thus preventing any one from getting at the boxes to open them.

About 6 o'c, the enemy set fire to the hospital and the few men who had been detailed to defend it fought bitterly to secure the rescue of the patients who were too ill to help themselves, but I am sorry to say a few men were killed and also Joseph Williams one of the defenders, the bravery of these men cannot be put into words each room was held to the bitter end. Victoria Crosses were awarded to Privates H. Hook, R. Jones, W. Jones and J. Williams, and Lieut Gonville Bromhead. These with Corporal Allen and Pte F. Hitch were also awarded the V.C. I think I am right in saying that I am the only Colour Sergeant in the army that ever have 7 holders of the V.C. in his Company.

The fight continued until 4.00 on the morning of the 23rd Jany. when the enemy withdrew but re-appeared again about 7 o'c and then quickly disappeared.

The remainder of the Column from Isandhlwana reached us about 8 a.m. thus giving a temporary rest after twelve hours strenuous fighting but we had the great satisfaction of having one the fight.

I said at the beginning that our fighting strength was about 100, that of the enemy was estimated by Lieut Chard as 3000, by others between 3 - 4000, I think 3,500 is nearly correct.

Our losses I regret to say were 17 killed and 10 wounded, that of the enemy was 351 killed, which we buried, and one man wounded who afterwards died, their wounded cannot have been between 3 to 400 which evidently they took away under cover of the night.

The results of this 'Defence' were, 1. that the Zulus never made a big stand again until Ulundi was fought on the 4th July '79 when they were so badly defeated that Cetewayo, their King, was taken prisoner and departed, and his warriors disarmed and dispersed. 2. That the whole of Natal was saved from invasion, murder, pillage & arson and perhaps worse.

I am sure you will all be interested to know that at the request of General Sir Alexander Wardrop the GOC in C, Northern Command, my old Regiment, the 2nd Battalion the South Wales Borderers (late 2/24th Regt.) has been requested to reproduce the 'Defence of Rorke's Drift' at the Northern Command Tattoo to be held at Newcastle on Tyne from the 7th to the 14th July this year *

I want to say one word in conclusion it is this, that so long as a Regiment maintains its glorious traditions should a Squadron or a Company ever find itself in the same position as my Company did they will fight it out to the end - and will win -

Good Night

There are 10 Survivors of the 'Defence', namely Sergt. Saxty, Privates Buckley, Cooper, Edwards, Jobbins, Lewis, Martin, Mason, Wood and myself

* He has also intimated his intention to invite the Survivors to attend the Tattoo"

A full transcript of his 1936 radio broadcasts for the BBC as published in "The Listener Magazine" [appears courtesy of the British Broadcasting Corporation]

"I WAS THERE" Sunday 20th December 1936. at 7pm.

Let me begin by telling you a little of my early days of soldiering and the sort of men we were in Rorke's Drift. I enlisted into the 24th Regiment in December 1872, I was 18 and I received the princely pay of 6d a day, of which 3.1/2d was deducted for messing and washing, leaving 1s.5.1/2d a week for luxuries, and I went to bed hungry every night but quiet happy and it made a man of me.

The Regiment had just come home from India after fifteen years, and the "A" Company of any Regiment in those days was always called the " Grenadier Company", supposed to be the biggest men. I think the Sergeant-Major must have been a wee bit humorous, as he posted me to our "A" Company although I stood only five feet six inches and was painfully thin.

The recruits appeared only on church parade, and the first I attended I asked Partridge, the old soldier who was teaching me the traditions of the Regiment, and how to keep my equipment clean, where I should fall in, and I received the crushing reply "In the centre of the rear rank, where do you think" - The smallest place in the Company.

Well, after five years of home service, in February, 1878, the Regiment received sudden orders to proceed to the Cape of Good Hope to take part in the Kaffir War. This was my first experience of active service, and shortly after, my Colonel promoted me to Colour-Sergeant of "B" Company - 100 strong. I was only twenty-three, very nervous, sensitive, and afraid of my new responsibilities.

Several men of the Company were of my own age, others older, and some old enough to be my father, but after a few months I felt more secure and though I was getting along quiet well. I also found myself "unpaid private secretary" to several men who could barely read and write, and I read and answered their letters home, feeling quiet happy in our relations. One day I heard a man named Wall, ask my batman outside my tent "if the kid was in", and a day or two later I asked Partridge casually who "the kid" was, and received the answer, "why, you are of course", and my stock slumped at once. I think it does us all good to have our swollen heads reduced, but we were a very happy family. You can't live in tents, and on mother earth, for two years on active service without knowing your men intimately.

Well, the Kaffir War ended in June 1878, and we were moved to Pietermaritzburg, Natal, to assist in the curtain being raised on the Zulu drama. On the 11th of January, we crossed the Buffalo River at Rorke's Drift into Zulu country, our Commander-in-Chief was Lord Chelmsford. Our strength was four thousand five hundred men including thirteen Companies of my Regiment, of the 24th, now the South Wales Borderers. One Company was left behind at Rorke's Drift to guard the hospital, stores and pontoons at the drift on the Buffalo River. This was my Company and at the time I was bitterly disappointed. I did not know we were going to have a battle to ourselves. Well, we saw the main column under Lord Chelmsford engage the enemy at once, and I watched the action, along with my four Sergeants, from a little hill by Rorke's Drift, then we saw them move on again, and they disappeared.

Now I must tell you what happened to them during the next ten days. Although I shall be telling you something that we didn't know ourselves, back at Rorke's Drift. They made their camp under a hill called Isandlwana, about ten miles away. Then days later, on the twenty-first, Lord Chelmsford learned that the enemy was in force ahead of the camp, and he moved out on the morning of the twenty-second with nearly half his force to attack them. But as he advanced they disappeared, and in his absence his camp was attacked and overwhelmed by fourteen thousand Zulus.

As regards the fighting in camp that day, little is known. So swift was the disaster that the few survivors who got away could give no reliable account of it, but the evidence of the dead who were afterwards found and buried where they lay told the unvarying tale of groups of men fighting back to back until the last cartridge was fired. After the war, Zulu witnesses all told the same story:- "At first we could make no headway against the soldiers, but suddenly they ceased to fire, then we came round them and killed them with our assegai's". According to one account, the last survivor was a drummer boy who flung his short sword at a Zulu. [This was the last occasion that band drummer boy's were taken on active service]. Lieutenants Melville and Coghill lost their lives that day trying to save the Queen's Colours. Fully twelve hundred men were killed, and by half past one, no white man was alive that day in Isandlwana Camp.

Well, of course, back at Rorke's Drift we knew nothing of this disaster, although my Sergeants, and I, on our hill above it could hear the guns and see the puffs of smoke, but an hour later, at two o'clock, a few refugees arrived and warned us what to expect.

One man whispered to me, "Not a fighting chance for you, young feller." Up to that time we had done nothing to put our small post in a defensive position, as our force in front was nearly five thousand strong and had six guns, and the last thing that we expected was that we should be saviours of the remainder of that force. The strength of our small garrison at the drift was two combatant Officers, six departmental Officers and one hundred fighting men. Remember that twelve hundred men had just been massacred at Isandlwana. Can you then be surprised that, flushed with their success the Zulus were making for our small post confident that we should be easy victims to their savagery.

Well having had the warning, but only two hours, as it turned out - we set to work to loophole the two buildings and to connect the front of the hospital with a stone cattle kraal by sacks of Indian corn oats, and to draw up two Boer transport waggon's to join the front of the commissariat stores with the back of the hospital. These proved excellent barricades, but by no means impregnable. The native has often been credited with deep cunning, but luckily for us, if the Zulu possessed any he did not use it, for as the sacks connecting the hospital had to be laid on a slope of the ground, he could have safely crept along, cut the sacks open with his assegai's, the corn would have rolled out and he could have walked in and I should not now be telling you this story today. When Lieutenant Chard of the Royal Engineers joined us he approved of what we had done, but considered that our inner space was too big, and suggested a line of biscuit boxes, this was done and proved of great value when the enemy set the hospital on fire. I was instructed to post men as lookouts, in the hospital and at the most vulnerable points, and to take out and command a line of skirmishers.

Shortly after 3.30pm an Officer Commanding a troop of Natal Light Horse arrived, having got away from Isandlwana, and asked Lieutenant Chard for instructions. He was ordered to send detachments to observe the drift and pontoons, and to place outposts in the direction of the enemy to check his advance.

About 4.15pm the sound of firing was heard behind the hill on our front; the Officer returned and reported the enemy close upon us. He also reported that his 100 men would not obey his orders and had ridden off. About the same time another detachment of 100 men belonging to the Natal Native Contingent bolted, including their Officer. I am glad to say he was brought back some days later, court-martialled and dismissed from the service. The desertion of these detachments of 200 men at first sight seemed to be a great loss, with only 100 of us left, but the feeling afterwards was that we could not have trusted them, also that our defences were too small to accommodate them anyhow.

We knew now that whatever might happen we had to fight it out alone, and about 4.30pm the enemy, from 500 to 600 strong, came in sight round the hill to our south, driving in my thin red line of skirmishers, and made a rush at our south wall, they were met, and held, by a steady and deliberate fire for a short time, but being reinforced by some 100's they made desperate and repeated attempts to break through our temporary defences, but were repulsed time and again. To show they had no fear, and their contempt for the red coats, and small numbers, they tried to leap the parapet and at times seized our bayonets, only to be shot down. Looking back, one cannot but admire their bravery. About 7pm they succeeded, after many attempts, in setting fire to the hospital. The small numbers we were able to spare, defended it room by room bringing out all the sick who could be moved before they retired. Private's Hook, R. Jones, W. Jones and J. Williams, being the last to leave, holding the door with the bayonet as all their ammunition was expended. Owing to the way the rooms communicated, and the burning of the house, it was impossible to save all. The Victoria Cross was awarded to these men, and they fully deserved it. The attack lasted from 4.30pm on the 22nd to 4am on the 23rd - twelve exciting hours - and when daybreak came the enemy was out of sight. But about 7am they appeared again to the south west. The Zulus had collected the rifles from the men they had killed at Isandlwana, and had captured the ammunition from the mules which stampeded and threw their loads; so our own arms were used against us. In fact, this was the cause of every one of our casualties, killed and wounded, and we should have suffered many more if the enemy had known how to use a rifle. There was hardly a man even wounded by an assegai their principal weapon. But help was at hand; Lord Chelmsford with the other half of his original force, was only an hours march away. On the previous afternoon he had learned of the destruction of his camp, at Isandlwana.

A certain commandant; Lonsdale had chanced to ride back to the camp and been fired at by Zulus wearing our men's uniforms. He escaped by a miracle and was able to report the news to Lord Chelmsford. He at once addressed his men and said:- "Whilst we were skirmishing ahead the Zulus have taken our camp; there are 10,000 in our rear, and 20,000 in our front, we must win back our camp tonight and cut our way back to Rorke's Drift tomorrow". The men of the 24th answered with a cheer. "All right, Sir, we'll do it."

Well they got back to the camp that night, but, I cannot tell you now the grim silent scene they found as they cautiously approached. The next day they resumed their march and appeared at Rorke's Drift, and our enemy retired, we were saved.

In his dispatch afterwards, Lord Chelmsford said:- "To our intense relief the waving of hats was seen from hastily erected entrenchment's, and information soon reached me that the garrison had for twelve hours made the most gallant resistance I have ever heard of against the determined attack of some 3,000 Zulus, 350 of whose dead bodies surrounded the post". As I've said our fighting strength at Rorke's Drift was about 100 of all ranks and the Zulus 3,500. Our losses were 17 killed, 9 wounded, theirs 351 killed that we buried, their wounded must have been between 400 and 500, which they removed under cover of the night.

There are two things which I think have made Rorke's Drift stand out so vividly all these years. The first, that it took place on the same day as the terrible massacre at Isandlwana, and second, that Natal was saved from being overrun by a savage and victorious foe. We were just one Company of the Regiment which is now the South Wales Borderers, seven VC's were awarded to this Company, in the same action, which must be a record. I should like just to give you their names; I have told you the names of four of them already, the men who held the door in the hospital. The other three were Lieutenant Bromhead, Corporal Allen and Private Hitch The VC, was also awarded to Lieutenant Chard. RE, Surgeon Reynolds and Corporal Schiess, but not one, I regret to say, of those VC's., is alive today. In fact, there are only six survivors of Rorke's Drift alive today, Ex-Private's, Cooper, Edwards, Martin, Owens, J. Williams and myself, and some of them are listening to me now. Lieutenant's Chard and Bromhead and the men received the thanks of Parliament, the Officers being promoted to the rank of Major. I was awarded the D.C.M., with an annuity of £10 - the same as awarded to the VC, and awarded a commission, but as I was the youngest of 8 sons, I had to refuse it that time.

The following year, Queen Victoria received at Windsor Castle a Colour Party of the Regiment and decorated the Colour with a Silver Wreath of immortalise in memory of Lieutenant's Melville and Coghill, " For their devotion in trying to save the Colour's on the 22nd January, and for the noble defence of Rorke's Drift". The wreath presented by her Majesty is now in the Regimental Chapel of Brecon Cathedral. If there are any service or ex-service men listening, may I say this to you; that if your Company had found itself in the same position as we were, you would have done the same as we did, fought and won. The following verse from Macaulay's "Lays of ancient Rome", can, I think be applied appropriately to the 24th Regiment on that fatal day, 22nd January 1879.

For how can man die better than facing fearful odds, for the ashes of his fathers, and the temples of his Gods.

Good night

"The Sunday Express," January 22nd, 1938

HERO OF RORKE'S DRIFT LIVES
The Battle Over Again At 83.

SIXTY YEARS ago eighty-eight men were sleeping the sleep of the valiant in the shadow of a little hill in South Africa. For fifteen hours B Company of the 24th Regiment, now the South Wales Borderers, had put up one of the most magnificent stands in the fighting history of England.

One of the eighty-eight who survived Rorke's Drift was Colour-Sergeant, now Lieut.-Colonel F. Bourne, of Stone Roof, Dorking, who was awarded the D.C.M.

Last week, talking to a Sunday Express reporter, he lived the battle over again.

He is eighty-three now.

"The odd thing," he said smiling, "was that it was our company that was left behind to look after the stores while the other twelve went into battle."

Overwhelmed

"Our main column, under Lord Chelmsford, camped at Isandlwana. Ten days later they heard that the Zulus were ahead and Lord Chelmsford took half his force to attack them.

While he was gone 14,000 Zulus descended on the unprepared 1,200 Britons, overwhelmed them when the ammunition was spent, and wiped out the lot.

At two o'clock a few refugees arrived and told us the news. They said we were next. At half past four the triumphant Zulus came, first 600 of them, then more until there were 4,000 against 100!

They charged right up to our parapet, even trying to leap over it and clutching our men's bayonets in their hands.

They hurled all their assegais. Then they stated to use the rifles and ammunition they had captured from our men at Isandlwana. They fired the hospital.

All night the battle went on, but we had only seventeen killed and nine wounded, and we had won. The Zulus retreated, leaving behind them 350 dead. We buried 351".

The last pair of figures sounded odd.

Colonel Bourne chuckled.

"I don't think the story of that one Zulu has ever been told", he said.

Left for dead

"One Zulu who was alive had been left for dead.

Later in the day Lieutenant Bromhead sent for me and said, very urgently. 'Where's that man who was here just now with a prisoner? Find that man and bring him here'.

"I went round asking. 'Who's the man who's got a prisoner?' They said. 'Ashton, of course'. Ashton was a lusty Irishman. I found Ashton.

"What have you done with your prisoner?" I said. He pointed to a tree from which the Zulu's body was hanging.

"I took him in to Lieutenant Bromhead", said the innocent Irishman. "And he told me to get the hell out of here with him, and I did."

"The Daily Mail," August 24th, 1932

RORKE'S DRIFT SURVIVORS

"Sir,

The death is reported of 'the sole British survivor' of Rorke's Drift, the famous engagement of the Zulu War of 1879.

Will you kindly allow me to point out that there are at least five survivors of the Rorke's Drift defence - viz., Sergeant Saxty, Privates Buckley, Cooper and Williams V.C., and myself

F. Bourne, Lieut. Col.,

Late Colour-Sergeant B Company 2/24th Regt., which defended the Drift.

Stoneroof, Dorking, Surrey

"The Dorking and Leatherhead County Post," May 18th, 1945

Fought at Rorke's Drift
An Epic in British Military History
Death of Lieut.-Col. Bourne.

...Describing the fight in a soldier's simple language during a talk to the Dorking Rotary Club, Col. Bourne said;

"By five o'clock in the afternoon we were completely surrounded. They made rush after rush, but we kept them at bay. Still they carried on. There was no question of quarter. They asked for none and they gave none. About seven o'clock they set fire to the thatched roof of the hospital. This was an advantage to us, because it lit up the countryside. We got most of the patients out of the hospital. I think that there was only one Zulu who got into our inner line of defences. He was killed instantly. The Zulus kept us going the whole night. Rush after rush came, but we kept them down. And when daylight broke the next morning they had disappeared. The losses among the British were 17 men killed and nine wounded. Of the attacking Zulus, 351 who had been killed were lying in heaps around the compound. The Zulus removed their wounded numbering between four and five hundred before retreating."

25B/1184 Private Thomas Buckley, 'B' Company, 2nd/24th Foot

"The Times," Saturday, February 2nd, 1924

Rorke's Drift Survivors

A recent reference to the fact that there were two survivors of the defence of Rorke's Drift by the 24th Regiment South Wales Borderers, in the Zulu War, has prompted a military correspondent to write to The Times to say that there is another survivor. He is Mr. T. Buckley, a London man, who figures on the roll of those at the defence of the Drift as a private with the regimental number of 1184 in the B Company of the 24th Regiment. He is now 65. The other two survivors, Private John Williams, V.C., and Sergeant Evan Jones, are both Welshmen.

"The Natal Witness," Saturday, January 21st, 1961

A Rorke's Drift Hero And Two Dogs Of The 2/24th Regiment.
By Capt. G.F. Court.

One sunny May morning in 1930, Mallelieux and I sat on a park bench in Brook Green, Hammarsmith, London, chatting and watching very good tennis played by Chinese students on the public courts.

At the end of our bench sat a moustached elderly gentleman reading a newspaper. Suddenly he uttered a loud "agh!" in a contemptuous voice, at the same time striking the paper angrily with his right hand, and glared at us over his spectacles, evidently much put out. Seeing us looking at him inquiringly, he spoke in a deep toned Irish voice saying: "I have just read here" - thumping the paper - "that a survivor of Isandhlwana has died in Natal. Every year I read of a survivor of this battle dying in Natal. I tell you that there were none, every man fought, died on the battle field. There were no survivors except a dog owned by our Colonel. The only living thing to come through the fight that day. 'I'm telling you."

"Are you speaking about the Zulu war battle of Isandhlwana, Sir ?" I asked.

"Yes I am! The day of the battle I was at Rorkes Drift, Private Buckley of 'B' Company the 2/24th Warwickshire Regiment. Lieut. Bromhead commanded us." The old soldier proudly declared.

"Surely there were survivors, about forty Sir ?" Mallelieux asked.

"There were none, those that got away left the field early in the fight. Some came to us at Rorkes Drift, a few stayed and fought with us: others rode on to Helpmekaar where two Companies of our First Battalion were posted. In the Regiment, we always said that Flip, a dog owned by Colonel Degacher, was the only living thing to survive, the other dog, Kreli, was never seen again."

"So there were only two dogs in the fight Sir ?" I enquired.

"Yes, of my Regiment, but only one when the Regiment sailed from Cork to the Cape in January 1878, to engage in the Kaffir war. He was a Dalmatian, one of those black and white spotted dogs, owned by our C.O., Colonel Degacher. Flip was his name. The Regiment disembarked at East London and then went inland to King

Williams Town to take part in the war with our First Battalion.

"The morning after a fight, we found a Kaffir dog tied up in a deserted kraal. He was a young yellow haired greyhound with kind black eyes. We named him Kreli, after the Kaffir king, our enemy. He chummed with Flip, they kept together through the war and he became a favourite in the Regiment.

"After the war we lay at the Kaboosie River for orders. When they came, it was, that the Regiment embark at East London for Natal.

"Orders were issued that no dogs could be taken, because by this time many had been collected by the men as pets.

"We entrained and left for East London on the new railway, with perhaps forty dogs of all breeds, sizes and colours galloping alongside the train, encouraged by men shouting, calling and cheering them on, and the dogs all barking and whining at being left behind. The dogs gradually fell out or they became tired, until after a few miles the only one left was Kreli the yellow dog, who continued to keep up with the train midst the cheers of the men, and barking of his chum Flip, who was on the train.

"At last the Colonel ordered the train to be stopped for Kreli, and he was helped on to rejoin Flip. The Colonel's kind act was loudly cheered by everyone.

"The Regiment landed at Durban and proceeded inland to Pietermaritzburg and then on to Helpmekaar to join Colonel Glynn's column about to invade Zululand, both dogs being with us.

"When we got to Rorkes Drift, my Company 'B', commanded by Lieut. Bromhead, was detached for line of communication duties. The main column entered Zululand and camped at Isandhlwana mountain.

"Early one morning Colonel Degacher left camp with six companies of the Regiment to fight the enemy. Flip and Kreli were left in camp with the company ordered to guard the camp together with five companies of our First Battalion commanded by Colonel Pulleine. The camp was attacked that day and all killed, no man survived.

"That night when our Colonel with six companies arrived back at the decimated camp to find everyone killed, the dogs were not found and it was assumed they had been killed.

"The following morning, Lord Chelmsford the Commander-in-Chief returned to Rorkes Drift with all that remained of Colonel Glynn's column, including the six companies of my Regiment under Colonel Degacher and camped.

"A few hours later Flip came into camp with a rope tied to his neck, and a severe spear wound in the shoulder. Everyone crowded to see and to cheer Flip, the only living thing to survive the battle where we lost a thousand killed that day.

"Apparently after being wounded a Zulu led Flip off, and the dog broke away and returned to his master. The yellow dog, Kreli, was not seen again. In the Regiment Kreli was not forgotten, we spoke of him affectionately for many years, this common kindly Kaffir dog that we found in one war and lost in another."

The old soldier indicated that was the end of the story.

Mallelieux said: "What became of Flip Mr. Buckley?"

"After the Zulu war the Regiment went to Gibraltar and afterwards to Burma, and Flip of course with the Colonel. When the Colonel retired from the army and went to live in the old family home in France, he took his dog, where he died of old age, so I was told."

We got up and introduced ourselves and thanked this old Irish soldier, hero of Rorkes Drift, for this story about Flip and Kreli. At the same time telling Mr. Buckley that we too had served in South Africa - Mallelieux at King Williams Town in Kaffirland and Pondoland in the Cape Mounted Rifles and myself in Pietermaritzburg in Natal and Zululand, a member of the Natal Police.

"This is very interesting indeed. I was in the siege of Ladysmith in the Imperial Light Horse." Mr. Buckley replied.

I added that I had been to Rorke's Drift and Isandhlwana several times.

"The devil you have!" Mr. Buckley exclaimed looking at me with a happy smile, "You are a lucky one."

We shook hands, said "Good morning," leaving the old hero opening up the paper, perhaps again to scan the item that made him angry - "Survivor of Isandlwana dies in Natal."

25B/906 Private John Connolly, 'G' Company, 2nd/24th Foot

File RA VIC/034/64: The Royal Archives, Windsor Castle. [appears courtesy of H.M. Queen Elizabeth II]

Case inquired into & following statement made, at Lady Frere's request, to Capt. Liddell, R.N. of H.M's Transport 'Tamar' - by John Conolly - invalided home -

Governement House,
Cape Town

Statements of John Conolly
Private 2nd Battalion, 24th Regiment as to the manner in which he escaped at Rorkes Drift 22.1.79.

I am 20 years of age having been born at Castletown, Berehaven, County Cork in 1859.
My father, of the same Christian name, was a fisherman at that place.
Enlisted 24.11.76 at Newport Monmouth, where I was working as a labourer.
I came out in the Himalaya last year leaving Portsmouth Feb 2.
Having been injured in the left leg at the knee when loading a waggon at Tugela River (5.1.79) I was in the Hospital at Rorke's Drift under treatment and in bed, when the position was attacked by the Zulus on the 22nd January.
Attack commenced about 5 p.m. but my bad leg prevented me from being of the

slightest use in the defence.

Attack was made on the hospital at 6.30 p.m. but the men defending it having expended all their ammunition, they retreated to the main body, leaving the hospital in charge of 2 men.

There were 7 invalids in the hospital 5 with fever (3 belonging to the 24th, 1 to Natal Contingent and 1 to Police) 1 belonging to the Natal Contingent having an assegai wound to the thigh, and myself.

State appearing hopeless, I crawled out of the window by placing mealie bags and at 7.30 p.m. made for the bush by sitting down and pushing myself along feet first. After going 50 yards I got into the bush and laid down to keep out of sight.

The hospital was set on fire at 7.45. The Zulus kept passing me all night, but either did not see me or thought me dead.

Our own men kept firing into the bush till 4 a.m. from a distance of 150 yards, but I was I not hit by any bullet.

About 5 a.m. on the 23rd, I crawled back into the entrenchment and then learnt that all the 5 poor patients had been burnt to death, the wounded patient escaped.

The Surgeon states that, the injuries sustained by John Conolly is of so serious a character that it will permanently interfere with his earning a livelihood, as he will be lame all his life.

His mind was at first a good deal affected by melancholia and he still suffers from attacks of the same.

William W Liddell
Captain

HMS "Tamar,"
May 3rd, 1879.

Extract from "The Natal Mercury," c. 1880

A Rorkes Drift Hero in Trouble

Some of the warriors who have recently returned to England have got into difficulties. Edward Connolly, one of the 24th Regiment and one of the heroes of Rorke's Drift, who on that famous conflict in the Zulu campaign was shot through the body and invalided, is one of these. He got six weeks hard labour for violently assaulting a policeman with his crutch (he is lame for life) and biting the man's finger nearly off. His brother got a month and his mother 14 days for being involved in the same offence.

25B/2453 Private William Cooper, 'F' Company, 2nd/24th Foot

Extact from "The South Wales Borderers Regimental Journal," c. 1942

Obituary

No. 25th Bde. 2453 ex-Private William Cooper, died at Worthing, Sussex, on the 19th February, at the age of 86. He was at Rorke's Drift on the night of 22nd and 23rd January, 1879. He belonged to F. Coy., but formed one of a ration party sent to B. Coy. the day before from Isandhlwana. He is number 113 in Lieutenant Chard's roll published in the History of the Regiment and in No. 7 of the Journal.

It is regretted that his family did not inform us of the death until May, as it is the unanimous wish of the Regiment to show respect to such veterans, consequently no representatives were present at the funeral. It would have been quite easy to have sent representatives as more than one of our units were then stationed in the vicinity.

25B/971 Private Thomas Driscoll, 'B' Company, 2nd/24th Foot

"The South Wales Argus," January 22nd, 1929, page 3

Ebbw Vale Hero.
Experiences of Private Thomas Driscoll.

Ebbw Vale may be proud of the fact that one of their inhabitants is ex-private Thomas Driscoll (familiarly known as Tom Tambourine), one of the survivors of Rorke's Drift. Driscoll is living at the Cambrian workman's home, Briery Hill, Ebbw Vale and has reached the advanced age of 73. He is now very feeble, suffers from indifferent health and is practically blind. He is in receipt of a pension from the war office, also the old age pension, he is a bachelor and has no relatives living.

Mr. Driscoll was born at Lower High Street, Dowlais, and went to the Catholic School there. At the early age of 12 he went to work at Dowlais Works, he served 13 years in the army and was discharged in 1888. For 40 years he was working as a labourer under the Ebbw Vale Company. Shortly after the death of Queen Victoria, he met with a severe accident at No.1 Mill, the property of the Ebbw Vale Company, when a portion of the roof fell on him and broke his right ankle, he was incapacitated for nearly six months. He enlisted in the 2nd Battalion of the 24th Regiment on December 6th 1876.

IN Feeble Health

A South Wales Argus representative who interviewed Driscoll at the Cambrian Workman's Home, found him in a very feeble condition and suffering from bad health, but he informed the reporter that they were fighting from 3.30 on January 22nd to daybreak the next morning. Driscoll said he could well remember the Zulus firing the hospital. They had to exist for two days on a few biscuits and corned beef.

Driscoll has done no work since 1925. He had the misfortune to be knocked down by a motor-car in the street at Ebbw Vale during last year and was taken to the Tredegar Infirmary where he remained for two months. This accident severely shook the old man, and he has never completely recovered. Driscoll has been made a life member of the local branch of the British Legion, but owing to his failing eyesight, rarely attends the institute.

"The South Wales Argus," c. June 1931

Death of Gwent Hero of Zulu War.
Survivor Of Epic Battle.
Death of Ebbw Vale Man Who Fought at Rorke's Drift.

MR. THOMAS DRISCOLL, the last of the Ebbw Vale survivors of the gallant stand made by the 24th Regiment (the South Wales Borderers) at Rorke's Drift, died on Tuesday at the age of 77 years.

Mr. Driscoll's sight failed him some months ago and he was rarely able to get out.

Mr. Driscoll was born at Lower High-street, Dowlais, and went to school there until he was 12, at which age he started work at Dowlais Works. He enlisted in the 2nd Battalion of the 24th Regiment on December 6, 1876, and served for 13 years.

The Epic Fight

When seen by a *South Wales Argus* reporter some time ago, Mr. Driscoll recalled the epic fight on January 22, 1879, at Rorke's Drift. He could well remember the Zulus firing the hospital. The defenders had to exist for two days on a few biscuits and tinned beef, and they fought from 3.30 on January 22 until daybreak next day.

Thirty years ago Mr. Driscoll met with an accident at the No.1 Mill of the Ebbw Vale Company, and six years ago he was knocked down by a motor-car. He never completely recovered.

Mr. Driscoll, who lived at the Cambrian Workmen's Home, Briery Hill, Ebbw Vale, worked for the Ebbw Vale Company for 40 years as a labourer. He was unmarried.

25B/972 Private George Edwards (Orchard), 'B' Company, 2nd/24th Foot

"The Bristol Observer," Saturday, March 29th, 1879

A Bedminster Man at Rorke's Drift

It appears from a letter just received by Mr. Orchard, of St. Luke's Road, Bedminster, that George Orchard formerly of Bedminster, and now in the B Company of the 2-24th Regiment, was one of the gallant band who, under Lieutenants Chard and Bromhead, held the post at Rorke's Drift against the Zulus on the night of the 22nd January. Writing to his brother, at Bedminster from Rorke's Drift, on the 29th January, he says:

I have no doubt that you will see by the papers before you receive this that we have had some warm work with the Zulus, they have cut up five companies of our first battalion, and one company of ours. We have had about 800 of our two battalions (1st and 2nd 24th Regiment) killed besides Volunteers, mounted Police, &c. - a terrible slaughter, I can assure you. We have lost everything except what we stand upright in, the enemy having captured everything, and two big guns from the Royal artillery, with all our rifles from our men who were killed, and also our camp. All this happened on the 22nd of this month (January). Our company was fighting hard from three o'clock in the afternoon until 6 o'clock the next morning, when we beat them off, losing 14 killed and 11 wounded, and it was the hardest fight since we have been out. We killed about 500 of the savages, our company being only 80 strong and the enemy was about 1,000 or more, so you see we fought them 12 to 1 and then beat them after all. These Zulus are a strong, savage, determined race of people, and we have not enough British troops out here for the war, so it will take a long time before it is over unless we get more troops as the enemy come in such large numbers.

"The Somerset Guardian," c. 1939.

Helped to Defend Rorke's DRIFT.
Paulton Veteran's Recollections.

To-day there must be very few survivors of that comparatively small and gallant band of British soldiers who took part in the famous defence of Rorke's Drift, in the Zulu campaign of 1879.

One of them is Mr. George Orchard, who resides at New Pit, Paulton, and is a well-known and highly-respected parishioner.

A native of Bristol, Mr. Orchard enlisted in H. M. Forces in Newport in 1876, and became a private in the 2nd. 24th Foot Regiment (after the South Wales Borderers). He was then 21 years of age.

Shortly after joining up he was sent with his Regiment to the Kaffir War in South Africa (1877-78). He went right through this campaign, and was present when Sandelli the chief of the Kaffirs, was captured, together with several 100 head of cattle, etc.

After this experience he went on to Zululand with his Regiment, under the command of the late Lord Chelmsford. They were sent up country under a forced march, and he has vivid recollections of marching 25 miles in one day - it was Christmas Day - without a "sup or a bite," because the bullock wagons were unable to get in consequence of the mud and slush and otherwise difficult state of the road track.

TERRIFIC FIGHTING

Upon arrival they at once became engaged in heavy fighting with the Zulus, and then came the famous Defence of Rorke's Drift, on the Tugela River, comprising about 14 hours hard fighting, during which Private Orchard's company of the 24th Foot, under the command of Lieut. Bromhead, was badly cut up.

No fewer than six times did the blacks charge the defenders, only to be repulsed each time. The only means of defence available to the little band of Britishers consisted of rice bags, biscuit tins and such like.

During this terrible fighting the 24th Foot lost their colours, and several guns, their band and drums. The company had 13 killed and 17 wounded.

It was during this fighting that Pte. Orchard saw one of the missionaries serving out ammunition to the British troops.

For the Defence of Rorke's Drift no fewer than six V.C.s were awarded.

GIBRALTAR AND INDIA

At that time Pte. Orchard was only 23 years of age, and he was personally presented with an illuminated address inscribed, "Presented to the Officers, N.C.O.s and Privates of the 24th Foot, Company, for their splendid defence at Rorke's Drift, which saved the Colony of Natal from being over-run by Zulus."

This he later sold to the officers of the 2nd. Batt. South Wales Borderers when they were stationed at Aldershot, and he has reason to believe that it is still hung in the Officers' Mess of that Regt. at Aldershot.

After the Zulu campaign he was sent to Gibraltar where Lord Napier, of Magdala, presented, in the name of Queen Victoria, a silver laurel wreath to be carried on the Queen's new colours of the 2nd. Batt. S.W.B., presented to replace the colours lost at Rorke's Drift.

While at Gibraltar they were ordered out to reinforce Gen. Fred Roberts (afterwards Lord Roberts) who was then in India for the Afghan War, but by the time they reached Bombay they received orders that they were not wanted because Gen. Roberts had succeeded in getting through from Kabul to Kandahar.

During the Zulu campaign Pte. Orchard and another comrade, simultaneously fired at and wounded in the knee the brother of the King of the Zulus, and he was taken prisoner in consequence.

FUNERAL ESCORT FOR A PRINCE

Pte. Orchard was present beyond Lant Man's Drift in Zululand when the Prince Imperial was killed, and was one of the escort of his body in the mule wagon down to Ladysmith, Natal.

He returned to England in 1888, and left the service in 1889, after 13 years with the Colours. When the South African War broke out, he re-engaged for 12 months for home service.

Mr. Orchard's elder son, Mr. William Orchard, served in the Great War, while at present his youngest son, Lance-Corpl. Herbert Orchard is serving with the 1st. Somersets in India.

Mr. Orchard also has a son-in-law, Mr. George Coughlan, who was among the first batch to be called up in Paulton at the outbreak of the Great War, and was one of the

"Old Contemptibles" who took part in the Mons retreat and was severely wounded. Mr. Orchard was 82 years of age last November, but nevertheless, he still retains a military bearing, and is comparatively active.

He is of the opinion that there must be very few alive today who served at the Rorke's Drift Defence, but if this article should meet the eye of any of the survivors he would be delighted to hear from them.

"The Somerset Guardian," c. 1939.

Bristolian survivor of Rorke's Drift relives his battles.
Is he only one now remaining of the great African epic?

Nearly 59 years ago a Bristolian won a life pension for gallantry at Rorke's Drift. Now after hearing of the death in South Africa, at the age of 90, of Mr. G. W. Mabin, who fought in the same engagement, he is wondering whether he is the last survivor of this famous battle.

He is 83 year old Mr. George Edward Orchard who was born at Charles Street, St, James's, Bristol in 1855, and who now lives with his wife in a little cottage at New Pit, Paulton, Somerset. He can remember January 22, 1879 - that fatal day when a British force were slaughtered at Isandhlwana and the Zulus descended on Rorke's Drift - as clearly as though it were yesterday.

Mr. Orchard's father, a tailor, apprenticed him originally to a shoemaker in John Street, Bristol, but this man died, so he moved to a boot factory near Stone Bridge. The factory closed down and off he went to South Wales to work for a builder who proved unsuccessful.

"I was only 21", Mr. Orchard told an Evening Post reporter, "and there I was out of work with a week's wages owing me and not a penny in my pocket."

Queen's Shilling

"So I took the Queen's shilling and enlisted in the 24th Regiment of Foot - now called the South Wales Borderers - at Newport (Mon.) in 1876".

"I remember they sent me to the 2nd Battalion just in time for my Christmas dinner! The Battalion was ordered to South Africa for the Zulu War, and I was one of those who assisted in the capture of Sandilli the Kaffir chief, whose son we kept with us until he was killed at Isandhlwana."

"My Regiment lost their colours, their band and their drums and practically every man present was killed. I was at Rorke's Drift, about 12 miles away, with B. Company which had been left behind to defend the hospital, where there were 30 or 40 wounded and the commissariat."

"There were only about 80 of us, and their victory at Isandhlwana several Impis of the Zulu army, about 4,000 all told, came down to the drift to attack us."

Saved Natal

"We fought them for about 12 hours, and six times they nearly got through our entrenchments. However, the fact that we were able to defend that ground saved the whole of Natal from being over-run by Zulus."

"We had about 17 men killed and 10 wounded by the time they withdrew. I remember I myself shot the Zulu chief, who was their second in command. I should have liked to have brought home his paisley shawl as a souvenir, but there was nothing left of it. The Zulus began to withdraw when, apparently, they heard that Lord Chelmsford and his relief column were coming into sight."

"I remember well that when Lord Chelmsford rode in on the morning of the 23rd, I was sitting on a biscuit box drinking a cup of cocoa. For some reason he stopped to speak to me and asked me my opinion about the defence we had put up. There was only one answer I could make to him, and that was; 'It was an act of providence.'"

Six V.C.s.

"Six of my company were given V.C.s for their bravery during this engagement. I was given a pension of 10s. a week for life for my services. Moreover, I was also presented with an illuminated address by the Mayor and Burgesses of Natal, who entertained those of us who survived to a banquet. The address is hanging to-day in the mess of the 2nd Battalion of my Regiment."

Mr. and Mrs. Orchard have 12 children, 10 of whom are still living, they have 19 grandchildren. The family are well known in the Whitehall district of Bristol, since grandson William Orchard, has a business in Whitehall Road.

25B/954 Private Thomas Evans, 'H' Company, 2nd/24th Foot

A letter written, in Welsh, to his wife which was subsequently translated and published in unidentified Welsh newspaper, c. 1879

A Rhondda Valley Man at Rorke's Drift

It appears that among the heroic hundred men who made the memorable defence at Rorke's Drift, under Lieutenants Chard and Bromhead, was a young married man named Thomas Evans, native of Tonypandy, Rhondda Valley, The following is a translation of a Welsh letter sent by him to his wife;- .

Rorke's Drift, Jan. 28, 1879

Dear Wife,
I send you these few lines to inform you that I was not among those unfortunate men belonging to our regiment who were killed on the 22nd of this month.
The camp was left in charge of some 850 privates and officers, and when they were

out they were attacked and killed excepting 20. The Zulus crossed into Natal and attacked another station; but another company of our regiment poured out such fife against them that they failed to force an entrance, and when they saw what number of men among them was being killed they set fire to the hospital and then retreated. I was in the midst of this fight, and about 100 of us killed about 600 of the enemy with only a loss of 15 men among ourselves. On the following morning, what remained of our regiment came to us, and we are now waiting for others to come and take our place, because we have neither clothes nor anything else. I do not suppose we shall go to the battlefield again because our companies are so cut up that it will be hardly possible to form us into a regiment. I shall write again when that be possible, and will give you full particulars -

Your affectionate husband

Thomas Evans

25B/81 Sergeant Henry Edward Gallagher, 'B' Company, 2nd/24th

An unidentified Hampshire newspaper, c. 1931.

Hero of famous defence dies at Portsdown Hill, Hampshire.
Officers attend West Country Funeral.

Members of the South Wales Borderers Regiment, recruited from Bristol and District, will learn with regret of the death of one of the few surviving hero's of the defence of Rorke's Drift, Zululand in 1879. He is Mr. Henry Gallagher, late Regimental Sergeant-Major of the 24th Regiment of Foot, who collapsed and died at his home at Drayton, Hants. It is believed that only two other members of the defence are still living, one of these is Mr. Charles Hitch VC who sent a wreath to the funeral, which took place with semi-military honours, at Christchurch, Portsdown Hill, Hampshire. A bugler sounded the last post and reveille on a silver bugle presented to the Regiment by Queen Victoria. Officers, Warrant-Officers and Sergeants of the 2nd Battalion 24th Regiment attended the funeral as well as family mourners. There were wreaths in the form of the regimental Cap Badge and forming the numerals of the Regiment in Roman figures.

Extract from the reminiscences of Major (Retired) Edward Lane, R.E., (Grandson of Henry E. Gallagher). [Appears by kind permission of Major Edward Lane, and Mr. Roger Lane]

H.E. Gallagher, my grandfather, gave graphic pictures of the defence of Rorke's Drift and the way in which B Company withstood the attacks so fearlessly. He remembered the initial horror felt at the sight of the first wave of the attack as so many Zulus in battle array came down on them. But as the fighting progressed all fear left him because he was so busy shooting. He was in-charge of the south wall of bags and waggons, and was latter stationed in the mealie-bag redoubt.

All the defenders were in a state of collapse when the fighting was done. He carried the scars of the defence with a permanent blue mark on the right side of his nose, which was a powder burn caused by the back flash each time he fired his rifle.

My mother, his eldest offspring, told me that when they were stationed in Egypt and he was Garrison Sergeant Major, how particular he was in his (turn out). She was responsible that no blemish was visible on his red tunic, blue trousers, belt, and highly-polished boots, before he left their quarters for his daily duties throughout the garrison. I am sure he was the terror of any soldier who appeared to be idle or slovenly - in spite of his short stature.

He retired from the army in 1897. I remember him from about 1919/1920 until his death. During that period I regularly spent two or three weeks annually at his home in Augustine Road. He was very fond of his grandchildren, and we loved him.

He had a great sense of humour and a real Irish sense of fun. When I first got to know him he would tell me stories of his soldiering, especially South Africa and Rorke's Drift in particular. He was proud of his regiment, the 24th, and maintained his soldierly smartness and appearance all his life. He was a great story-teller on any subject true or fictitious. He was very fond of walking, especially on the Portsdown Hill. He would walk many miles on what he called (Campaigning), me asking questions, and him giving the answers - which I fully believed. But sometimes his deliberate exaggerations gave the clue that it was all his (Irish blarney) coming out. He loved his small garden, where he grew most of his vegetables and kept chickens. He died very suddenly in 1931, when strangely, I was stationed with the Royal Engineers in Eire, quite close to Thurles, and from where I kept up correspondence with him.

On the anniversary of the defence of Rorke's Drift each year my grandfather requested to be left alone with his memories.

25B/1062 Private John Harris, 'B' Company 2nd/24th Foot

Extract from his army service and discharge papers: [WO97/1983, The National Archives, (P.R.O.), London]

Proceedings of Discharge

Gibraltar 16 July 1880
...his character has been good and he is in possession of one good conduct badge. present at Defence of Rorkes Drift...

...compensation loss of kit at defence of Rorkes Drift
signed Bvt. Major C.J. Bromhead, 2/24th
[the President of the Regimental Board assembled to consider his discharge]

2-24/2067 Drummer Patrick Hayes 'B' Company, 2nd/24th Foot

"The News of the World," Sunday, January 22nd, 1939

Jubilee of Rorke's Drift Epic
When 131 Britons Held Back 5,000 Zulus
("News of the World Special")

Sixty years ago to-day, on Jan. 22, 1879, a band of 131 British soldiers, many of them sick and wounded, held 5,000 Zulus at bay during a 16 hour attack on Rorke's Drift.

No fewer than 11 Victoria Crosses were won on that day of epic struggle. One of the few survivors of the noble defence force is Drummer Patrick Hayes, then an Irish lad serving in the South Wales Borderers, and now a grey-haired veteran living in cosy house in Riverhall Street, Wandsworth Road, London.

He told the "News of the World" a thrilling story of the battle in an interview at his home yesterday.

"My company was left to guard Rorke's Drift while the rest of the battalion went forward nine miles with Lord Chelmsford's column to Isandhlwana, where they camped," he related.

"Lord Chelmsford divided his force, taking the main part of his column on a reconnaissance and leaving the 24th to guard the camp and stores. That provided the opportunity for which the Zulus had been looking, and they attacked the British camp."

Britons Massacred

"The defenders fired back vigorously until the 50 rounds each man carried were exhausted. There was spare ammunition in plenty but it was stored in boxes, the lids of which were screwed down tightly and before it could be served out the enemy rushed camp and massacred the British.

News of the disaster was brought to Rorke's Drift by a twenty-year-old subaltern destined many years later to play a great part as a military leader. He was Horace Smith-Dorrien, who commanded an Army corps during the retreat from Mons in 1914.

He warned us to prepare, and, in the short time at our disposal, we worked frantically to fortify the place we held, which was a combination of hospital and store depot.

A young Royal Engineer officer named Chard directed the barricading of the buildings; our own subaltern, Lieut. Bromhead, posted the men at various points behind the barricade so that we might put up a desperate defence and the medical officer, Dr. Reynolds arranged shelter for the sick and wounded.

Suddenly the cry went up 'Here they come', and a black yelling mass of frenzied savages could be seen crossing the Buffalo River a short distance away and rushing towards us brandishing rifles and spears. It was a terrifying sight, but the enemy halted as we poured a deadly volley into their midst and followed it up with well-directed independent firing.

But they soon recovered from their surprise, and came on with a rush, but steady volleys drove them back, and they then started to reply with rifle fire from a distance."

Hand-To-Hand Fight

"Gradually they advanced again and some of them reached the building, which they entered again and again, only to be beaten back by our bullets and bayonets.

It was a hand-to-hand fight, and it seemed every moment that we would be overwhelmed, but the knowledge of the awful massacre of our comrades earlier in the day impelled us to do our damnedest. It was discipline and leadership against weight of numbers, but 50 to 1 are heavy odds when fighting savages already flushed with victory.

During a lull in the fighting we saw to our horror that the enemy were lighting firebrands in order to set alight the thatched roofs of our buildings. But that move perhaps proved our salvation, for night was closing in and the glare shed by the burning roofs showed us where the enemy were lurking, enabling us to keep up an effective fire and bayonet all who came too close.

So the battle dragged on throughout the night. As dawn approached we were at our last gasp, but the enemy were tired also, and after a few more half-hearted rushes at our defences they began to drift away."

Zulus' Red Coats

"Meanwhile Lord Chelmsford had heard the heavy firing at Isandhlwana and had sent back to find out the cause. He was told that the camp was still standing and that men in red coats could be seen walking about. Little did he think that those red coats were being worn by Zulus who had stripped them from the force they had slaughtered.

When the truth reached Chelmsford at last, he brought his worn-out column back towards the camp, and then pushed forward to Rorke's Drift. On the way the column passed the Zulus, but each side was too exhausted to give battle.

It was a great and welcome surprise to the head of the column to see our men perched on the blackened rafters of the hospital waving to them now that they knew the peril was over.

Altogether 11 Victoria Crosses and four D.C.M.s were won that day. Lieuts. Chard and Bromhead were among the V.C.s, and they were not only promoted majors at once, but they received the thanks of both Houses of Parliament.

After I completed my Colour service I continued to live in barracks as a civilian workman until I was well over 60, so that my experience at Rorke's Drift did not quench my love for army life."

Two other Rorke's Drift survivors Ptes. Lockhart and Dunbar, reside in South Africa, and another Pte. John Thomas, now lives in Canada.

Extract from "The South Wales Borderers Regimental Journal," c. April 1941

Obituary

No 3949, 25th Brigade, Drummer H. Hayes, formerly of B. Coy., 2nd 24th Regiment, and a survivor of Rorke's Drift, died in London on 4th October at the age of 84, and was buried there on the 8th October. The Colonel of the Regiment, Lieut.-Colonel F. Bourne, O.B.E., D.C.M., and Mr. Tom Press attended the funeral and the latter laid a wreath on the grave from all ranks of the Regiment.

The East Surrey Regiment kindly supplied a bearer party and a bugler, who sounded the Last Post and Reveille. The widow has presented to the Regiment Dr. Hayes' Zulu War medal, discharge certificate, and Rorke's Drift bible, which will rest finally in the Regimental Museum. Dr. Hayes joined the Regiment at 14 years of age on the 9th September, 1868, and was discharged to pension on 30th November 1892, after 24 years, 180 days total service, over 17 years of which was spent abroad.

Bob. S. Head, a soldier of the 2nd/24th Foot

"The Irish Times," November 26th, 1932

Mr. John Williams, a hero of Rorke's Drift, and stated to be the oldest surviving holder of the Victoria Cross, died at Cwmbran (Mon.) yesterday, at the age of 75.

John Williams (who enlisted under the assumed name of Bob Head) was one of the eight defenders of Rorke's Drift who were awarded the Victoria Cross. All his officers and comrades are dead.

After the fight he wrote a remarkable letter to his brother, F. Williams, who was at that time employed in Grafton street, and it was printed in the Irish Times in 1879. It is reproduced here in facsimile. The paper cost Williams a shilling, and he used up both sides.

John Williams enlisted in the South Wales Borderers in 1877, and joined the 2nd Battalion. The account of his winning of the Victoria Cross was published in the London Gazette of May 2nd, 1879, and relates how Williams and a comrade made a desperate stand against the Zulus in a hospital, and brought eight patients to safety.

Dear Brother,

I now send you these few lines to inform you of what I daresay you will have seen in the paper before you receive this we under Lieut Chard and Broomhead had a nice night of it at Rookes Drift I call it I never shall forget the same place about as long as I live I daresay the old fool in Command will make a great fuss over our two officers commanding our company in keeping the Zulu Buck back with the private soldier what will he get nothing only he may get praise of the public now I shall if

God spares me live and see dear old England again I shall find what I say to be true so now as I had to give a Shilline for this bit of paper you will only be able to know I am ready & willing to lose my life to win back for our sister Battalion 1-/24 Renown so Kindest love to all I am jolly only short of a [a drawing of a pipe] and Bacca

Your loving Brother
Bob S. Head 2/24

25B/1061 Private John Samuel Jobbins, 'B' Company, 2nd/24th Foot

"The Monmouthshire Beacon," March 29th, 1879

THE ZULU WAR
Letter From A Pontypool Man

"Rorke's Drift, Natal, South Africa.
Feb. 6th, 1879.

"Dear Father and Mother, -
I now have the pleasure to send you a few lines, hoping they will find you quite well, as they leave me at present. Since I wrote to you last we have had a deal of hard work and terrible fighting. But before you receive this letter I expect you have heard something about it by the newspapers. But I will tell you a little about it, what I have seen myself.

"On the 22nd of January, about four o'clock in the morning, the General left camp with about half the Division in search of the Kaffirs; they threw out a few thousand men as a decoy for our troops to follow, which they did do instead of following the main body of the Kaffir army; when our men got about 16 miles out of the Camp they could see large numbers of the enemy approaching the Camp which they had just left.

"But our wise commanders did not think it necessary to turn back to protect the Camp until it was too late; they still kept marching on after the other few men in front. Well, there were about 20,000 Zulus attacked the Camp (but mind, I was on detachment about 12 miles away with our company in charge of the commissary stores) There was left in the Camp five companies of the 1-24th, one company (G) of ours on picquet, and a lot more men of ours on guard, and the staff officers' servants, and cooks, five little band boys, and our new bandmaster just come to our regiment, and there were a lot of volunteers left in Camp. and two guns of the Royal Artillery The guns opened fire on them, but it was no use; as fast as the fire mowed them down their place was filled up again by more of them. All our men that fell and especially the little boys were cut to pieces by the Zulus; they are not satisfied with killing us but they mutilate the body afterwards.

"These names I mention are known very well by me and you. Poor Alf Farr, Charlie

Long, George Morrison, Harry Smith, who used to live at Sohill, Dick Treverton, and Will Reece, they have all been killed. There were about 16 white men escaped from the Camp out of about 900 men; all the others - officers and men - were killed. "There were two officers who escaped on horseback with the colours of the 1-24th. They got down to the river called the Buffalo, when they were both knocked over, the colours were found a few days after in the river at the side of the two poor officers. All that did escape were on horseback.

"At night the General received a messenger from the Camp to say it was taken and the ammunition, 2 guns and about 1000 rifles, and thousands of pounds in cash. Well, the General says to the men, 'We must take the Camp at the point of a bayonet' and they first had to shell the Camp with the 6 guns which the General had out with him. When the men got back to Camp they could see the Zulus retiring and the men had to sleep that night amongst the dead, and some terrible sights there were; but there were, say, about 10 black men killed to each white man.

"Before it was daylight the next morning what was left of our poor soldiers had to retire upon the stores, where I was with about 120 men - our Company and Volunteers. The day before 4 men on horseback arrived at the stores who escaped from the Camp and told us what had happened, this was about 3 o'clock in the afternoon of the 22nd January. We at once let our tents fall to the ground and got inside the stores, and made a small fort with sacks filled with grain. Just as we had finished our little fort we could see thousands of niggers coming down on our little body of men. At the end of the fort was a large house which had been turned into a hospital the owners which were Swedes who fled as soon as the Zulus were in sight. There were lot of sick men in the hospital at the time, one - poor Sergeant Maxfield - was insane and he was burnt alive, or killed and then burnt. Well we fought hard from about 3.30 p.m. till the following morning when they retired, but they killed about 12 of our men but we killed at least 450 of them. They were charging over the sacks but we repulsed them. All that night a minister was praying in the fort that they would go away. God helped us and gave us the victory.

In the morning we could see in the distance a large body of men approaching; we did not at first recognise them but after a bit we could see the welcome red coats retiring on us from the other unfortunate camp. Then we all gave hearty cheer as we felt safe when we were all together. Nothing important has happened since the 22nd, but we have ever since been making the fort stronger, and we sleep in our clothes every night on the look out. One of the poor fellows who was wounded is a Corporal Lyons, him who used to go about with Jim Sullivan but he is expected to get over it. Poor M. Morgan is here very bad with the fever, but he seems to be getting over it. The General has sent to England for 10,000 more troops. We shall advance no further till they come out here. I send my kind love to brothers and sisters and Mrs. Sullivan and all friends thanking God I am well, and hope you are all, the same. Your affectionate Son, J. Jobbins.

"When you write address:- No. 1061. J. Jobbins, B. Company 2-24th Reg., Natal, South Africa.

"Good bye and bless you all."

(The above is a son of Mr. Jobbins the post boy at the Crown Hotel, Pontypool. The Sergeant Maxfield in this interesting letter was we believe a Monmouth man.)

"The South Wales Argus," c. *September 1934*

Rorke's Drift Survivor
Death of Pontypool Veteran

Private John Jobbins, one of the last of the heroes of Rorke's Drift, is dead.

As reported in the *South Wales Argus* just over a week ago, Mr. Jobbins, whose home was at Machine Meadow, Pontnewynydd, was taken ill after visiting a military tatoo in July.

As a soldier of the 24th Regiment of Foot (now the South Wales Borderers) he took part in the gallant defence of Rorke's Drift on the night of January 22nd, 1879, when behind hastily-made defences fewer than a hundred men of the 24th successfully resisted the attacks of thousands of Zulus.

Private Jobbins participated in the rescue of wounded men, some of whom were hauled through holes in the wall.

He served 19 years in the Army - 16 of them in the South Wales Borderers. The Zulu War medal, with three clasps, and long service and good conduct medals were awarded him. When he lost his Zulu War medal he was presented with a new one. Mr Jobbins was 79.

Private John Williams, of Cwmbran, who won the V.C., for his gallantry at Rorke's Drift, died on November 25, 1932.

25B/1428 Private Evan 'Gibby' Jones (Cosgrove), 'B' Company, 2nd/24th Foot

"The Montgomery County Times, Shropshire and Mid-Wales Advertiser," *Saturday, February 27th, 1915.*

A Welshpool Veteran.
Over 40 years service and still in the army.

For long military service, Drummer Instructor Evan Jones, 18, Union Street, Welshpool, now with 7th Bn RWF (Res) at Aberystwyth has a remarkable record. He is probably the oldest drummer in the army. He has over 40 years service to his credit, and now a veteran approaching 60, he is still in khaki having even volunteered for Imperial Service. The age limit however, forbade although he looks hale and hearty, and to use his own words to a County Times representative as he recounted rather wistfully how he was not accepted for active service, he feels as fit as when he first enlisted. He served in two hard campaigns, including the heroic defence of Rorke's Drift, and is entitled to a high place in the Roll of Honour of Montgomeryshire men who have rendered worthy service to their country.

Drummer Jones entered on his military career in 1874, when he joined the Monmouthshire Militia, with whom he served for three years. In 1877 he enlisted in the famous 24th Foot Regt (now the SWB) and fought through the Kaffir War of 1877-78. He also served in the Zulu War of 1879 and as stated above, was one of the band of heroes who took part in the defence of Rorke's Drift, one of the most brilliant episodes in the history of British Arms. The British numbered only 104 and for nearly two days kept an army of some thousands of Zulu's at bay. Drummer Jones escaped unhurt although the assault on the part of the defences where he was engaged became so hot that they all had to retire to another position. All the defenders were recommended for the VC, but only about fourteen were granted including seven to the men who rescued the patients from the hospital in which the Zulu's succeeded in firing.

From Africa, Drummer Jones accompanied his regiment to Gibraltar where they were stationed for about 6 months. They were then ordered out to India to take part in the Afghan War, but peace was declared before the 24th saw any more fighting. They did not enjoy barrack life for very long however for in 1887-89 Drummer Jones saw active service again in the Burma War.

In 1893 after 17 years foreign service he returned home, and 6 years later was discharged. Most men would then have considered that they deserved a rest. Not so Drummer Jones, however. In 1900 he joined the Royal Northern Reserve with whom he served 12 months followed by 2 annual training's with the 3rd Monmouthshire's. He then joined the Montgomeryshire Yeomanry, with whom he served until last May - a period of 12 years. Then when war was declared the veteran again responded to the call and though denied leave to go abroad, engaged as Drummer-Instructor with the 7th RWF. He is a complete master of both the big drum and the side drum and when in India was accounted the best player among the troops in the country. He played for 3 years in the band of the Governor of Bombay and also in the bands of the 24th and the Mont. Yeo. Under his expert tuition the drummers of the 7th are making great progress and are rapidly becoming the pride of the battalion and at the same time the envy of the other regiments in the town.

Drummer Jones possesses the South African Medal, 77-78-79, the Burma Medal, 87-89, and the Territorial Long Service Medal, and when discharged from the Regular Army he possessed five good conduct badges - the maximum possible.

Another soldier with local connections who fought at Rorke's Drift is Sgt. Wilson, stepfather of Mr. J. McKenzie, Berriew Street, Welshpool and Capt. Black, who was the last quartermaster with the 4th SWB at Welshpool and was detailed to bury the dead after Rorke's Drift and Isandlwana. Capt. Black who is now on active service with a Yorkshire regiment. Enlisted when a young boy and served about 30 years with the Regular Army - mostly with the 1st and 2nd battalions SWB. He left Welshpool about 7 years ago to become quartermaster of a territorial regiment, so that by this time he has about 40 years service to his credit. He has three sons also serving.

A private letter written by Jones in 1925, [courtesy Mr. Bill Jones, grandson of Evan Jones]

18 Union St
Welshpool
16 Aug 1925

Dear Sir,

I received your most kind letter and enclosed cutting with photo and am most pleased to hear that there are still a few left in South Africa who can recall the part taken by my old Regt the 24th...

...Dear Sir talking now about Rourkes Drift all that now survive as far as I know are Col Bourne Williams V.C. myself and a man of the name of Tom Driscoll who I saw last year and who is living in Ebbw Vale, Mon.
As regards the defence of Rourkes Drift. I was the sentry on outpost who first saw the two survivors of the Isandulana disaster struggling in and reported to Lieut Bromhead and after their story we set too at once to put the place in a state of defence. After the Zulu war was over we went to Gibraltar and was sent to the Afghan Campaign but were too late as peace was proclaimed. Previous to the Zulu War I have been through the Kaffir war and East London was where we landed in serf boats a very nice doing...

Yours sincerely
Evan Jones

An unidentified Welshpool newspaper, c. 1931

Death of Rorke's Drift Veteran
Sergt. Evan Jones of Welshpool

One of the few survivors of the fight at Rorke's Drift, died in Welshpool on Wednesday, in the person of L/Sergt. Evan Jones, of 18, Union Street, Welshpool. Sergt. Jones who was 78 years of age, was a native of Abervale and had a romantic career as a soldier. Joining the Army when quite a boy, he saw service in many parts of the world, and had a very fine record. He was naturally very proud of his experience at Rorke's Drift, and frequently described it in graphic terms.
The garrison of Rorke's Drift was 'B' Company of the 2nd Battalion of the 24th, (now the South Wales Borderers). It numbered 80 effectives and 30 or 40 sick. This little body of men was attacked just after the disaster of Isandlwana by a Zulu impi of 4,000. They attacked just after mid-day on January 22, and the fight went on till nine o'clock the next morning. The Zulus reached the breastworks many times, but on each occasion they were beaten off with bayonets. The dead lay in heaps before the breastworks and were found for miles around after the beaten impi retired. Their losses were estimated at 350, and the loss of the British was 17 killed and ten wounded.

Sergt. Jones, who was on sentry duty at the time the attack began, told a *County Times* reporter some time ago that he would never forget the sight of the Zulus charging to the attack in the well-known crescent formation, the young fleet runners on the wings closing round until the garrison was surrounded by attackers, a fearful spectacle in their savage panoply or war - black ostrich plumes, cowtails, bull-hide shields, with their assegais gleaming in the sun, "A warm soup," was how he summed up the position.

The survivors of the fight, in addition to Sergt. Jones, known to be alive at the 50th anniversary of the fight in 1929 were;- Lt. Col. F. Bourne, O.B.E., D.C.M., Beckenham, Kent (24th Regiment); Sergt. H.E. Gallagher, Drayton, Hants (24th Regiment); Sergt. A. Saxy (24th Regiment); Pte. T. Driscoll, Ebbw Vale (24th Regiment); Pte. J.S. Jobbins, Pontnewydd; Pte. Will Osborne, Blaenavon; Pte. J. Williams, V.C., Cwmbran (24th Regiment); Acting-Commist. Officer Dalton...

Extract from an unidentified Welsh newspaper, c. July 1931

...On the morning of January 22nd, 1879, Drummer Jones was on sentry duty at the outpost of Rorke's Drift, with some ninety rank and file of the 24th Regiment, under Lieutenants Bromhead and Chard, when he heard the firing of guns, and drew the attention of Sergeant Lyons, who was in charge of the guard, to the sound. Not long afterwards he saw some horsemen coming over the brow of the hill, who reported there was a battle raging at Isandlwana some miles away, between the Zulus and a small British force...

The reminiscences of Mr. Stan Morris, (formerly Captain in the 7th Battalion Royal Welsh Fusiliers), who knew 'Drummer Jones'.

As a youngster
My Recollections of Mr. Evan Jones

He was a strong sturdy character.

On a Saturday morning he would often call at my father's saddler's shop in Berriew Street, Welshpool for a chat and a beer next door in the Wellington Inn. Afterwards he would think nothing of making a tack to the village of Llanfyllin and back - a distance of some 20 miles or so - to visit a friend and no doubt have a couple more beers.

He was an expert at playing the side-drum and was known throughout Welshpool and district as "Drummer Jones" and in this capacity he took part in all military parades held in the town. He taught his skill to a friend of mine, Mr. Jim Evans - Jim says during his instruction if he made a mistake he would receive a severe tap on the knuckles so he would avoid doing the same again!

Evan Jones was a perfectionist, whatever he had anything to do with had to be one hundred per cent correct.

No doubt he inherited this trait as a result of his long service in the army and the discipline he shared in the battle of Rorke's Drift.

When he died he had one of the largest funeral processions ever seen in Welshpool, which was escorted by a detachment from his old Regiment - The South Wales Borderers.
You know what, you can keep all your Stanley Bakers and your film Zulus - I knew a man that was actually there, and that's good enough for me!

Stan Morris, age 91 years
Welshpool
November 2003

Some reminiscences from Mr Bill Jones, grandson of Evan Jones.

My father, used to tell me that my grandfather often sat in his house practising with his drums, much to the annoyance of his neighbours although no one ever dared to complain. I will always remember my mother, who tended Evan Jones up until his death, teling me that I was born in the very bed in which he had died.I remember also being told that once year a group of old army friends, including several "Rorke's Drift men" would gather at Jones' house to sit and talk about days gone by, my father and the other children being ushered out of the room, as they were to young to listen to such things.

25B/970 Private John Jones 'B' Company, 2nd/24th Foot

"The Merthyr Express," March 29th, 1879, page 3

The Zulu War
Letters from Merthyr soldiers at Rorke's Drift

By the mail which was delivered at Merthyr on Friday, a number of letters were received from soldiers who are serving in the campaign against the Zulus. The receipt of these letters from the Cape has imparted general joy in the neighbourhood where the young men formerly resided, and which, with a few exceptions, was at Caedraw. There are however, many families in the district who have suffered bereavement by the affair at Isandula, and the grief of the parents at the loss of their sons is still very great. The letters are though-out of such an interesting nature; and bring the feelings which animate on soldiers so graphically before the reader, that the copies of the letters, most of which were written in pencil on scraps of paper, cannot but be read with the deepest interest.
This letter is from 970 Private John Jones whose mother lives at Caedraw

Rorke's Drift, Natal.
January 28, 1879.

My Dear Mother,
I now take my pen in hand to write you a few lines, as I dare say you will be anxious to hear from me before you receive this, as you will hear of the disastrous battle which we had on the 22nd of this month with the enemy.

But, dear mother, I am happy to inform you that I came through it all right without being touched. The enemy came down on our camp, 20 men to one of us, as the most of our column had gone out 15 miles further up the country, expecting to have an engagement, but they out-flanked us and came down on the camp which was defended by 1,000 men only and two guns, and the enemy's force being over 20,000 strong warriors. They came so numerous that every man in camp was slaughtered, but happily to me I was out with the column, so I was saved, but Billy Terrett, Hughey Perkins, James Cantlon, commonly called "Jimmy knocked the house down", were all killed on the field, as five companies of the 1st Battalion and one company of ours, besides 100 Artillerymen, and a great number of Mounted Volunteers of the colony, in all nearly 1,000 perished at the mercy of the enemy, but we took back our camp by 10 o'clock at night, after marching about 35 miles that day, but mostly everything in camp was lost, lost to us, as the enemy had our valises, blankets, big coats, tents, and, in-fact, everything excepting what we stood in. There is no one that knows where James Terrett, is. He is supposed to be up in the Diamond Fields with the mounted troops, but they will be called down here now as reinforcements, so I don't know how things will turn out as yet, and no one knows what number of lives will be lost by the time it is finished; but I trust in God to return home safe some day.

But this is a fearful war, and the havoc will be great among our troops, as it is such a fearful hill country for marching; and now, since we lost our camp, we are obliged to sleep on the ground in the best way we can, without anything to cover us, and its very cold and wet here now the rainy season is on, but the heat of the sun is so scorchingly hot in the day that it has already caused a great deal of sickness amongst our troops; but in a few days, as soon as we get reinforcements, we will make a further advance into the country towards the King's kraals where he is supposed to have about from 40,000 to 58,000 troops, and we expect to have a great engagement when we get there as no mercy is to be shown them any more, owing to the manner they cut and mutilated our dead bodies. The enemy has already lost nearly 20,000, and before we finished with them we hope to kill them to the last man. Our loss up to the present is about 1,000.

So now I beg to conclude. I shall write again soon with more particulars. Hoping I shall hear from you soon, and hoping also that you are all at home enjoying the best of health, give my best respects to all inquiring friends, and accept my kindest love to all at home. - Believe me to remain your very affectionate son, John.

Please address - No. 970. Private John Jones.
B. Company. 2-24th Regiment.
Rorke's Drift, near Helpmakaar, Natal, South Africa.

2-24/2381 Drummer James Keefe, 'B' Company, 2nd/24th Foot

"The South Wales Daily Star," Tuesday, September 19th, 1893

The interest excited by the annihilation of the 24th Regiment in the Zulu campaign some years ago is well remembered as, too, is the song that was composed bringing honour to this Regiment of "Glorious Renown", and calling upon England to "Defend her countrymen and strike the foeman down". A reminder of the campaign comes to notice by the demise at Ebbw Vale of Sergeant-Instructor Keefe, who was a survivor of Rorke's Drift, and took part throughout the campaign in which the celebrated Cetshwayo was a conspicuous figure. The deceased soldier spent no fewer than 22 years in the 24th Regiment, coming to Ebbw Vale about a couple of years since.

Death of a Rorke's Drift Hero At Ebbw Vale

We regret to announce the death of Sergeant-instructor Keefe, which took place at his residence at Ebbw Vale on Monday. The deceased was about 40 years of age, and took part throughout the Zulu War, being one of the survivors of Rorke's Drift. He was a sergeant in the 24th Regiment, serving 22 years, and came to Ebbw Vale about two years ago. He leaves a widow and family, for whom much sympathy is felt.

25B/963 Private David Lewis, (James Owen), 'A' Company, 2nd/24th Foot

"The South Wales Evening Post," July 27th, 1938

Death Of Swansea Man Who Was At Rorke's Drift

Mr. James Owen, who died to-day at the home of his son, 12, Kemble-street, Brynmill, Swansea, aged 87, was one of the now minute band of survivors of Rorke's Drift. He was a veteran of the old 24th Regiment of Foot, now the South Wales Borderers, and his military career was one of romance as well as one of periods of privation on active service.

As a young man he joined the regiment in the name of David Lewis, after running away from home in search of adventure. Mr. Owen was a weaver by trade, and was a native of Whitland.

He had lived for many years in Swansea, and he retired at the age of 73. Up to about three years ago, he was active, but ill-health overtook him.

It was in the 70's that he was posted as a recruit to "A" Coy., 24th Regiment the Foot.

He served through the Kaffir and Zulu wars of 1877-78-79, and during the Kaffir war he was a member of the burial party at the burial of the Kaffir chief, Sandala. He took part in the famous march to Isandhlwana, and was present at the relief of troops at Rorke's Drift. He was also present at the capture of Ulundi, and recalled seeing the Zulu chief, Cetewayo being led to the British headquarters as a captive. Famous figures whom he came into contact personally during these campaigns were General Thesiger (Lord Chelmsford), Colonel Wood, who later became Field Marshal Sir Evelyn Wood; and Major Buller, subsequently General Sir Redvers Buller; while he had also served directly under Lieutenants Chard and Bromhead, the heroic defenders of Rorke's Drift.

He leaves two daughters and one son - Mrs. Edwards, Tondu; Mrs. Jenkins, of Grandison-street, Hafod; and Mr. David Owen, of Kemble-street.

25B/1112 Corporal John Jeremiah Lyons, 'B' Company, 2/24th Foot.

A letter written to his mother: [Lyons family archive]

Helpmakaar
February 7th 1879

Dear Mother,

I now take the pleasure of writing home these few lines, to let you know that I happened to be one of the unlucky ones that got wounded on the 22nd of last month, but thank God that I am getting around favourable again. Dear Mother, the Zulus attacked the camp of the 1/24th on the 22nd and slaughtered five companies of them, and slaughtered one company and a half of the 2/24th. They also attacked the company I belonged to on the same day, at half past 3 in the afternoon. We were stationed at Rorke's Drift, guarding the commissariat and hospital. We were warned that they were going to attack us about one hour before they came. We did the best in our power to make a laager to defend ourselves. There were about eighty of us, all told, and we fought like men and kept four thousand of them at bay until morning. Dear Mother, I do not know who all the boys are that got killed from Pontypool, but I know that Farr, the butcher, and young Harry Smith were killed. Dear Mother, I will be able to let you know more in my next letter. I am getting around alright at present. I suppose that I shall be on the road home soon. Give my best respects to Thomas and all my enquiring friends, and you must accept the same yourself,

I remain, your dear son,
John Lyons
ps. Write soon.

"The Cambrian," June 13th, 1879

The Massacre At Rorke's Drift
(Narratives By Survivors)

Corporal Lyons, another of the wounded men tells the following story:-

I belong to the B Company of the 2-24th, under Lieutenant Bromhead. I went up to Greytown with Private Hitch, who was one of the same company. We arrived at Rorke's Drift about Jan 5. I saw Private Evans, of the Mounted Infantry, riding up at full gallop, without either coat or cap on, and I of course thought something was up. Hitch had by this time reported that the Zulus were in sight, and we were scarcely finished before they were on us. We were told not to fire without orders. This, I suppose was to make sure that the advancing force was really Zulus. Only a few seconds elapsed before the real character of it was made known to us. The Zulus did not shout, as they generally do; but, after extending and forming a half-moon, they steadily advanced and kept up a tremendous fire. I took up a position to check the fire from the enemy's right flank, as it was thought the crack shots would go up there.

Corporal Allen and several men were with me, and we all consider we did good service. Lieutenant Bromhead was on the right face, firing over the mealies with a Martini-Henry. Mr Chard was also very busy, I only turned round once to see this, and in that brief interval I saw Private Cole shot, and he fell dead. Seeing this I kept myself more over the bags, knowing that the shot which hit him had come over our heads, and I was determined to check this flank firing as much as possible. I became thus more exposed, and so did Corporal Allen. We fired many shots, and I said to my comrades, 'They (the Zulus) are falling fast" over there; and he replied 'Yes, we are giving it to them.' I saw many Zulus killed on the hill. About half-past seven, as near as I can tell, after we had been fighting between two and three hours, I received a shot through the right side of the neck. The ball lodged in the back, striking the spine, and was not extracted till five weeks afterwards. My right arm was partially disabled. I said, 'Give it to them, Allen. I am done; I am dying,' and he replied, 'All right, Jack;' and while I was speaking to him I saw a hole in the right sleeve of his jacket, and I said, 'Allen, you are shot,' and he replied 'Yes; good bye.' He walked away, with blood running from his arm, and he helped to serve ammunition all night. All I could do as I was lying on the ground was to encourage the men, and I did so as long as I was able to open my mouth. Every man fought dearly for his life, but we were all determined to sell our lives like soldiers, and to keep up the credit of our regiment. Mr Dalton, who has since received a commission, deserved any amount of praise.

CORPORAL LYONS

Our readers are already aware that our brave townsman, Corporal John Lyons, was badly wounded in the neck, by a Zulu bullet, at Rorke's Drift, on the 22nd of January last. The bullet which remained in the neck until the 27th of February, causing intense pain, is supposed to be made of Zinc or a similar metal; it is round and unproved, roughly cast, having a shank left by the hole in the bullet-mould still upon it, measuring 2 ins in circumference, and weighs within a trifle of three-quarters of an ounce.

The operation was performed by Dr. D. Blair-Brown, F.R.C.S., Ed., A.M.D., from whose "Surgical notes on the Zulu War", published in the Lancet, we have extracted the following:-

Case of gunshot injury to the Cervical Vertebrae with lodgement of the bullet. - No. 1112. Corporal. J. Lyons, of the 2nd-24th Regiment, when engaged in the defence of Rorke's Drift, on the night of 22nd January, received a bullet in his neck, near the posterior margin of the -mastoid of the left side, about the upper portion of the middle third of its length. Only one wound, that of entrance, was present. He complained of great pain in the neck on the slightest movement. While in bed the pillow caused an increase of this. He had lost almost all use of arms and hands, especially the right one, which he describes as "quite dead". Painful "twitchings" were experienced in the arms. Whenever he moved his head from the bed someone had to support it between their hands before he could do so. At Rorke's Drift several surgeons tried to find the bullet, but were unsuccessful. In the above condition he arrived at Helpmakaar on the 26th of January. Next day, assisted by several surgeons, I got him under chloroform, I made a prolonged attempt to find the bullet. The course I found it had taken was in a direct line with the spinal cord. I made a free opening in the middle line, as far down the course as possible, and again attempted to reach the bullet. I found by digital examination now that the processes of two adjacent vertebrae's were smashed, and I felt a soft, smooth, cord-like substance under my finger beyond. Pressure on this instantly caused the patient to turn very pale and the pulse to be almost imperceptible, and necessitated the immediate withdrawal of the chloroform and adoption of artificial respiration. I have no doubt but that it was the spinal cord. I took away several pieces of vertebrae which were very loose, but had to give up attempting to reach the bullet. The case continued much as described for some time. He was sent to the base hospital at Ladysmith. On taking over medical charge thereof, on the 27th of February, I found my old patient much in the same condition as before described. He was suffering greatly from the pain in his arms, and wished to have them both off to relieve him from it.

On examination I found a distinct hard substance on firm pressure beneath the ligamentum nuchae, which was not present on former occasions. On consultation with the Surgeon-General of the forces, who happened to be on a tour of inspection at the time, I cut down upon it, and without much difficulty enucleated an ordinary round bullet, with a rather long rough process extending from its smooth surface. The wound healed rapidly; but the original one still continued open and discharged a little pus. In a few days the pain entirely disappeared from his arms, and their use nearly returned. The right arm was not "quite the thing" when he was sent to head-quarters at Pietermaritzburg. He has since, I learn, sailed for the Royal Victoria Hospital at Netley.

Those of our readers who are acquainted with Corporal Lyons will not, perhaps, be surprised to hear that the gallant fellow bore the excruciating pain of the operation without making the slightest murmur, although he was not under the influence of chloroform or any other anaesthetic...

"The South Wales Argus," Thursday, May 3rd, 1923

A Newport V.C.
Hero Of Rorke's Drift

A claim is being sent to the War Office for a Victoria Cross on behalf of Corporal J. Lyons, late of the South Wales Borderers, for conspicuous bravery at Rorke's Drift 44 years ago. Lyons is said to be on the Horse Guards' roll of Victoria Cross heroes, but he has never received the award.

A pathetic feature in connection with the matter is that the gallant old soldier died at Newport on Wednesday without knowing the result of the belated claim. He enlisted in the 57th Foot of the old "Die-hards" in June, 1864, served in New Zealand through the Maori War in 1865-6-7, and, after a subsequent short stay in England volunteered for service for the 63rd Foot in India, and later joined the 24th Foot (South Wales Borderers). He was present at the battle of Haynes Hill, Rabula Heights, and Perie Bush in the Kaffir war in South Africa.

When the Zulu war broke out he embarked for Durban, and marched from there to Pietermaritzburg and on to Rorke's Drift, where on January 22, 1879, he was wounded in the neck by a bullet. He continued to fight and serve out ammunition in spite of his wound. He was 78 years of age, and leaves a widow, two sons, (both of whom are in Australia), and two daughters.

The funeral will take place from Oxford Street, Newport on Saturday morning next.

"The South Wales Argus," May 5th, 1923, page 6.

An Old Warrior, Death of Rorke's Drift Survivor.

Another of Newport's old warriors was laid to rest at Newport Cemetery on Saturday in the person of Corporal John Jeremiah Augustus Lyons, of the 24th S.W.B., and a survivor of Rorke's Drift. The coffin, which was of un-polished oak, was conveyed to the cemetery on a gun carriage supplied by the 3rd Battery R.F.A. The chief mourners were Mrs. Lyons (Widow), Helen and Gladys Lyons (Daughters), Mr. Ernest Prothero and Mr. Will Evans (Brothers-in-law) and Mrs. M. Young (Sister-in-law). A number of deceased's old comrades were present including Sergeant J. Murphy, of the old 24th S.W.B., who served throughout the campaign and was present at Rorke's Drift with the late Corporal Lyons. Mr. Alfred Morgan carried out the funeral arrangements.

"The Daily South Wales Argus," c. May, 1923.

Newport Widow's Claim To Posthumous V.C.

The late Corporal John Lyons, Newport, the Rorke's Drift hero, for whom a Victoria Cross is being claimed (after a lapse of 45 years), on behalf of his widow, Mrs. Lyons of 22, Oxford Street, Newport.

"The Daily South Wales Argus," Tuesday, January 22nd, 1929.

Notes by the way.

With reference to the Rorke's Drift roll, which appeared in the Military column of the *South Wales Argus* on Thursday, Mr. T.C. Hislop, of 22, Oxford Street, Newport, writes:
"You have left out two old Newport veterans, my father-in-law, also Private Murphy. My father-in-law was in "B" Company, and fought through the whole time at Rorke's Drift with a bullet wound in his neck - the self-same bullet we now have. As it is intended to preserve this Regimental Roll. I should like my father-in-law's name on it." The writer will have observed our remark that we published the Roll (prepared as a record from the Regimental pay list for January, 1879) to help in clearing up little controversies, and possibly also to assist in tracing a few others. The roll was reproduced as it stood, but it was pointed out there was a suggestion the official record omitted a few names, probably accounted for by some stragglers having drifted into the base between the detailing off the party for its protection and the mass attack by the Zulus. The attention of the South Wales Borders Regimental Association has been drawn to the statement of Mr. Hislop.

25B/756 Private Henry Herbert Martin, 'B' Company, 2nd/24th Foot

"The Glastonbury & Axbridge Gazette," Friday, January 29th, 1937.

Rorke's Drift Hero's Death.
Wells visit recalled

The death has taken place of Mr. Harry Martin at his home at Gurney Slade. Mr. Martin was one of the last of the Rorke's Drift heroes. Monday was the 59th anniversary of the Zulu War. When the King and Queen, then Duke and Duchess of York, visited Wells and inspected the annual parade of Somerset British Legion, Mr. Harry Martin was introduced to the Duke and Duchess. The funeral will be on Saturday with military honours.

25B/1480 Private William Osborne, 'B' Company, 2nd/24th Foot

"The Free Press of Monmouthshire," January 21st, 1927.

Rorke's Drift Hero.
Mr William Osborne,
Blaenavon.
Description of the Fight

Yet another Rorke's Drift hero has been "discovered," and on this occasion at Blaenavon, in the person of Wm. Osborne, who resides with his wife at 79, Cambrian Row. Mr Osborne, who will be 69 on Feb. 20th, saw active service in the Kaffir War of '77, and the Zulu Wars of '78 and '79, in the old 24th Foot (South Wales Borderers).

Born at Duke's Street, Blaenavon, Mr. Wm. Osborne (the son of Mr Thomas Osborne, who was employed at the Blaenavon Co.'s Mills), when quite a youngster, joined the Regular Army, and took the Queen's silver coin at Pontypool. He was at once transferred to Brecon and shortly afterwards moved to Chatham. In November of the same year he was put on draft for Africa, and sailed from Portsmouth in the old Himalaya. Mr Osborne distinctly remembers that one of the first jobs when going on board was to empty the ticks of the old straw, which were then taken to the quarter master for refilling. The voyage, which lasted about five weeks, was a good one, no heavy weather being encountered. Upon landing the troops entrained and travelled via Durban to Kingwilliamstown. From here a march lasting between two and three weeks brought them in touch with the enemy.

The incident at Rorke's Drift is graphically described by Mr Osborne. A fatigue party of about 100 were told off for commissariat duties and preparing the food for the main column. The small company was in the charge of a captain and no untoward incident happened for some time. The "kitchen" was an outdoor one, adjacent to a house which had been occupied by a Dutchman who carried on the business of a shoemaker. This house, with a thatched roof, had been vacated when the British reached it, the only living things left being a domestic cat and an old sow. Sixteen hoggets (or small pigs) had been drowned, evidently by the Savages, who were afraid of the swine.

"But we saved the old pig," said Mr. Osborne, "and had some fine meat from her."

An interesting description of the method of baking the bread was given. Large ant-hills, were dotted all around the place. At the top of each of these a hole would be made, and, at the bottom, a cavity, into which a fire would be placed, and soon the ants would emerge in millions from the hole at the top. The fire would then be taken out and leavened dough placed in the cavity, which would quickly bake. (This is a principle employed even today, and is known as the "Aldershot oven.")

The first intimation that the enemy were approaching the camp was given by one of the company, who had been washing at the river, and it was discovered that the camp, or dump, had been cut off from the main column. Preparations were rapidly made for defending Rorke's House, which, besides being used for a store for food, was also a hospital. Including the "casualties" there were in all about 100 men. The Zulus, numbering between 3,000 and 4,000 and practically naked, attacked the drift with great courage in face of deadly rifle fire. Their weapons were mostly assegais (spears), but that they were in possession of some ammunition is proved by the fact that Corporal Jack Lines (at one time a postman in the Eastern Valley) received a bullet-wound in the back of the neck, "which bullet his wife still possesses," said Mr Osborne.

"We had seventeen hours' of hard fighting," continued the narrator of the story, "If we were all third-class shots it would have been all over with us. They came on in their thousands, and we made them jump! We took six or seven prisoners, but we sent them out into the open again. If you didn't catch 'em smart as they put their hands up, they were gone like a dart! Jack Lines and I were firing together with our ammunition placed on the wall besides us. The corporal was in the act of raising his rifle when his arms dropped helplessly to his sides from a bullet wound in the back of the neck The enemy set the thatched roof afire, but we pulled the roof off during the night to stop that little game." It was 17 hours before the relief came.

Mr Osborne remembers a few of those who were in the engagement, including Captain Browning and Jack Williams, V.C. (Cwmbran).

From Africa Mr Osborne was sent to Gibraltar, and from there to India, where he completed his six years' regular service. He returned to Blaenavon in 1883 at 26 years of age, and began work underground for the Blaenavon Co. After his return he married Miss Martha Whitcombe, daughter of Mr and Mrs Joseph Whitcombe of Abersychan. There is one daughter (Mrs S. Williams) and an adopted son, Mr Wm. Osborne (Wm. Bumell), the latter who figures in Blaenavon billiards circles.

Africa A Great Country

Asked his opinion of the countries he had visited, Mr Osborne sang the praises of Africa, which, he thought, was the greatest country in the world.

There are two things which he treasures. One is his medal with three bars which Mrs Osborne wears as a brooch, and the other is a Bible, presented by the ladies of the Rorke's Drift Testimonial Fund, and signed by "Miss Wilkinson."

25B/1284 Private Frederick (Charles) Mason, 'B' Company, 2nd/24th Foot

A letter written to his parents [appears courtesy of the Mason family]

Pietermaritzburg Natal South Africa
Septr 24th 1878

Dear Cary & Mary and Charly
I received your kind and affectionate letter on the 24th of September and I was very glad to hear from you again Dear Cary I quite forgot to tell you in the last letter that

those stamps which you sent me I could not get them changed so I have enclosed them in this letter at the same time returning many thanks to you for your kindness towards me Dear Cary you will be able to change them again so you wont be nothing out of pockit Dear Cary I return you many thanks for the songs you sent me. Dear Cary I must tell you that I have given up drinking altogether now - because the last drop of beer I had done me up - so I thought I would leave it off and see how that acted with me I find that I can get on a great deal better without it so I think I shall continue the same Dear Cary as soon as I can get a few shillings by me I shall have my Photograph taken and I will send it home to you hopeing this letter will find you all in good health as it leaves me at present with my kind love to you Dear Cary give my kind love to Mary and Tom and all the children and I hope they are all quite well give my kind love to Charly & Mrs & Mr Schooley & Dick I hope they are all quite well and have plenty of work to do give my kind love to Hannah Robertson I hope she is quite well and plenty of work to do. I remain your affectionate brother Fred

A second letter written to his family, [appears courtesy of the Mason family]

Rork,s Drift Natal South Africa
Feby 8th 1879

Dear Cary Mary & Charly
I write these few lines to you hopeing this will find you all in good health as it leaves me at present thank God.
Dear Cary whe are at war with the Zulus the Regiment crossed the bufloe river into Zulu land on the 10th of January and camped there they had a bit of a skirmish on the 11th of the month but very few negoes were killed on the 15th the Regt moved further into Zulu land to a place called izila valley that is between two very high hills and camped there there was not much fighting done till the 22nd of January they received orders that the 2nd 24th and 4 guns of artilery, and mounted troops mounted police and voluntiers and carbiniers leaving in camp 5 Companies of the 1st 24th and 1 Company of the 2nd 24th that was G Company and 2 big guns of artilery and mounted police and Native contingents and servants and cooks numbering all about 900 well you must understand the enemy had been watching the movements of the troops and early on the morning of the 22nd there was a number of kaffers showed themselfs for the intention of drawing the troops out Well the Generall, on seeing this advanced in persuit of them with the column as I stated before well you must understand there was thousands of Kaffers behind a hill watching the column leave the camp they watched them till they got some 10 miles away then we are told by those who escaped that the enemy sent a small body of kaffers into camp to lay down their arms and give themselfs up well you know that was only done for a blind to see how many there were in camp and how these were situated the troops in camp they lay down their arms and the colonel in command let them go away well from what we hear, they whent back again to the main body of the enemy and told them how

many was in camp the tropps that were in camp thought no more about it not thinking they were going to be attacked well there were all over the camp some asleep some washing there clothes others cooking servants busy waiting on the oficers well, Dear Cary the alarm was given that the enemy was advancing on them every man flew for his rifle and amanition then they could see that the kaffers where surrounding them they commenced fireing on them whe hear there where about 15 thousand kaffers well every man faught till the last there a few escaped but not many they faught for some hours but all was in vain the kaffers got possesion of they camp and murdered every poor fellow that was in camp they took the big guns and amanition and rifles and every thing they could get hold of there were 5 boys belonging to the Band poor little fellows they where left in camp the black buggers got the boys and tied them up by the hands to the waggons and butchered them cut their privates off and stuk them in there mouths

Dear Cary I forgot to tell you that my Company was left behind to take charge of the Commersery Stores at Rorks Drift well whe was all busy the time of the fight I was on guard myself that day whe had news the kaffers where coming to attack us well you can guess how whe felt about 100 of us sick and all well whe made a bit of a fire round the Commersery whe managed to make some sort of fort true enough they came to murder us the same as the poor lot in the other camp but they got took in there was about 4-000 of them and 130 of us sick all those that could get out of the hospital got out the best way they could there were two or three poor fellows that were very bad in hospital and whe could not get them out because the kaffers set fire to it and got in the hospital and cut the four fellows up to pieces well we faught bravely from 3 o Clock an the 22nd till day break 23rd when reinforcements came the loss on our side where 13 killed and 4 wounded thank God I am alive myself that is all at present I dare say you have seen in the paper about the cut up of the 1st & 2, 24th 5 Compys of the 1st-24 & 1 Compy of the 2/24 G Compy

Give my kind love to Mary Tom all the children & Charely & Dick & Mr & Mrs Schooley and all the children Dear Cary I have not had my clothes off since the 22nd of Jany Dear Cary, you excuse the writering because I could not get any ink no more at present, from your affectionate Brother Fred. God Bless one and all of you good by

1284 Private Charles Mason
B Company 2/24 Regiment
Rorkes Drift Natal

25B/662 Private John Murphy, 'B' Company, 2nd/24th Foot

"The South Wales Argus," June 3rd, 1914.

Newport veteran's story - 662 J. Murphy.
A rescue from burning hospital:

Survivors of the small Company who gallantly held Rorke's Drift against an overwhelming force of victory flushed Zulus are few in number, but the discovery of one apparently leads to the discovery of others, Private John Williams V.C.; of Cwmbran, was no sooner thrust into the limelight than Private Sam Pitt, of Nantymoel was unearthed, and now it is learned that there is living in Newport another member of the brave band which added such lustre to British arms. Mr. John Murphy, of 41, William Street, Newport, belonged to the old 24th Regt; and after going through the Kaffir War played his part in the Zulu campaign. He tells a very similar story to that narrated by Private Sam Pitt, and January 1879, he declares, has never been, and is not likely ever to be, effaced from his memory.

Handful against thousands:

It was on January 22nd that the messenger from Isandlwana reached them with direful tidings that the British advance force had been almost wiped out. They knew then what to expect, but handful as they were, there were no cowards amongst them, and they determined either to thrash the Zulus or die fighting to last. Indeed, he says, there was no other thing to do, for Cetshwayo's warriors had few notions in the way of dealing mercifully with a foe they had the power to slaughter.

To fix up defences worthy of the name did not appear to be a very hopeful task, for they had no fortifications, simply two old mission rooms, one of which was used as a hospital and the other for storage of provisions, ammunitions ect. Apart from invalids, the British force numbered 84, and it was realised that their visitors would make them look a little lot indeed, bags of biscuits and mealies formed a hastily improvised entrenchment and this was all that was between them and the advancing horde.

Early in the afternoon the enemy were sighted, and soon the country around was black with them. In another hour they were within rifle range, and the ghastly fun began. The fire, however, seemed to make no difference, and on they rolled, the defenders having eventually to retire to an inner "fortification." It was a terrible struggle, but nothing to the fight at close quarters as darkness set in. Private Murphy described the fight at length, but as this is a matter of history - familiar, it is to be hoped, to all - the details need not be given further.

Rescue from hospital:

One incident, however, shall be narrated. When the hospital caught fire, and it was necessary to get the inmates out, Private Murphy did his full share of the work, and one difficult task which fell to his lot was pulling through the window a Private named Conolley, who had a broken leg. The next man near that particular spot was shot through the head. Meanwhile the battle continued to rage, but eventually the fine defence prevailed, and the enemy drew off. The British casualties were few, the Zulus had lost hundreds – for in the morning the ground was covered with their dead and dying. Private Murphy was very emphatic on one point, and, though he may be in error it is perhaps worth recording that he thinks the part played by certain officers was unduly extolled at the time and since. They were not he declares, nearly so conspicuous in the fight as they have been made out to be. Murphy (who at Rorke's Drift was slightly wounded in the foot) was 24 years in the army, and then, having reached the age of 60, had to leave, but declares that at the time he felt fit to serve another 24.

"The Western Mail," Wednesday, August 3rd, 1927.

Rorke's Drift Hero.
A Military Funeral at Newport:

Sergt. John Murphy, of 81, Witham Street, Newport, one of the few survivors of Rorke's Drift and a veteran of the Zulu War, who died aged 71, was buried with Military Honours in Newport Cemetery on Tuesday. Sergt. Murphy served in the old 24th Regiment of Foot. John Williams V.C.; of Cwmbran, who fought side-by-side with Sergt. Murphy at Rorke's Drift, attended the funeral with several other comrades who fought in the Zulu War.

The coffin, covered with a Union Jack, was borne on a Gun-carriage from the Newport Barracks. The committal rites were performed by the Rev. Father Feves.

The chief mourners were:- Mr. & Mrs John Murphy (Son and Daughter-in-law), Mr. & Mrs Joseph Morgan (Son-in-law and Daughter), Mrs. Florance Bennett (Daughter), and Mr. Fred Murphy (Nephew).

Among others present including members of the 24th Regiment Monmouthshire group of Old Comrades Association were, Capt. H. M. Thomas (Chairman of the Association), Sergt. John Williams V.C.; Ex-CQMS. F. Williams (Secretary of the Association), Messrs. Houghton Bros. were the Undertakers.

25B/1186 Private Samuel Pitt, 'B' Company, 2nd/24th Foot.

"The Western Mail", May 11th, 1914

ANOTHER RORKE'S DRIFT HERO.
Nantymoel Man's Story Of Zulu's Attack

It appears that Private John Williams, V.C., of Cwmbran, is not the last survivor of the gallant band which defended Rorke's Drift. There is at least one other in South Wales in the person of Private Sam Pitt, of Nantymoel, who looks hale and hearty enough to go through another campaign, and young enough to enjoy a few more decades of life.

A Western Mail man enjoyed an hour or two in the company of Private Pitt. The word 'enjoyed' is used advisedly, for to be in Pitt's company is to be quite at ease and interested. He has a pleasant, homely way, and his stories are mellowed with age and ripe experience.

His account of the terrible struggle against overwhelming numbers at Rorke's Drift was perhaps the more thrilling because it was told in simple language.

The Zulus' Attack

"Our first news that the Zulus were advancing into British territory," he said, "was brought to us on January 22, 1879, by a messenger from Isandhula, where our advance force had been almost annihilated. We at once set about making preparations for a defence. There was no fortifications, merely two old mission rooms, which were used as a hospital and for the storage of provisions and ammunition. Our total strength, apart from invalids, was 85, and there was no time to throw up entrenchments, but we knocked up a rough defence of bags of biscuits and mealies.

It was about half-past two in the afternoon when we first caught sight of the enemy rounding the bend of a hill from the direction of Isandhula, and the country was soon black with them. We were without artillery, and it was an hour before the enemy was within rifle shot. Then we pounded away for all we were worth, raining bullets among them, but on they came, not fearing death. They were sharp enough, however, to take advantage of every bit of cover they could.

Fire away as we could, it was impossible to keep them at a distance, and we were forced to retire to an inner enclosure.

By nine o'clock, when darkness had set in, they got to close quarters, and were gripping our bayonets through the spaces left between the bags for firing. It was 'touch and go' at that time, and how they were kept out was almost miraculous. Just when the fray was at the thickest a loud 'Hoo-hoo' sounded from the hills, and we had quiet for a while. They seemed to lie under cover for a time. Then there was sound all round, and a renewed attack was made."

Hospital In Flames

"The hospital, which was situated, outside our defences, and from which the invalids had been removed, was ablaze, and in the glare the Zulus held up their dead comrades for us to fire at, the idea, I think, being to get us to expend our ammunition. Somehow or other, we kept them at bay, and only one got over our defences. Needless to say, he did not live long. By-and bye they took themselves off. We found we had come off luckily with only five casualties.

In the morning we found the ground strewn with the dead and dying. We reckoned we had accounted for 875, but the school books tell you 400 or 500."

Private Sam Pitt is 58 years of age, and enlisted in the Warwickshire (now the South

Wales Borderers) at Cardiff on February 9, 1877. He saw active service in the Kaffir War the same and following years, and in one of the engagements was shot through the head. His total service in the Army and Reserve was twelve years, and his discharge is marked. 'Conduct - very good.' He holds the South African medal with the clasp, dated 1877-8-9, and an illuminated address presented by the burgesses of Durban.

At the age of 58, he toils as a labourer underground at the Wyndham Colliery, pensionless. Is not this an instance in which the War Office should recognise Pitt's service to his country?

25B/1185 Private Edmund Savage, 'B' Company 2nd/24th Foot

"The Manchester Weekly Post," July 19th, 1879

Interviewing Invalided Soldiers

"On Wednesday several privates belonging to the ill-fated 24th Regiment arrived in Brecon from the seat of war..."

"...Private Savage says he was in the hospital at Rorke's Drift when the Zulus came, and experienced that terrible onslaught of the enemy, whom he described as treating the English dead in a horribly cruel manner. Savage describes the warning given to the unfortunate inmates of the hospital. Seeing the danger drawing nearer, though suffering from an injured knee, he jumped out of the window into the fort. He assisted in the defence, lying on his side and taking aim at the Zulus through an opening in the biscuit boxes. Lieutenant Bromhead assisted to open a cartridge box. In doing so, in the dark, Savage cut his hands. He, however, kept 'pegging' away, and did some execution. An officer standing beside him shot dead a Zulu who had made no little havoc in the English ranks. In the night time, when under fire, Savage heard a fellow soldier of the name of Fagan cry out for water, and managed to crawl along to help his disabled comrade-in-arms, who died before daylight next morning. Savage says he never spent such a miserable night in all his life. There was momentary danger of being shot dead, and the likelihood of perishing from cold and hunger. He has no recollections of ever having gone through such hardships as while invalided at Rorke's Drift. After succour arrived he went down country, and as he proceeded his health so much improved that he hopes to be able again to see active service if this is required..."

2-24/1387 Sergeant George Smith, 'B' Company, 2nd/24th Foot

A private letter written to his wife, published in "The Brecon County Times," March 29th, 1879.

The two following letters are written by Sergt. Smith, who was present at the defence of Rorke's drift, to his wife, who lives in Little Free street, Brecon.

Rorke's Drift, Natal, 24th January 1879.

My Dear Wife,

I now have the pleasure of writing these few lines to you, hoping to find you al in the enjoyment of the very best of health, as I am happy to say it leaves men. I am thankful at having been saved from the cruel slaughter and bloodshed that we had all gone through the last four days. I have some very bad news to tell you. Our regiment, that is the 2-24th, left here five day's ago to go to Cetawayo's kraal, to fight the Zulus. They had left my company at this place to protect the commissariat stores, and encamped about eight miles from here, and on the 22nd the troops went out reconnoitring the country, and had only left one company in camp to protect the ammunition and baggage. They went out about 16 miles, and while they were out the camp was attacked by 6000 of the enemy, and cut to pieces.

The 1st battalion has lost 17 officers killed and missing, and nearly all of the men. The Zulus got hold of four boys of the band 1-24th, and cut them up in bits, and destroyed everything they could lay their hands on, and our colors are missing, and all the ammunition is taken from us. After destroying all they could, they made for Rorke's Drift, and at about 2-30 p.m. on the same day we were attacked by about 3000 of them, and had to build up a fort with bags of meal, oats and boxes of meat and biscuits. How we ever escaped I can hardly tell you. There were only about 100 of us, all told. We kept up a continual firing for 15 hours, from 3 p.m. on the 22nd until 6 a.m. on the 24th when the two battalions of the 24th (what was left of them) came to our relief, and four guns of the Royal artillery. We had 13 men killed and about 8 wounded. Amongst the former was poor Drummer Haydon, that lived at the top of John street. He was stabbed in hospital in 16 places, and his belly cut open right up in two places, and part of his cheek was cut off.

I am afraid poor Mulroy is dead, for there is only about four men of his company left now. Corporal Allen was shot through the shoulder. It is only a flesh wound, and he is coming round very well. Poor Sergeant Williams is said to be killed. One company of ours, No. 7, were cut up to bits. I myself had given up all hopes of escaping. My company was very highly praised for the noble stand they made in keeping the place, and the cool manner in which we defended it, and I heard the general say that the colonel should take the two battalions home again after it was over, and that we were to be formed into one regiment, and a new 2nd Battalion 24th Regiment was to be formed at home. Out of the 1-24th there is only 1 company left, and I fear there will be a good many sore hearts in Brecon, for we have lost Colour-Sergeant Chambers of the 1-24th. His wife is in Cape Town, and her brother, who is in the Royal Artillery, was left in hospital sick with the fever. The Zulus took one of the band boys and hung him up by the chin on a hook, and cut him up in bits. One of our men was shot through the lungs, and he stuck to his post, and fired away for an hour, when he dropped down dead from loss of blood. It is said that Pt. Orlopp, and Sergeant Johnson, who lived in John street are among the slain. I cannot tell you one quarter of the horrors that have taken place. We have lost nearly everything that we had, and we have to return back to Pietermaritzburg to get a fresh supply of clothing, and everything else, for we have only got what we stand up in now.

G. Smith

B Company, 2-24th Regiment,

Rorke's Drift, Natal.

P.S. - We have counted the number of the blacks that were killed and shot by my company, and they were over 800, so that they paid dearly for what they killed of our men.

Rorke's Drift, February 1879

My Dear Wife,

Since I last wrote things have been very quiet. The only thing fresh is that the draft has arrived to make up the company which was cut to pieces in the late fight with the enemy at Isandula. The draft are all quiet well, but they don't seem to like the country at all, and they all say they would rather be in the depot at Brecon than out here. I see another old face in the draft, young Probert, of John street. He came out as a corporal and is posted to G Company, and also there is a nephew of Mr. Yates, the Landlord of the Clarence Inn, The Watton. Since my last letter I have found out the total number of men killed in the battle of the 22nd. Altogether we have lost about 1,600 men, and the people of Pietermaritzburg are so well pleased at the manner in which my company kept the stores from being taken by the enemy that they think they cannot do enough for us. They have subscribed £150 for us to buy the troops a lot of clothing, and pens, ink, and paper, matches, pipes, and a lot of everything, and sent them to us to be given to the troops at Rorkes Drift. They also sent word that they consider we have been the means of saving the whole of the colony from being taken by the Zulus, and I don't think they were far wrong, for if we had left the place and let the enemy take it nothing would have saved the other parts of the colony from the Zulus' raid.

G Smith

B Company, 2-24th Regiment, Rorkes Drift, Natal

25B/777 Private Thomas Stevens, 'B' Company, 2nd/24th Foot.

"The Merthyr Express," c. *April 1879, page 3.*

The following has been copied from a letter written by Private E. Stevens B Company 2nd/24th Regiment, dated Rorke's Drift, February 5th, addressed to his parents, who reside at the Robin Hood Inn, Dowlais. We may add that enclosed in the letter is a feather, described by the writer as; "…a feather, part of a head-dress of the chiefs of the enemy…"

Dear parents,

I now take the opportunity of writing to you a few lines, hoping it will find you in the enjoyment of good health, as thank God, I am happy to say I am. Dear Mother, no doubt you will read of our late disaster. I must tell you as near I can. On Sunday, the 12th, our regiment and five companies of the 1st/24th, and volunteers and natives, crossed the river into Zululand, leaving our company - that's B, and 300 of the native troops behind to guard the stores and provisions. All went well till Tuesday, the 22nd, and horrors, it was an unlucky day of it. Our column went out for an attack, leaving one company of the 2nd/24th, G. Company, and five companies of the 1st Battalion, and a lot of volunteers to guard the camp.

About two hours after they had gone another party of the enemy attacked the camp. After a long struggle they took possession of the camp, and killed every one of our men, butchered them, and even hung the little boys up by their heels, where they hung the meat; destroyed the waggon's and all the clothes and band drums and even took our colours away; drank all the rum, and even went mad with drink. Well, the General was about 15 miles from them, and could not get to them. This occurred about 10 or 11 miles from where our company is staying. Well, one or two escaped at about two o'clock to our camp, and reported that the Zulus had taken possession of the camp, and they were making for us little lot.

Dear Mother, a farthing would have bought our lives. Then we got our guns and ammunition, struck camp, and barricaded the old storehouse as well we could. Some were posted one place and another, and about an hour elapsed when we could see them coming. They say it was 4,000 altogether. Every man went to his post, and all the 300 natives we got ran away, and there was 146 of us altogether. We kept steady firing; it began about three o'clock - kept on for two hours- when they succeeded in setting fire to the little house used as an hospital. It was getting dark then, and we expected help. We thought the General would come to us, but not so. We said we would die brave. We kept it up until day-break, and, thank God, they ran away, and we went around to bury the dead, and we killed a good number, and we lost four, and three wounded.

Dear Mother - We worked hard all day, and about three in the afternoon we saw the General and the remainder of the regiment coming. Dear Mother, - The General was pleased to see that we had kept the place. We lost everything. I must tell you that poor Blake and Johnny Shearman and several of the Dowlais lads, is killed, worse luck. Remember me to all friends. I think, we are going back to Pietermaritzburg again. The General has sent to England for more troops. I think we shall stand a good chance of coming home after this is over. I will send paper if I can get one. We are sleeping out still, we have no blankets or big coats now, and not a second article to wear. Cheer up we shall yet meet again. I think B Company will get a good honour and name for what they did - they saved all Natal -

I remain your affectionate son.

E. Stevens. B. Company 2nd/24th Regiment.

25B/889 Private Thomas Edward Taylor, 'B' Company, 2nd/24th Foot

Extract from an unidentified Runcorn newspaper, c. 1924

Another Runcorn Hero
A Second Survivor of Rorke's Drift

A second Rorke's Drift hero has been discovered in the Runcorn district. This is ex-Private Thomas Taylor, of St. John's Cottages, Weston, who, no doubt, will be given a place of honour, along with ex-Private Thomas Moffatt and "Todger" Jones, V.C., when the King passes through Runcorn on Wednesday.

Until last week it was thought that Thomas Moffatt was the only survivor of this historic defence living in the Runcorn area, but the news of a second hero will be received with the greatest pleasure. It is learned that a few years ago there were only three survivors of the Rorke's Drift incident, so that it is a peculiar circumstance that Runcorn should be the home of two out of three survivors of the incident which thrilled the whole of the civilised world, details of which were recorded in our last issue.

Ex-Private Taylor has unfortunately been off work at the Weston quarry for a considerable time owing to a damaged arm due to blood poisoning.

25B/1398 Private Joseph Williams, 'B' Company, 2nd/24th Foot

"The South Wales Argus," January 29th, 1924

Rorke's Drift
The Story of a Newport Man's gallantry
How Joseph Williams died

To the older generation, the story recently told by Private John Williams - and published in the South Wales Argus - was a spur to memory. Many of us remember the disaster of Isandhlwana and the heroism of Rorke's Drift; - at the mere mention of those names we hear again the song with which all England rang - "All honour to the Twenty-Fourth" - we recall thrill with which we first heard of the heroism of the men who held out at the Drift. It has led Mr. R. Jenkins, of 4, Raglan Street, Newport, to recall amazing gallantry of one of the defenders who fell. He writes:-

I was much interested to read in your issue of last Friday one more account of the

Battle of Rorke's Drift. In this narrative Private John Williams mentions the name of an old playmate of mine - Private Joseph Williams, a man who took a prominent part in the Battle of Isandhlwana at the cost of his life It may be interesting to the rising generation of Newportonians to know that Joseph Williams was a fellow-townsman of theirs. Joe and I were born in close proximity to one another, we went to school together, and we started the battle of life together at a very early age by working in the Dos Works. After a few years of this [both of us were motherless], we started to ferret for our own living. I went to sea, Joe joined the Army - two not very rosy occupations in those days, I can assure you.

Now, we will refer to Joe's gallantry. It appears that Private Joseph Williams was posted on guard single-handed at the door of the temporary hospital and store-room when the Zulus rushed it, coming on in the dusk of the evening. Joe, with bayonet and butt-end of rifle, managed for a short time to keep them at bay, but in beating them and following them up he became surrounded. When poor Joe was found at the dawn of the following morning his body was full of Assegai stabs as there are holes in a riddle. Beside him lay dead 14 Zulus. Joe was supposed to have accounted for the lot. It was reported of him at the time that for single-handed bravery it surpassed everything in the annals of British warfare. His gallantry was recognised by the late Queen Victoria, inasmuch as she forwarded a letter of condolence to his father, accompanied by a sum of money to compensate him for the loss of so gallant a son. May he rest in peace!

"The South Wales Argus," January 22nd, 1929

How a Newport Man Died

...Pte. Joseph Williams, referred to, was a Newport man who started life at the Dos Works. It is believed he was on guard single handed at the door when the Zulus rushed it., but, in beating them off with bayonet and butt end of rifle, he was surrounded. When found at dawn next morning his body was riddled with holes from assegais, and beside it were 14 dead Zulus; he is supposed to have accounted for the lot. Queen Victoria forwarded a letter of condolence to his father, accompanied by a sum of money as act of grace for the loss of so brave a son...

25B/1316 Private Caleb Wood, 'B' Company, 2nd/24th Foot

An unidentified Nottinghamshire newspaper, c. February 1935.

Made Hosiery For The Royal Family
Ruddington War Veteran's Funeral

A veteran of Rorke's Drift - that memorable battle between a small but heroic band of British soldiers against the Zulus in January, 1879 - was buried in Ruddington this afternoon.

He is Mr. Caleb Wood, 77, of 2, Distillery-street, Ruddington, who died on Wednesday.

Mr. Wood's soldiering career began at an early age when he and another youth of the village, the late Mr. Robert Tongue, enlisted in the South Wales Borderers, and with that regiment took part in the Zulu campaign.

Mr. Wood also served in the South African War, and in 1914, though 56 years of age, he volunteered for service in the Great War, but was not accepted.

Recently he received an invitation from his old regiment to take part in regimental celebrations which are to be held in Brecon, and he was keenly anticipating this event.

A frame knitter by trade, the veteran soldier had made hosiery for members of the Royal Family, and he remained at work until he was well over 70.

He leaves a widow, three sons and a daughter, three grandchildren and a great-grandson. Two sons, a son-in-law, and two grandsons all served with the Army during the Great War, one son being awarded the Military Medal. A grandson served in the Dover patrol and later visited Russia and other war zones.

By an unidentified defender

"The Times of Natal," c. February 1879

The Rorke's Drift Action

Yesterday's Times of Natal says it is permitted to publish the following extract from a private letter, written by one who was present at Rorke's Drift station when it was attacked:-

Colonel Glyn's Column,
Jan. 28, 1879

We have had an eventful time since I last wrote on the 21st inst. On the 22nd we heard from the advance company (I was then here at Rorke's Drift, on the Natal side of the river) that the Zulus were awaiting the advance of our column in force, and a battle was imminent. soon after luncheon, I took my binocular glasses and went up a very big hill, and then I heard firing in earnest, and saw crowds of kafirs around the distant camp, and coming towards us. I thought they were our native allies, and the more so because I saw knots of horsemen in uniform galloping in the same direction. I saw several minor battles, the natives driving everything before them. When they got to the foot of the hill, I found, but could scarcely realise the fact, that they were the Zulus. Down the hill I went, to warn the little garrison, and found them hastily constructing a barricade of sacks of grain round the house (used as a hospital) and the store-house close by, but within twenty minutes the enemy appeared round the hill, and opened fire upon us. While half the men returned the fire, the rest went on forming a barrier across our oblong enclosure, dividing it in half, in case of losing any position. There were about 95 able-bodied, and 35 in hospital, a doctor and a parson. It was four in the afternoon. In about twenty minutes they were crowding in on our left, within 200 yards, and then they made a rush, came on in a dense mass, and swarmed over the parapet. Driven from this end, our men took up their position behind the biscuit boxes and mowed them down; but they got shelter from the barricade that we had lost, and our men began to fall. Between 7 and 8 p.m. the brutes set the hospital on fire; and by the light of the burning pile, our defenders kept up a deadly fire, but had to use great care, as our supply of ammunition was getting low. Then the house burned out, and on past midnight they rushed upon us with their hideous yells, and fired from caves and rocks upon the hill above our position. The firing was kept up all night, desultory at times, and then rapid again; and every minute we expected some desperate final rush to storm our position. but daylight dawned at last, and at about 5.15 a.m., the last shots were fired, and our enemies were gone. We do not know how many wounded or dead were carried off the field, but we found about 200 dead bodies. Our own loss was 17 killed and 12 wounded. The determined and successful resistance which, by God's help, we were able to make seems to have surprised them; and, although we have been on the alert day and night since (and reinforcements of 500 men have arrived), no fresh attempt has been made by them; but, terrible to relate, the column on that day met with fatal disaster, and it was a mighty wave of victorious barbarity which was checked by our little band.

Had we lost our position here, I believe the wave of destruction would have gone on into the colony. Now, thank God, I do not myself anticipate any renewal of their attack, or any serious inroad into Natal. I am thankful to say that the health of the camp has been fairly good; but the whole place being barricaded by sacks of mealies, which are getting wet and rotting, may produce typhoid fever any day. What our movements may be, I do not know. My native servant bolted on my own horse, which I have since recovered.

An unidentified defender, wounded in the battle

"The Lancet," March 8th, 1879

The Gallant Defence At Rorke's Drift

One of the wounded men states as follows:-
"After the niggers surrounded us we fought like tigers. I saw Dr. Reynolds (A.M.D.) blazing away at them, cheering the ones that were hit, running to the fellows, dressing their wounds, then fighting away like a hero. He and the Hospital Corps men defended the hospital to the last moment. When the Zulus got in they charged through them and got into the laager behind waggons and mealie bags, where they all fought like true Britons until daylight. They made several sorties, and drove them off splendidly."

Surgeon Reynolds, writing the next day, reporting the loss of hospital stores, never mentions a single word about himself, but simply states, 'I am glad to say that the men of the A.H.C. behaved splendidly; and I am almost certain that Lieutenant Hall,

A.H.C., and several men were killed.' They were with Dr. Shepherd. But for the magnificent defence by that one brave company, the victorious Zulus would have swept down upon Greytown, and would have certainly have destroyed Helpmakaar, laying everything to waste before them.

By an unidentified defender

An unidentified South African newspaper, c. 1879

We have been kindly permitted to make the following extract from a private letter, written by an officer who was present at the defence of Rorke's Drift:-

"Rorke's Drift was splendidly defended. Not a man in it who did not fight for his life from the very commencement of the attack made upon us. The people who escaped from Sandhlwana and came to inform us of the disaster there assured us again and again there was no chance for our escape from certain death, except by rushing away without a moment's reflection: that the Zulus were in myriads; that they had taken our camp only seven miles away, which was then running with the blood of nearly 1,000 white men, not one of whom had escaped. I assure you that these people, four or five of them, coming in madly in ones and two, shouted and screamed at the pitch of their voices all the miseries which had just taken place at Sandhlwana and, worst of all, in the midst of our men. However, by the time the Zulus did come, all our panic was over, and you cannot imagine a lot of men settling down to their work more coolly and methodically. Firing commenced from our men at about 700 yards, and I really think we did more damage then in proportion than afterwards; every shot seemed to fall among the enemy; but the devils did not care for us or our guns. They came on trotting, as if nothing extraordinary were happening, and without returning a shot until they arrived at our laager.

Our business at this time became very, very desperate. It was all round the hospital, and the slaughter of the Zulus in the morning in this vicinity showed how well our labour told, and how desperately the brutes fought. I can't conceive any human courage equal to theirs; it amounts simply to madness. But there is one thing seems worthy of notice in their mode of fighting. They shoot comparatively little, but believe in their own overwhelming crowd breaking down any opposition by firearms or other weapons, and they go in purely for doing the 'eating up' dodge, at which , I admit, they are very clever. On the other hand, I think the Zulus must have suffered severely, and some of their mad ardour must have cooled a bit. They cannot continue to fight as they have done. A few defeats will demoralize them, and then they will sink in character to the level of the common Kafir."

By an unidentified defender

Extract from "The World Of Adventures."

Tales Of The Victoria Cross: The Defence Of Rorke's Drift

...this further description by another of the defenders is well worth the reading:-

"...Our men opened fire at five hundred yards. The first man to fall was the chief. He was shot by Private Dunbar, and fell off his horse headlong. Numbers of the enemy fell at once. They hesitated, broke, and the greater number scattered to their left, and occupied the garden and orchard where there was plenty of cover. A few got up close to the houses, and lay behind the field oven and kitchens that, there were built. Scarcely any of these men had guns or rifles. Others came in a continuous stream, occupied the hill above, and gradually encircled the two houses. All the men who had guns were stationed on the hill and kept up a continuous and rapid fire on the yard. It caught our men in their backs as they were guarding the garden side, and five men were thus shot dead. Had they been good marksmen the place was untenable, but they fired wildly and badly for the most part, as if the noise had as much effect as the bullets. It now became dusk. The Zulus crept up nearer and nearer. Under cover of the bushes and long grass they were able to get within five yards of the hospital without being seen. From this point in parties of fifteen to twenty they repeatedly attacked the end room of the hospital.

"At length they forced the hospital door by sheer weight of numbers.

"Thirty of the patients were got out in time. Most of them were pushed and pulled through a window which opened on the yard. Sergeant Maxwell, a fine young soldier, was ill and delirious with fever. He could not be moved, and he was killed in his bed. They now set fire to the hospital. The roof was thatch, and it quickly blazed. By its light our men were enabled to see their faces better, and many fell before they retreated to better cover. After a pause, encouraged or commanded by a chief who from time to time shouted his orders from the hillside, they came on again. The fighting in places became hand-to-hand over the mealie-sacks. Once or twice the Zulus actually seized. the bayonets and tried to wrench them off the rifles. One of our men loaded whilst a Zulu was tugging at his bayonet. He pulled the trigger and blew the plucky fellow to atoms. They next tried to set fire to the thatched roof of the store. In face of a hot fire they got up to the house, and one fine savage had his brains blown out as he was holding a brand against the eaves..."

CHAPTER 3: The Other Defenders

12046 Driver Charles John Robson, 5th (Field) Company, Royal Engineers

A letter written by JRM Chard, dated November 17th, 1879: ["The Noble Sapper on the Box - Charles Robson RE," by L. Stevenson, The Royal Engineers Journal, Aug. 1995]

Moredon
Taunton
17th November 1879

Driver Charles Robson Royal Engineers, served with me in the 5th Compy R.E. as my batman, for some months before and during the whole of the Zulu Campaign. His conduct has been very good & he has given me great satisfaction - He was the only Royal Engineer with me at Rorkes Drift on the 22 Jany where he did good service. He was also present at the action of Ulundi.
I sincerely hope he may get on & do well
John R.M. Chard
Capt & Bt. Maj., R.E.

Extract from Robson's service & discharge papers: [WO97/3762 The National Archives, (P.R.O.),London]

Campaigns: Present at the Defence of Rorke's Drift 22 & 23 Jan. '79, and
             Battle of Ulundi 4 July '79

Extract from "The Royal Engineers Journal," November 1st, 1879. (reporting on Chard's truimphant arrival in North Curry, Somerset)

"...Major Chard was accompanied by his military servant in full regimentals and the appearance of this soldierly young fellow bearing an armful of Zulu assegais and other trophies of the campaign excited much interest..."

Extract from "The Somerset County Gazette," October 4th, 1879, (reporting on Chard's speech made at the same occasion)

The Heroes of Zululand.
Arrival of Major Chard and the 24th Regiment

...He was sorry that Major Bromhead, who was still serving his country in South Africa, and that Dr. Reynolds, who yesterday landed with him at Portsmouth, were not with him on that occasion to see how much was thought of what they did at

Rorke's Drift; but he was glad to say that there was one there beside himself (alluding to a driver in the Engineers, named Charles Robson, who was occupying the box-seat) who had the opportunity of seeing how greatly their services were appreciated, and what a splendid reception had been accorded him, for which he thanked them one and all very sincerely...

A private letter written for the author by the late Mr. Edwin P. Ewart, the only grandson of Charles Robson, October 1992

Life With My Grandfather
Charles Robson In His Retirement
A Page of Reminiscences
October 1992 - E.P. Ewart

In order to think back to the time when I lived in the same house as my grandfather, Charles Robson, my memory has to span more than seventy years. Indeed, it is not easy to bring back those days before the spread of electricity and the microprocessor. This was a time of parlours and aspidistras when 'respectability' was important - the tail end of the Victorian era.

It helps if I recall the physical environment in which we lived in the twenties and early thirties - it is very different today. No.43 Swingate Lane, Plumstead, SE18 was a modest working-class dwelling set in the middle of a terrace of a dozen houses, fronted by a low brick wall topped with decorative wrought iron railings, which disappeared for ever to make guns during World War Two. The usual tidy privet hedge was about all there was room for in the tiny front garden. The back garden compensated for this as it was quite a good size with a chicken house at the bottom. My grandfather always kept chickens and reared his own chicks. My mother used to tell me that when I was three, I was attacked by a fierce cockerel in the garden and grandfather had to beat it off with a shovel. I have no recollection of this. My grandparents always kept a dog- usually called 'Gyp' - and I have recollections from the earliest years of an enormous cat who was named 'Buller' after General Sir Redvers Henry Buller who had taken part in the Zulu Campaign.

Our part of the street was on the extreme south eastern perimeter of Greater London and a short walk brought us into North Kent. Immediately beyond the back garden was farmland owned by Mr. Callow who grew vegetables and brought them round the streets on his cart. Beyond the farm it was countryside and woodlands as far as the horizon, a very pleasant outlook from the back windows. When my grandfather was in his early seventies, somebody bought the cabbage field and established half-a-dozen tennis courts on it and after this he used to enjoy sitting by the fence watching the play on a fine day. It was about this time that we began to hear gramophone music booming across the grounds with contemporary songs of the time such as "Aint it grand to be bloomin' well dead"! By walking west up Swingate Lane, you came to the place where the original swing-gate had been which gave the lane its name; after that it was open countryside and farmland for four or five miles until you found yourself climbing the side of Shooters Hill, where the highwayman Dick Turpin was said to have carried on his nefarious activities two centuries before. It was in about 1919 when I was three years old that we went to live at No.43 - my grandparents had already taken the house some years before. We occupied part of the upper floor. My father had married Annie Lilian, only daughter of Charles Robson in 1915 and was buying a house in Bournewood Villas, some twenty minutes' walk away; then he had fallen on hard times and was force to give it up. My grandparents had evidently come to the rescue. No. 43 eventually became our permanent home after grandfather's death in 1933 when we took over the whole house.

Charles Robson was retired when I knew him - he had reached the age of sixty-five in 1919. When I was old enough to know what was going on around me I gathered that he and my grandmother, Jane Elizabeth, had worked in the nearby Woolwich Arsenal during the 1914-18 War. He probably as a labourer and she in the danger buildings doing some thing connected with cordite.

I remember my grandfather as a solidly-built man, not tall but well nourished on the substantial meals which my grandmother regularly provided. All the neighbours seemed to be aware that he had been present at Rorke's Drift. They did not need to know precisely what part he had played in that unique defence action. It was enough that he had been there and that in itself had made him a hero. Not everybody knew that he had been batman to the officer in command, Lieut. John Chard. I never heard him speak about his part in this affair. When Major Chard wrote him a brief testimonial on 17th Nov. 1879, all he said was that Charles Robson had been his batman during the whole of the Zulu campaign, that he was the only other Royal Engineer besides himself who had been present at Rorke's Drift on 22nd Jan. and that he had 'done good service.' An entry in his paybook states that he 'distinguished himself and is in possession of medals for 1879 Battle of Ulundi 4th July and the defence of Rorke's Drift 22nd Jan.' I still have the medal, made of solid silver with a clasp '1879' hinged to it, and '12046 Driver Charles Robson, R.E.' deeply etched round the edge. The ribbon is gold with blue stripes.

Although my grandfather was a bit rough and ready in some ways, he carried himself with a quiet dignity as befitted one who, in the past, had faced mortal danger and survived. He had been only twenty-five years old at that time and now, forty or fifty years later, the aura still hung about him. My grandmother seemed to bathe in his reflected glory and she too, had an air of quiet confidence about her, which was no doubt partly due to her own experiences in India where she had been nursemaid to the children of a Colonel Atkinson at Mussoorie until 1882. She then returned to England and worked for a Mrs. Napier at No. 14 Hall Crescent, Farnham, who stated in a reference dated 20th September 1882 that she was only parting with her because her husband had been ordered to Egypt and 'I am breaking up my establishment. The housemaid's name is Jane Ferrand. She is honest, clean and obliging, waits well at table and is a good needlewoman.' It was probably during this period that she and my grandfather became acquainted and they married in 1883 when he was twenty-nine and she twenty-three. They spent the early years of their marriage living at 23 Orchard Road, Dorking and their only daughter Annie Lilian, my mother, was born in 1891...

...I remember the kindness which my grandparents invariably showed towards me. although my family lived upstairs, I used to go down and spend time with them, and I remember particularly the evenings, just before bed-time when I would share their supper which regularly consisted of thick slices of grandmother's home-baked bread with cheese and pickled onions. I find it impossible to describe the superb flavour of these simple viands, but the memory lingers still!

I often went for walks with grandfather, particularly on the sabbath - which was strictly observed as a day of rest at that time. He would not have dreamt of leaving the house wearing anything but his Sunday best with a flower in his buttonhole and carrying his choicest walking cane with the silver knob. He would sometimes take me to a lake on Wynne's Common just up the road; there I would sail my small boat and admire the flashier craft belonging to other folk who could afford such things. Wynne's Common was a gravelled space with a mound in the middle which was occasionally used by the Royal Artillery for manoeuvres with field guns (then horse drawn). Opposite the Common was a public house called 'The Woodman' where my grandfather had an occasional pint; he was not a heavy drinker. He took me more than once into Woolwich to watch the Artillery on parade and I well remember one occasion when an artilleryman was tied to a field gun and made to run with it as the horses galloped around the parade ground. I never knew for what crime he was being punished.

One of my favourite outings was when my grandfather took me down to Woolwich Free Ferry. I was fascinated by the churning paddles as the boat approached the side and when we were on board we would always go into the engine room to watch the enormous brass beam turning over and over - I still remember the smell of steam and hot oil that accompanied the adventure. Our destination on these occasions was the North Woolwich Gardens on the other side of the Thames - there we would sit and eat our sandwiches while watching the activity on the river, which flowed alongside the park railings.

In retirement my grandfather devoted himself to tasks about the house and in particular to his garden in which he grew the most succulent vegetables. He had trained a grapevine which covered the whole off the back yard and was fixed to a point just above the kitchen window. It bore a crop of uneatable grapes every Autumn and made the kitchen very dark. There were two flourishing apple trees at the lower end of the garden which he had planted years before - I believe they were transplanted from Dorking where my grandparents had lived previously. The garden was so well tended and fertilised - with the help of passing horses! - that when I was in my teens I remember noticing that the soil was a good six inches higher than that of the neighbouring gardens.

One of the things that sticks in my memory is the peculiar noise that grandfather always made when using a brush to clean boots and shoes in the back kitchen. I later learnt that this was the sound made by all grooms who had spent a large part of their lives rubbing down horses. My grandmother was always very busy, too. She specialised in high-class laundry work and was able to deal with starching, stiff collars and dress shirts etc, with an expert touch. Consequently the house often smelt like a laundry, particularly when she was boiling clothes in the copper in the back kitchen. This was long before the washing machine came into it's own. One of my jobs was to help with the collection and distribution of these articles from time to time.

My grandfather was very much devoted to the enjoyment of tobacco. He regularly smoked pipes of all shapes and sizes from an eighteen inch 'churchwarden' to clay pipes only about four inches long with the mouthpiece wound with string. I remember a favourite briar of his which had a bowl shaped like a bull's head complete with horns and glass eyes. I still have a cigar holder of his with an amber mouthpiece, a silver collar and an ivory carving of two hunting dogs; this was used only on special occasions, such as Christmas. He never touched cigarettes which were an abomination to him. This is probably one of the reasons why he survived in full possession of his faculties until the age of seventy-eight.

It is now a matter of extreme regret to me that my grandfather and I never discussed his army experiences. Had I known then a fraction of what I know now, I would have taken any opportunity to get first hand accounts of battles and other events. I am thinking here especially of the occasion when, in the aftermath of the Zulu campaign he accompanied Major Chard on a triumphal tour of the country. The newspaper accounts had been available then, but as far as I know my grandfather did not have copies, I wonder if he was ever aware they existed. Occasions such as that at Taunton when Sir Percy Douglas (who had been General of the forces in South Africa before Lord Chelmsford) called for 'three cheers for the Sapper on the box' must have given a fillip to his pride and self-esteem that lasted the rest of his life.

2076 Gunner John Cantwell, 'N' Battery, 5th Brigade, Royal Artillery

"The Times," March 9th, 1880

Court Circular
Windsor Castle, March 8

The Queen decorated Gunner John Cantwell, of the Royal Artillery, in the corridor at Windsor Castle to day, with the distinguished service medal for gallantry displayed by him at the defence of the hospital at Rorke's Drift...

A letter written by Cantwell in 1900: [NAB ref. 1975/00, Kwa-Zulu Natal Archives, Pietermaritzburg]

Sir,
I joined Her Majesty's Service in 68 and served until 19th July 87 - where I left as a full N.C.O. of the R.A. with a very good discharge.
I am one of the heroes & defenders of Rorke's Drift, & am in receipt of the War Medal for, 77-78 + 79 - together with the Medal for Distinguished Service for gallantry at the defence of Rorke's Drift presented to me by the hands of Her Most Gracious Majesty the Queen at Windsor 8th March 80 - also the Medal for Long Service & Good Conduct...

2077 Gunner Arthur Howard, 'N' Battery, 5th Brigade, Royal Artillery

A statement of unknown origin reads;-

"In his fevered state he made a dash for the verandah but being confused turned the wrong way and jumped the wall of mealie bags. He lay by a bush feining death until it was safe to return to the barricade."

"The Daily Telegraph," March 25th, 1879.

The following letter is from Gunner Howard, servant to Colonel Harness, to his family in England. A telegram published in the Cape papers, dated Pietermaritzburg, January 29, states tat Howard had a narrow escape, but got away from the hospital and sat in the bush all night, exposed to the fire from both sides:-

Helpmakaar, Feb. 7 1879.

Just a line to let you know that I am still in the land of the living. I daresay before you got this you will have heard of the massacre. They killed just half of our battery, and nearly all the 1st-24th Regiment. The awful black devils watched the General out of camp, and then, as soon as his column had got clear away, they came down,

- about 1,500 of them, - like bees out of a hive, and there was awful slaughter. They took everything belonging to officers and men, - all but what they stood upright in, - burnt the huts, and scattered the provisions all about the place. There was a deal of money in camp, - my Governor lost a bit, but, as it was Government money to pay the battery with, he will get back again.

I was not in the camp, for I had the diarrhoea and was left behind at a place they call Rorke's Drift, where there was a temporary hospital. One company of the 24th, ninety strong, was left to protect it. Well, the same day as the other affair happened about which I have just told you, four thousand or so of them paid us a visit at the hospital. But we had about three hours notice, and plenty of sacks of oats with which we threw up a temporary fortification round this old place. When the Zulus arrived, about five in the evening, they did not find it quite as comfortable as they thought, for they expected that they would have nothing to do but assegai us at their pleasure, and possess the place, but we had knocked holes through the house to fire through. So what with the sacks and the holes through the house, we had very good cover. Boxes of ammunition were placed beside us. Forty men were in hospital, and nearly all able to fight when it came to the pinch; I had a rifle belonging to a sergeant who was too ill to use it. The Zulus made short work of him.

When waiting for the approach of the enemy we would see them half a mile before they got to us. When I beheld the swarm I said to myself, "All up now," but I was wrong, and we all agreed to fight till only two were left, and these were to shoot themselves. Well, we all got behind our ramparts, and when the Zulus were about 400 yards off, like a wall coming on, we fired the first volley. The rifles being Martini-Henry's, our firing was very quick, and, when struck by the bullets, the niggers would give a spring in the air and fall flat down. The enemy advanced to within 300 yards, and then it did not seem healthy to come any nearer, so we continued to fire at them till it got dark. Then, as the roof of the hospital was of thatch, they crept up and set it on fire. When the flames burst out it was all the better for us, for we could see the niggers and their movements, though they could not see us. Didn't we give it to them then, anyhow!

They sheared off, all but a few who hung about us all night; but as soon as it was light we finished off all we could see, and I can tell you that when I saw the general's column coming to our relief I was glad. The general said we were a brave little garrison, and that this showed what a few men could do if they only had the pluck. I had a letter and a paper, and was glad to see that you got the clock. I shall not be able to write very often.

"The Times," February 11th, 1930

A Survivor Of Rorke's Drift

The death is announced in a Reuter telegram from Sydney, of Mr. Howard, a survivor of Rorke's Drift. Mr. Howard who was 74, arrived in Australia in 1906. As recently as Friday he complained of an assegai wound received in the fight. In addition to Neuville's famous painting of the defence of Rorke's Drift, the Sydney Art Gallery has a picture showing Mr. Howard assisting and carrying a wounded man from the blazing hospital...

"The Daily Mirror," Friday, February 14th, 1930

Told He Was Dead
Rorke's Drift Survivor and a Newspaper Report
Picture Mystery

Mr. Arthur Howard, a hero of Rorke's Drift, has just learned that his own death has been reported.

It was announced in the newspapers several days ago that he had died in Sydney, Australia, after complaining of an old assegai received in the historic Drift fight.

Mr Howard expressed great surprise to a Daily Mirror representative when he was informed of the report. Although he is now seventy eight years of age and blind, he is an active and alert man, and takes a keen interest in present day affairs.

"I cannot understand how there can be any mistake," he said. "I have been living in Kent now for forty years, and I have certainly never been to Australia.

As you can see for yourself, I am quite alive and able to tell you about the battle. I was at Ulundi too, where we beat the Zulu armies in forty minutes.

My relatives tell me that the photograph in the papers is of me all right.

I never received a wound of any sort from an assegai, or from anything for that matter, though I was in the hospital with fever when the Zulus burned it during the battle."

Picture of Rescue
"I never Carried Anyone to Safety at Famous Battle," says Mr. Howard

"At Rorke's Drift, 4,000 Zulus attacked eighty six men of them South Wales Borderers under the command of Lieutenants Chard and Bromhead. Half of the men were in a small farmhouse which had been turned into a hospital.

How Sydney Art Gallery can have a picture of me leaving the burning hospital carrying another man over my shoulder is more than I can understand. It certainly cannot be a picture of me. It was as much as I could to leave the building myself, without carrying anyone else.

There were only eighty six of us all told, and I don't think it is at all probable that there was another Arthur Howard among us, though of course it is possible. I knew most of the men, and I never met anyone of my own name.

I think the Australian report must be incorrect in the name."

1643 Gunner Abraham Evans, 'N' Battery, 5th Brigade, Royal Artillery

"The Free Press of Monmouthshire," April 18th, 1913.

RORKE'S DRIFT

Sir,

After hearing different statements concerning the battle of Rorke's Drift, which I think should be corrected, I beg a short space in your paper to do so, in the interest of Justice to those left alive after their heroic defence. I, Gunner A. Evans, "N" Battery, 5th Brigade R.A., of which battery half was lost at Isandhlwana, when the terrible disaster occurred to that notable regiment, the 24th Warwickshire's, now the South Wales Borderers, feel it my duty, being one of the number, to correct the statements I read time after time in the papers.

First of all let me say that anyone who would like to criticise this statement is at liberty to do so while I live, so that I may answer any questions they would like to ask me. I beg to state that after the disaster of Isandhlwana I saw the scout from Isandhlwana gallop to Rorke's Drift to warn them that the Zulus were advancing on that place. This scout was minus any arms or clothing but Jersey and pants, and knowing the danger we were in, made all haste to come to us.

This message was first given to Dr. Reynolds, between 2 and 2.30 in the afternoon. Then he at once set the men to work to form a laager from the hospital to the shore. Meanwhile Lieut.s Bromhead and Chard were giving orders elsewhere and making preparations for the best resistance possible with so small a number of men, and many of them sick. I may say that under adverse circumstances as these were, this laager and defences was built from 4 to 4.30pm. I was then standing in the doorway of the hospital, and witnessed five Zulus come in front of the doorway, jumping in their mad frenzy, flushed with their late victory.

Just at this moment my newest mates were Adams and Jenkins, of the 24th Regt. What became of these men I can't say. I never saw them after. There were in all 30 casualties, 17 killed, and 13 wounded, out of the 96 men. The number of rifles in action was 85, and every man a man, and when you know that 17,000 rounds of ammunition were fired during the action, I think you will agree with me that all men were heroes of the first water. Yet there is a lot said now that is not true. There were killed at this battle 700 of the bravest tribe in South Africa, within six hundred yards of the hospital, therefore the ammunition was well spent.

No doubt many wonder what I, a R.A. man, was doing at Rorke's Drift. I was left there sick, but not too sick but that I could not help my comrades in arms to defend our position, and could say many things about it. I beg to inform the Editor of the "Daily Sketch," who published the account of the funeral of V.C. Hitch, that Major H.J. Williams is not a survivor of Rorke's Drift. There was no officer of that name at all. There are several men left alive today, myself included, in the immediate neighbourhood in which I live, one of them a V.C. man. On the 23rd January I witnessed the burial of those men who were killed on the 22nd, in this historic battle, in two large holes, which our native pioneers had dug for that purpose, and which was done on the return of the Column under General Chelmsford from Isandhlwana. My position at this time was on the parapet, alongside Lt. Chard, and watching them, the Column, coming down to the pontoon which Dr Reynolds and other officers, Lieut.s Bromhead and Chard, thought were Zulus dressed in our men's clothing, and they asked me to mount the sack and look through the field glasses. As soon as I got there I told them I did not want the glasses for I could see it was our men, and I could see a division of grey horses in the middle of the Infantry. I took up my former position alongside Lt. Chard, on the parapet, until Lord Chelmsford came and spoke to Lt. Chard, thanking him for the way we held the position during the night. Shortly after this our brave men followed up to the laager and into the bush, where they found heaps of dead bodies, and I shall never forget the sound of the click as they fixed bayonets, and there took some revenge for Isandhlwana.

Mr Editor, this statement is made by one who was presented to her late Majesty Queen Victoria - with three others, making two from Rorke's Drift, and two who escaped from Isandhlwana. This was in July, 1882.

(signed)
A. Evans,
Spring Gardens, Varteg, Mon.

"The Western Mail," May 20th, 1914

ANOTHER SOLDIER HERO
THIRD RORKE'S DRIFT SURVIVOR IN SOUTH WALES.
HONOURED BY QUEEN VICTORIA.

As well as Mr. John Jones, the Merthyr veteran, and Private John Williams, V.C., of Cwmbran, whose reminiscences were published in the Western Mail recently, there is living in South Wales another of the heroes whose wonderful defence of Rorke's Drift astonished the Empire. He is ex-Gunner Evans, Spring Gardens, Varteg, Pontypool.

It was in 1874 that the ex-gunner joined the Army, for in that year he enlisted in the Royal Field Artillery at Newport. His first campaign was in the Kaffir War of 1877, and it involved long marches and much bush fighting. Then came the Zulu War. His battery marched with the field column to Isandula, leaving him in hospital at Rorke's Drift. One day while he was there a survivor from Isandula, a Natal Carabineer, came there at full gallop to tell the story of the disaster, and to warn them that the Zulus were moving on the drift. Immediately preparations began, and under the directions of Lieutenant Bromhead and Dr. Reynolds, Army surgeon, a laager was formed. Ex-Gunner Evans helped in its formation and in the removal of helpless invalids from the hospital, and later in the gallant twelve-hour defence, which ended in the repulse of the enemy.

Apart from Rorke's Drift, ex-Gunner Evans has many tales to tell. He was one of the firing party at the burial of the Prince Imperial. no volleys were fired - ammunition was scarce, and all that was done was to snap the triggers. Afterwards the ex-gunner served in the first Boer War, and in the defence of Potchefstroom, which was besieged by the Boers, he was wounded in the back by a bullet which came through an embrasure into the gun-pit. Evans suffered from enteric during an epidemic which caused many deaths, including that of Captain Justice, of Newport. The succession of deaths led the pipers of the Scots Fusiliers to march round camp on many evenings at tattoe, playing laments.

On return to England the battery was ordered to Windsor Park for inspection by the late Queen Victoria. As a veteran of three campaigns and as a defender of Rorke's Drift Evans was specially brought under the notice of Queen Victoria, who spoke a few words to each. About this time one of the officers of the battery was Captain Rundle, now Governor of Malta. Evans was on the point of being discharged from the Army when the Egyptian War broke out. At once he applied to have his discharge cancelled, and volunteered for the front. He served at Tel-el-Kebir, and remembers having to drink water from canals in which floated the dead bodies of men and animals. Within a short time cholera broke out in the camp.

Evans possesses the South African medal with dates 1877-78-79 - the full significance of which only soldiers can understand - the Egyptian medal, and the Khedive's Star.

Some years ago much was done by the public for the Crimean veterans. surely the time has come to do something for the survivors of later campaigns. The Welsh survivors of Rorke's Drift have a strong claim on the Principality. Another claim is for a bar for Rorke's Drift. Pressure by Welsh members of Parliament on the Secretary for War could right this neglect.

"The Western Mail," c. 1914.

Rorke's Drift Hero
Varteg Man's Interesting Career

To have served your country and have got nothing for it is the fate of many men. Pensions, recognition, honour, only go the way of the few. After years of faithful service Gunner Abraham Evans is spending the evening of his days at his pretty cottage home – Spring Gardens, Varteg, which is situate on the mountain above Pontypool. Evans' career is one full of brave deeds. He has been in three wars and yet has no pension.

The ex-gunner joined the army in the year 1874, when he enlisted in the Royal Field Artillery at Newport, Mon. three years later his first war campaign was entered upon, for he took part in the Kaffir War of 1877 which involved long marches and much bush fighting. Following that came the Zulu War. Evans was an artilleryman and he can thank heaven that he was to ill to proceed with his column to Isandlwana where a camp had been formed. That illness saved his life for even though he was left in hospital at Rorke's Drift he managed to escape alive.

For guarding the hospital many brave men have received the Victoria Cross. Evans was recently seen by our representative to whom he described the terrible onslaught by the Zulus at Rorke's Drift. One day a Natal Carabineer came to Rorke's Drift at the gallop to tell the story of the disaster at Isandlwana and to warn them that the Zulus were moving on towards the drift. Immediately preparations were made for safeguarding the place against the expected attack. Lieut. Bromhead and Dr. Reynolds superintended the formation of a laager. Evans was well enough to help in this work. He also helped to carry out some of the helpless invalids from the hospital, and he took his part later in the twelve hours defence which repulsed the enemy. The news from Isandlwana was that "our fellows" had been "cut up" by the Zulus. The attack on the hospital at Rorke's Drift, Evans described with tear stained face. He did not like talking about the fight. He was all praise for what the others did.

He described how he and his fellow soldiers kept at it with bullet and bayonet until six or seven patients had been got out of the hospital. Dr. Reynolds' bravery he said, was marvellous, Dr. Reynolds was on a sort of verandah, and there under heavy fire, and a cloud of assegai's he kept up a constant attendance on the sick and wounded. The Zulus would make a rush on the little fort every now and then, but the men did not trouble, they just kept on fighting in the knowledge that they were protecting woman and children who were in Natal just over the river. The hospital was being set on fire and the flames from it illuminated a picture terrible to behold. When day broke it could be seen that the Zulus had had enough and were clearing away over a hill in the distance.

It was six o'clock in the morning when relief arrived, Colonel Russell and some mounted infantry going to their assistance. Later Lord Chelmsford arrived with the remainder of the 3rd Column. The Zulus came as if to make another attack but soon went of when they saw relief had arrived.

Apart from Rorke's Drift, Evans has many a tale to tell. He was one of the firing party at the burial of the Prince Imperial. No volleys were fired, ammunition was scarce, and all that was done was to snap the trigger. Afterwards the ex-gunner served in the first Boer War and was in the defence of Potchefstroom, which was besieged by the Boers, he was wounded in the back by a bullet which came through an opening into the gun. Evans suffered from enteric fever during an epidemic which caused many deaths. The succession of deaths lead the pipers of the Scots Fusiliers to march round the camp on many evenings at tattoo playing laments.

On their return to England the Battery was ordered to Windsor Park for inspection by the late Queen Victoria. Evans a veteran of three campaigns and a defender of Rorke's Drift was specially brought under the notice of Queen Victoria, who spoke a few words to each.

Evans was just about finished with the army when the first Egyptian War broke out. At once he applied to have his discharge cancelled, and volunteered to go to the front. He served at Tel-el-Kabir.

60B/1123 Corporal James Graham, (Daniel Sheehan), 90th Light Infantry

"The Aldershot News," Saturday, March 4th, 1899

Death of Mr. Sheehan
A Rorke's Drift Hero

There is a halo of romance about the men who defended the little river station at Rorke's Drift. This fact has been brought home once more by the death of one of the gallant band of heroes. Mr. Daniel Sheehan, a foreman in the Mobilisation Stores. The deceased was forty-six years of age and died on Friday of pneumonia, at Winchester-street, Farnborough, after ten day's illness. He was a familiar figure in Aldershot and has been an honoured guest at more than one South African celebration. He belonged to the 2nd Scottish Rifles, in which he was a colour sergeant on completing for pension. He was present at Rorke's Drift by an accident, having been sent up in an escort to a convoy after recovery from sickness himself. He was a modest man and it is said that this quality kept his share in the defence quite in the background...

3359 Private Michael McMahon, Army Hospital Corps

"The Queens Submission Book for the Distinguished Conduct Medal" [WO103/13 The National Archives, (P.R.O.), London]

Most humbly etc., That a Silver Medal for Distinguished Conduct in the field, granted without annuity or gratuity to 2nd Corporal Michael McMahon of the Army Hospital Corps, as a reward for his gallant conduct in rescuing Private Cole 2/24th from the Zulus during the attack on Rorke's Drift post on the night of the 22nd January 1879.

Assistant Commissary Walter Alphonsus Dunne, Army Commissariat Department

Two letters written to his parents, published in "The Irish Times," March 5th, 1879

The Defence of Rorke's Drift.

We have been permitted, through the courtesy of the writer's family, to publish the following extracts from letters received, within the last few days, from a young officer who took part in the gallant defence of the post at 'Rorke's Drift':-
Camp, Rorke's Drift, Natal
January 20th 1879
....I have not had a moment I could call my own to tell you of my adventures in coming here on horseback from Luneburg - how I had to swim a river, how the next day my horse sank up to the girths in mud, and how finally I completed in safety the

ride of over one hundred miles. When I got here I was so done up that I could do nothing for two or three days, but I son came round again, and now feel as well as ever. As has been long expected war has begun with the Zulus, and we are beginning another campaign with greater difficulties to face than the last. I am in charge of the commissariat of the column, which is a very serious responsibility entailing a great amount of work and anxiety, the roads and transport are so bad. So far things have gone well. In addition to this column are two others of about equal strength entering Zululand. This column crossed the River Buffalo this morning, taking food &c. for fifteen days. I remain here in charge of the depot, which is protected by some of the 2-24th Regiment and 400 natives. This is the first quiet day I have had for some time, and I was very glad when they moved off from the camping ground. It was a busy and picturesque scene to look on - the rows of tents and waggons, with crowds of oxen and men winding to and fro. The waggons were carried across the river on pontoons; the men went in boats. From our side of the river the view was very fine and impressive, as the strains of the band and the notes of the native war song were wafted on the breeze. Now the spot is deserted. There is a large farm house for commissariat stores, outside of which grain is raised high in bags, covered with tarpaulin. Inside boxes of biscuits are piled to the roof, with tea, coffee, meal, sugar, flour, &c. We are in the midst of a fine country, and the weather is cool, but there has been a great deal of rain, which is a disadvantage, as it cuts up the roads and damages our supplies.....A part of our column had a small engagement the other day, the first of the war, and captured 400 head of cattle, some sheep, goats and horses. Some of the 4th Foot are expected here shortly...

Camp, Rorke's Drift, Natal
24th January 1879

...As you may have seen in the papers alarming accounts of the sad reverse which has happened to a part of our force. I hasten to let you know that I am quite safe and well. The Zulus lured the General and most of his column away for some miles from his camp, and then another large body, which had not been seen, fell on the camp and about 500 men left behind, and killed nearly all of them. Twenty officers are missing. We got notice here of the disaster, and that the Zulus were coming towards us. We fortified the store with bags and boxes, and in about two hours they attacked us. The soldiers fired steadily and continuously on them, but they came on to within about a few yards, where they were shot down in scores. We were surrounded on all sides, and they remained all night, but when morning broke they had disappeared, leaving 370 dead on the ground. soon after the General returned with the column, and we were rejoiced to see them. The men fought splendidly, and the first words the General spoke were - 'I congratulate you all on the gallant defence you have made'. Everything was lost that was left in the camp, so that the officers and men have scarcely a thing besides what was on their backs...

"Eyewitness in Zululand," by Lt. Col. I. Bennett, Greenhill Books, London, 1989
[Dunne's account were originally published in the Army Service Corps Journal of
1891, it reproduced here by kind permission of Lt. Col. Ian Bennett]

The force that was to invade Zululand in three columns from three different points on the border, under command of Lord Chelmsford, numbered 12,000 men, including the Native contingent, but Cetewayo's army was known to be about 30,000 strong, well drilled, organised in regiments and held under strict discipline.

I was attached to No. 3 Column, commanded by Colonel Glynn, CB, under the personal supervision of Lord Chelmsford, who accompanied it, and was instructed to form a Supply Depot at Rorke's Drift, the site of a Swedish Mission Station on the banks of the River Buffalo, 12 miles from Helpmakaar. The house and school of the mission, which had been abandoned, were utilised as a hospital and store respectively. The strength of No. 3 Column was over 2,000 whites and 2,500 natives, composed as follows: - one Battery of Royal Artillery, N/5 RA, one Company of Royal Engineers 1st and 2nd Battalions of the 24th Regiment, one Squadron of Mounted Infantry, one Squadron of Natal Mounted Police, the Natal Carabiniers, Newcastle Mounted Rifles, Buffalo Border Guard and the 3rd Regt. of Natal Native Contingent under European officers. The Transport comprised 1,500 oxen, 70 mules, 220 waggons, and 82 carts.

The quantity of Supplies to be stored was very large and my work was very arduous, the staff placed at my disposal for supply duties being very inadequate; but I did not then fully understand the magnitude of the task before us. An Acting Commissariat Officer (Assistant Commissary Dalton), a civilian clerk, Mr. Byrne, and Corporal Attwood of the Army Service Corps were all the assistants I had at first. I mention their names as they all took a gallant part in the defence of Rorke's Drift Post and are now no more. To these were subsequently added 2nd Lieut. Griffiths, of the 24th Regiment, a most promising young officer, and a sergeant and three privates as issuers, etc.

The once quiet Mission Station was now a busy scene. Heavily laden ox-waggons constantly came and went, accompanied by the usual yelling, whip cracking, and bellowing; piles of corn bags, biscuit boxes, etc. rose up; detachments of troops were continually arriving and pitching their tents - all the bustle of a large camp and depot was apparent.

On the 10th January, 1879, the first portion of the Column crossed the river and encamped on the Zulu side, and for the next ten days was engaged in road making. On the 20th the remainder of the Column crossed with the exception of the small garrison left to guard the Depot; the camps were struck and a general advance was made to Isandhlwana, about 12 miles distant, where a fresh camp was formed. On that day we said good-bye to friends and comrades, so many of whom we were destined never to meet again in this world - all of them, both officers and men, as fine fellows as the British Army has ever numbered in its ranks.

Our post at Rorke's Drift seemed silent and lonely after they had left; but we expected to join them soon, and to hear of some fierce but successful fight with the enemy. Alas for human hopes and expectations! Before daylight on the 22nd January, Lord Chelmsford advanced in force from Isandhlwana, leaving his camp there in charge of Lieut. Colonel Pulleine, of the 24th Regiment, who had under his command about 800 of all ranks, including five companies of 1st 24th and one company of 2nd 24th. Colonel Durnford, RE., arrived at the camp later on the same morning with about 500 of the Native Contingent and took over the command. What followed at the camp was learnt afterwards by putting together the accounts given by the few survivors and from the Zulus themselves after the war.

Early in the morning reports were brought in of bodies of the enemy being in sight. The troops turned out to meet them a mile or two from the camp, but were soon obliged to fall back, for fresh regiments of the enemy were continually arriving at the scene. About 11 a.m. a force of 20,000 Zulus advanced simultaneously to the attack and gradually surrounded the defending force, developing the movement with great swiftness and bravery, undaunted by their heavy losses. The Native Contingent gave way before their determined assault and fled, thus exposing the rear and flank of the British force, whose ammunition was nearly all expended, while they found themselves unable to obtain a fresh supply, as they were cut off from the camp. A desperate hand to hand fight now ensued. The Zulus suffered enormous losses; but numbers prevailed. Surrounded on all sides by crowds of the enemy the small British force was finally overwhelmed: very, very few escaped from that dreadful melee.

How Melville and Coghill of the 24th tried to save the colours, and how they were overtaken and killed in the river is well known. How groups of men formed back to back and fell to a man where they stood was shown only too well by their corpses when the battle-field was revisited.

On that ill-fated day, 51 officers and 786 non-commissioned officers and men, including both regulars, police and volunteers, were killed. The 24th suffered most, having lost 21 officers and 433 men. Twelve days' supplies for the Column and all the transport fell into the hands of the Zulus, besides two guns, hundreds of rifles and large quantities of ammunition. It was one of the most complete disasters that had ever occurred to a British force. In the meantime we at Rorke's Drift were all unconscious of the tragedy which was being enacted only twelve miles away.

The story of the engagement at Rorke's Drift has already been graphically told by the gallant Chard; but there are probably many readers of the journal who have never read it.

The little garrison consisted of one company of the 2nd 24th Regiment, under Lieut. G. Bromhead, and a number of details, regulars, police and volunteers, making a total of 138 officers, non-commissioned officers and men, besides 300 of the Natal Native Contingent under an officer named Stephenson. They were variously employed on their different duties on that morning. Lieut. Chard, RE, who commanded the post, was down at the river repairing the "pont," which had got out of order; poor young Griffiths, too eager for fighting to remain at Rorke's Drift, where there seemed to be no prospect of seeing any, had asked permission to ride out to Isandhlwana and had left the night before - never more to return! Bromhead and I were resting after luncheon under an awning which we had formed by propping up a tarpaulin with tent poles; everything was peaceful and quiet, when, suddenly, we noticed at some distance across the river a large number of mounted natives approaching, preceded by a lot of women and children and oxen. We were going down to find out what they were, but had not gone many steps when we were called back by one of the men who said that a mounted orderly wished to see the officer in command. Turning back at once we met a mounted man in his shirt sleeves riding hurriedly towards us. His first words were "The camp is taken by Zulus!" When I heard the words a strange feeling, which I cannot account for, came over me that I had heard of this somewhere before. Though we could not realise it fully at first, we soon gathered the truth that a great disaster had befallen that portion of No. 3 Column which was left to defend the camp at Isandhlwana, and that the Zulus, flushed with victory, were advancing to attack our post.

Dalton, as brave a soldier as ever lived, had joined us, and hearing the terrible news said "Now, we must make a defence!" It was his suggestion which decided us to form a breastwork of bags of grain, boxes of biscuit, and everything that would help to stop a bullet or keep out a man. An ox-waggon and even barrels of rum and lime juice were pressed into the service.

Bromhead at once ordered the men to fall in; outposts were thrown out, tents were struck, ammunition was served out, and the work of putting up the barricade was begun by all hands. Other preparations were also made: a water barrel was filled and brought inside, and several boxes of ammunition were opened and placed in convenient places. It was well for us that we had the help of the 300 natives at this juncture, otherwise the work could not have been accomplished in time. Chard had now come up from the river and heartily superintended the progression of the fortification, making many improvements. The men knew what was before them - a struggle for life; but they one and all displayed the greatest coolness, though some of them were very young soldiers. On all faces there was a look of determination which showed that they meant to "do or die."

In about two hours a wall breast high had been made nearly all round, taking in the hospital and store. When I went to look at the progress made at the former place, I saw that this was the weakest point, for there was nothing but a plank to close the opening at one part; but before anything could be done to strengthen it a shot was fired outside. Turning round, I saw one of the outposts running back, and at the same moment a single Zulu appeared, standing out against the sky on the top of a high hill which rose up about 100 yards in rear of the store.

Immediately they heard the shot our 300 natives took up their assegais and made off towards Helpmakaar, followed by their officer! Chard, seeing that we could not now hold the original line, immediately had the space curtailed by drawing a row of biscuit boxes, two high, across the middle. This probably saved us later from destruction, for it afforded shelter for the men when they were obliged to retreat on the hospital being taken.

Very soon the Zulus appeared round the foot of the hill in a black mass, coming on without a sound at a steady trot. The men on that side, without waiting for any word of command, opened fire on them at once at about 800 yards range and dropped many of the foremost, causing the remainder to swerve away to their left and thus round to the front of our position. Soon they were all round us, and all sides of the square became hotly engaged. The store, which had been loopholed, afforded shelter to some of the men, who were able to do great execution on that side; but the heaviest attack was made on the hospital, which was soon captured after a very stubborn resistance on the part of the few men defending it who were forced back by numbers, fighting all the time with their bayonets, Ptes. Williams, Hook, and R. and W. Jones, of the 24th, greatly distinguishing themselves in their efforts to save the sick. Those of the sick who were able to move escaped by running back to the second line of boxes; but some of the poor fellows were stabbed to death with assegais in their beds.

All this had not occurred without loss on both sides, numbers of the Zulus having fallen, and on our side Pte. Cole ("old King Cole") and another man of the 24th had been shot dead, and three of four wounded. The doctor, Surgeon Reynolds, was busy attending the wounded as they fell. Early in the fight Mr. Byrne was shot through the head, and later Dalton, when firing standing at full height, received a bullet in the chest, but the wound fortunately did not prove fatal.

About five o'clock some of us who were on the look out for help from Helpmakaar, noticed a cloud of dust on the road some miles away, and we felt little doubt that the two companies of the 24th quartered there were coming to our aid. The news passed round like wildfire, putting new spirits into all, and was welcomed with loud cheers, which must have astonished the Zulus. But the dust was dispersed by the wind, and the longed for help never came.

As darkness came on we saw that the hospital had been set on fire; but this proved fortunate, for the blaze gave light through the greater part of the night, thus enabling the men to take better aim. Several times the foremost Zulus rushed right up to the barricade, but were always driven back with heavy loss, many being stopped only by the bayonet. The men behaved with splendid coolness and bravery. It was a soldier's battle - each man fighting for his own hand; and well did they avenge the slaughter of their comrades at Isandhlwana.

However, the position was a desperate one and our chance of escape seemed slight indeed, so Chard decided to form a sort of redoubt of mealie bags, where a last stand could be made. We laboured at this till we dropped with exhaustion; but succeeded in building it up to about eight feet on the outside, and here the wounded were brought for protection. It was hard work, for the bags of mealies weighed 200 lbs. each. Overhead, the small birds, disturbed from their nests by the turmoil and smoke, flew hither and thither confusedly.

As the night wore on the attack slackened from time to time; all firing ceased for the moment and profound silence reigned, broken only by the words of command of the Zulu leaders, which sounded strangely close. How we longed to know what they said! Every man was then on the alert straining eyes and ears to detect the rush which was sure to follow, only to be checked each time by a withering volley. Luckily the supply of ammunition was very plentiful and it was served out as required, the chaplain, the Rev. George Smith, being very active in helping to distribute it.

Towards morning there was a longer pause than usual, causing us to wonder what devilment the Zulus could be planning; but when the pale dawn, glimmering in the east, lit up the scene they had disappeared! Without a sound to betray their movements they had gone - beaten; carrying their wounded with them: all except a few whose case was hopeless. Then the garrison gave vent to their feelings in ringing British cheers, while the hearts of all were full of gratitude to God for their escape from what seemed certain death.

The scene we beheld was a strange and sad one! On one side stood the blackened walls and still smoking ruins of the hospital. Around it and in front of that side of the barricade lay the bodies of Zulus in rows, as if literally mown down, showing how brave had been the assault and how unerring the fire that had laid them low. Inside, were our own dead comrades - stark and cold, one still kneeling in a natural position against the wall- while the wounded excited pity by their sufferings, patiently borne. The ground was strewn with trampled grain which had run from bags pierced by bullet or assegai, and every face was black with smoke and sweat of toil and battle. No words of mine can do justice to the gallant soldiers who kept overwhelming numbers of those brave savages at bay all through the afternoon and long hours of the night with a steadiness which has never been surpassed. I am glad to. say several of them in due time were awarded the Victoria Cross; but every private present deserved a special reward. Our casualties were 17 killed and 10 wounded.

We could not believe that the Zulus would quietly accept their defeat, so we set to work to repair, as far as possible, the damage that had been done during the fight, and to prepare for another attack. One party proceeded to tear down the thatch from the roof of the store, which might easily be set alight; another collected and destroyed the muskets and assegais strewn about the ground, while a third had the painful task of decently laying out our dead in a corner of the enclosure. We walked round the scene of the fighting, finding everywhere dead Zulus - all "ring kop," that is married men, who alone wear a black ring woven into the hair of the head.

While this was going on a pale white face suddenly appeared like a ghost from some small out-buildings, where the Commissariat ovens had been established. "Who and what is it?" we asked. To our intense astonishment it proved to belong to a man of the Artillery, who, in some unexplained manner, had been out all night while the fight had been raging round him, and who, strange to say, had escaped the notice of the Zulus. Just then one of the apparently dead Zulus rose up, fired his musket at us and walked away! We were too surprised for the moment to do anything to stop him, and, though a couple of shots were fired after him, he got away round the base of the hill.

About 7 a.m. our attention was drawn to a large column of men advancing towards us some miles off in Zululand. We all scanned them anxiously, fearing that they might be a fresh body of the enemy, and we felt, and said to each other, that in that case our doom was sealed. Even at that distance there was something strangely silent and solemn about them which depressed our hearts. In time suspense was turned into relief when, through glasses, we could descry the familiar red jackets of the infantry, and then once more the little garrison burst forth into wild cheering, while many helmets were waved aloft, for there could now be no doubt that this was the Column returning under Lord Chelmsford. But they, seeing in the distance the smoke still rising up from the ruins of the hospital, feared that the post had been captured, and that the signalling which they saw was a ruse of the enemy.

Approaching cautiously at first, a mounted officer, when re-assured, galloped up and anxiously inquired if any of the men from the camp at Isandhlwana had escaped and joined us. Sadly we answered "No!" Overcome by emotion at the terrible certainty conveyed by that short word, he bent down to his horse's neck trying in vain to stifle the sobs which broke from his overcharged heart. No wonder his grief mastered him, for he had passed during the night by that camp where hundreds of his brave comrades lay slaughtered, and the hope that some portion might have fought their way through was crushed for ever.

Lord Chelmsford next rode up. No one could envy him then, for in defeat, as in success, all thoughts centre on the commander. His first words were, "thank you all for your gallant defence." Then the main body of the Column began to arrive. Strange arrival! No train of waggons to park - no tents to pitch - weary and sad they looked from fatigue, hunger and anxiety. Fortunate it was that we were able to provide them with food, for they had been without any for eighteen hours.

They had no change of clothes, no blankets, no great coats, no cooking utensils, except what we could lend them. Empty sacks suddenly became most valuable: slit open at the bottom and with holes made for the arms, they were worn by the men in lieu of great coats, and under different circumstances it would have been laughable to see British soldiers gravely mounting guard in such a costume. But one sees strange things on active service.

The day after the fight our dead were buried near the foot of the hill, not far from the spot where they nobly fell. The little cemetery was afterwards enclosed by a wall and a monument erected, on which was recorded their names and how they died fighting for "Queen and Country." For the bodies of the Zulus two huge excavations were made in front of the hospital and therein were interred 351 corpses.

Death has already thinned the ranks of the survivors of the little band that fought at Rorke's Drift: Bromhead, who was beloved in his regiment; Dalton, the lion-hearted, and Corporal Attwood, who received the Distinguished Conduct Medal, having since passed away.

The Garrison having been increased to 800 men and strengthened by two guns, the remainder of the Column left next day en route for Pietermaritzburg, whither Lord Chelmsford proceeded direct to telegraph home for reinforcements, and to make arrangements for a fresh advance on their arrival.

Pending the arrival of tents and blankets, most of the Garrison at Rorke's Drift had to sleep on the ground without shelter, crowded together within the barricade, and as heavy rains came on, which turned the ground into deep mud, their wretched plight may be imagined. Fever and dysentery broke out which the Medical Officer had no means of combating, for all the medicines had been destroyed in the Hospital when it was burnt by the Zulus. Things improved after a time, but not before many men had been laid low. I, too, sickened with typhoid fever and was sent off, early in March, in an ambulance to Helpmakaar, where a field hospital had been established..."

A letter by JRM Chard written in response to a request from Commissary E. Strickland for corroboration of Dunne's bravery prior to a recommendation for a V.C. being made: [WO32/7386, The National Archives, (P.R.O.), London]

To Sir Edward Strickland K.C.B.
Durban
20th Aug 1879

My dear Sir Edward,
I have very much pleasure in writing at your request the following short account of Mr Dunne's services on the occasion of the attack on Rorke's Drift 22 - 23 Jany. 1879 -
Mr Dunne from the first gave valuable assistance in superintending and working at our defences, and with Mr Byrne was greatly instrumental to forming the retrenchment of biscuit boxes which was in all probability the means of our successful defence, & that at a time when the firing in the distance being heard, there was every necessity for the work being completed as quickly as possible. -
At one time during the attack, & when the Hospital was burning, it appeared as if the enemy would also succeed in setting fire to the Commt Store - and it became of the greatest importance to have some point to rally round in case they succeeded. -
It was then that we formed our inner defence of the two heaps of mealies in sacks - Mr Dunne worked hard at this until the little redoubt was completed; his height, in addition to the fact of standing on the heaps which were high above our outer walls, causing him to be much exposed. - The enemy's fire was very heavy at the time, and in addition to any shots aimed at those working, from the usual Zulu fault of firing high, the place was one of particular exposure.

Believe me
Dear Sir Edward
very faithfully yours
John R. M. Chard
Capt & Bt. Maj R.E.

Extract from "Officer's Service Registers: Army Commissariat Department."
[WO25/3922, The National Archives, (P.R.O.), London

Mentioned in despatches Lond. Gaz. 14.3.79 for affair at "Rorke's Drift"
Promoted Depy Cmy in recognition of his service at Rorke's Drift Zululand

C/2469 2nd Corporal Francis Attwood, Army Service Corps

Extracts from two of a series of letters written by Cpl. F. Attwood to his aunt and uncle in the U.K over the period of a year of his stay in South Africa: [F. Attwood Papers, MS.455, The Brenthurst Library, Johannesburg]

Dear Uncle & Aunt,
I have to thank God for being now alive, as I told you in my last letter I was stationed at a place called Helpmakaar, 12 miles from Zululand. I was sent from there to a place called Rorkes Drift on the Border of the River Buffalo that divides Zululand from Natal. I arrived all safe and was so until the 22nd January when news came to us that our Camp was taken and about 800 men of ours killed.
I should have said that I belong to Col Glyns Column consisting of the 1st/24th and 2/24th Regts some Mounted Infantry, Police, and Native Contingent and a few others, I was with a Company of the 2/24th Regt about 90 men, in charge of Commissariat Stores &c, the News was too true, and 4 Regiments of zulus attacked us with the idea of taking the stores, we immediately looped holed the house and put up a kind of fortification of sacks of oats &c, all at once they came down upon us and fired, we returned it and it lasted from 4 in the afternoon till 6 the next morning Thank God I escaped unhurt but we lost 13 men killed and 10 wounded.
Shortly after it commenced they set fire to the Hospital and I am sorry to say that some of the poor fellows were burned to death, we killed 390 we found them on the ground the next morning after they retired we came out to look round well such a sight met our eyes, all the white men that were killed were cut open and their entrails protruding, the stench of the Burning bodies was something awful, we all made up our minds for the worst, such a night, and the next, although we were not attacked we had to be up watching.
I should have said that we were relieved by the remainder of the Column and got some more ammunition we have no tents or any camp equipage we have plenty of food for the present. I should have said that the zulus fight with spears (called assegai.) and all kinds of guns from the oldest pattern to the latest, they do not seem to have much fear, they are very daring, coming right up to the guns, such horrid looking brutes, quite naked except a string of something about their loins, we do not know the moment we may be attacked. I do not know how we may fare but their

abilities as fighting men have been sadly under estimated, and we have a very big debt to wipe out. I cannot write any more I am too tired no sleep at night and working issuing rations all day, Love to all - up to now thank God I am quite well and remain

Yours affectionately

F Attwood

<u>Rorkes Drift</u>

<u>25.1.79</u>

I have not heard from you since I have been out here. F A.

Extract from a second letter written to his aunt and uncle, dated "Rorkes Drift 14 April 1879"

...such a horrible night, I never shall forget. I am specially recommended for promotion, and I was the only one of my Corps, at the attack on the Commissariat under Lieuts Bromhead & Chard. I must tell you that I made an awful mess of one fellow, he was running towards the house in a slightly stooping position, when I let fly at him and struck him in the Crown of the head the effect of which was to blow the entire side of his face away. I must tell you that I was at an upper window the only one in the <u>Barn</u> I call it...

Extract from "The Natal Witness," Saturday, November 15th, 1879

Medal for Distinguished Conduct.
Decoration of a Rorke's Drift Hero.

An interesting parade took place in Maritzburg on Thursday morning, when a medal for distinguished conduct, was presented to Corporal Attwood, Army Service Corps, by A.C.G. Healy, in the presence of the whole corps.

The Commanding Officer remarked that it was an unpleasant morning on which to perform a very agreeable duty, but that he would not, in consequence of the rain, detain them long. He proceeded to say that more than 2,000 years ago, as well as his recollection served him, a great barbarian host invaded, and ravaged some of the provinces of ancient Greece. Between them and her richest and fairest possessions lay a mountain range, and in that mountain range a small pass. In that pass stood a small and devoted band of heroes, and though the barbarian host swelled and surged and fought against them and threatened to overwhelm them, those intrepid men stood their ground and died at their post, but the pass was held. - Why, said the gallant officer, do I mention this? To show you that such noble deeds are never forgotten, ever since poets have sung, painters have painted, and nations have declaimed of that gallant little band of Spartan heroes and their noble leader Leonidas, and whenever noble and heroic deeds have been told, the defence of Thermopylæ is spoken of as the noblest of all. Now. what do we come to? Not twelve month's ago a savage horde gathered on the borders of this beautiful country and threatened to overrun it, but there stood at Rorke's Drift a small but intrepid band of men who fought and died, but held their ground against this savage foe. and the country was saved, and long as history is read and written the deeds of those noble few will live and be acclaimed. It may be that 2,000 years hence this fair land will be covered with fertile productions and rich cities and towns, and be filled with appliances, arts, and industries hitherto undreamed of, but if that should be so, depend upon it the men of that day would still speak with pride and boasting of the glorious defence of Rorke's Drift, and the heroic men who took part in it. One of them is among you now - Step to the front, Corporal Attwood. The order conveying Her Majesty's pleasure was then read:- "I have it from an eyewitness," said the A.C.G., "that he was conspicuous for the cool and intrepid manner in which he performed his duty. It is now my pleasing duty, Corporal Attwood, to fasten on your breast the highest decoration that a soldier can win, and I wish you long life, and happiness to wear it, and I am proud of you as belonging to the Army Service Corps."

Corporal Attwood then resumed his place, and the officer continued to say he hoped that all present would look upon their comrade not with envy, but with emulation, and that whenever any of us are called upon to act under the same incentives, we should not forget his example. I think, continued the gallant officer, we may venture on this occasion to show our admiration of our comrade's conduct by giving three cheers for Corporal Attwood and the gallant defenders of Rorke's Drift.

The parade then terminated, and Nos 3 and 4 Companies of the Army Service Corps marched off the ground on their way to Durban, where they are to give in their equipment. The horses of the corps, which are in excellent condition, will then return to be sold in the City on the 6th of December.

1566 Colour Sergeant George William Mabin, 'Staff of the Army'

"The Cape Times," Thursday, January 22nd, 1914

"Lest We Forget"
Anniversary of Rorke's Drift.
A Survivor's Story
How the Defenders Triumphed.

As the 22nd of January comes round, the number of gallant men who took part in the defence of Rorke's Drift and stemmed the tide of invasion which threatened to overwhelm the colony of Natal grows smaller and smaller.

One of them - Mr. G.W. Mabin, of Woodstock - probably the only one remaining in South Africa - was interviewed yesterday by a representative of this journal. Mr. Mabin was at the time of the affair staff-sergeant on General Chelmsford's staff. He accompanied Col. Glynn's column on the invasion of Zululand, and in his capacity as staff clerk found himself at Rorke's Drift on the occasion of that memorable impi attack, which the men of the 24th Regiment, now known as the South Wales Borderers, so gloriously frustrated.

Lord Chelmsford had formed a station at Rorke's Drift, on the Buffalo River, which formed the centre of communication between his base at Helpmakaar and his advance force in Zululand. The post was under the command of Major Spalding, to whom Staff-Sergeant Mabin was appointed clerk.

Lord Chelmsford, with his advance column, consisting of the Second Battalion of the 24th Regiment, Lonsdale's Light Horse, and a battery of artillery, were in Zululand. The post at Rorke's Drift was held by one company of the 24th Regiment, under the command of Lieut. Bromhead. Rorke's Drift was also used as a hospital base for the advance column, and at the time there were a number of patients in charge of the Medical Corps. It will be remembered that the advance column had reached Isandhlwana, twelve miles from Rorke's Drift, and on the morning of the 22nd of January, 1879, the greater portion of this column was out on reconnaissance, under the personal supervision of Lord Chelmsford.

An Eventful Day

During their absence a large Zulu impi, said to number nearly 20,000, attacked the camp at Isandhlwana, and after a severe fight overpowered the troops, resulting in almost a general massacre, only six escaping with their lives. A portion of the successful impi, numbering, it was computed, between 4,000 to 5,000, made their way to Rorke's Drift, where they arrived at about four o'clock in the afternoon. Prior to their arrival Lieut. Adendorff, of the Natal Native Contingent, who had escaped from Isandhlwana, reached the drift, and gave warning of the approach of the Zulus. "I was sitting at my office tent door," said Mr. Mabin, "Major Spalding had gone to Helpmakaar that morning with a view to arranging for reinforcements. At the station we did not expect any trouble. Just after three in the afternoon a man, hatless and bootless, rode up on an exhausted horse. He halted at the tent, and I immediately asked what had occurred. He exclaimed, 'Good God, the camp is taken, and they're coming on here.'"

Sergeant Mabin took the bearer of the news to Lieut. Bromhead, who at the time was in charge of the camp. The latter then brought in Lieut. Chard, R.E., who was superintending the working of the ponts on the river half a mile away. Steps were taken at once to put the camp in a state of defence. The windows and doors of the hospital were blocked up with mattresses and other things, loopholes made through the walls both of the hospital and store-house. A wall of mealie and other grain bags was made, enclosing the front of the hospital and running along the edge of the rocky terrace to the stone wall of the kraal. Three or four bullock wagons were utilised to stop gaps between the existing buildings and the barricade of biscuit boxes. Ammunition was then served out.

A Forlorn Hope

"We had scarcely finished our preparations," went on Mr. Mabin, "when the approaching Zulus were observed coming round the spur of the Oscarberg Mountains. There were 86 of us bearing arms, and we were prepared to sell our lives as dearly as possible."

The enemy were now upon them, and were pouring over the right shoulder of the hill in a dense mass, and making straight for the connecting wall between the store-house and the hospital. But when they got within fifty yards the firing was altogether too hot for them. Some half of them swerved round to the left, and passed the back and right end of the hospital, and then made a desperate attempt to scale the barricade in front of that building. But here too they were repulsed. They dispersed to find cover amongst the bushes and the stone wall below the terrace. The others found shelter amongst the numerous banks, ditches and bushes and poured a continuous fire on the camp.

"The first man I ever killed in my life," said Mr. Mabin, "was a big Zulu, carrying an assegai and shield, and as he advanced he took cover behind anything that presented itself. He dropped behind a rock prior to making another rush, when I covered the rock with my rifle, and as he rose to come on again I pulled the trigger, and he leaped at least five feet into the air and dropped dead."

Mr. Mabin went on to say they afterwards found that the area of defence was too large to be adequately defended by the small force, and about half was discarded, and Lieut. Chard ordered the construction of a biscuit box re-entrenchment which, unfortunately left the hospital outside the line of defence. But there was nothing else for it if the station was to be saved. Attack after attack was repulsed by the gallant defenders.

Lighted Tufts Of Grass

"About seven in the evening," went on the narrator, "the Zulus attempted to fire the hospital, lighting tufts of grass and attaching them to their assegais and throwing them on to the thickly-thatched roof of the building, which was soon afire. The flames , as a matter of fact, aided us, because by their light we were able to distinguish the Zulus as they formed into bodies for succeeding rushes."

While the building was in flames many gallant acts were performed in saving and attempting to save patients, the greater part of whom were borne to a place of comparative safety.

The attacks of the Zulus were continuous. Hardly had the defenders repulsed one, than another body would move forward and fling itself on the stockade, and on one or two occasions the gallant body of defenders were almost overwhelmed. The Zulus forced themselves fearlessly up to the points of the bayonets, where they met their fate by bayonet thrust or ball. But the stream of savages was never quite sufficient to swamp the camp, and between nine and ten in the evening their rushes became fewer. At intervals of about twenty minutes, however, fierce assaults on the stockade were kept up.

Then one of the chief buildings, once used for mission work, became the centre of the attack, but the assaults were successfully repelled by the handful of defenders by a steady fire through the loopholes which were constructed earlier in the day. Then attempts were made to set fire to the building, and one of the Zulus, more daring than his fellows, rushed with a lighted assegai, and getting in between the loopholes, reached up and attempted to fire the eaves of the thatched roof. Corporal Attwood, of the Army Service Corps, pushed his carbine through a loophole, and fired downwards on the off chance of getting his man. And so it proved, for on the following morning the Zulu who had made the attempt was found immediately under the wall with his head split open by the bullet.

An Anxious Night

"Probably upon his this incident," said Mr. Mabin, "hung the preservation of the camp." Desultory firing was kept up during the whole of the night, and in the early dawn the enemy was seen to be assembling some six hundred yards away, and this was judged as to be the preparations for the final onslaught. By this time their ammunition was running short, and it was found that only a further 13 rounds per rifle remained.

"Just about this time I was on look-out," said Mr. Mabin, "and discovered a movement on the Zululand side of the river. Owing to the light I could not determine what was happening - whether they were friends or enemies approaching. But on the next ten minutes I found they were mounted men, and to our intense joy it proved to be the General at the head of the remained of the column, and their approach was the signal for the full flight of the Zulus."

The defenders lost 15 killed, two mortally wounded, and 10 others less seriously hurt. No fewer than 386 of the Zulus were buried in a donga, while many bodies were found day by day in isolated spots. He believed that the besiegers lost quite 500 men.

Mr. Mabin, who was sixty-five last birthday, looks hale and hearty, and certainly belies the number of his years. For his share in the defence of the river post Lord Wolseley promoted him to the warrant rank. After going back to Pietermaritzburg, the trouble with Joubert's Boers developed, and as chief clerk he accompanied Sir George Colley to fields destined to be less glorious that Rorke's Drift, but almost as noteworthy. At Laing's Nek and Ingogo he fought, and one night the ill-prepared force, with seventy rounds and three days' rations. marched to Majuba Hill, and scrambling up the crags got into position, where the Boers found them at dawn. The Boers' Council of War decided to attack, and they advanced up the hill fairly well covered. When the ammunition of the British was expended they had only stones to fight with, and they (the Boers) got possession of the crest. Mr. Mabin was near Colley when the latter fell, shot through the head. Amongst the many medals which

Mr. Mabin holds is the gold medal presented on the occasion of the Diamond Jubilee, and this was presented to him for the longest and most meritorious service in South Africa.

An unidentified South African newspaper, possibly "The Natal Mercury," January 22nd, 1937

'The Fighting Clerk,' as ex Sergeant-Major Superintending Clerk G.W. Mabin was called in the '80's, is living with his daughter at 20 William Street, Woodstock, Capetown.

Big, heavy-jowled clear-eyed, with a moustache which droops at the corners of his mouth, he still has the bearing of a soldier of the line.

His voice retains the resonant power of that of the sergeant-major of the parade ground. His hearing is good. He walks about, he sees, and he remembers...

In an interview with 'The Natal Mercury' he recalled that late afternoon nearly 60 years ago at Rorke's Drift. He was a colour-sergeant then, in the 24th Regiment. He had accompanied colonel Glyn's central column at the invasion of Zululand.

Well he remembers the impi's attack, and the desperate 12-hour battle 104 British soldiers had with 4,000 Zulu warriors. Six times during that night the Zulus got within the entrenchment of the little river-side hospital base camp. Each time they were driven back at bayonet point.

And at dawn Colour-Sergeant Mabin and 86 other weary, dirty, blood-bespattered men gazed at the shambles about them.

Seventeen of the garrison had been killed. Ten had been wounded. And all about them lay the half-naked, war-plumed bodies of 350 of the warriors of Dubulamanzi, Cetewayo's brother.

The rest had fled. And Natal had been saved from invasion...

...One of his most cherished souvenirs of the Battle of Rorke's Drift is a copy of a Natal newspaper published shortly after the battle. It contains a full account of it, running into several columns. And it also has the names of all the soldiers who were there.

"You see, son," he said, "there's a lot of people who say they were at Rorke's Drift during the Zulu War. They probably were - months after the battle. But all our names are here...."

"The Cape Argus," Monday, October 24th, 1938

Rorke's Drift Veteran
"Old Dad" Mabin Dies Aged 90
Took Part In Many Battles

"Fighting Clerk" (ex-Sergeant-Major G.W.) Mabin, the last known survivor of the 124 of the defence of Rorke's Drift 59 years ago, died at his home at 20, William-street, Woodstock, in the early hours of yesterday morning. Ailing since August, he reached on October 3 the 90th birthday which he had set his heart on living to celebrate, with the good wishes of his 45 descendants and host of military friends, to whom he was also affectionately known as "Old Dad" Mabin.

Born in Bristol in 1848 Mr. Mabin enlisted in the British Army in 1868, and took part in many historic battles before he retired after 30 years of service. Although it was for his part in the battle of Rorke's Drift that he was most celebrated, it was in the 1881 Boer War that he won the soubriquet of "The Fighting Clerk."

Beside Colley

At the battle of Majuba he was standing only a few feet away from General Colley when that leader fell with a bullet through his forehead.

"Old Dad" Mabin retired from the army in 1898. The later years of his life he spent with a daughter in Woodstock. Active until a few months ago he spent his time between his garden and the Castle and other meeting places of military folk, among whom, regardless of rank, he was held in the greatest affection.

Until his death he remained in full possession of a remarkable memory. He was able to give a most graphic description of how, at dawn on January 23, 1879, 124 grimed and bleeding men stood surveying the shambles around them and the ruin of the little riverside hospital base at Rorke's Drift, which, for 12 hours, they had defended against the repeated onslaughts of 3,000 picked Zulu warriors.

Dubulumanzi's Impi

Among them lay the bodies of nearly 400 black warriors, belonging to the impi of Dubulumanzi, Cetewayo's brother, who had led the attack on Rorke's Drift after 800 British soldiers had been wiped out at Isandhlwana. Among the biscuit tins and mealie sacks of which the Rorke's Drift laager was hurriedly improvised lay the bodies of 17 men who had fallen in the battle which saved Natal from massacre at the hands of Cetewayo's hordes.

Rorke's Drift was a small depot of provisions established with a hospital base on the banks of the Buffalo River to keep the line of communication with Natal open. It was left in charge of two young officers, Lieutenants Chard and Bromhead with 141 men.

The post was attacked by one of the Zulu king's "crack" impis a few hours after 800 men left by Lord Chelmsford at Isandhlwana (the hill of "The Little Hand") had been wiped out.

In that memorable battle "Old Dad" Mabin, who fought also through the thick of Ingogo, Majuba and Laing's Nek, got off with only a slight wound in the shin, caused by a spent bullet.

Sunset Parade

At 6 p.m. to-morrow a "Sunset Parade" will be held in memory of "Old Dad" Mabin by the Moths organisation of which he was a life member.

2260 Sergeant Frederick Augustus Millne, 2nd/3rd Foot

"The Manchester Evening Chronicle," Saturday, December 2nd, 1905

A Life's Adventures
Story of Rorke's Drift Hero,
Who Drew A Cheque for Forty Thousand Dollars

On an eventful morning in January, 1879, the remains of a British column moved down from Isandhlwana to Rorke's Drift. The Isandhlwana camp had been, in the forcible language of the Zulus 'eaten up,' and the savage warriors, primed with victory, made straight for the guard of white men on the Buffalo River. No one in the ranks of what proved to be the relieving force expected to find a living soul at Rorke's Drift, for the Zulus were seen retreating from the place, and volumes of smoke were rising from the hospital.

But the Union Jack was still flying, and a British cheer rang out as Colonel Russell and his men galloped into the beleaguered encampment at the Drift. One of the men who kept the flag flying is in Manchester today, and chatted recently to an 'E.C.' representative of his experiences on that memorable occasion.

WAR AND FORTUNE

Ex-Colour Sergeant Fred. A. Millne, who is now caretaker of Princess Road Higher Grade School, has seen not only the fortune of war but also the "war of fortune". One day, when out in the Far East, some Shanghai policemen rushed up to him excitedly with the story that he had drawn the winning number in a lottery, and was worth forty thousand of dollars. It was true. The sergeant is also one of the few men who have seen reports of their own deaths in print. Further he has been shipwrecked. So to the tale.

As a lad of eighteen he joined the 2nd Battalion of the Buffs in 1872 at Dover. He went to Ireland with his Regiment, and later gained the certificate as an instructor in field works at Chatham. Proceeding to South Africa in 1879 he was wrecked in the

St. Lawrence on Paternoster reefs. Everybody on board was saved, and the regiment was stationed then Durban, and then at Pietermaritzburg.

When hostilities became likely with the Zulus, the sergeant was sent with the pontoon stores and equipment of the 3rd column which was to enter Zululand by Rorke's Drift. Arriving there about a week in advance of any other soldier, he accomplished his work, and on the 12th of January, the troops had passed over, and pitched their camps at Isandhlwana.

NEWS OF DISASTER

Firing was heard in Rorke's Drift camp on the morning of the 22nd, and about eleven o'clock a party of native women and children with a few decrepit old men, came to the river bank and wanted to be put across, as 'Cetewayo had killed all the white men.' A transport rider soon after galloped into camp with news of the Isandhlwana disaster. Under the superintendence of Lieutenants Chard and Bromhead, a breastwork of sacks of Indian corn was raised between the hospital and the stone kraals. Wagons were pulled in on the others side. The Natal Native Contingent and some Basutos left foe safety.

"While this was going on," said the sergeant, "Daniels and I were getting things in order on our pontoons. We wanted to moor in mid stream and, if need be hold them back." Behind the modest statement lurks the heroic. A leading authority of the time interpreted the incident thus - "The pont guards Daniels and Sergeant Millne of the 3rd Buffs, with five or six men, volunteered to moor the ponts in midstream and keep the ford against the whole Zulu vanguard. They volunteered for a more than forlorn hope, for there was not a chance that one of them would survive the encounter. Lieutenant Chard did not accept that offer. He had other uses for such soldiers."

ZULUS' ASSAULTS

"We joined the remainder of the force", continued the sole representative of the Buffs, "and the firing was pretty heavy as we scrambled over into the enclosure. Just after we got into the laager the enemy advanced in force. Silently they came, taking advantage of every bit of cover that presented itself. Their men dropped fast under our fire. A stalwart Induna yelled out an order. It was his last. On came the mass with a rush, shouting 'Usutu, Usutu.'

They hurled themselves on our feeble defences, to be repulsed by our concentrated fire and by bayonets. Again and again they came on. Assegais clashed against rifle barrels. They shouted their war cries and we gave British cheers. At first I felt nervous, but the savage instinct, the blood thirst came on top. So close was the conflict that one soldier felled two Zulus with his fists."

VICTORIA CROSS WON

"All the afternoon the fight waged, and in the evening the hospital was fired by the Zulus fixing burning bunches of grass on their spear ends aiming at the thatch. Six times did the Zulus try to rush the place and in my opinion they would have wiped us out had they not provided the light which enabled us to perceive their movements. A desultory fire was kept up till dawn."

Next morning the little garrison saw more natives advancing and thought they were to have another day's fighting. But Russell's mounted men were also observed coming from the same direction and the Undi fell back.

Sergt. Millne served afterwards three years with his regiment in Singapore, and took his discharge in Hong Kong in 1883, being appointed instructor to the Shanghai municipal police force. When his engagement was nearly completed he drew half of the winning ticket in a Manila lottery, getting for his six dollars £8,000. "Had I put it in the bank" he said, "I should not be in Manchester now."

HOME WITH HIS FORTUNE

He came home to England and started a big grocery business with a partner.

"It's like this" qouth the ex soldier, "You've read Mark Twain. In the first instance I have the money and you have the experience; in the second I have the experience."

Married life, however, toned down his disappointment. He was afterwards assistant labour master at Crumpsall Workhouse, and in 1895 took up his present duties.

It was in the regimental paper of the Buffs in August 1890, that Sergeant Millne was reported as having died on his way home to enjoy his fortune.

Sergeant Millne has a little daughter born on the anniversary of Rorke's Drift. She was christened Ada Rorke. The sergeant figures in the Sixth Standard readers in use at Princess road, and with such a history is it any wonder that his name is underlined or that the boys occasionally gather round him in admiration and say, "Oh Mr. Millne we've been reading about you."

The Reverend George Smith, Vicar of Estcourt, Natal

"The Natal Mercury," April 7th, 1879

The Defence of Rorke's Drift
January 22nd 1879
(By an Eye-Witness)

Descending the steep and circuitous road from Helpmakaar, the valley of the Buffalo River, at and above its junction with the Blood River, is comparatively open; whilst below, on the right, just at Rorke's Drift, a spur of the Biggarsberg shuts it in completely. Upon an elevated terrace of rock (which forms a sort of pedestal for the terminating hill of the range) stood a neat homestead, about three-quarters of a mile from the drift.

The buildings were erected by a former border agent named Rorke, and, together with the farm, were recently purchased by the Rev. Otto Witt, on behalf of the Swedish Church, for the purpose of establishing a Zulu Mission; and the fine hill at the back was named Oscarsberg, in honor of the King of Sweden.

The house stood within a few feet of the edge of the rocky terrace, overlooking a well-enclosed garden of two or three acres in extent, planted with standard grape vines, and many fine orange, apricot, apple, peach, quince, fig, pomegranate, and other fruit trees. There was a road running parallel with the front of the house, between the garden and the terrace, with a strong stone wall along the terrace side; whilst the sloping ground between the walk and the summit of the terrace was occupied by a grove of fine Cape poplars, some large gum trees, and a luxuriant growth of bushes and shrubs of various kinds.

The dwelling-house standing as above described was over eighty feet in length, the side wall on the left running back nearly 60 feet.

Forty paces to the left, but with its frontage line of 80 feet running parallel with the extreme back wall of the dwelling-house, was another block of buildings, consisting of large store-rooms, wagon-house, stable, &c. These buildings extended back 52 feet. Almost parallel with the extreme left wall of this block of buildings, with only a space of ten or twelve feet, intervening, a stone wall extended to the edge of the ledge of rocks, forming the right wall of a kraal some 50 feet square, which was divided in half by another similar and parallel wall.

Passing out of the semi-enclosure to the left, between the store-house and the kraal, one saw the neat double row of tents occupied by B Company, 2-24th Regt., under the command of Lieut. Bromhead; whilst all along at the back, and running parallel with the buildings, juts out another and very precipitous rocky ledge, some 30 or 40 feet high, full of caves, thoroughly overlooking, and within 350 yards of the premises.

The dwelling-house had been fitted up by the medical authorities as a base hospital for the column, and nearly all the rooms, as well as the large verandah in front, which had been carefully screened with blankets, were occupied by patients - 36 in number, including some who bad been wounded at the taking of Sirayo's kraals, on Jan. 12th. The large store-house was occupied by the Commissariat department, and was full of provisions of all kinds.

On Wednesday afternoon, January 22nd, after the slaughter at the camp at Isandhlwana, three companies (or regiments) of Zulus were formed upon the neck of land above the late camp, and marched towards Rorke's Drift; each company appeared to be from 1,000 to 1,500 strong. No. 1 company (we will call it) marched on in advance in open order, and drove every mealie garden, firing heavily all the while, killing many Europeans and natives who were trying to escape from Isandhlwana. They crossed the Buffalo River about four miles below Rorke's Drift, just below where the river makes a bend, almost at right angles, between precipitous rocky sides, firing repeatedly into every cave, bush, and crevice that might have afforded shelter for refugees. Being satisfied with the result, so far, they came on to a small green hill, sat down, and took snuff all round.

Companies 2 and 3 then followed the example of No. 1, keeping some distance apart; They also advanced in open order - after going through various exercises, dividing off (apparently) into hundreds, then into tens, wheeling and quickly reforming; they crossed the river just above the bend, repeatedly firing amongst the bushes and rocks on both sides. They remained a long time in the river, forming a line across it, either for bathing or to assist one another in fording the stream.

By the time they had gained the rising ground upon this side, and had sat down to take snuff, up started 10 men of No. 1, and ran on in advance up the valley, which lies between the high ground at Helpmakaar and the hills at the back of Rorke's Drift.

In the meantime another party of Zulus, who must have crossed the river some miles lower down, had set a European house and a kafir kraal on fire, about four or five miles away at the back of Rorke's Drift.

No. 1 Company followed their advanced guard at an easy pace. No.2 Company started off, bearing away to their left, apparently to join and support No. 1.

No. 3 company started off two men straight for Rorke's Drift, who ran as hard as they could, followed by ten others who took it more easily; and then came on the rest, headed and led by two very corpulent chiefs on horseback.

Whilst these Zulu warriors, reeking with British blood, are pressing on "like a steady rain," to plunder the Government stores, and (incidentally, of course) "wipe out" the handful of men that may attempt to defend them; let us see what preparations for defence have been made by the little band, if only they have been warned in time.

About three p.m. or shortly after, several mounted men arrived from the camp at Isandhlwana, and reported the terrible disaster which had occurred.

Lieut. Bromhead, commanding the company (B) of 2-24th Regt., at once struck his camp, sent down for Lieut. Chard, R.E. (who was engaged with some half-a-dozen men at the ponts on the river), to come up and direct the preparations for defence, as in the absence of Major Spalding the command of the post devolved upon him.

The windows and doors of the hospital were blocked up with mattresses, &c., loopholes made through the walls, both of the hospital and store-house. A wall of mealie and other grain bags was made, enclosing the front of the hospital, and running along the edge of the rocky terrace to the stone wall of the kraal, which has been described as coming from the far end of the store-house at right angles to the front of that building, down to the edge of these rocks. Other mounted men arrived from the late camp, and told of the horrors they had escaped, and the dangers that were about to overwhelm us. Doubtless the poor fellows had seen terrors enough for one day, and were possessed by an earnest desire to warn the people at Helpmakaar in time, and so, like many before, and several after, on they galloped to carry out their laudable intention.

A praiseworthy effort was made to remove the worst cases in hospital to a place of safety; two wagons were brought up, after some delay, and the patients were being brought out, when it was found that the Zulus were so close upon us that any attempt to take them away in ox wagons would only result in their falling into the enemies' hands. So the two wagons were at once utilised and made to form part of the defensive wall connecting the right hand front corner of the store-house with the left hand back corner of the hospital - about 40 paces long; sacks of mealies forming the remainder, and being also used as barricades underneath and upon the wagons. A barricade, filling up the small space between the left front corner of the store-house and the stone wall of the kraal !before referred to, and the blocking up of the gates of the kraal itself made the outer defensive work complete. The men worked with a will, and were much encouraged by the unremitting exertions of both the military officers, the medical officer, and Assistant-Commissary Dalton, all of whom not merely directed but engaged most energetically in the construction of the barricades. The water cart in the meantime had been hastily filled and brought within the enclosure.

The pontman Daniells and Sergt. Milne, 3rd Buffs, offered to moor the ponts in the middle of the stream and defend them from their decks with a few men. But our defensive force was too small for any to be spared, and these men subsequently did good service within the fort.

About 100 men of Durnford's Horse, who came in from the camp, had been drawn up for an hour or so, up on some rising ground, half a mile off. As soon as firing was heard, they rode off in a body to Helpmakaar, and then the noble body of some 350 loyal natives, who had been left specially to protect this post, and had consumed one or two oxen daily, at the expense of a paternal Government, and had got fat in the process, were seen hurrying away like a flock of sheep to the summit of a distant hill. The anxiety which had been displayed fur the safety of Helpmakaar, Fort Pine, Dundee, and other distant places, had considerably lessened the number of those whose help had naturally been calculated upon for the defence of the place. Seeing this, Lieut. Chard had a retrenchment of a double row of biscuit boxes placed from the right hand front corner of the storehouse, straight down, and at right angles to the barricade, running along the ledge of rocks in front, thus dividing our whole enclosure (roughly speaking) in half.

Between this retrenchment and the kraal wall on the left, were two large pyramids of sacks of mealies and oats standing side by side.

About 4.30 p.m., the Zulus came in sight, coming round the right hand end of the large hill in our rear; only about 20 at first appeared, advancing in open order. Their numbers were speedily augmented and their line extended quite across the neck of land from hill to hill. A great number of "dongas," on their line of approach, a stream with steep banks, the garden with all its trees and surroundings, gave them great facilities for getting near us unseen. The garden must have soon been occupied, for one unfortunate Contingent corporal, whose heart must have failed him when he saw the enemy and heard the firing, got over the parapet and tried to make his escape on foot, but a bullet from the garden struck him, and he fell dead within 150 yards of our front wall. An officer of the same corps who had charge of the 350 natives before referred to, was more fortunate, for being mounted, he made good his escape, and "lives to fight another day." But the enemy are upon us now, and are pouring over the right shoulder of the hill in a dense mass, and on they come, making straight for the connecting wall between the store-house and the hospital; but when they get within fifty yards, the firing is altogether too hot for them. Some half of them swerve round to their left, past the back and right end of the hospital, and then make a desperate attempt to scale the barricade in front of that building but here too, they are repulsed, and they disperse, and find cover amongst the bushes and behind the stone wall below the terrace, The others have found shelter amongst numerous banks, ditches, and bushes, and behind a square kafir house and large brick ovens, all at the rear of our enclosure. One of the mounted Chiefs was shot by Private Dunbar, 2-24th, who also killed eight of the enemy, in as many consecutive shots, as they came round a ledge of the hill; and as fresh bodies of Zulus arrive they take possession of the elevated ledge of rocks overlooking our buildings and barricades at the back, and all the caves and crevices are quickly filled, and from these the enemy pour down a continuous fire upon us.

A whisper passes round amongst the men - "poor old King Cole is killed." He was at the front wall, a bullet passed through his head, and then struck the next man upon the bridge of the nose, but the latter was not seriously hurt. Mr. Dalton who is a tall man, was continually going along the barricades, fearlessly exposing himself, and cheering the men, and using his own rifle most effectively. A Zulu ran up near the barricade; Mr. Dalton called out "pot that fellow," and himself aimed *over* the parapet at another, when his rifle dropped, he turned round quite pale, and said that he had been shot. The doctor was by his side at once, and found that a bullet had passed quite through, above the right shoulder. Unable any longer to use his rifle (although he did not cease to direct the fire of the men who were near him), he handed it to Mr. Byrne, who used it well.

Presently, Corporal C. Scammell, N.N.C., who was near Mr. Byrne, was shot through the shoulder and back; he crawled a short distance and handed the remainder of his cartridges to Lieut. Chard, and then expressed his desire for a drink of water; Byrne at once fetched it for him, and whilst giving it him to drink, poor Byrne was shot through the head, and fell dead instantly.

The garden and the road - having the stone wall and thick belt of bush as a screen from the fire of our front defences - were now occupied by a large force of the enemy; they rushed up to the front barricade and soon occupied one side whilst we held the other; they seized hold of the bayonets of our men, and in two instances succeeded in wrenching them off the rifles, but the bold perpetrators were instantly shot. One fellow fired at Corporal Scheiss of the N.N.C. (a Swiss by birth, who was a hospital patient), the charge blowing his hat off; he instantly jumped upon the parapet and bayoneted the man, regained his place and shot another, and then repeating his former exploit, climbed up the sacks and bayoneted a third; a bullet struck him in the instep early in the fight, but he would not allow that his wound was a sufficient reason for leaving his post, yet he has suffered most acutely from it since. Our men at the front wall had the enemy hand to hand, and besides, were being fired upon very heavily from the rocks and cans above us in our rear. Five of our men were here shot dead in a very short space of time; so by six p.m., the order was given for them to retire to our retrenchment of biscuit boxes, from which such a heavy fire was sent along the front of the hospital, that although scores of Zulus jumped over the mealie bags to get into the building, nearly every man perished in that fatal leap; but they rushed to their death like demons, yelling out their war-cry of "Usutu," "Usutu." Shortly after, they succeeded in setting the roof of the hospital on fire, at its further end. As long as we held the front wall, the Zulus failed in their repeated attempts to get into the far end room of the hospital; Lieut. Bromhead, several times, having driven them back with a bayonet charge. When we had retired to the retrenchment, and the hospital had been set on fire, a terrible struggle awaited the brave fellows who were defending it from within. Private Joseph Williams fired from a small window at the far end of the hospital. Next morning fourteen warriors were found dead beneath it, besides others along his line of fire. When their ammunition was expended, he and his companions kept the door with their bayonets, but an entrance was subsequently forced, and he, poor fellow, was seized by the hands, dragged out, and killed before their eyes. His surviving companions were Private John Williams, No. 1395, and two patients. Whilst the Zulus were dragging forth our men's late brave comrade, the latter succeeded in making a hole in the partition with an axe, and got into another room, where they were joined by Private Henry Hook, and he and Williams, turn about, one keeping off the enemy, the other working, succeeded in cutting holes into the next adjoining rooms. One poor fellow, Jenkins, venturing through one of these, was also seized and dragged away, the others escaped through the window looking into the enclosure towards the storehouse, and running the gauntlet of the enemy's fire, most of them got safely within the entrenchment.

Trooper Hunter of N.M.P., a very tall young man, who was a patient in the hospital, was not so fortunate, but fell before he could reach the goal. In another ward Privates 593, Wm. Jones, and 716 Robt. Jones, defended their post until six out of the seven patients in it had been safely removed. The seventh was Sergt. Maxfield, who was ill with fever, and delirious. Private R. Jones went back to try and carry him out, but the room was full of Zulus. and the poor fellow was dead. The native of Umkungu's tribe who had been shot through the thigh at Sirayo's kraal, was lying unable to move; he said that he "was not afraid of the Zulus, but wanted a gun," When the end room in which he lay was forced, Private Hook heard the Zulus talking with him; next day his charred remains were found amongst the ruins.

Corporal Mayer, N.N.C., who had been wounded under the knee with an assegaied, at Sirayo's kraal, Bombardier Lewis, R.A., whose leg and thigh were much swollen from a wagon accident, and Trooper R. S. Green, N.M.P., also a patient, all got out of the little end window within the enclosure. The window being high up, and the Zulus already within the room behind them, each man had a fall in escaping, and had then to crawl (for none of them could walk) through the enemy's fire, inside the retrenchment. Whilst doing this, Green was struck in the thigh with a spent bullet.

Some few escaped from the front of the hospital, and ran round to the right to the retrenchment, but two or three were assegaied as they attempted it.

Gunner Howard, R.A., ran out of the hospital, and managed to hide himself in the long grass, on the upper side of the stone wall below our front parapet. He covered himself as well as he could with twigs and grass, and there, in company with a dead pig, and four of our horses (which had been shot where they were tied up), he lay unobserved all night, and came in unharmed at daylight. Another, Private Waters, 1-24th, secreted himself in a cupboard in the hospital, and killed many Zulus who entered the room, he himself getting wounded in the arm. At last he put over him a black cloak, and ran out of the burning building amongst the bushes, in one of which he lay concealed and unharmed until morning, with hundreds of Zulus moving about during the night upon all sides of him.

Whilst the hospital was being thus gallantly defended, Lieutenant Chard and Assistant-Commissary Dunne, with two or three men, succeeded in converting the two large pyramids of sacks of mealie into an oblong and lofty redoubt, and, under heavy fire, blocking up the intervening space between the two with sacks from the top of each, leaving a hollow in the centre for the security of the wounded, and giving another admirable and elevated line of fire all round. About this time the men were obliged to fall back from the outer to the middle, and then to the inner wall of the kraal, forming our left defence.

The Zulus do not appear to have thrown their assegais at all, using them solely for stabbing purposes.

Corporal Allen and Private Hitch both behaved splendidly. They were badly wounded early in the evening, and incapacitated from firing themselves, but never ceased going round and serving out ammunition from the reserve to the fighting men.

The light from the burning hospital was of the greatest service to our men, lighting up the scene for hundreds of yards around; but before ten p.m. it had burned itself out. The rushes and heavy firing of the enemy did not slacken until past midnight, and from that time until daylight, a desultory fire was kept up by them, from the caves above us in our rear, and from the bush and garden in front.

At last daylight dawned, and the enemy retired round the shoulder of the hill by which they had approached. Whilst some remained at their posts, others of our men were sent out to patrol, and returned with about 100 rifles and guns, and some 400 assegais, left by the enemy up on the field; and round our walls, and especially in front of the hospital, the dead Zulus lay piled up in heaps. About 350 were subsequently buried by us. They must have carried off nearly all their wounded with them.

Our loss was 15 killed, two mortally wounded, and 10 others less seriously wounded; but we were not to be left alone, for between 7 a.m. and 8 a.m. the enemy re-appeared in great force, in the same direction as before, when, fortunately, the General, with the remainder of the column, was seen coming in the opposite direction, and, crossing the Buffalo, came straight to our relief, and the Zulus made off as they approached.

Whilst all behaved so gallantly, it was hardly possible to notice other exceptional instances, although all their comrades bore testimony to such in the conduct of Colour-Sergeant Bourne, 2-24th, Sergeant Williams, 2-24th (wounded dangerously - since dead), Sergeant Windridge, 2-:24th, and Privates McMahon, A.H.C., and Roy, 1-24th.

It was certainly of the utmost strategical importance that this place should not be taken. Perhaps the safety of the remainder of the column, and of this part of the colony, depended on it.

The determined and successful resistance which by God's help the brave fellows were able to make, seems to have surprised the enemy, who have not shown themselves near the place since.

Whatever signs of approval may be conferred upon the defenders of Rorke's Drift from high quarters, they will never cease to remember the kind and heartfelt expressions of gratitude which have fallen both from the columns of the colonial press and so many of the Natal colonists themselves.

A letter written by the Reverend Smith with regard to the death of Corporal W. Anderson, N.N.C.: [NAB ref 3012/1879, Kwa-Zulu Natal Archives, Pietermaritzburg]

W. Anderson was killed just outside the laager at Rorkes Drift, at the commencement of the Zulu attack on Jany. 22nd.

I buried him on Jany. 23rd & was told, concerning him, that he was a Corporal in the Natal Native Contingent, who had been left in Hospital; that he had been engaged in working the surf-boats at East London & had been also a performer on the wire slack rope.

He was shot through the head, by the natives who had gained possession of the garden on our front, his body was otherwise untouched.

Geo. Smith
Chaplain
2nd Division

Head Quarters
2nd Division
Upoko Valley
July 16/79

"The Times," c. 1879

Our Chaplains In The Zulu War
(United Service Gazette)

The duties of an army chaplain during war, though arduous, rarely involve the personal risks which combatants are exposed. But in the late Zulu war this was far from being the case. There our forces moved through the enemy's country, liable to attack at any moment.

The lines of communication along which, in civilised warfare, non-combatants can move in absolute safety, were as dangerous to the latter as the most advanced posts are, as a matter of course, to the fighting branches.

The Zulus knew not of, nor did they make, any distinction between combatants and non-combatants. To them every white man was a foe. Even in the day of battle the peculiarity of the situation , the fact that we were numerically inferior, and could not move with the rapidity of the Zulus, necessitated our acting always on the defensive. Thus every action reduced itself to a white island, against which an angry sea of black men beat themselves in vain; and within that island all alike were exposed to the hostile fire. This was a war in which there were no non-combatants, for all fought with their lives in their hands. Our chaplains have never been backward in fulfilling their calling, and in the late Zulu war they have certainly maintained their old reputation.

Amongst the gallant defenders of Rorke's Drift, the Rev. G. Smith, who afterwards acted as chaplain to the 2nd division, was as conspicuous for his cool conduct as anyone of the garrison...

"The Times," c. March 1879

The Zulu War
To The Editor Of The Times

Sir,

It is meet that among the names of the brave men who saved Natal at Rorke's Drift the name of a non. combatant should not escape notice.

The Rev. George Smith, aware of the approach of the enemy, when there was yet time to fly, preferred to remain where death was before him. Through the night of the attack he lent his gallant help to our soldiers; and yet again he held his life of small account when, as one of Major Black's little band, he volunteered to search for the bodies of Lieutenants Melvill and Coghill, that they might receive, as they did receive Christian burial at his hands.

Surely the State will not permit this hero to go without reward.

I write on behalf of an old comrade.

Yours faithfully,

S.B. Tristram

Union Club, March 24

"The Preston Guardian," November 30th, 1918

Hero of Rorke's Drift
Death of Rev. Geo. Smith, of Fulwood

The death took place yesterday morning, at his residence in Fulwood, of the Rev. George Smith, one of the heroes of Rorke's Drift, the historic siege in the Zulu campaign of 1878-79 immortalised by the painting of Lady Buller. The deceased, who originally went to South Africa as a missionary, and was ordained there by the Bishop of Maritzburg, had spent many years as a chaplain to the forces, and during later years, from 1899, with slight interruptions, he had been stationed at Fulwood Barracks. He retired about nine years ago, but continued to live at Fulwood, and with his patriarchal beard he was one of the most familiar and popular figures in the social and religious life of the town for a long period.

At the time the Zulu War broke out Mr. Smith was rector of Estcourt and St. John, Mooi River, Natal, of which he had been in charge six years, and he volunteered to act as chaplain to the troops, a step which led, on the advice of Archibald Forbes, the war correspondent, to him deciding later to devote himself to service in the army. He was one of the first to enter Ulundi during that campaign, and he participated in the ever-memorable defence of Rorke's Drift, the story of which has stirred the British heart through successive generations.

Afterwards he took part in the Nile Expedition and all the Egyptian campaigns from 1882 to 1887, including the battle of El Kebir, and subsequently was chaplain at Aldershot, Cork, Shorncliffe, Woolwich, Netley, Malta, and Preston. His period at Fulwood was twice broken, first when he went to Caterham between 1900 and 1901, and again when he undertook temporary duty at Harrismith, Orange River Colony, in 1903-4.

One of the incidents in his career during the Zulu war was at the burial of the Prince Imperial. In the absence of Father Bellord, the Roman Catholic padre, Mr. Smith conducted the first part of the ceremony, but before it was concluded Father Bellord appeared and carried out the commitment.

Mr. Smith, who was a native of Docking, Norfolk, and never married, had lost his two elder brothers within a short period of his death, and he himself had been in indifferent health for a few weeks. He was a member of the Junior Constitutional Club, in London, where he was well-known, and highly esteemed, and although he did not take a prominent part in events outside his duties he may be said to have been one of the most universally respected of all Army padres.

Trooper Henry Lugg, Natal Mounted Police

"The North Devon Herald," April 24th, 1879. His letter also appeared in "The Times," under the heading; "An Oktonian At Rorke's Drift."

I know you were surprised to hear from Fred that I had been at Rorke's Drift. I should have written you the same morning I wrote to Fred, but I could only find an old envelope and a small piece of paper and then only a piece of pencil to write with. I shall not profess to give you an exact account of the fight but will give you just the heads. It must have been about two forty p.m. when a carbineer rode into the little yard, without boots, tunic, or arms, and leading a spare horse. All we could glean from his excited remarks was, 'Everyone killed in camp, and 4,000 Kaffirs on their way to take the mission station,' (or rather hospital) - not pleasant tidings for a hundred men, you may be sure. When he came to himself a bit he said, 'You will all be murdered and cut to pieces,' and the only answer he received was, 'We will fight for it, and if we have to die we will die like Britishers.'

All those who were able began to throw up sacks and knock loopholes out with pickaxes, and otherwise make preparations to receive them. We had some 2,000 Native Contingent there on a mountain, and occupying the krantzes and caves. Noble savages! As soon as they heard the Zulus were to attack us they made a great noise, had a big dance, clashing their assegais against their shields, and otherwise showed their warlike spirit. Now I must describe the fort, It consisted of two small houses, one used as a store and the other as a hospital and mission station. These houses were about 40 yards apart, and our ramparts were composed of mealies three sacks high, and running from the corners of one house to the corners of the other, but the one great danger being thatched roofs to both. There were two missionaries (Swiss) living in the hospital. They were absent for some twenty minutes, out for a ride, and no one could help laughing at their gesticulations when they came back on seeing the best parlour paper being pulled down and loopholes being knocked out, while splendid furniture was scattered about the rooms. His first question was, in broken English, 'Vot is dish?' Someone replied that the Zulus were almost on us, upon which he bolted, saying, 'Mein Gott, mein wife and mein children at Umsinga! Oh, mein Gott!'

In the meantime a mounted infantryman and two of our men, Shannon and Doig, came in excited and breathless. Upon my asking, 'What is it, is it true?' Doig replied, 'You will all be murdered.' and rode off with his comrade. Consolatory, certainly, but nothing remains but to fight, and that we will do to the bitter end. A man named Hall, of Natal Mounted Police, *[Compiler's note: This is actually written as 'P.M.B.' in "The Times" version],* rode out to see if he could see anything of them, and on going about 1,000 yards out he could see them just a mile off, as he described it, 'as black as hell and as thick as grass.' 'Stay operations and fall in!' My carbine was broken, or rather the stock bent. I found a piece of rein, tied it up, and fell in with the soldiers. I thought if I can get somewhere to sit down and pop away I shall be all right, because my knees were much swollen. I was told off in my turn to take a loophole, and defend the roof from fire. At about three thirty they came on, first in sections of fours then opening out into skirmishing order. Up came their reserve, and then they were on us. The place seemed alive with them. No orders were given, every man to act as he thought proper. I had the satisfaction of seeing the first I fired at roll over at 350, and then my nerves were as steady as a rock. I made sure almost before I pulled the trigger. There was some of the best shooting at 450 yards that I have ever seen.

Just before dark we had beaten them off with great losses, and only a few casualties on our side, two killed and one wounded. One of our fellows named Hunter, also ill with rheumatism, was assegaied in the kidneys and five wounds in the chest. Before it got really dark the fiends lit the hospital thatch, which being very closely packed did not burn well. At about ten they came on tremendous force, sweeping the fellows before them and causing them to retreat to the store. But Providence favoured us. The thatch roof burst out flames, and made it as light as day, and before they had time to retreat we were pouring bullets into them like hail. We could see them falling in scores. Then you could hear suppressed British cheers. They kept up the attack all night with no better luck. We knocked them down as fast as they came. At five a.m., 23 January, the last shot was fired, and the last nigger killed; he had a torch tied on his assegai and was in the act of throwing it into the storehouse thatch, but he was 'sold'. The column came to our relief about five thirty and real British cheers went up, I can tell you. When the major saw me he said, 'I never thought of seeing you alive again, my boy.' The tears were standing in his eyes. He said, 'We saw the fire last night, and thought you were all murdered.' Thank God it is not so. I have sustained no damage beyond the loss of everything (except letters) and a little weakness of the eyes, I suppose from peering out of the loophole all night, and the constant straining of the eyesight.

Trooper Sidney Hunter, Natal Mounted Police

A letter written by his father to the Master Supreme Court, Pietermaritzburg: [NAB, MSCE 5/84 Kwa-Zulu Natal Archives, Pietermaritzburg]

Union Street
Barnet Herts
England
June 29th 1880

Sir,
I have received a letter from Sergt. Maclaren of the Natal M. P. to inform me that the Balance due to me in the Estate of my late son, Sidney Hunter.....
...my wife who is now on her Death Bed has never fully recovered from the shock of the sad news of his death...
Yours Respectfully

R. Hunter
Union Street
Barnet Herts
England

P.S. I am truly a great sufferer from that Cruel & uncalled for Zulu War

Robert John Hall, a civilian meat contractor attached to No. 3 Column

"The Natal Witness," c. January 1879

"...A private letter from one of the Carbineers gives the name of Robert J. Hall as amongst those he saw dead..."

"The Natal Witness," January 30th, 1879, page 3

...Since our last Mr. R.J. Hall. who was reported missing, has turned up all well...

Hall's own letter written in 1906, "Kingdom and Colony at War," by J. Laband & P Thompson, 1990: [KCM 42358, Killie Campbell Africana Library, Durban, Kwa-Zulu Natal]

To the Editor of the Natal Witness

Sir,
I notice in your issue of today an account of the defence of Rorke's drift, and wondered whether another account, written by one who was there, would be of interest to your readers. Lieut. Chard is mentioned in your article as having fortified

the place etc. but the man who really saved Rorke's Drift was Mr Dalton of the A.S.C.

When Mr Alfred Henderson and myself arrived at Rorke's Drift from Isnadhlwana about 1 or 2 p.m. on that fatal day, Mr Dalton asked us if we couldn't get the native contingent back to build a laager. These natives were emptied by the A.S.C. with their waggons etc. but had just bolted. We got on to our horses, fetched them back and stood over them while the laager was built under the direction of Mr Dalton. Chard and Bromhead were not there. The former was down by the river near the punt and the latter was smoking his pipe above the house. When the laager was completed, Mr Dalton asked Mr Henderson and myself if we go and reconnoitre over the hill, and we saddles up and went off At that time all the native contingent had again disappeared, also some natives Mr Henderson had brought with him, mounted boys from Edendale.

We went over the hill and as we were returning we saw some Zulus making a rush for Rorke's Drift House. I remarked, 'The Zulus are upon us,' and we galloped towards the house. My horse was the faster of the two, and I got to the house first above the fence, and as I passed within a few yards of the Zulus, the first shots were fired from the hospital and whizzed about my ears. Mr Henderson went round below the fence and we met outside the wall of the Commissariat shed and the cattle kraal. Here we took shelter and there we stayed and fired away at the Zulus as they came down the hill and squatted themselves in the garden under the peach trees and among the mealies.

I must now tell you that when the Zulus first attacked Rorke's Drift, there were not more than twenty five of them and they kept coming on in batches of twenty five to fifty and so they continued rolling up, until they set the hospital on fire. At this time Mr Henderson and I had exhausted all our ammunition and had to move further away to a thorn tree about 500 yards below the house. It was getting dusk, and as we saw no .chance of returning to the laager, as the whole place would soon be on fire, we decided to leave, and started to ride to Helpmakaar. On the way we fell in with a convoy taking ammunition to Rorke's Drift and quietly trekking along in complete ignorance of what had happened there. Mr Henderson stayed with them the night, and I went off after my cattle at Helpmakaar.

Now, I am not saying anything against the bravery of Lieuts. Chard and Bromhead after the Zulus attacked Rorke's Drift. But I know they did nothing before the attack. Mr Dalton was the man who saved the place. Captain Dunne was also there, and well I remember his words to Dalton, 'Do whatever you think best.' Carbineers, Mounted Police, Edendale Mounted Natives, many who had escaped from Isnadhlwana before us, had been there but would not stay, and no laager would have been built had Mr Henderson and myself not turned up as we did, to make the native contingent return and work at the laager. These natives numbered about 100, and only a few soldiers and A.S.C. men were there, not sufficient to do the work required.

Reading over yoyr account in the 'Witness' today, I could not help comparing to myself the ghastly failure of that campaign with the list of unbroken successes achieved by our men in this last native rebellion. All honour to Colonel McKenzie. As an eye witness I know what happened at Isandlwana and Rorke's Drift, up to the time the hospital was fired, and well can I see the whole thing as it commenced and ended. This I can safely say without fear of contradiction. I was the last white man to leave Isandlwana camp alive. Mr Henderson, some Natal Police, and Edendale Mounted Natives, were also eye witnesses and we fired several shots at the Zulus who were blocking the way. When we left the hill where I caught up Mr. Henderson and the Police, the whole of Isnadhlwana Nek and hills were covered with the Zulu army. One or two gun carriages were caught just over the Nek, and we watched these being taken back and then we rode on to Rorke's Drift, to end our day working at the laager and eventually being shut out after all.

So ended that day of tragedy, January 22nd 1879. Some other day I will tell you about Isandlwana.

Yours etc.

R.J. HALL

Boschfontein, Brakwal.
October 25th.

Lieutenant Gert Willem (or Wilhelm) Adendorff, Natal Native Contingent

Extract from the recollections of the battle of Isandlwana, by Walter H. Stafford, late Captain in the N.N.C., c. 1939: [Killie Campbell Africana Library, Durban, Kwa-Zulu Natal]

...Reverting to Rorke's Drift, a friend of mine, Lieut. Odendorff, and another man, as both could not swim, hugged the bed of the river up to the punt and were ferried across the river. It was them who gave the alarm to Rorke's Drift. Lieut. Odendorff escaped again but I think his friend was amongst the 18 that were killed. I met Odendorff in 1883 and he told me that Rorke's Drift was saved through two Godsends. The first was that the Zulu retired in the middle of the night, apparently to hold a consultation and that gave the garrison time to strengthen the weak parts of the little fort, and the Martini Henry carbines to cool off. The other was the Zulus setting fire to the thatch building which gave a bright light round the little fort and when the Zulus came volley after volley was poured into them.

He also told me that Rev. W. Smith was a great help. You will always find that in a tight corner there is a hard case and there was one at Rorke's Drift. This man was cussing all the time. The Rev. Smith went to him and said. 'Please, my good man, stop that cussing. We may shortly have to answer for our sins.' The reply he got was, 'All right Mister, you do the praying and I will send the black B's to Hell as fast as I can.' Odendorff told me that there were 460 Zulus killed at Rorke's Drift. Although it was a case of do or die it was one of the most noble and glorious defences put up by 114 men against approximately 2000. I often wondered why there was no Rorke's Drift Day!"

Extract from the diary of Lieutenant Pogge of the Kaffrarian Rifles: [courtesy Mr Ron Lock]

...Lieut. Adendorff left us in PMB as he had been offered a post in local regiment, later in the defence of Rorke's Drift he excelled himself but I have not seen him since...

Extract from "Reminiscences of the Zulu War," by John Maxwell, Capetown, 1979 (referring to the escape from Isandlwana of Lt. Higginson of the N.N.C.)

On his arrival in Maritzburg, he and the only two others of the 3rd N.N.C. who got out of the fight, Lieutenants Vane and Adendorff, were placed under arrest and ordered back to Rorke's Drift. In the case of Adendorff, his escape must have been most miraculous, according to his own acocunt, but considering he managed to get along the road to Rorke's Drift, it was the opinion of most of us that he left the field rather early. Lieutenat Vane came out by the Refugees' Drift and gave his horse credit for his escape...

Lieutenant Thomas Purvis, Natal Native Contingent

A minute paper filed by Major Genl. Clifford, enquiring after the state of health of Lieut. Thos. Purvis N.N.C.: [NAB 2264/1879, Kwa-Zulu Natal Archives, Pietermaritzburg]

Statement of the case of Lieut T. Purvis N.N.C

Lieut Purvis aged 27 single an offr in the NNC was present at the actions at Sirayo's Kraal & Rorkes Drift & recd. a bullet wound thro the deltoid muscle of the left arm. This healed satisfactorily but dysentery of an acute form set in & for this he was invalided. He was passing numerous motions of a dysenteric character with blood .... & accompanied with pain in the abdomen increased on the slightest pressure. This caused great exhaustion and ....& debility but the disease succumbed to large doses of Specacuanha (3 frs) twice & three times a day proceeded by MXXV of Laudanum other astringents such as Tannia [?], lead & opium was used with advantages but he still remains weak & debilitated altho the motions are now healthy both in character & number. His wound has disabled his arm & he suffers great pain from it. His wound & disease was caused by the service.

V. Ash AMD Surgeon in charge
Fort Napier 22.4.79

p.s. This officer is not likely to be fit for service within a less period than a year

The Reverend Otto Holger Witt, Swedish Mission Society

[NAB CSO vol. no. 679, ref. no. 1879/172, Kwa-Zulu Natal Archives, Pietermaritzburg]

To The Hon'ble Colonial Secretary - Natal
1 Jany. 1879.

Sir

I am directed by H.E. the Lt General Commanding to request you will have the goodness to request to H.E. the Lieut Governor, that in his opinion it is a military necessity that the house and outhouses near Rorkes Drift, the property of Mr De Witte, should be handed over for imperial purposes.

Lord Chelmsford believes that Mr. de Witte proposes bringing his family there, which in his opinion should not be permitted, as it is in a very exposed position.

If the Lieut Governor accedes to this request, Lord Chelmsford would suggest that the rent should be decided upon by the Resident Magistrate, and an Officer of the Royal Engineers, and Commissariat Departments, and that the Lieut General should be empowered to take possession of these buildings. He is not aware whether it is necessary to place the border under martial law to enforce this.

Mr. de Witte was in negociation with Col. Glyn, but the rent he demanded, viz:- £12 per month for 2 Rooms. and an outhouse, was so exorbitant, that it is evident he is only trying to make a good bargain out of the necessities of the Government.

I have the honor to be,
Sir,
Your most obedient Servant,
[signed] J North Crealock
Assistant Military Secretary

"The Irish Times," March 6th, 1879. [This account also appeared in, amongst others,"The Times," c. March 1879, & "The Illustrated London News," c. March 8th, 1879]

(Press Association Telegram)
PLYMOUTH, WEDNESDAY MORNING.
The Donald Currie mail-ship Warwick Castle, with the latest news from Zululand, arrived in Plymouth Sound this morning shortly before one o'clock. she brings home Mr Witt, missionary, who saw the fight, and whose house at the time was occupied as a hospital and the back parts as a Commissariat store. Mr Witt escaped on his horse, and to the many members of the Press who saw him this morning he stated that as he had lost all his property he would sell his account of the fighting. This was eagerly bought. It is as follows;-

It was on the 22nd of January, 1879. Bright and warm rose the sun over my station, Oscarsburg, situated at the Buffalo River. On the Natal side, at the farm, is a drift in the Zulu country, known by the name of Rorke's Drift. Ten minutes walk from the drift were my houses, two large buildings situated at the border of the Zulu country, and at the very place where the greatest resistance from the Zulus was expected. These buildings were found very fit, indeed, for military purposes, and at the request of the General Commanding the Forces I had left them at his disposal. A large outhouse, 80 by 20 feet, which I used as a church, was turned into a commissariat store; and my dwelling-house, 60 feet by 18, was made a hospital, in consequence of which I had to send away my wife and three children. I myself stayed and acted as interpreter between the doctor in charge and the black people. Before the above-mentioned day all was quiet, waggons arriving constantly, augmenting the store of provisions, and the only variation in this monotony was the report of skirmishes occurring on the other side of the river. But a heavy storm is often preceded by sudden calm. The 22nd came, and witnessed the battle in which the warriors on both sides showed, or, perhaps, were compelled to show, a courage that cannot be denied either by contemporaries or by posterity. Behold on the one side a thousand soldiers, reinforced by equal their number of black ones, leaving their camp to attack an enemy more than ten times their number. Behold on the other side this mass of Zulus, who, close together, walk straight against the mouths of the cannons. Look how thousands after thousands are killed, and nevertheless the mass presses on without fear over the dead bodies of their comrades against the destroying weapons. Behold on the one side a few dozen white troops, the only ones remaining of that thousand. Look how they, after having shot away all their ammunition, keep close together, trying yet awhile to fight for their lives with their bayonets. Behold on the other side the black ones, how they are fighting against the intruder and oppressor, fighting for liberty and independence, coming close to the bayonets, and making them harmless, by taking the corpses of their brethren and throwing them on them. Who wins your warmest sympathy - the captain who, knowing that he is lost, stops a moment to spike the cannon and die, or the Zulu, who, in his excitement, leaves his fellow soldiers behind and alone makes the attack on the hospital at Rorke's Drift, resting his gun on the very barricade and firing on those inside? Is your admiration greater for those 95 who entered the commissariat store at Oscarsburg, and defended it against the 5,000 Zulus, than for those 5,000 who fought outside the whole night, trying to overpower the whites, and who withdrew at day break, leaving 1,000 dead, hundreds of whom were lying even on the very verandah of the house? Indeed, your admiration ought to be as great for the one as for the other. Where did you find greater courage or contempt of death than theirs?

Doctor R. and myself had in the morning made up our minds to pay a visit to a missionary in the neighbourhood. When about to start, at noon, we were told that a great fight was taking place over the river. In company of the chaplain of the forces, we ascended a hill, five hundred feet high, between the station and the river, from where we had an excellent view of what was going on at a distance of 3 miles as the crow flies. We saw the place where the camp was made. The whole of the spot swarmed with black figures, swarming about. The valley down below us, though very hilly and broken, contains a large flat between us and the camp; and on this flat we saw three lines drawn - the one end reaching the camp and the other the river. The whole of it was a strange sight. The heavy firing from the rifles, mixes with the rollusing sound from the big guns and the movements of the lines. All this caused a nervo feeling that something terrifying was going on. What struck us in the beginning was that a good many of the officers of the native contingent had one by one crossed the river some miles below the mission station, and came galloping towards it as fast as their horses could carry them, and on the left hand side we noticed some of the mounted natives crossing at the drift, and driving some cattle before them. Although we could not clearly comprehend this movement, we did not pay much attention to it, our minds being far from dreaming of the real facts.

In the meantime the three lines had drawn themselves more closely to one spot. Here was a large Kaffir kraal, which was gradually surrounded and fired at. How many had entered it I do not know, and will probably never learn, because what were inside there were certainly killed by the Zulu bullets. After twenty minutes' heavy firing the resistance ceased and the attacking ones divided themselves again; and half of them returned towards the camp, the other half - from five thousand to six thousand - approached the river and the place where I was, firing every now and then. They reached at last the river, where another skirmish occurred. The spot where they crossed was half a mile below the drift and was defended by a few Natal Kaffirs. A tolerably good force could have easily prevented them crossing. Having killed these few Natal Kaffirs they crossed one by one. This done they sat down for half an hour in order to get some rest and to strengthen themselves from the snuffbox. Then they separated again, divided into two parties, the one following the course of the river and the other taking its way towards us. We now perceived that the house of a neighbouring farm on the Natal side was put on fire, but we were so far from fancying that the Zulus would cross the river that we never had the slightest idea of the real state of things, but still were thinking that the approaching black people were our own troops. They now were so close to us that their bullets could easily have reached us, and we saw that they were all naked. Reality then, also stood naked for us. The thick mass that swarmed in the camp was the Zulus who had taken possession of it; the eight lines firing at the kraal were Zulus; and finally, those who had crossed the river and were approaching were Zulus. The few whites whom we had seen galloping now and then to the Natal side perhaps were the only survivors of all those who a week before had entered the Zulu country. Our eyes were opened, but why had they not been before? How had the idea or possibility of a disaster on our side been so far from us that the clearest facts had been unable to make it enter our minds? The officers' flight! the burning farm! the immense masses (say 20,000) moving to and fro in eight lines! Why had this not long ago told us that the Lord's thoughts are not our thoughts, nor our ways His? These ideas were crossing my mind while we speedily descended the hill followed by the Zulus.

Arrived at the houses we saw at once a new proof of the sad truth for which our eyes had just been opened. The tents which surrounded the houses, and were used by a company left there, under Major Spalding for the protection of the hospital and the commissariat store, had been pulled down, and temporary barricades of meat sacks were made between the houses, at a distance of 20 yards from one another. Here we were met by anxious questions from many lips - "Do the Zulus come here?" and compelled to answer, "In five minutes they will be here," and in the same moment the fighting began in the neighbourhood.

Though wishing to take part in the defence of my own house and at the same time in the defence of an important place for the whole Colony, yet, my thoughts went to my wife and to my children, who were at a short distance from there, and did not know anything of what was going on, and, having seen one part of the Zulus going in that direction, I followed the desire of my heart, saddled my horse, and started to warn my family. What my poor family had to suffer before, after five days' journey, towards Martizburg, chased by the Zulus, and frightened by all sorts of reports, I will pass over as of no interest for other people.

The attack on Oscarsburg had been awful. Before I started I saw a Zulu alone at the barricade kneeling and firing. The whole force drew nearer. The battle grew heavier. Soon the hospital was on fire. Our people found it impossible to defend themselves inside the barricade. They must retire within the walls, thus entering the commissariat store. The sick people were brought here except five who could not be removed, and who were stuck by the Zulus and burnt. That the hospital was put on fire was certainly a great personal loss for me, as all my property was burnt; but it was of great importance for the whole colony, and especially for the people in the commissariat store, as the flames of the burning house enabled them to aim properly at the Zulus and thus keep them at a fair distance. If the Zulus had known what they did they should never have set fire to the house, and the heavy darkness of that dreadful night would have made our troops unable to defend themselves as they did.

Extract from Witt's letter accepting compensation for damages: [NAB CSO vol. 949, Kwa-Zulu Natal Archives, Pietermaritzburg, South Africa]

Rev. Otto Witt, Rorke's Drift

Accepts on behalf of the Swedish Mission society, the sum of £450 in compensation for the damage done during the Zulu War & £200 for himself personally. Acknowledged 13.2.84

To G Nicholls, Esq., Act Ass. Col. Secrety.
Rorke's Drift, Feb. 9. 1884

Sir,
I beg to inform you that I am in receipt of your letter of Feb. 4th stating that the Lord Commissioner's of Her Majesty's Treasury have been pleased to sanction the payment of the sum of £450 on account of damage done during the Zulu War to the Swedish Mission House at Rorke's Drift, and of the sum of £200 to me personally.
Further I beg to state that I will accept the above named amount viz £450 and £200 in full satisfaction of all demands in connection with these claims, as well from the side of the Mission Society as from my own side.
Please be good enough to inform me what I have to do in order to get possession of the money.
I have &c.
(signed) Otto Witt

"The Heroic Defence of Rorke's Drift"

A coloured lithograph by Henri Duprey
[Ron Sheeley]

Clockwise from top left; John Rouse Merriott Chard, V.C., Gonville Bromhead, V.C.,
[Ron Sheeley],

George Smith, James Henry Reynolds, V.C.
[Lee Stevenson]

Private Robert Jones, V.C. *(bottom right)*, and his brothers.
Clockwise from top left; Charles 24th Regt.; Philip Royal Marines; Thomas, 24th; John 2nd
S.W.B.; Robert Jones, V.C., 2nd/24th. Each being photographed on their respective 21st
birthdays. *[© Mrs Rose Morgan 2003]*

Bottom left; An early portrait of a newly decorated Private Alfred Hook, V.C.,
[Keith Reeves]
Bottom right; Hook as a Sergt. in the 1st V.B. Royal Fusiliers,
[Alan Baynham Jones]

"The Defence of the Drift"
A rather stylised 1940's sketch of the battle.
[Lee Stevenson]

Clockwise from top left; Frederick Hitch, V.C., Patrick Hayes,
George Edwards (Orchard), Frederick Augustus Millne.
[Alan Baynham Jones & Lee Stevenson]

"The Man Whom Plymouth Delights to Honor"
A contemporary caricature of John Chard, c. 1879
[Lee Stevenson]

Charles John Robson, and his grandson, Edwin Peter Ewart
[Ewart family & Lee Stevenson]

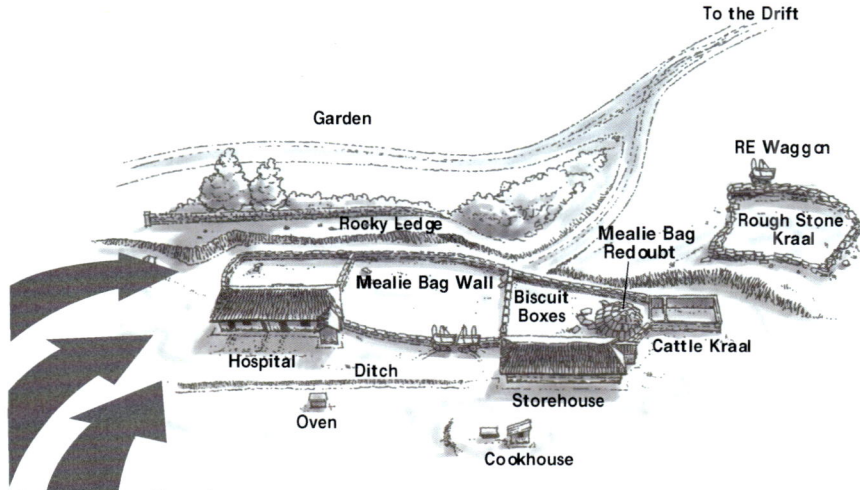

To the Drift

Garden

RE Waggon

Rocky Ledge

Rough Stone Kraal

Mealie Bag Redoubt

Mealie Bag Wall

Biscuit Boxes

Cattle Kraal

Hospital

Ditch

Oven

Storehouse

Cookhouse

Line of Initial Zulu Attacks

Above; The defences at Rorke's Drift, showing the line of the first Zulu attacks on the afternoon of the 22nd January 1879

Below left; "Victoria Cross Heroes" - Private Hook at Rorke's Drift. *[Lee Stevenson]*
Below right; Evan Jones, recently arrived from India, and his son, Gilbert,
[Mr. Bill Jones]

Prince Dabulamanzi kaMpande (centre) and his attendants.
[Ron Sheeley]

"A Zulu Warrior - Veteran of Isandula"
[Alan Baynham Jones and Ian Knight]

Although it dates from the turn of the century, this striking scene of three Zulus by a riverbank captures something of the appearance of the Zulu army of 1879.
[Lee Stevenson]

The original caption for this photograph reads simply,
"Swearing Fealty"
[Lt. Col. (ret'd) Henry Pickering]

Above; A veteran of the uThulwana, Ngaikana kaYenge, Chief Laduma, photographed in Pietermaritzburg c. 1916 when aged 85.
[appears courtesy of the Campbell Collections of the University of Natal]

Below; A fine study of seven Zulus in full ceremonial regalia, photographed at the turn of the century
[Lee Stevenson]

Memorials to the dead at Rorke's Drift.
Above; The British memorial and cemetery

Below; The oldest of three known and marked Zulu mass graves -
"In Proud Memory of the Zulu Warriors who fell at the battle of Rorke's Drift
22nd January 1879, some of whom lie buried here."

CHAPTER 4: Finished up at Jim's; The Zulu view of Rorke's Drift

by Ian Knight

In 1882, the traveller and writer, Bertram Mitford, undertook a tour of Zululand 'with the object of making the round of the battlefields in succession - which, till then, had not been done by anybody - mixing with the people, observing their character as well as manners and customs, and gathering their opinion on the subject of the recent campaign' (1). Mitford would prove an interested and perceptive observer, and his account of his adventurers offers a rare insight into the condition of the Zulu country in the immediate aftermath of the Anglo-Zulu War. It also encapsulates many of the difficulties and frustrations faced by modern historians who try to glean from sources such as Mitford any sort of Zulu perspective of the fighting. During his travels, for example, Mitford made a point of visiting Prince Dabulamanzi kaMpande in his reconstituted eZulwini homestead near Eshowe (2). Typically, Mitford has left us a good physical description of the Prince and a realistic appreciation of his military reputation. His opinion of Dabulamanzi's personality, however, had clearly been prejudiced by the prevailing resentment reserved among white traders and officials for Africans who were not intimidated by European culture;

> Before leaving Eshowe I paid a visit to Dabulamanzi, whose principal kraal is about six miles off. This worthy, whose name came greatly to prominence before the war, is one of Cetywayo's half-brothers. Why he should have been made so much of it is difficult to understand, seeing that he is not an induna in any sense, and whatever lustre may be reflected on him is solely due to his relationship with royalty, except that everyone, having got hold of the name of one man of rank, was determined to make the most thereof. Accordingly, in Natal, Dabulamanzi was forthwith constituted commander-in-chief of the Zulu army, and its leader in every battle, quite irrespective of such trivialities as time and place.
>
> ... creeping through the low doorway [I] stood in the presence of the doughty 'Divider of Water' (3). My lord looked decidedly cool and comfortable, squatting on a mat, without a rag of clothing but his mutya, and the inevitable head-ring encircling his shaven poll. Two of his sons, boys of about ten or eleven, stopped in their play to stare at the umlungu (white man) as I entered. One side of the hut was piled up with trunks; and heaps of rugs, topboots, brass candlesticks, lanterns, and other odds and ends were lying about, the whole suggestive of Isandhlwana loot.
>
> Dabulamanzi is a fine looking man of about thirty-five, stoutly built and large-limbed like most of his royal brethren. He is light in colour even for a Zulu, and has a high, intellectual forehead, clear eyes, and handsome, regular features, with jet-black beard and moustache. But although a handsome face, it is not altogether a prepossessing one, for it wears a settled expression of cunning which would

cause you to have little doubt as to the deservedness of public opinion about him if you had heard it, and if you had not, readiness of belief when you should come to do so. That opinion I have heard expressed by those who knew the man, in two words, 'a blackguard'. With missionary and trader alike he is in disrepute, and many are the tales of sharp practice, if not downright rascality, which were told me about him; nor is he popular among his countrymen.

We shook hands, and sitting down opposite the chief, I produced a substantial piece of tobacco, which was promptly transferred to his side of the field. Then he told Andries to bring in my gun – which, in accordance with Zulu etiquette, I had left outside - as he wanted to look at it. He examined it with the air of a connoisseur (the fellow has the reputation of being a good shot), bringing it to his shoulder, trying the hammers, handling the weapon as if he could not bring himself to part with it… (4)

After an attempt to barter with Dabulamanzi for personal souvenirs, Mitford turned the conversation to the war. Here, however, his account is bitterly disappointing for modern historians. Granted a rare opportunity to obtain command insights from the senior Zulu officer at Rorke's Drift, Mitford merely noted that,

We talked a good deal about the war and subsequent events, but I elicited nothing new in the way of information or incident from Dabulamanzi, who, like many other Zulus of rank, was reticent in matters political to a degree bordering on suspicious - and after a couple of hours indaba (talk) I left him. (5)

Mitford's account of this interview in many ways typifies the record of contemporary Zulu comment on Rorke's Drift. Where a Zulu voice has survived, it is usually by chance, recorded at the whim of a rare passing European, and it is often anecdotal, and almost always incomplete. This is true, of course, of all the battles of the 1879 war, but particularly so of Rorke's Drift. If a remarkable number of accounts have survived from among the tiny garrison who defended the position at Rorke's Drift, only a handful still exist from the many more who were on the other side of the barricade.

There were a number of reasons for this, and the first is simply demographic. The number of men who survived the attack on Rorke's Drift was small compared to the size of the Zulu army as a whole - perhaps 3000 men at most. Although the four amabutho who took part in the attack - the uThulwana and its associated regiments, the iNdlondlo and the iNdluyengwe, together with the uDloko - were badly demoralised by their failure on that occasion, they continued to fight throughout the remainder of the war. At the battle of Khambula (29 March 1879) they had formed the 'chest' of the attacking army, and had charged close to the main British redoubt, suffering heavy casualties as a result. At Ulundi (4 July) they had been committed late in the battle, but had still been exposed to Gatling and artillery fire. Thus many individuals survived Rorke's Drift only to be killed later in the war, and the upheaval which followed the post-war settlement of the country thinned their ranks still further. In 1883, when the British restored King Cetshwayo to his throne, the king had attempted to reassemble what remained of his old regiments. Many individual Zulu no longer recognised his authority, and mustered instead in the service of regional chiefs opposed to Cetshwayo. Nevertheless, allegiance to the amabutho system remained strong among precisely those regiments like the uThulwana - middle-aged and conservative - who had been associated with the king since his youth. Large number of uThulwana had assembled at the reconstituted oNdini in response to the king's call in June 1883; they were still there on 3 July when inkosi Zibhebhu launched a devastating attack upon the royal homestead. King Cetshwayo was forced to flee, and over fifty of the most important men of the kingdom died in the ensuing rout. Some of the uThulwana attempted to stand among the huts of oNdini itself, but were surrounded and killed. Thus, at the very time that white penetration of Zululand increased, the numbers of Zulu who had experienced the events at Rorke's Drift dwindled. Moreover, the men who had attacked Rorke's Drift were mostly in their mid-forties at the time of the battle in 1879; those who survived the ensuing violence were in their sixties by 1900, and most had passed over to join their ancestors by the 1920s.

All of this was in stark contrast to the much larger army of essentially young men who had carried the camp at Isandlwana - some 20,000 of them. Although thousands of these, too, would be killed resisting the British invasion and during the subsequent civil war, thousands more were still alive and vigorous at the turn of the century, and indeed many hundreds survived into the 1930s. For these reasons alone, surviving Zulu accounts of Isandlwana, while small compared to the numbers involved, are plentiful compared to those of Rorke's Drift. There were more veterans of Isandlwana alive for much longer, and some indeed lived to see the birth of modern media interest in the war, which arguably began on the fiftieth anniversary in 1929. Yet there were psychological reasons, too, why the Zulu preferred to talk about Isandlwana rather than Rorke's Drift. Isandlwana had had an enormous impact on the population of Zululand as a whole; with so many young men taking part, there were few homesteads which did not include at least one veteran of the battle. The importance of the victory was immediately apparent to the nation as a whole; so, however, was the terrible price which had been paid. For most Zulu, the attack on Rorke's Drift was a minor mopping-up operation which had gone badly, tarnishing a great strategic success, and it seemed all the more absurd because it had not been authorised by the king, nor had it been fought to secure any clear objective. In stark contrast to the heroic status accorded the British participants in the battle, the Zulu survivors were mocked and derided by the nation as a whole for their folly. It is scarcely surprising, therefore, that their voice has been largely forgotten.

Even the names of very few participants in the attack have survived, and, as Mitford had wryly noted, only Prince Dabulamanzi achieved any celebrity among his enemies at the time. Even so, Mitford's description is typical of the missed opportunities which characterise white interaction with the Prince. Although

Dabulamanzi's surrender to British troops during the closing stages of the war was widely reported, and his role in the post-war movement to restore King Cetshwayo to Zululand was conspicuous - actions which provided ample opportunities to elicit his views on the battle - and he was well-known to white traders in the Eshowe district, very few accounts were elicited from him. Perhaps the most telling of those which have survived was given by King Cetshwayo himself, who received the Prince's report of Rorke's Drift shortly after the battle occurred. Like unsuccessful commanders the world over, the Prince sought to temper the news of his defeat by stressing his successes;

> Of the Rorke's Drift fight, Cetywayo received most imperfect news. Dabulamanzi reported that he had successfully stormed and taken 'the house'; he attacked, and then retired, but admitted he had suffered heavily. (6)

According to optimistic reports in the Natal press, the King was so disappointed with the news that he had promptly ordered Dabulamanzi to be executed;

> In our last, we mentioned a report which we believe to be well founded, that Cetywayo had put Matshana to death for disobedience of orders - attacking the camp instead of the General and his forces, whom he was ordered to stop. He is also said to have put to death the chief indunas who attacked Rorke's Drift, saying it was bad enough to take the army so far away as the camp, leaving him open to the General's army; but it was still worse, after the heavy losses at Isandhlwana, to go on to Natal, and lose more men there.
> Other reasons are assigned for these indunas being put to death: one, the disobedience of the King's orders that the river was on no account to be crossed; another, that he had forbidden the enemy to be attacked except in the open. The Rorke's Drift Post was not a properly fortified place, but the rapidity with which defences were thrown up, and the slaughter the Zulus there suffered, fully justifies Cetywayo's aversion to encounter English forces unless in the open, where the Zulu tactics could be employed... (7)

While the king was undoubtedly angry, there is no evidence that he ever contemplated such drastic action. In fact, Prince Dabulamanzi retired to his personal homestead near Eshowe, where he took a leading role organising the siege of the British garrison there. He was wounded in the thigh during the action at kwaGingindlovu on 2 April, but survived the war. Indeed, he was the subject of another interview, probably conducted in 1885 (8), by Walter Stafford, who, as a Captain in the 1/1st Regiment, NNC, had himself survived Isandlwana. Stafford, however, elicited little more information about Rorke's Drift than had Mitford;

> ...A few years after the war another man and myself had a store about 15 miles out of Vryheid. I heard that Dabulamanzi was at a kraal nearby visiting. I rode

over to see him, when I got to the kraal I told one of the men to tell him that a white man who escaped at Isandhlwana wanted to see him. He sent back word saying that I was lying - that no white men had escaped. I went into the hut and Kuleka him. I said 'Listen to me and I will convince you.' After I had spoken for some time he handed me a pot of beer and said 'puza'. I asked him if it had been his intention to invade Natal. He said 'No' that Cetywayo told him that the flooded rivers were a bigger King than what he was. I then said 'Then why did your men shout out, both at Isandhlwana and at Rorke's Drift- Nina manga - which means you are kidding yourselves, tomorrow night we will sleep with your wives and sisters in Umgungumhlovu (Maritzburg)'. He said that was only bravado - 'But had Rorke's Drift fallen I should certainly have taken my army into Natal.' If that had happened all the Natal natives and the Cape natives would have joined him as a matter of policy to save their own skins. It is too awful to contemplate what the result would have been (Hell upon Earth). (9)

This last comment should perhaps be taken to reflect deep-seated colonial fears rather than as a true statement of intent. Even had Rorke's Drift fallen, Dabulamanzi's troops would have been exhausted by their exertions on 22nd January, and, unsupported by the rest of the army, were in no position to launch a major incursion into Natal in the face of royal disapproval. Moreover, as many of the African groups in Natal had a long-standing antagonism towards the Zulu Royal House, and had supplied troops for auxiliary units such as the NNC, it seems unlikely that they could so easily have changed sides. A fear of a widespread rising among African groups was a common cause of settler disquiet, however.

Whether or not Prince Dabulamanzi might one day have had more to say of Rorke's Drift, the desperate nature of post-war Zulu politics robbed him of the chance. An ardent supporter of the exiled king, he was marked down in European eyes as a troublemaker, and in September 1886 he was arrested together with his son Mzingeli by Boers in the newly-formed Vryheid district on a trumped-up charge of stock theft. While en route to Vryheid, escorted by Wilhem Joubert and Paul van der Berg (known to the Zulus as Peula), Dabulamanzi and his son suddenly broke away. Both were mounted, and they galloped as far as a homestead on the Nondweni river belonging to a headman known to the Prince. This homestead lay in territory recently annexed by the British, and believing himself to be safe from his pursuers, Dabulamanzi entered the huts. The Boers caught up with him, however, and Van den Berg dismounted and threatened to shoot the Prince in the hut if he didn't surrender. Dabulamanzi protested that he was on British territory, and demanded that if the Boers took him anywhere, it be to the headquarters of Lt. Col. Cardew, the British Sub-Commissioner at Nquthu. What happened next was related the following morning (23 September) by Mzingeli;

The Boers replied, 'All right, come out, we will take you to the Colonel.' My father said, 'Will you swear that you will do me no harm if I come out?' to which

Peula replied, 'I swear.' My father then came out and after we had proceeded a short way towards the Colonel's office Peula, who had handed his rifle to Wilhelm, caught hold of my father and attempted to tie him up with reims, saying, 'Now I will take you to Vryheid.' My father resisted, saying, 'No, if you take me anywhere you must take me to the Colonel as I am.' Peula and my father then struggled together, my father seizing hold of Peula's bandolier. After a bit they separated, my father having possession of the bandolier and Peula of my father's knobkerrie. I was prevented from assisting my father by the other Boer who threatened to shoot me. Peula said, 'Give me back my bandolier.' My father replied, 'Return to me my knobkerrie'. My father threw the bandolier to Peula who then seized the gun from Wilhelm and said he would shoot my father if he wouldn't go to Vryheid. My father replied, 'You won't shoot me on Government ground.' Peula said he would and after some more words he shot my father who was standing within two or three yards of him, through the body, the bullet entering his stomach below the left side and coming out above the right hip. My father ran away, and as he was doing so Peula shot at him again twice, the first shot struck him above the left hip, the second passed through his right elbow and left wrist. Peula then fired two shots at me as I was riding away on which the horse bucked me off and I sprained my knee. My father, after receiving the second shot, fell close to me; he had only run about 200 yards. After this I saw the Boers seize our horses and ride away, and presently the people from the nearby kraal came up and carried us to their huts. It was dark by the time we arrived at the kraal. My father was then in a very weak state. This morning about sunrise he died. His last words were, 'I don't know why they killed me on Government ground.' (10)

It was a squalid end to a man whose name, in 1879, had been the terror of Natal.
It was left to ordinary Zulu to offer more detailed accounts of the fighting. Many, like Mehlokazulu kaSihayo, a junior commander in the iNgobamakhosi ibutho, had fought at Isandlwana rather than Rorke's Drift, and knew the story of the latter second-hand;

The men who fought at Rorke's Drift took no part at Isandhlwana; they were the men of the Undi regiment, who formed a portion of the left wing. When the camp at Isandhlwana had been taken, these men came up fresh and pursued the fugitives right over the Fugitives' Drift into Natal. There was a long line of stragglers, as we supposed, making for Jim's house. The other reserve regiments, intending to cut them off, crossed the Buffalo at the point where the Bashee flows into it, and came round crossing the road near the kraal of Inswarele. These reserves complained that they had had no opportunity of taking part in the battle of Isandhlwana, and therefore they went on to Rorke's Drift, and fought there. These were men with rings. I only followed the fugitives a little way, I did not go as far as the Buffalo. We who had fought at Isandhlwana were as tired as the

Englishmen, and many more of the English forces would have escaped if the reserve regiments had not come up. (11)

Mehlokazulu said of the Zulu losses at Rorke's Drift that they numbered 'about 300'. He seems to have shared the prevailing Zulu view that the attack was ill-conceived; asked whether Prince Dabulamanzi was a good general, he replied 'no; he is too hasty.' (12)

One man who had apparently fought at Rorke's Drift, a warrior named 'Umtyololo', was interviewed shortly after being found wounded by the British on 23 January. He confirmed Mehlokazulu's impression of how the attack had developed;

> ...A few [survivors of Isandlwana] were met and killed by the Undi, but that Corps, believing that the Camp was already plundered, decided to make the best of their way to Rorke's Drift, and plunder it, never dreaming that any opposition could be offered by the few men they knew to be there. The loss of the Zulus must have been exceedingly heavy...
>
> ...and the loss of the Undi at Rorkes drift cannot be less than 500. They killed all their own wounded who were unable to get away. Much astonishment was expressed by the Zulus at the behaviour of our soldiers - firstly regarding their death dealing powers considering their numbers, secondly because they did not run away before the enormously numerical superiority of the enemy. (13)

An unidentified 'Zulu Deserter', also questioned by the British, offered much the same story;

> ...When at last we carried the camp our regiments became mixed up; a portion pursued the fugitives down the Buffalo, and the remainder plundered the camp, while the Undi and Udhloko regiments made the best of their way to Rorke's Drift to plunder the post there, in which they failed, and lost very heavily, after fighting all the afternoon and night... (14)

Sofikasho Zungu, who fought with the iNgobamakhosi at Isandlwana, saw something of the pursuit, and recalled details of the fight that were typical of those told by returning survivors;

> ...I saw quite a lot of white men escape on horseback soon after we attacked, they rode off on horseback to Jim's place at Rorke's Drift. Jim was a storekeeper. These men who rode away were dressed in black, they were cowards to leave their brothers behind.
>
> I know that that night there was a big fight at Jim's place. Two regiments who were too late to fight at Isandhlawana, the Mbhoza and the Lulorga (15) attacked at Jim's place at night. I know that the Mbhoza threw lighted grass attached to Mkontos into the roof of a building there and set it alight but the soldiers fought bravely and the Zulus never got in to kill them... (16)

Those accounts of the battle which have survived from Zulu participants offer little in the way of tactical detail, but instead conjure up what must have been the overwhelming impression of those who took part – that of a desperate and confused struggle fought out at close-quarters and mostly in the dark. Perhaps the most graphic description was given by Muziwento ('Umsweanto'), a 'Zulu boy' who was interviewed in 1883. Muziwento's family lived close to Isandlwana, and at the start of the war had moved away from the danger posed by the advancing British troops. Muziwento's father had fought at Isandlwana and later at Ulundi. Muziwento himself heard the story of Rorke's Drift from Munyu, a friend of his father who had fought with the uThulwana. This account, recorded in idiomatic style, focused on the brutal fighting at the very doors of the mission buildings, and commented wryly on the way in which both sides, coming close to exhaustion after dark, expressed their defiance in war-chants and cheers. It describes, too, the bitter response of the nation as a whole to the battle;

> ...Presently they [the uThulwana] said, 'O! Let us go and have a fight at Jim's! The white men had by this time made their preparations; they were quite ready. The Zulus arrived at Jim's house. They fought, they yelled, they shouted, 'It dies at the entrance! It dies in the doorway!'....They stabbed the sacks; they dug with their assegais. They were struck; they died. They set fire to the house. It was no longer fighting; they were exchanging salutations merely.
> The uThulwana regiment was finished up at Jim's - shocking cowards they were too. Our people laughed at them, some said, 'You! You're no men! You're just women, seeing you ran away for no reason at all, like the wind!' Others jeered and said, 'You marched off. You went to dig little bits with your assegais out of the house of Jim, that had never done you any harm!...' (17)

A similar sense of a perspective limited by the frantic nature of fighting in a confined space is evoked in a description by Col. H.C. Lugg of a chance encounter which befell his father, Henry, who had fought in the battle as a Trooper in the Natal Mounted Police;

> ...Rorke's Drift was to have an interesting sequel some twenty-three years later, when in 1902, Henry was carrying out inspections of war graves at this spot and at Isandlwana, where by chance he met an old warrior bearing a number of obvious war scars. A bullet had seared his scalp, another his left shoulder and two through the calf of his leg, all received at Rorke's Drift. Being anxious to hear the old man's version of the affair, Henry got him to tell his story, being careful not to disclose his own participation in the affair. And what a story! Told as it could only be by an old Zulu in language rich in allegory and metaphor.
> Soon the old scene came back to life as the old fellow recounted the sounds of rifle fire, the shouts of the Zulu war cry, "Usuthu!, Usuthu!, Inkomo ka baba," as they rushed to the attack, determined to prove their worth as worthy sons of a

worthy sire, for this is what the cry implied (18); the crackling of flames from the burning building, the groans of the wounded, and the din of battle generally. How often, in turn, I have been privileged to hear such stories, and told in just such a way!

One of the stories Henry used to recall was of a Zulu, who during the height of the fight, availed himself of the semi-darkness to creep into the kitchen to light his smoking horn or gudu from the glowing embers, and was promptly shot by Henry (19). When the old man had come to the end of his story, Henry casually asked him who the man was who had met his death in the kitchen. Greatly taken aback, he exclaimed, "Kanti nawe wawukhena? Wafa uMngumle! Sizinja ngaphansi kwezinyao zenu."

"And were you there also? And so perished Mngamule. We were merely dogs under your feet..." (20)

During his expedition of 1882, Bertram Mitford also met a number of ordinary veterans of the battle. Like Lugg, he recorded little in detail of what they told him, perhaps feeling that Zulu accounts of Rorke's Drift could not easily be conveyed in writing. Exploring the battlefield of Hlobane one day,

...a snort from my pony caused me to look up. Within a few yards, leaning against a rock, stood a couple of stalwart savages calmly looking at me. I saw that one of them carried an assegai with a blade like a small claymore, and, seeing, coveted and resolved to have it if possible. I climbed to where they stood; the warriors greeted me as usual, 'Inkos!', and of course were anxious to know all about me. The one with the assegai was a fine, tall fellow, with a cheery countenance and hearty manner, and we speedily became friends; the other, dark, taciturn, and unprepossessing, I didn't much like the look of. But he of the assegai did his companion's share of the indaba and his own too. He belonged to the Udhloko regiment, and had been present at the attack on Rorke's Drift, which battle he proceeded to fight over again for my enlightenment with an effusiveness and pantomime accompaniment thoroughly Zulu; going into fits of laughter over it, as though one of the toughest struggles on record were the greatest joke in the world. At a judicious moment I produced some 'gwai' (21), which was received with acclamation, even my saturnine friend's dark countenance expanding into a grin. Then taking up the assegai I began to examine it, suggesting that we should make an exchange, and throwing out all sorts of inducements. Not a bit of it; the jovial warrior would about as soon think of parting with his head-ring - or his head. He had fought with that very weapon at 'kwaJim' (Rorke's Drift) &c. &c; no, he couldn't give it away on any account. It was a splendid specimen of a spear, but on no terms could I obtain it. (22)

It was one of Mitford's informants, nonetheless - part of a group of three, two members of the oNdini amabutho, and one of the iNgobamakhosi, with whom he discussed the war in a road-side encounter near Mthonjaneni - who offered the most perceptive observation on the battle;

> '...at Rorke's Drift - there were no big guns there, and the English could have stood here (making my hand into a hollow) while the Zulus were everywhere; how is it that you didn't make a better fight of it?'
> 'The soldiers were behind a schaans (breastwork), and,' added the narrator significantly, showing all his ivories, 'they were in a corner'. (23)

One thing that the Zulu were agreed upon was that the attack on Rorke's Drift had been hugely costly. Although the Zulu seldom offered figures for their losses, the most authoritative reports at the time suggested that they might have been as high as 600 men - at least fifteen per cent of those who took part (24). As one of Bishop Schreuder's informants suggested, the combined effect of exhaustion and these devastating losses left the attackers utterly spent;

> The detachment of the Zulu army seen by Glyn's column on its way, the 23rd January, back to Rorke's Drift, was part of the Undi corps and Utako retreating from the unsuccessful attack on the commissariat stores at Rorke's Drift. Amongst the horsemen was Udabulamanzi, who says that they were so tired and glad that Glyn's column did not attack them, for if attacked they would have bolted everyone... (25)

As one Cajana kaMatendeka put it,

> The Tulwana regiment then crossed and attacked the camp at Rorke's house, without success; they were beaten off, they say, with very heavy loss. Masipula's chief son, and a number of his brothers, Untabatu ka Maxoza, and his brother Uncuncwana, Umgamuli kaUmbaugulana (26) were killed and many other headmen. The dead are not to be counted there are so many. The whole Zulu nation is weeping and mourning. (27)

Captain Norman MacLeod, the British political agent operating on the Swazi border, reported simply that,

> ...they say themselves that the Tulwana Regiment (the King's Own), which attacked Bromhead, is gone. They say there is no Tulwana now... (28)

Cornelius Vijn, a trader who had entered Zululand before the war and was detained throughout under the king's protection, saw at first hand the suffering caused by the loss of so many family heads in the fighting of 22 January, particularly at Rorke's Drift;

About 2 P.M., while I lay in the hut, talking with one of the men of Ziwedu (Cetshwayo's brother), who had been sent by the king to learn about me, whether I was alive, and how it went with me, our attention was drawn to a troop of people, who came back from their gardens crying and wailing. As they approached, I recognised them as persons belonging to the kraal in which I was staying. When they came into or close to the kraal, they kept on wailing in front of the kraals, rolling themselves on the ground and never quieting down; nay, in the night they wailed so as to cut through the heart of anyone. And this wailing went on, day and night, for a fortnight; the effect of it was very depressing; I wished I could not hear it.

The reason of this was that the headman of the Kraal, Msundusi, a trusty person and the husband of four wives, had fallen at Isandlwana ... (29)

The heavy losses of 22/23rd January - including those from the simultaneous actions in the northern and southern parts of the country - had a deeply unsettling effect on the Zulu. It was obvious that Isandlwana had been an extraordinary victory, an act of concerted defiance which would alter the course of the war. Yet the brutal cost of that victory was equally obvious, and left the king and his councillors full of foreboding. Moreover, there was no such ambiguity about the lessons of Rorke's Drift; although it had been a minor affair, the Zulu had proved utterly ineffectual in the face of determined troops protected by even the most rudimentary barricade. 'The Zulus say', noted Schreuder, 'that the affair at Isan'lwana commenced with a victory and ended with a fight ...a defeat' (30). When a new phase of fighting began in March, a warrior named Mgelija Ngema of the uVe ibutho recalled that King Cetshwayo's instructions were quite specific on the matter of attacking British strongholds;

Cetewayo actually said you are not to go into the hole of a wild beast or else you will get clawed, wait until the soldiers come out of their laager and then fall on them. (31)

Tragically, for the young men who made up the bulk of the army, and who had not run the gauntlet at Rorke's Drift, this advice proved difficult to follow, and the lesson had to be learned again at Khambula, and finally at Ulundi - ultimately with devastating consequences.

Notes
1 Through the Zulu Country; Its Battlefields and Its People, by Bertram Mitford, London 1883.
2 The British had destroyed the original eZulwini homestead in April 1879, at the end of the Eshowe campaign.
3 The meaning of Dabulamanzi, so named by his father, King Mpande, to commemorate his passage across the river Thukela in 1840 – an act which secured

Boer support for Mpande's ultimately successful campaign to win the Zulu throne.

4 Mitford, *Through the Zulu Country*.

5 Mitford, *ibid*.

6 Quoted in *A Zulu King Speaks; Statements made by Cetshwayo kaMpande on the history and customs of his people.*, edited by C. de B. Webb and J.B. Wright, Pietermaritzburg and Durban 1978.

7 Cutting from an unidentified Natal newspaper, possibly *The Natal Witness*, c. 1879.

8 Stafford refers to the town of Vryheid. If his memory is correct, this would place the interview some time between the end of 1884, when construction of Vryheid began, and September 1886, when the Prince was murdered.

9 Captain Walter H. Stafford, late of the Natal Native Contingent in his own recollections of the battle of Isandlwana, typescript copy c. 1939, Killie Campbell Africana Library, Durban, KwaZulu Natal, South Africa.

10 Cardew's report, BPP C4980. Reproduced in C.T. Binns, *Dinuzulu; The Death of the House of Shaka*, London 1968.

11 Account by Mehlokazulu kaSihayo, war supplement to the Natal Mercury, 1879. Also see Charles Norris-Newman, *In Zululand With the British Throughout the War of 1879*, London, 1880.

12 Ibid.

13 'Statement made by natives regarding the action of the 22nd January at the Sandhlwana Hill' compiled by W. Drummond. 'Umtoyolo' was described as 'A Zulu well known to Mr. Longcast, Interpreter to the Lt. General'. WO32/7711, The National Archives, (P.R.O.), London.

14 Reported in the Natal Witness, 24 February 1879, and reprinted in F.E. Colenso and E. Durnford, *A History of the Zulu War and its Origin*, London 1880.

15 Mbhoza and uDloko. Mbhoza was another name for the uThulwana.

16 Bowden Papers, Natal Museum, Pietermaritzburg, reproduced in *Kill Me In The Shadows; The Bowden Collection of Anglo-Zulu War Oral History*, edited by Ian Knight, Soldiers of the Queen, issue 74, 1993.

17 G.H. Swinney, *A Zulu Boy's Recollections of the Zulu War and of Cetshwayo's Return*. London, 1884.

18 Inkomo kababa – my father's cow.

19 The smoking horn, igudu, was used for smoking cannabis, which was regarded by the Zulu as a stimulant.

20 A Natal Family Looks Back by H.C. Lugg, Durban, 1970.

21 Tobacco.

22 Mitford, *Through the Zulu Country*.

23 Ibid.

24 Seem, for example, Chard's revised estimate of their losses, and the assessment by Henrique Shepstone, letter to T. Shepstone, Shepstone Papers, KwaZulu/Natal Archives Depot, Pietermaritzburg.

25 J.C. Schreuder, letter to W. Littleton, Ntunjambili (Kranskop) mission, 2 March

1879. BPP C.2318.

26 It is interesting to speculate whether this is the same Mngamule referred to in the Lugg account.

27 'Statement of Ucadjana, son of Matendeka, belonging to Seketwayo's people, made to me, H.C. Shepstone, Secretary of Native Affairs, Transvaal', BBP C. 2260.

28 Norman MacLeod, 'Extract from a private letter addressed' The Honourable W. Littleton, Private Secretary to His Excellency the High Commissioner, Derby, February 8, 1879'. BPP 2308.

29 Cetshwayo's Dutchman, being the private journal of a white trader in Zululand during the British invasion, by Cornelius Vijn. London 1880. Entry for 25th January 1879; it is worth noting that while many senior men in command positions were killed at Isandlwana, and that elements of the uThulwana broke away from the reserve to join the attack, the bulk of the casualties were nevertheless suffered by the younger, unmarried amabutho who stormed the camp. Almost all of the men who died at Rorke's Drift, in contrast, were abamnumzana – married homestead-heads.

30 J.C. Schreuder, ibid.

31 Kill Me In The Shadows, SOTQ 74.

CHAPTER 5: The men of No. 3. Column

<u>**Lieutenant General Sir Frederic Thesiger, Lord Chelmsford**</u>

Extract from "The Times," March 12th, 1879

Lord Chelmsford's Orders

...Lord Chelmsford directs that every column and post must be made self-supporting, and the officers commanding are to be responsible both for the security of their positions and, for their supplies, so that they may be able to "withstand attack and advance or follow up the enemy at any moment."...

Extract from a private letter to Commissary General Sir Edward Strickland, Army Com. Dept., dated January 13th, 1879. [Chelmsford Papers, National Army Museum, London]

...I have been across the Buffalo R. today to see how the depot was going. I find that there is absolutely nothing there and this column cannot move until there is a months supply with the column.

Mr Dalton is the only representative of the Commissariat Dept. at Rorke's Drift, and for the first time today he has been given a sergeant of the 24th to assist him. Mr Dalton is too young to take the weight of responsibility which the charge of a column represents, altho I am sure he would do well under another.

You must send up one of the new Asst. Commissary Genls. who are on their way out, at once to Helpmakaar or we shall have a breakdown. There is no one here like Colonel Wood to keep everyone up to the mark and Helpmakaar appears to me to have been sadly neglected. Look after the interests of this column before you advance with No. 1. Column, leave PMBurg to be, what it is, merely a forwarding station. This column will advance very shortly, and it will be a sad disgrace to the Commissariat, if it is obliged to halt short of its destination for want of supplies...

A letter written to the Secretary of State for War, dated February 8th, 1879: [WO32/7710, The National Archives, (P.R.O.), London].
(see also the response to this letter by Col. the Hon. F.A. Stanley).

From the Lt. General Commandg. in S. Africa to the Rt. Honble. the S of State
Durban, Natal,
8th February 1879

Sir,

It is with much satisfaction that I have the honor to forward the report of the successful defence of Rorke's drift post on the 22d & 23d January.

The defeat of the Zulus at this post, & the very heavy loss suffered by them, has to a great extent neutralized the effects of the disaster at Insandlana, and it no doubt saved Natal from a serious invasion.

The cool determined courage displayed by the gallant garrison is beyond all praise & will I feel sure receive ample recognition.

As at the present moment the lesson taught by this defence is most valuable, I have thought it advisable to publish, for general information the report in question which I trust will meet with your approval.

I have the honor to be Sir
your most obedt. Servant
Chelmsford LG

From reports received since the date of Lt. Chard's letter it appears that that the Zulu loss greater than he knew of at the time.

A letter written to the Military Secretary, Whitehall which accompanied the original recommendations for the award of the first Victoria Crosses to members of the Rorke's Drift garrison: [WO32/7390 The National Archives, (P.R.O.), London]

<u>Military Secretary</u>
Submitted for the favourable consideration of his Royal Highness the Field Marshal commanding in Chief.

I would express a hope that the gallant conduct of Lt Chard R.E. and Lt Bromhead 2/24th may be taken with consideration in view, of possible, that these two officers should receive the Victoria Cross -

Had it not been for their fine example and excellent behaviour, under most trying circumstances, it may be assumed that the defence of Rorke's drift post would not have been conducted with that intelligence and tenacity which so essentially characterised it -

Whilst in no way desiring to deteriorate from the individual conduct of any of those who took part in this gallant defence, I cannot help feeling that its success must in all fairness be in a great measure attributable to these two young officers who exercised the chief commands on the occasion in question -

Chelmsford LG
PMBurg 23-2-79

Colonel Richard T. Glyn, 1st/24th Foot, commanding No. 3 Column

A minute paper issued by the Deputy Adjutant General; "Asks for six men to be provided accustomed to punt management for working ponts on Buffalo at Rorke's Drift, dated 13.1.79." [NAB CSO vol. 681 ref. 1879/378, Kwa-Zulu Natal Archives, Pietermaritzburg]

Rorke's Drift
January 13/79

Sir,
I have the honour to request that it may be brought to the notice of H.E. the Lt. General Commanding that as the ponts, now on the Buffalo at this point, will be required to be kept constantly in work after the 3rd. Column advances, a party of sufficiently experienced men in pont management should be provided for this service.
At present the work is being performed by the troops, but as it is not advisable to leave any men of the force behind, & as none can said to be experience in this work, I beg to suggest a party of civilians as per margin [6 men] be permanently engaged for this work.
I have the honour to be Sir
Your obt. servant
(sd.) R.T. Glyn, Colonel
Commanding 3rd. Column

To Mily. Secretary
D.A.G.

17.1.79
Deputy Adjt. General,
I fear it will be very difficult to procure other than Natives for this service. Can a N.C.O. R.E., or a Sapper be detailed to take charge of men if ordered out?
[signed] C.M. Mitchell

Lieutenant Colonel Henry J. Degacher, 2nd/24th Foot.

An official letter sent to Col. Glyn, Officer Commanding No. 3 Column. [WO32/7390, The National Archives (P.R.O.), London] - see also Bromhead's official letter.

From Officer Comdg. 2/24th Regt.
For Staff Officer 3rd Column.
Rorke's Drift, Natal 15.2.79

Sir,
I have the pleasure of forwarding the enclosed letter from Lt. Gonville Bromhead 2/24th Regt. and beg that the Officer Comdg. the Column will be so good as to forward the same to H.E. the Lt. General Commanding the troops in South Africa, in the hope that the conspicuous gallantry of the men named in the margin and mentioned in Lt. Bromhead's letter, may be brought by H.R.H. the Commander - in Chief to the notice of Her Majesty the Queen, and be deemed worthy of the Victoria Cross being awarded them

No. 1395 Pte John Williams 2/24th Regt.
No. 1373 Pte Henry Hook 2/24th Regt.
No. 593 Pte William Jones 2/24th Regt.
No. 716 Pte Robert Jones 2/24th Regt.
No. 1240 Corpl Wm Allen 2/24th Regt.
No. 1362 Pte Frederick Hitch 2/24th Regt.

I have the honor to be
Sir
Your most obedt. servant
H.J. Degacher
Lt. Colonel
Commandg. 2/24th Regt.

Rorke's Drift 17 Feby.
DA.G. P.M.B.

Submitted [signed] RJ. Glyn. Colonel
Commanding 3rd Column

The following letter has been sent by the Colonel Commanding the 24th Regiment in answer to the vote of condolence past by the Brecon Corporation.

Rorke's Drift, Natal
28th April 1879

Sir, on behalf of the officers, non-commissioned officers and men of the 2nd Battalion 24th Regiment, I beg to thank you and the gentleman of the borough of Brecon for the vote of condolence transmitted to me by the officer commanding the 25th Brigade Depot and which I have caused to be published in this night's Regimental orders.

I cannot close this letter without expressing to you the high esteem which I, in common with all the officers of the Regiment, hold the soldier-like qualities of the gallant fellows I have the honour to command, and who are now mostly your countrymen. No officer need wish to lead better and to his Excellency Lord Chelmsford's words to me when speaking of the steady, determined conduct of the men on that fearful night of the 22nd January.

"It was admirable; no troops could have done better." I am pleased to tell you that three of your countrymen have been recommended to her gracious majesty the Queen for the honour of the Victoria Cross, and a fourth, 1398 Private Joseph Williams, of Monmouthshire, South Wales, would most certainly have been recommended had the poor fellow been spared to reap the reward of his conspicuous gallantry at the defence of Rorke's Drift.

I have the honour to be, Sir,
your Worship's obedient servant,
H. J. Degacher.
Lieut/Colonel Commanding 2/24th Regiment.

Major Cornelius F. Clery, 32nd Light Infantry, principal staff officer with No. 3. Column

Extract from a private letter written to Lady Allison. ["Nothing Remains but to Fight," by Ian Knight, London 1993]

Wolf's Hill
Zululand
16 May 1879
My dear Lady Allison,...
...Reputations are being made and lost here in an almost comical fashion, from the highest downwards...
...Well, Chard and Bromhead to begin with: both are almost typical in their separate corps of what would be termed the very dull class. Bromhead is a great favourite in his regiment and a capital fellow at everything except soldiering. So little was he

held to be qualified in this way from unconquerable indolence that he had to be reported confidentially as hopeless. This is confidential, as I was told it by his commanding officer. I was about a month with him at Rorke's Drift after Isandhlwana, and the height of his enjoyment seemed to be to sit all day on a stone on the ground smoking a most uninviting-looking pipe. The only thing that seemed equal to moving him in any way was any allusion to the defence of Rorke's Drift. This used to have a sort of electrical effect on him, for he would jump up and off he would go, and not a word could be got out of him. When I told him he should send me an official report on the affair it seemed to have a most distressing effect on him. I used to find him hiding away in corners with a friend helping him to complete this account, and the only thing that afterwards helped to lessen the compassion I felt for all this, was my own labour when perusing this composition - to understand what it was all about. So you can fancy there was not one who knew him who envied him his distinction, for his modesty about himself was, and is, excessive.

Chard there is very little to say about except that he too is a 'very good fellow' - but very uninteresting. The fact is that until the accounts came out from England nobody had thought of the Rorke's Drift affair except as one in which the private soldiers of the 24th behaved so well. For as a matter of fact they all stayed to defend the place because there was nowhere else to go, and in defending it they fought most determinedly...

Extract from a private letter written to a 'Colonel', identified only as; "A Staff Officer in Ireland." [Appears courtesy of the South Wales Borderers Regtl. Museum, Brecon, Acc. No. L47.64]

Rorke's Drift
Buffalo River
Feby. 17th 1879

My dear Colonel,

...When day-light broke, what we saw in that Camp was sad to look at. For indeed, all our friends were there. But with the first glimmer we had to move, as the watchfires of the enemy on the hills between us and him, burned al night, and it was only too certain that the people with whom we had been engaged the day before, would now be on our backs as well. - Moreover we had no food or ammunition, except what the men carried of the latter - so we fully expected to have to fight our way to the river here. - But fortune gave us a turn, as the force told off to bar our passage had come on the evening before, to attack this post, but it was most gallantly defended by the one Company that held it, and after fighting from 4 o'clock in the afternoon till 5 o'clock the following morning, the enemy had to retire with a loss of close upon 500 men - no mistake about these numbers as we unfortunately had to bury them. So this enabled us to reach here without having to fight for it...

Captain Henry Hallam Parr, 1st/13th Somerset Light Infantry

Extract from "A Sketch of the Kafir and Zulu Wars," London 1880

...Soon we saw that the post at Rorke's Drift was on fire, and feared the worst, and made sure that at any rate the ponts had been wrecked.

We advanced on the river, and our scouts, to the surprise of all, reported the points standing. The cavalry crossed below them at the shallows, as it had done twelve days before, and the first files advanced up to where the mission station had stood, at the best gallop their weary and hungry horses could muster after having been under the saddle nearly thirty hours.

We expected to find a repetition on a smaller scale of Isandlwana camp, but as we came in sight of the commissariat stores, a cheer sounded from the top of a wall of mealie sacks, from a man on the look-out, and was taken up by the remainder of the little garrison, and to our delight we found that there was no more bad news to be expected, at any rate at present.

To relate what had occurred here we must retrace our steps. About 2.30 that afternoon, when the sack of Isandlwana was complete, when the Zulu regiments who had been engaged were scattered all over the camp - some helping themselves to booty and ammunition; some stabbing each dead man, so that the corpse should not swell (the Zulu superstition is that if this is not done, as the body swells and corrupts, the right hand and arm of its slayer also swells and corrupts); some carrying away those wounded Zulus who could be moved, and shooting those who could not; some throwing their dead into holes, ravines, and dongas; about this time the Undi corps, the crack corps of the Zulu army (which, with the exception of the Nkobamakosi regiment, had been held in reserve), arrived, fresh and eager for fighting, near the camp.

Finding there was nothing for them to do here, and being ignorant that the whole of the column was not destroyed, this corps continued its march in the direction of the Buffalo. After crossing, the corps split up into regiments. The crack regiment, the Royal Tulwana, in whose ranks Cetywayo had fought in his younger days, and to which he still nominally belonged, advanced to attack Rorke's Drift, accompanied by portions of three other regiments, making up a force of between three and four thousand men. The other portions of the Undi corps dispersed in search of the plunder and cattle.

At Rorke's Drift there was stationed, to guard the ponts, stores, and hospital, the B Company of the second battalion 24th, under Lieutenant Bromhead. The ponts were in charge of Lieutenant Chard, RE. News of the disaster at Isandlwana reached these officers about 3 p.m., and they began at once hurriedly strengthening the position which Bromhead had already begun to place in a state of defence.

A worse position could hardly be imagined. Two small thatched buildings, about thirty-nine yards apart, with thin walls, commanded by rising ground on the south and west, completely overlooked on the south by a high hill. On the north side an orchard and garden gave good cover to an enemy up to within a few yards of the houses.

The force which was about to defend this position against three or four thousand Zulus consisted of 104 officers and men, and 35 sick. Luckily the men were seasoned soldiers and were commanded by two capable and brave officers, who upheld indeed the prestige of the British subaltern...

Extract from "Major General Henry Hallam Parr: Recollections And Correspondence," c. London 1917

...The Zulu army began to disperse directly after Isandlwana, many returning straight from the field of battle with their booty to their kraals. This contrary to orders, but the severe fighting and the amount of booty which had fallen into their hands had entirely disorganised the Zulu regiments.

The Undi (the royal corps) however, preserved its discipline, and after sullenly and unwillingly retreating from Rorke's Drift, marched straight to Ulundi. The king, according to custom, received them in the grand kraal. He had only as yet received the news that the white man's camp had been taken, and that 'Somtseu's' column had been eaten up. He had not heard of the repulse at Rorke's Drift, nor was he prepared for the terrible gaps made in his regiments. As the men began to file into the enclosure, he saw there had been very different fighting to that he had known in the Swasiland or against the Amatonga.

The Tulwana (the crack regiment of the royal corps, in whose ranks, as already stated, Cetewayo himself had fought in his young days, and to which he still nominally belonged) was the last regiment, and it filed in and saluted. 'Why don't the rest come in?' cried the king impatiently. But the rest of the brave Tulwana could not hear him, for they were lying outside the mealie bags and biscuit-boxes at Rorke's Drift.

We left No. 3 Column on the morning of the 23rd of January, about half-past eight, recrossing the Buffalo River. The crossing this time did not take long. Harness's four guns and wagons, and one mule wagon, which had carried the biscuit, comprised our wheeled vehicles.

By half-past nine, the remains of No. 3 Column had marched up to Rorke's Drift, and were getting their breakfasts round the shattered buildings and temporary parapet, which for twelve hours had sustained so desperate an attack. This over, all hands set to work in putting things to rights; while the Headquarters Staff, the mounted men, and Harness's four guns continued their march to Helpmakaar.

One of the most necessary duties to be undertaken was the burial of the dead and the cleansing of the ground. This had to be taken in hand without a moment's delay, as decomposition comes on quickly under the hot African sun. The superintendence of this work happened to be my duty.

'It's your turn now, comrade, now we've cleared this rubbish out of your way,' said a 24th man to a dead soldier, who was found with two or three Zulus stretched almost upon him. 'I'm main sorry to put you away, mate,' continued he, laying the end of a torn sack gently over the dead man's face, 'but you died well and had a soldier's end.'

Homely words, but what soldier could wish a better requiem?

The dead of the little garrison were buried where the colonist who gave his name to the drift lies, and the burial place service was read over them by the chaplain...

Extract from a private letter written to Sir Henry Bartle Frere: [RAVIC/033/118, The Royal Archives, Windsor, by permission of Her Majesty Queen Elizabeth II]

Camp, Rorke's Drift
23.1.79

...The men & officers have behaved admirably working shoulder to shoulder. I finished burying the dead Zulus this morning - natives won't touch dead bodies so our men had to do it & I did not hear a grumble.

To a dead soldier I heard a man say as he was lifting him - "Come on, old comrade, I'm main sorry to put you out of sight, but ye had a soldier's death"...

Captain William Penn Symons, 2nd/24th Foot

"The Battle of Isandhlwana and The Defence of Rorke's Drift 1879," by Capt. W.P. Symons 2-24th Regiment. [Appears courtesy of the South Wales Borderers Regtl. Museum, Brecon] This appears to be Penn Symons' first draft for his account complete with numerous corrections and alterations etc. It runs to some 44 pages not including additional inserted pages for notes, etc., indicated here by an *. Those sections that he actually crossed out in the original have been, where relevant, included as <u>underlined</u>

Private
Read by Her Majesty the Queen, the Prince of Wales, the D. of Cambridge, Sir Charles Ellice, Sir A. Alison, the Intelligence Department, &c &c -

The Queen kept this for a fortnight at Osborne in January 1880 and I was <u>order</u> asked by Sir Charles Ellice, then Adjutant General, by, I understood, the desire of Her Majesty, & of H.R.H. D. of Cambridge that the account should not be published until after the death of Lord Chelmsford, & perhaps other persons mentioned.

21st February 1880

An Account of the battle of Isandhlwana and Defence of Rorke's Drift
(Written at Rorke's Drift February, March & April 1879)

...We arrived there, on the Natal side, at 8-30 a.m., without encountering any of the enemy, though two large bodies made their appearance on our left rear, without, however, coming near enough to enable us to fire at them. Fortunately the Pontoons had been left untouched & we crossed easily *i).

The appearance of the defenders, most of them were of my old Company "B", in which I had been a subaltern for nearly 15 years., surpassed my attention. Some after their desperate exertions were hysterical, & could not speak *ii). Others overjoyed at their escape & our arrival there threw their arms about, waved their caps, & cheered. All were begrimed with powder, & blood & smoke smuts from the burning Hospital.

Lieut Bromhead was cool & collected, & his first thought, when he heard that the remnants of the column was returning, was to issue rations, & get breakfasts cooked for us.

One mile from the Buffalo River, on the Natal side, Lieut Gonville Bromhead 2/24th Regt with his Company, letter "B", of that Regiment, had been left to guard Commissariat stores & the lines of communication. The Company numbered 90 men & besides these there were 40 Casuals, 35 of whom were patients in Hospital.

Lieut. Chard Royal Engineers was the senior officer present, & Lieut Bromhead & his Company fought & acted under his able superintendence & orders.

The Post had been desperately attacked by great numbers of Zulus from 4. p.m. on the 22nd until daylight of the 23rd...

...At 3 p.m. on the 22nd January, Lieut Bromhead received the startling news from two fugitives that the General's Camp at Isandhlwana had been taken, & that the Zulus were on the way to attack his post. These men, after giving warning, lost no time in galloping off towards Helpmakaar <u>in continuing their journey & it is fortunate for them that Lt Bromhead was not able afterwards to recognize them</u>. Half an hour afterwards the intelligence was confirmed by a hastily written note received from Captain Gardner 14th Hussars...*iii)

...The above warnings gave the Officers at Rorke's Drift a short hour for preparation. It was badly needed, as nothing had been done to prepare the place for defence; the arrangements for so doing having been put off "by order" until the arrival of the expected reliefs of the Royal Engineers & 4th Regt.

The tents of the Company were pitched outside the Farm House or rather houses, as there were two; one, was used by us as a store, the other, as a "Base Hospital," & they were 40 38 yards apart -

At this time Lieut Chard was engaged with the Pontoons down at the river, & receiving like intelligence of the disaster & intended attack from another fugitive from Isandhlwana, moored the Pontoons in the middle of the stream, & made the best of his way back to where Lieut Bromhead & Acting Commissariat Officer Dalton were doing their utmost to render the Post defensible. -

The tents were struck, & the Store House loopholed & occupied. Biscuit boxes & sacks of mealies were piled so as to form a parapet towards the garden on one side, & along the other, facing the Hill, three wagons were drawn up, & the gaps between them were filled up with more boxes & sacks of grain. These "lines" connected the two Houses & formed what we will call "the Yard". It was a broken & imperfect barricade at the best. On the garden side the parapet was nowhere more than 3 ft. high; towards the hill in places it was raised to 4 & 4? feet. *iv).

The advance guard of the Zulus first appeared about 4-30 p.m. They came round the South Corner of the Hill in a body 500 to 600 strong, led by a chief riding a grey mare. They halted a moment, & then advanced quietly but quickly, at a run, taking advantage of every bit of cover. It seems as if they had expected to surprise the Post & capture it with a rush. Our men opened fire at 500 yards. The first man to fall was the mounted chief. He was shot by Private Dunbar, & fell from his horse headlong. numbers of them fell at once. As soon as the enemy felt the fire, they broke, & the greater part scattered to their left, & occupied the garden & orchard where there was plenty of cover. A few got up to the Houses & lay behind the Field Ovens & Kitchens. Most of these men were soon shot. It was quickly perceived that a very few only had of this advanced guard of the enemy had either guns or rifles. In a continuous stream more warriors followed the advanced party, occupied the hill, 400 yards distant & gradually encircled the two houses. Most of the men who had <u>guns</u> rifles were stationed on the hill, & they kept up a rapid fire on the yard.

It caught our men in reverse as they manned the parapet on the garden side, & 5 men were thus shot dead. As the evening set in, the <u>dusky foe</u> enemy crept nearer & nearer. Under cover of the bushes & long grass they were able to get within <u>five</u> a few yards of the Hospital without being seen. From this point in parties of 15 to 20 they repeatedly attacked the far corner of the Hospital.

They made these attacks in the most deliberate manner. As in their dancing, they stalked out of their concealment, pranced up with a high stepping action, & caring nothing for the slaughter, endeavoured to get over the barricade, <u>and into the end room of the Hospital.</u> Many times, seven or eight at least, Lieutenant Bromhead, collecting a few men together, had to drive them off with a bayonet charge. On being repulsed they would retire to better cover, shout in chorus & strike their shields with their assegais. Our men cheered in response & let them have it. How deliberate & telling was the fire may be gathered from the following incidents.

Private Joseph Williams, a young Welshman of under two years service, <u>had</u> was posted at a small window in the far end of the Hospital <u>to shoot from.</u> Next morning fourteen dead Zulus were found outside his window, & many more down his line of fire - As soon as his ammunition was expended, he & the other men in the room with him defended the door with their bayonets till it was broken & force open. Poor fellow, he was seized by the arms & hands, dragged out & assegaied<u>, & mutilated before the eyes of his comrades.</u>

Another instance - Private Dunbar, a Canadian by birth, the same man who had shot the Chief on horseback, was told off to watch the hill. As the Zulus streamed round the foot<u> from their right,</u> this man of even less service than Williams, got the right distance, & shot eight of them in as many consecutive shots. Lieut Chard was standing by him as he did it.

At last by sheer weight of numbers the enemy burst in the doors of the Hospital & effected an entry. Twenty eight of the patients were got out in time. most of them were pushed or pulled through a window which opened on the yard. A few escaped by making a bold dash from the Verandah, round & over the parapet. Two or three were caught & assegaied as they attempted this. An <u>artilleryman</u> gunner, a patient, by name Howard, a servant of Colonel Harness, *v). ran out of the Hospital, & hid himself in the long grass growing on the bank outside. He covered himself with grass & twigs <u>as well & quickly as he could</u> & remained there all night. He came in unharmed at daylight, although for many hours, the Zulus were constantly around & about him. A small pig was shot dead by his side. *vi).

Sergeant Maxfield of the 2/24th, a fine young soldier was down with fever & delirious. He could not be moved, & was killed in his bed. -

The enemy now set fire to the roof of the Hospital. Being thatch it blazed up at once. By its light our men were enabled to see the<u>ir foes</u> Zulus better, & many fell before they retreated.

After a pause, commanded and encouraged by an "Induna" or Chief, who from time to time shouted his orders from the hill side, they came on again most pluckily, shouting their war cry "Usutu, Usutu".

The fighting now became desperate, constantly hand to hand along the line of defence. The assailants only used their assegais as stabbing weapons. They seldom threw one. Any of our men showing themselves over the parapet were instantly trust at. Owing to want of flanking fire, there were places where the Zulus could crouch beneath the barricade in safety. They even seized the men's Bayonets, & tried to wrench them from the muzzles of the rifles. One soldier to whom this happened had just loaded; he pulled the trigger of his Martini, without putting it to his shoulder & blew the plucky fellow to atoms.

At first the hurriedly made & rough lines of defence were constructed to hold a very much larger body of defenders than actually were engaged. A large number of natives & some white men having in the most cowardly manner, at the first whisper of danger, deserted the post & bolted. Lieut Chard with admirable forethought & readiness of resource no sooner grasped the fact that he set men to construct a "retrenchment" or inner line of defence of biscuit boxes, connecting the corner of the store with the parapet on the garden side, & son after the roof of the Hospital fell in all our men had to take refuge behind this. Had he not done so it is probable that the Zulus, at this period of the attack, would have <u>rushed </u>captured the position. The immediate safety of the little garrison being secured, Lieut Chard, able assisted by all available hands, constructed inside the inner line of what may be termed a "crow's nest" of mealie sacks. From this commanding position the fire of the defenders was rendered much more effective. Acting Chaplain the Revd. George Smith of Estcourt, Natal; & Assistant Commissary Dunne contributed greatly to the construction & success of these little works.

The enemy now endeavoured to fire the roof of the Storehouse. One <u>fine savage</u> splendid fellow was shot by Corporal Attwood, of the Army Service Corps, as he was holding a lighted brand against the eaves.

And so the fight continued till midnight, from which time the attack gradually slackened, & the enemy, carrying away as many of their dead & wounded with them as possible, according to their custom in battle, withdrew. Some days afterwards, 50 large shields covered with blood were found by the river side, marking the spot to which they had carried their dead, & cast them into the river.

The last of them left just before dawn. The numbers composing the attack were estimated at 3,000. Many of the bodies by their shields & other distinctive marks, such as plumes, head rings &c were identified as belonging to one of the King's chief & favourite Regiments, & one which bore a great reputation.

Our loss was thirteen killed & ten wounded; three of the latter died soon after of their wounds. Of the enemy, these had all fallen close round the Post, we buried 376, & after days over 100 more skeletons were found lying here & there in the long grass & bush between Rorke's Drift & the spot where the Zulus recrossed the Buffalo River. -

The larger proportion, in fact 5 out of 6, of the bodies found were those of old men, many of them quite wizened, & all spare & thin. Very few could be called fine men, & one or two only approached six feet -

 - Already I have stated that many of them were heaped up contorted - and many others saw being dragged off by a fatigue party, to bury, with a wagon rope attached to the heel of the corpse only -

We must now mention the names of those who in this memorable fight defence especially distinguished themselves. It must be understood that it was essentially a soldiers fight. Given all credit to the Officers who used the best judgement under the circumstances, & exhibited prompt action & readiness of resource; given also the confidence with which Lieutenants Chard & Bromhead, young officers both, inspired their men, we repeat that it was a fight at the long odds of one white man to 30 black savages frenzied with success & slaughter. Each individual soldier stuck to his post, did his work & duty grandly.

No 395 Private John Williams, with the Joseph Williams before mentioned, was posted in the end room of the Hospital. They held it for more than an hour, as long as they had a round of ammunition left. As they were unfortunately cut off from the rest of the Company they could get no more ammunition. After Joseph Williams was dragged out of the room, John Williams & two of the Patients were the only men left alive. The Zulus left them alone for a while to butcher Joseph Williams. Taking advantage of the lull, these three made a hole in the partition wall with an axe, & getting into the next room joined Private Henry Hook, who still at his post was covering the escape withdrawal of the sick. John Williams & Hook, one working, whilst the other kept the enemy at bay with his bayonet, cut holes through three other partitions, & so working their way from room to room, succeeded in getting all the remainder of the sick out through the window into the yard. Private Hook was the last man to leave the Hospital & then it was all in flames.

In another ward Privates 593 William Jones, & 716 Robert Jones had been placed by Lieut Bromhead. They defended their post to the last, & held the ward until 6 out of the 7 Patients entrusted to their charge had been safely removed. The seventh was

Sergeant Maxfield. He was left for a while lying delirious & wounded on his bed. Private Robert Jones giving up his rifle went back to try & carry him out. The room was full of Zulus, & he saw them stabbing the body on the bed. It was entirely owing to the personal pluck & exertions of these four men that the last of the Patients escaped.

Acting Commissariat Officer Dalton, until badly wounded in the shoulder, & Corporal Schiess of the Natal Native Contingent, a Swiss by birth, also wounded, deserve the highest praise for their cheery encouragement of the soldiers, & the good work they performed in the Defence. *vii).

Corporal W. Allan, & Private Hitch, both 2/24th men, must also be mentioned for their courageous work & assistance. It was chiefly due to these two men that communication with the Hospital was kept up at all. Holding at all costs a most dangerous post, at the N.E. corner of the Hospital, raked in reverse by the enemy's fire from the hill, they were both severely wounded, but their determined conduct enabled the Patients to be withdrawn from the Hospital. When incapacitated from firing themselves, they continued, as soon as their wounds had been dressed, to serve out ammunition to their comrades during the night -

It was a gallant defence. The young soldiers backed each other up & fought splendidly. They never wavered for an instant. Most of them Welshmen by birth, by a few months of drill & training, & infusion of "Esprit de Corps", had become the best & pluckiest of "Warwickshire Lads", & gloriously upheld the traditions of the old 24th.

It was of the utmost importance that Rorke's Drift should not have been captured by the enemy. Had it fallen, Helpmakaar would probably have gone also, and not only would a probable invasion by a triumphant enemy followed by a great panic have fallen on the Colony of Natal, but the safety of the remainder of Colonel Glyn's Column would have been imperilled.

When Lieut General Lord Chelmsford K.C.B. left Rorke's Drift on the morning of the 24th January 1879 for Pieter-Martizburg, he desired Lieut Colonel Degacher C.B. commanding the 2/24th Regt. to address the men of his Battalion at the first opportunity as follows - "Not having time myself I wish you to tell them how highly I think of their conduct, it was admirable, no troops could have been steadier or more collected, especially during that trying night of constant alarms, the 22nd.As for Lieut Bromhead & his Company nothing that I can now say can express my admiration of the gallant defence they made".

Notes made on separate pages

i). Major Russell of the 12 Lancers was the 1st & I was the second officer of the column to reach Rorke's Drift Post, and the sight there presented was astounding. Several hundred dead Zulus were lying close round the houses & defences. In some places they were heaped together, 5 or 6 one on top of the other. The limbs of many of the bodies were strangely contorted almost tied in knots, giving the idea of the Martini Henry bullet at very close range causing severe muscular contractions before death.

ii). Private Michael Minahan, the right hand man of the Company, & a great pal of mine, who knew his drill well, & had often kept me straight on parade, took me off to show me where he had been stationed in a corner of the cattle kraal. He could scarcely speak from excitement, but suddenly catching sight of his bayonet, which was fixed at the time, & seeing it covered with blood, he appeared to remember something, & groping about in the straw a yard or two from where he had been posted uncovered the naked body of a dead Zulu, with a broad bladed assegai still in his hand. He then related, chiefly with signs, that this Zulu must have crept in over the wall of the kraal, & crawling under the straw had suddenly seized him by the leg. My friend Minahan had then, as he said, prodded the straw, & one prod right through the body had got home.

*iii) Lieut. Bromhead stated that on the 10th January, when he with his Company to their intense disappointment were detailed to remain behind & occupy & guard Rorke's Drift commissariat store & base hospital, he twice asked permission to place the post in a state of defence, but sanction was refused him by Lord Chelmsford's Staff. Afterwards when the Column had moved on, he became so persuaded of the risk & danger of inaction, that he made up his mind what to do if occasion should arise. & Hence followed on the sudden alarm the promptness & correctness of his preparations, which had the warm approval of Lieut Chard an officer of the Royal Engineers.

*iv). The hill was 400 yards from the post, & it commanded the houses & enclosures.

*v). when it was dark

*vi). He told me next morning that his greatest fear was that the red stripes on his trousers would be seen

*vii). It was told that when the Zulus first endeavoured to rush the Post & were checked, Mr Dalton who had charge of the wagon barricade, stood up on one of the wagons & jeered at the Zulus, daring them to come on; and that when thus standing he had no more ammunition left, he threw his helmet at some of them crouching behind the ovens.

Corporal Schiess, they said, "fought like a little tiger". He could not restrain himself, but more than once dashed over the barricade, bayoneted a Zulu, & got back again.

Lieutenant George S. Banister, 2nd/24th

Extract from a letter written to his father, Surgeon General Banister, dated January 27th, 1879: [Appears courtesy of the South Wales Borderers Regtl. Museum, Brecon]

...When we reached the top of the last rising ground between us and Rorke's Drift our hearts again sank, for where our little camp of one Company used to be was now to be seen nothing but a column of smoke and no tents. Then we gave up all hope for Gunny Bromhead and his Company who had been left there. We crossed the river in the punts, which to our surprise had not been destroyed, but before our turn came we heard a cheer from those who had gone first to the house, which had been used as a store. But how much or how little it meant of course we could not tell. At last we crossed and went up there and found old Gunny as cheery as ever and not a scratch about him. All round was a scene of awful confusion. What had been a hospital was a misshapen mass of smoking cinders - dead niggers everywhere...

Lieutenant Henry G. Mainwaring, 2nd/24th Foot

Extract from "Isandhlwana Prelude and Aftermath," January 22nd, 1895:
[Appears courtesy of the South Wales Borderers Regtl. Museum, Brecon]

...On arriving in sight of Rorke's Drift, we saw the house in flames, also far over the country we observed various homesteads ablaze. This led us to believe that the Zulus had invaded Natal. We naturally thought that the garrison had fallen. Great therefore was our relief when the cavalry, who were the first to cross the river, galloped up to the house and sent up a ringing cheer. Soon afterwards, the infantry crossed by the Pontoons and I shall never forget seeing 'Gonny' Bromhead (then Lieutenant) come out to meet us as we formed in quarter column outside the gate. He told me afterwards he felt as if he was walking on air as he never expected to see daylight again. After giving me some food Bromhead took me round the scene of the fight. In front of the verandah outside the hospital and near the two blue gum trees the Zulu bodies were lying three deep. 'Gonny' especially pointed out a young Zulu Induna with a plume head-dress, telling me that he was a very gallant man, and had headed a charge three times. 'But we got him the third time' he added. Inside the hospital he pointed out the remains of Sergeant Maxwell who I knew well - a good fellow.
Within the yard and right in front of the Rorke's Drift house was an inner defence - a sort of redoubt. This was suggested by Lieutenant Chard. It consisted of a circular pile of mealie bags, about 20 feet high. I climbed up to the top and looked down into the well space inside and there saw a soldier lying - dead as I first thought but after calling up 'Gonny' we found he was fast asleep from exhaustion. As a matter of fact we were all well played out.
But there was much to be done. The dead were buried - we lost 15 men and we buried between 300 to 400 Zulus...

A letter written to the Editor of the "Morning Post," c. 1921: [Appears courtesy of the South Wales Borderers Regtl. Museum, Brecon, Acc. No. L40 57]

Army and Navy Club,
Pall Mall, S.W.1
28 May 1921

Sir,
ISANDHLWANA and RORKES DRIFT.

I have recently spent several months in Natal, South Africa, and whilst there I was able on the 8th March this year, through the great kindness of Mr. Plowman, C.M.G., Administrator of Natal, (who made all the arrangements) to revisit the battlefield of Isandhlwana.

For the information of those who lost relations and friends, I wish to state that I found the place very little changed. The graves were well kept and in good order. The stones over each grave were whitewashed. This gave the appearance of innumerable little monuments over the battlefield.

The 24th Regimental Memorial is in very good position - could not be better.

We next went on to Rorke's Drift. This Drift is now seldom used, and the roads leading to it have become out of repair, some almost obliterated.

We crossed the river in a boat and on the other side found horses waiting for us.

Fort Melvill is now nothing but a ruin.

Within 300 to 400 yards of Rorkes Drift house I could recognise <u>nothing</u>. The old place, as we who were stationed there remember it, has been swept away, not a vestige of the old house remains.

In its place is a small modern villa of a style to be seen in the suburbs of London, an aggressively red-faced little building with a blue slate roof. The old yard round which our defences were formed is now occupied by a Church. The hospital has been rebuilt almost the same. The two blue gum trees are still there, but the right-hand tree, so I was informed, is new.

The place is now in possession of a Swedish missionary. He did not appear to take much interest in the records of that gallant outpost fight - nor did he evince any kindly feeling for the memory of the men who formed the little garrison - 180 British against 4,000 to 5,000 Zulus.

We relieved them at 7 a.m. the following morning. In defeating this attack they undoubtedly saved Natal from invasion by a Zulu Impi.

The Minister replied to a question from me asking to see the graves of the 24th men, "We don't mind looking after the graves of the English soldiers". As a matter of fact the graves are really in Government charge.

The obelisk made by Bandsman Melsop, 24th Regt., I found in good order, but the graveyard is choked up with bushes. These should be cleared away.

The whole surroundings of Rorke's Drift and ground not occupied by buildings is covered with a untidy jungle of fruit trees. I am sorry I saw it and regret still more that this historic spot should have passed into alien hands.

Yours faithfully,

H.G. Mainwaring
Brig. General,
late Comdg.
1st South Wales Borderers, 24th Regiment

Lieutenant William Weallens, 2nd/24th Foot

Extract from "The Uppingham School Magazine, c. October 1879: ["The Red Soldier," by Fred Emery page 123]

...Since I last wrote I have heard some particulars of Lieutenant Bromhead's fight here. You must know that he only had 90 men, and that he was occupying exactly the same extent of ground that 600 or 700 do now, with the exception that it was not nearly so strongly fortified. As he had so few men, he could not afford to fortify any one place very strongly, but there was one building used as a hospital which he determined to defend to the last, as there were about twenty sick men in it. Strange to say, the Zulus made most persistent attacks on this one point, and seemingly not caring how many of their men were killed in the attack. They got possession of one room and, having accomplished this, fired the building. This is what was most dreaded; however, most of the sick were removed in safety. One man, named Williams, did a very plucky thing; he got into a small room by himself, and from the window fired away all the ammunition he had. He then tried to make a bolt for it into the fort, but unfortunately fell in getting out of the window. He got up, however, and tried to join the fort, when he was wounded by an assegai. He was caught by the Zulus and literally cut to pieces, as they were so infuriated at the number of them he had killed. He had only about six yards to run to get into the fort, as the hospital was in the same line of defence. It seems very hard that he should have lost his life after fighting so well.

I only hope Bromhead will be well rewarded for his defence of this place, as there is but little doubt that if the Zulus had beaten him it was their intention to attack our line of march, when we should have been taken at a great disadvantage and in country suitable to them, and with their numbers we might possibly have been cut to pieces...

Lieutenant Archibald B. Milne, Royal Navy

Extract from "Report of proceedings of 21st, 22nd, 23rd & 24th Jany. 1879." [ADM1/6486, The National Archives, (P.R.O.), London]

...There was seen the gallant defence made by the small garrison of 80 men. The dead Zulus were lying about in <u>scores</u> close up to the parapet. Firing was still going on at wounded men trying to escape. For a long time the garrison held the hospital but at last found they had too much ground to defend for so small a number, and the enemy kept creeping up in the bushes in the garden, and coming upon them in rushes. So at last they were obliged to leave it. The sick defended it for an hour longer when at last the enemy managed to burn it with all its inmates.

The officers who so gallantly defended this store were Lt. Bromhead 2/24 and Lt. Chard, RE.

As soon as our column had had some food, they were immediately set to work to improve the defences. The parapet was heightened and continued along to the edge of the hospital, the thatching of the store was taken off, and all the trees round about cut down. The guns were brought inside, three were mounted pointing towards the river, and the fourth towards the right of the krantz and the direction in which the enemy came the previous night...

[In addition to this statement Milne also left the following as "No. 12" of his accompanying 'Notes on the Report of Proceedings'];-

12/.

"At Rorkes Drift, one of the prisoners taken gave these undermentioned names as the Regiments who attacked at Isandhlwana...

...Undi Regt. - Kraals Toulwan, Inhlohonhlo, Inhluyegwe - Strength 8000 (Cetywayos own Regt.)...

Attacking force at Rorkes Drift consisted of from 4 to 5,000 men of the Undi Regt.

This prisoner also stated that they were obliged to fight, should they not do so they would be killed by Cetywayo

The Undi Regt. consists entirely of Ringtops or married men about 35 years of age.

A private of the 2/24th took from one of the prisoners captured at Rorkes Drift some of his own property taken at Isandhlwana the day previous...

Arch. B. Milne
Lieut. R.N.

Extract from a letter written by Milne to Commodore Sullivan, R.N., in Durban: [ADM1/6486, The National Archives, (P.R.O.), London]

Fort near Rorke's Drift
23rd January 1879

My dear Sir...

...Started again at daylight this morning & reached this place at 7.0. Found that the Hospital had been attacked by 2,000 Zulus last evening at 5 p.m. it was garrisoned by 1 Company 2/24th who held out until the Zulus withdrew at 4 a.m. this morning. They lost 13 killed. Zulus 100 killed. We have lost everything, camp &c. &c. being taken away by the enemy. Be good enough not to make this public until something Official comes out. This is what Crealock thinks best.

Sincerely Yours
Arch. B. Milne.
Extract from a second letter written to Commodore Sullivan, R.N. in Durban: [ADM1/6486, The National Archives, (P.R.O.), London]

Ladismith,
Saturday morning

My dear Sir
We left Rorke's Drift yesterday morning at 8 a.m. we had an anxious night in the Commissariat store which we had fortified or rather improved upon the fortifications which had been hastily thrown up the night previous by its small garrison of 70 men. They behaved in the most gallant manner. A force of 3,000 Zulus attacked them at 3 p.m. on Wednesday afternoon, the engagement continued until 4 a.m. Thursday morning.
The Zulus came over the embankment of mealie bags surrounding the store 6 times and were each time driven out at the point of the bayonet, our loss was 12 killed and 13 wounded. 351 dead Zulus were counted round the store. They were carrying away a good many dead and always their wounded so their loss must have been great its no doubt if the Zulu force had been successful against Rorke's Drift, they would have gone on to Helpmakaar...

...Sincerely Yours
A.B. Milne

Lieutenant Horace Lockwood Smith-Dorrien, 95th Regiment

Extract from "Memories of Forty-Eight Years' Service," London, 1925

...The next day I rode down to Rorke's Drift, some twelve miles, to resume charge of my depot. There was the improvised little fort, built up mostly of mealy-sacks and biscuit-boxes and other stores which had been so gallantly defended by Chard, Bromhead, and their men, and Parson Smith, and all around lay dead Zulus, between three and four hundred; and there was my wagon, some 200 yards away, riddled and looted, and there was the riem gallows I had erected the previous morning. Dead animals and cattle everywhere - and a scene of devastation! To my young mind it appeared impossible that order could ever be restored, but I set to work and next day, whilst sitting in my wagon, I saw two Zulus hanging on my gallows and was accused by the Brigade Major, Clery, (afterwards General Sir Francis Clery), of having given the order. I was exonerated, however, when it was found that it was a case of lynch law performed by incensed men, who were bitter at the loss of their comrades. Other incidents of the same sort occurred in the next few days before law and order were re-established...

1404 Lance Corporal William Adams, 'D' Company, 2nd/24th Foot

The following letter was sent to his family in Abertillery, Wales. Is is reproduced here with the kind permission of Mr Frank V. Hughes Esq. who owns the original.

Rorke's Drift, March 6th 1879.

My Dear Mother,

I write these few lines to you, hoping to find you in good health, as I am very proud to tell you I am myself at present. I received two newspapers from Joe, and one from George, and when you get a newspaper with the account of the disaster out here, please try and send me one. I sent you £1 in December last, and you have not sent to say whether you received it or not.

We lost one mail altogether when our camp was taken on January 22nd, at Isandlwana, and there might have been a letter for me then. I will send you some more money as soon as I can, but things are all of an uproar now. We have not received any pay this year yet. We are still in our little fort at Rorke's Drift, and have not had our boots or clothes off (except when we can manage a bath) since January 22nd, and not likely to yet for some time to come. We can see but very few Zulus at present. One of our columns, 3rd Buffs, Naval Brigade and 99th Regiments are hemmed in, but they are strongly entrenched, and receiving half rations. Everything is at a standstill until reinforcements arrive from England.

There are 500 sailors landed from the 'Shah' man-of-war, to try to relieve Colonel Pearson. As soon as troops arrive from home the General says he will send us back to Pietermaritzburg, to get fresh equipment, as it appears we shall not be in much danger during the remainder of the Zulu War. I sent the account of the losses to Joseph. We have about 40 men in hospital, 60 more attending hospital, all sick of dysentery and fever, resulting from the unhealthiness, because of so many dead buried around.

We have just had a collection for the widows and orphans of the killed. We generally have about two men die every week. Jordan, Frowen, Ellis and Gleeson are all right. Please remember me to all the family and inquiring friends. Stamps and paper very scarce. Will write to George, when I get another stamp. I must now remain your ever affectionate son,

William. D Company, 2nd/24th Regiment, Rorke's Drift.

PS. We have plenty of live stock on some of us.

25B/1125 Private James (John) Cook, 2nd/24th Foot

Extract from a letter to his parents & subsequently published in "The Brecon County Times," March 29th, 1879.

Rorke's Drift, Feb. 2nd, 1879 ...We came to this place next morning, which we thought to have seen all ransacked, but the company we left here had succeeded in beating the enemy and killing 1,000 of them. It took us two days to bury the dead. We have now a fort made out of meal and oats and boxes of biscuits...

25B/1605 Lance Corporal Courtney Frowen, 'G' Company, 2nd/24th Foot

A letter to his parents, published in "The Citizen," & "The Forester, Mercury & Guardian," c. 1879

A Forester in Zululand

Rorke's Drift, February 2nd, 1879

Dear Parents,

...I am glad to tell you that I am very well, but do not think the place we are in is very healthy, as it is like a graveyard all around us. We have buried hundreds of bodies, and we put as many as 40 Zulus into one hole at a time, and there are hundreds of bodies both black and white, now on the other side of the hill, but the officers will not let us go to bury them...

1481 Private John James, 'G' Company 2nd/24th Foot

Extract from a letter to his parents which was published in "The Western Mail", c. 1879

Rorke's Drift
February 2 1879

...Dear Mother, after they done slaughtering up there they went down to where B company was with commissary - about 12,000 of them, and they set fire to it, but our boys had the best of them. Here they killed about 1,200 of them. The loss on our side was 11 killed and two wounded. William Osborne had a narrow escape. They had to fight hard for their lives that night. William Osborne, Edward Murphy, T. Parry, and William Davies, all send their kind love to you. George Slasher got killed in the battle. So no more at present -
From your loving son,
John James
Thank God that I am alive to tell the news
Private John James, 1481, G Company 2/24th Regiment, Natal, South Africa

25B/295 Private David Jenkins 'G' Company, 1st/24th Foot

"The Merthyr Express," Saturday, March 22nd, 1879

Letter from a Welsh Survivor of Isandula
Survivor of Isandlwana, from Aberdare

The following letter has been received from Zululand, written by David Jenkins, son of Mr. Thomas Jenkins, tailor and draper, Tanner's Arms, Davynock, and nephew of Mr. W. Davies, saddler, of Aberdare, in which town the writer was well known;-

Zululand
January 26, 1879

Dear Father, -
Just a few lines to let you know that I am one of the ten that escaped out of the five companies. The remainder were cut to pieces, - in fact cut in bits- with those savages. About 15,000 of them came on the camp when the column was out. All in camp were killed - 495 of our regiment and about 300 of different corps. Oh I never saw such a sight. Please to pray to God to continue to save my life. There are only 240 men remaining in our regiment. So no more. I shall write again soon if alive. Dear Father, please go personally or write a letter to Isaac Lewis, Pendra, Brecon and tell him that his son in law Sgt. Chambers is killed. His son Thomas is alive but is still in hospital with the fever. He had a very narrow escape . He crept on his hands

and knees and came from the hospital to the fort through all the firing. Please give my love to all, and write soon. -

Your affectionate son.

D. Jenkins.

P.S. I think we will go down to the colony to get re-fitted, as we have lost everything.

No.295 David Jenkins.
'G' Company, 1-24th Regiment
Pietermaritzburg, Natal.

25B/934 Private Harry Lang, 'B' Company 1st/24th Foot

Extract from "The Northern Echo," c. May 1934

**Rorke's Drift Survivors
Invited to Tattoo:
Horden Man's Memories.**

...Lieut. Col. Frank Bourne, one of the survivors, who is now 85 and lives at Dorking, Surrey, made this announcement on Saturday night when he broadcast a graphic account of the defence of 100 men against between 3,000 and 4,000 Zulus. Among the survivors are ex-Sergt. A. Saxty and ex-Privates T. Buckley, Cooper, G. Edwards, J. Jobbins, D. Lewis, H. Martin, C. Mason, C. Woods and H. Lang.

"Now Only A Name."

Mr. Henry Lang is now living in retirement with his wife at 6, Aged Miners' Homes, Horden. Mr Lang told a Northern Echo reporter that he was a keen listener and had heard the broadcast talk. "There cannot," he said, "be many survivors left. The battle took place 55 years ago, when I was only 20."

He had never met any of the survivors until in 1918, after dismissal from the Brighton Military Hospital, he saw a comrade walking on the Brighton front. A medal such as Mr. Lang, himself proudly wears on his watch chain was the only means of identification.

"Rorke's Drift," Mr Lang said, "is now only a name. Very few people appreciate the stubborn courage and devotion to duty displayed by the 100 or so British soldiers who beat off thousands of Zulus in a skirmish lasting all night and all day. It is a thing I shall never forget."...

1939 Private William Sweeney, 2nd/24th Foot

"The Oldham Weekly Chronicle," April 26th, 1879

...About 3,000 Zulus came on our chaps about three on the same evening. Our boys made a fort of all the bags of corn, and bags of flour, meal, and all sorts of stuff. The enemy came on in rushes times out of number, and our chaps mowed them down as fast as they came up. Several of the Zulus got over the fort, but our chaps on the inside were waiting for them with the bayonet. You would be surprised to see the horrible murders as ever were committed. Those 80 men kept them off from three o'clock in the afternoon on the 22nd, until six a.m. on the 23rd for the loss of 14 men. One of them had a most horrible death. He was assegaied with long knives. His name was Billy Horrigan. He joined the regiment in Cork. Each of the men in the fort that night used 150 rounds of ammunition. The General said if he had 1,000 men like those he would face any 10,000 Zulus...

Major John G. Dartnell, Commandant of the Natal Mounted Police

His own account [NAB 1/BLR, Vol. 6, ref. P90/1879, Kwa-Zulu Natal Archives, Pietermaritzburg]

Colonial Secretary to Resident Magistrate
Ad. Nat. Law Ipolela

The following short account of the Action at Rorke's Drift, written by Major Dartnell, is sent you, in order that you may explain to those in your District how practicable it is for a few determined men to repulse the attacks of large bodies of savages if advantage is taken of cover.
By command,
C.B.H. Mitchell,
Colonial Secretary Recd
15 Febry. 1879

DEFENCE OF THE POST AT RORKE'S DRIFT.

At Rorke's Drift a detachment of one company of the 2-24th Regiment (80 men), under the command of Lieutenant Bromhead, was stationed in charge of Commissariat stores, &c., Lieutenant Chard, of the Royal Engineers, being the senior officer present. The buildings at this post consisted of two stone and brick houses, with *thatched* roofs, about 20 yards apart, and a small square stone cattle kraal, with walls about 5ft. high, adjoining one of these buildings.
The detachment was encamped close to these buildings, one of which was used as a hospital and the other as a Commissariat store. There were also great quantities of other stores, principally mealies, oats, &c., in sacks, stacked outside.
About 4 p.m. on the afternoon of the 22nd of January, notice was given at the post by some fugitives of the disastrous attack by the Zulus, upon the Headquarter Camp of No. 3 Column at Isandhlwana, and the probability of an attack being immediately made upon the post at Rorke's Drift.
No preparation for defence having been previously made, the Officer in command at once commenced to enclose the buildings, as far as possible, with sacks of grain, and, being assisted by willing hands, had so far completed the work that in an hour's time a wall of sacks about 4ft. high was formed into an enclosure of about 20 yards

square, flanked by the cattle kraal on one side and by the Commissariat store upon another. the store was loopholed, and the thatch was partially removed to allow the men stationed in the roof to fire through.

There was no time to complete the entrenchment so as to include the Hospital within the enclosure, for the enemy came down about an hour after the first warning was received, and immediately rushed to the attack. On the one side were 80 men of the 2-24th Regiment, assisted by a few others, behind a very hastily-constructed barricade of sacks filled with grain, and on the other were over 2,000 Zulus armed with guns and assegais, and flushed with recent success, who imagined that they would easily make a prey of the small European force.

The gallant and devoted little garrison, however, behind their weak barrier of sacks, received the assault with a cheer and a volley, and maintained their ground for twelve hours, notwithstanding the persistent and determined attacks of the enemy; the flames of the burning Hospital which was fired by the Zulus, fiercely lighting up the scene of the raging conflict. No less than seven organised attacks were made during the night, the Zulus on several occasions rushing right upon the bayonets of the defenders.

The enemy finally retired about daylight, leaving over 300 dead around the enclosure; the defenders having suffered the small loss of 13 killed - including those cut off in the Hospital - and 9 wounded.

The gallant defence of Rorke's Drift shows with what confident hopes of success a small party of Europeans, well armed, and behind some sort of entrenchment, may protect themselves from an apparently overwhelming number of Kafirs.

Should any thatched buildings be within the lines of defence, the thatch should be, if possible, removed or well covered with mud before the enemy's arrival.

The advisability of destroying thatch so removed must be determined by circumstances. If there were any wooden or other inflammable materials in the composition of the entrenchment, it would be well to destroy the thatch, lest it be used by the enemy as a means of igniting them; if, on the contrary, there were nothing of the kind, it might be well to deposit the thatch at a short distance, to be available for giving light in ease of a night attack.

Care should be taken that the entrenchment is not too large for the number of men to defend it; there should be at least one man to every loop-hole, or yard of wall, besides a reserve sufficient to take the places of wounded men, and to issue ammunition, &c.

(Signed)

J.G. Dartnell, Major

Commandant Mounted Police and Volunteers.

Trooper William James Clarke, Natal Mounted Police

Extract from Clarke's own reminiscences entitled "My Career in South Africa," (c. 1878-1919): [File 1, Clarke Papers, Killie Campbell Africana Library, Durban, Kwa-Zulu Natal]

...On reaching the summit of the hill overlooking the Drift, we could see men moving about round the hospital, so Colonel Russell sent on the Mounted Infantry to reconnoitre. After they had crossed the river we saw them gallop up to the buildings and we then knew that the Zulus had been unsuccessful. As we approached the Commissariat Store the first dead man we came across was a N.C.O. of the N.N.C. who had attempted to run away and had been shot by our own men before the flight had commenced.

One of the N.M.P., Trooper Hunter, had been killed in the space between the Hospital and the Commissariat Store. Hunter had shot his assailant dead while receiving two assegais in his chest. When we searched his pockets before burying him we found two pounds of gold. Altogether we buried 375 dead Zulus and some wounded were thrown into the grave.

Seeing the manner in which our wounded had been mutilated after being dragged from the Hospital (men who were wounded in the skirmish on the 12th January) we were very bitter and did not spare wounded Zulus. One man of the 24th, in escaping from the burning hospital, had rushed through the Zulus in the darkness and had hidden in a cave within a few yards of the spot where the mutilations took place and which he witnessed. Another man had dashed into a mealie garden and had remained there unseen.

As soon as we had off-saddled we were paraded to draw rations and a tot of rum, the first food I had had since the morning of the 20th, nearly three days ago. I managed to comsume a 2lb. tin of corned beef and a 3lb. loaf of bread whilst walking round looking at the slaughter.One man, Sergeant Maxwell, of the 24th, had been burnt alive. As soon as we had buried all the dead, we laid down and slept until evening...

Trooper Fred Symons, Natal Carbineers

Extract from "The Farmer", March 3rd and 10th, 1933", reprinted in "The Journal of the AZWRS, Vol 4, No.1." [Killie Campbell Africana Library, Durban, Kwa-Zulu Natal].
(He picks up the story as he and the remainder of Lord Chelmsford's column are returning to Rorke's Drift on the morning of the 23rd January 1879)

...'What's that on the wall?'
It was a man waving a flag. There was another. The place was full of them! 'Are they friends or are they foes?'
'Perhaps they are the Zulus and the waving of flags a ruse to get part of the force

across the river and then fall upon us.'

This suspicion was roused by the sight of a large force of natives on the spur of the Biggarsberg beyond the Mission Station where the flag waving was going on.

Rorke's Drift

Pushing on to the Buffalo as fast as possible, Col. Russell ordered the Carbineers to line the bank, dismount and cover the retreat of the Mounted Infantry, if necessary. Fixing the sights of our carbines at eight hundred yards, we stood waiting for the Mounted Infantry to be fire upon, but soon one came back to say, 'All right. They're our men'...

...The first corpse that met our gaze was that of a N.N.C. officer who was shot by the 24th for deserting them in the hour of danger. His men fled at the approach of the Zulus but that was no reason for deserting too. Thrice they called him to come back, but he would not. He was a foreigner. Around the ruins of the hospital lay in heaps the bodies of dead Zulus, some burnt to ashes. A strong smell of roasting flesh pervaded the place.

A trooper of the Police, who had been in hospital with fever, tried to reach the laager of mealie bags from the burning.... A Zulu followed him. The soldiers shouted to the trooper to drop down so that they could shoot the Zulu, but he either did not hear or understand, for the Zulu stabbed him.

In endeavouring to reach the others from the burning building a young soldier was also stabbed from behind.

One patient flung a blanket over himself, smeared his face with ashes, and escaped into the orchard, where he escaped observation and came out safely in the morning. But the first question we put was;

'Where are our men, have none escaped?'

The only ones they had spoken to was trooper Fletcher of the Carbineers and R. Hall, the meat contractor...."

About the Camp

"...Each man was here served out with bread and a rum ration. Then we began to saunter round. Beneath the trees, still fastened by reins to the tree trunk, lay the carcasses of three horses, and everywhere lay bodies of Zulus.

The men on the spur of the mountain turned out to be the regiment of N.N.C. deserts who were on their way back to see how the fight had gone. When they saw it was all right, they came down and were brave as ever they were when no enemy was about!

The greater part of the day was spent in collecting the dead Zulus, of whom about seven hundred were buried on that and the following day.

The men of the 24th, who defended the place, spoke very highly of the Rev. Geo. Smith, who, they say, carried ammunition round in his hat for the men. One man told me that a private was swearing because he could not get any ammunition and the Rev. George reproved him, saying he should not swear at such a time as this but put his trust in God. Patting his rifle the soldier replied; 'I shall put my faith in this now and God afterwards.'

The palms of their hands were scorched by the heated rifle barrels and over and over again the Zulus would seize the bayonets and try and wrench the rifles away."

Saved from Fire

"When the hospital was fired by the Zulus the men at once set to work to pull off the thatch from the dwelling house. A German, or some foreigner, who was with the garrison, saved the building from fire for he saw the Zulu with a lighted bunch of grass on the end of a stick just raising it up to the eaves and promptly shot him. Had that building caught alight it would have been all up with the garrison.

The guns and assegais were collected and thrown into a large hole below the laager and burnt. Most of the guns were loaded (muzzle loaders) and all day long these weapons were discharged in this hole. It is surprising no one got hit.

The men spoke very highly of Chard and another man named, I think, Milne. Of Bromhead they did not speak well.

Milne, if that was the man's name, ought to get the V.C., if any man deserved it; for when the men were distracted with thirst and parched with the dust from the thatch and smoke, they went to broach a cask of rum, but this man stood upon it and threatened to shoot the first who touched it. He also volunteered to go with a few men and guard the punt, but was not permitted to do so...

Trooper H. T. Simpson, Newcastle Mounted Rifles

Extract from his own account which appeared in an unidentified Natal newspaper, c. 1929: [courtesy Mr Ron Lock]

...A few hours' marching brought us to Rorke's Drift, so gallantly defended by Lieutenants Chard and Bromhead with 31 men of the 24th and 21 others. The previous night we have heard the terrific firing, and when we arrived about 9 o'clock in the morning and saw the hospital, where 35 sick men had been billeted, burning furiously, we thought the tragedy of Isandhlwana had been repeated.

"We were formed up in order and given the order to charge; but our feelings of relief can well be imagined when we saw a soldier climb on to the wall of boxes and bags and signal to us. We pulled up. Hundreds and hundreds of natives lay round the laager in heaps. One or two of them had even succeeded in entering the scanty enclosure, but they had been killed immediately.

"I think the firing of the hospital actually helped the defenders, who had been able to see the enemy much better by its glare. Their hands were scorched by their rifles, which had grown red hot with continual firing, and every man was utterly exhausted.

Their little bit of laager had undoubtedly saved them from sharing the fate of the 800, and at the same time taught us once and for all that in fighting the Zulu in those days a laager was not only advisable, but absolutely necessary...

Lieutenant & Adjutant Henry Harford, Natal Native Contingent

Extract from "The Zulu War Journal of Colonel Henry Harford, C.B.," edited by D. Child, Shuter & Shooter, Pietermaritzburg, 1978: [Appears by kind permission of the Local History Museum, Durban, Kwa-Zulu Natal, South Africa, who owns Harford's original handwritten manuscript]

...When the general advance took place, a few of our Natives under a corporal named Schiess were left at Rorke's Drift as part of the Garrison of the Fort under Lieutenant Bromhead, of the 2nd Battalion, 24th Regiment, and Lieutenant Chard, of the Royal Engineers. Schiess was subsequently awarded the Victoria Cross for very conspicuous bravery. Some of the men of the 24th Regiment told me that he fought like a tiger and at one time, when some Zulus actually managed to clutch hold of his bayonet, he got it out of their hands and, springing over the parapet, bayonetted some six or seven of them straight away...

...Throughout the night we could see the intermittent flashes of light from the firing at the Rorke's Drift post, which was only some three of four miles off in a straight line, though twelve miles by road. Everyone felt anxious for the fate of the little garrison after what had happened in the Camp, and longed for daylight to march to their relief...

...As we approached the Drift and reached the hill overlooking the river and the Post, the excitement became intense, all eyes were strained and field-glasses raised, to see if there was any sign of life in the Fort. Then, as we drew nearer, a man was seen on the bared roof of one of the buildings, signalling with a flag, which was hailed with a tremendous cheer from the whole Column as we knew then that the garrison had not been wiped out.

The General and his staff galloped off at once to the Fort and the troops got in by degrees, the selecting of their camping grounds taking some little time. We were the last to get in, and for some time it was quite impossible to keep the men in hand. They were all round the surroundings of the Fort in a second, crowding about the Zulu dead who were lying thick everywhere, partly, no doubt, from curiosity but I dare say some may have been looking out to identify friends or relations as many of the Natal Kaffirs are refugees from Zululand.

Commandant Lonsdale having gone to interview the General and to get something to eat, I also strolled into the Fort and helped myself bountifully to some biscuits, several boxes of which the thoughtful Commissariat Officers, Dunne and Dalton, had hauled out and opened for us hungry souls. What a Godsend it was, as it was over two days and two nights since most *of* us had had a mouthful of food. Hunger, however, luckily does not affect one like thirst, and one could have gone on much longer as there was plenty of good water.

As I ate biscuits I wandered about the Fort, looking at the wreckage which gave the appearance and feeling of devastation after a hurricane, with the dead bodies thrown in, the only thing that remained whole being a circular miniature fortress constructed of bags of mealies in the centre. Several of our dead lay just where they had fallen, and one of them - a youngster in the Natal Mounted Police - a very fine specimen of humanity, struck me particularly. Having given our natives ample time to exhaust their curiosity, they were got together and marched off to the position allotted to us at the back of the Fort, behind the Itchiane hill to guard the valley up which the Zulus had made their attacks, well hidden until the last moment. Outposts were at once posted and Mounted Patrols sent out, and the remainder of the troops not thus occupied were told off to clear the surroundings of the Fort and renovate the defences. As many of our men as could be supplied with picks and shovels were set to work to dig pits and bury the dead Zulus, and the remainder brought in stones for reconstructing and strengthening the barricades. Altogether, it was a stiff day, and officers and men worked alike...

...With the disbandment of our men, the officers and N.C.O.'s of the Contingent were brought into the Fort and given the N.E. corner of it to hold, and a very tight fit it was for everyone as the place was overcrowded with the number of men in occupation. To make matters worse we had a lot of rain, and the interior of the Fort became a simple quagmire from the tramping of so many feet. Fatigue parties were employed for the best part of the day in carrying liquid mud away and emptying the slush outside. In this state of filth we lived and ate and slept for more than two months, no-one being in possession of anything more than a blanket and the clothes that he stood up in. An exception was made, however, with B Company, 2nd battalion 24th Regiment, who had made such a gallant defence, and they were housed in the attic of Rorke's house with a tarpaulin thrown over the rafters (from which the thatch had been removed) to shelter them from the wet, a well-deserved honour. However, even they had their troubles in trying to keep dry, as the tarpaulin often bagged in between the rafters with a collection of water which had to be ejected, and I shall not easily forget one particular night when Dr. Reynolds, who got the V.C., and I met in the dark having been literally washed out of our sleeping place, and mooched about, endeavouring to find a more sheltered spot. Suddenly we hit upon the idea of lying down under the eaves of B. Company's roof, so coiled ourselves up in our soaking wet blankets, thanking our stars that at all events there would be no river running under us, when presently swish came about half a ton of water clean on top of us - B. Company were emptying their tarpaulin! It was useless moving, as we could not better ourselves, and wet as we were, thanks to the temperature of the atmosphere and the heat from our bodies, were comfortably warm as long as we lay still...

...Some 300 or 400 yards behind the Fort, and overlooking it, was Itchiane hill from the summit of which a splendid panorama of the country for a great many miles round could be obtained, and where, after the arrival of the relief column a heliograph station was established. On the morning of the Isandhlwana fight, the Rev. W. Smith went up there to see what was going on, as he had heard the guns in the distance, and a day or so after we got in he took me up to explain to me what he had seen. On the "neck" just below Isandhlwana hill he saw the artillery firing, and presently a large body of Natives moving round the hill towards them. Thinking it was our Contingent, he said to himself, "Well done, Lonsdale!", as they were moving with. such precision. Then shortly after, he noticed a number of horsemen galloping for their lives, away on his right, making towards the Drift, which made him think that Lord Chelmsford's column were being driven back, and almost at the same time large numbers of Natives appeared away to his left front, coming up from the river very leisurely and massing in the valley. After taking a look at these, and seeing that none of them wore the red head-band of Lonsdale's men, his first impulse was to go down and parley with them, but noticing that their numbers were considerably increasing he hastened down the hill again to inform Chard and Bromhead who, however, had already received warning that a Zulu impi was advancing on the Fort. The horsemen he had seen were fugitives from the Camp and had passed the Post before he got down, and be it to their everlasting shame and dishonour, galloped on as hard as they could, refusing to stop a moment to assist the garrison, and merely shouted out that the Zulus were close on them. How far their flight took them, I don't think was ever ascertained.

The part which the Rev. Mr. Smith played in the defence, and the splendid example he set throughout that terrible night, ought to have earned for him the V.C. The same with the Acting Commissariat Officer, Mr. James Dalton, who in the absence of Lieutenant Chard, R.E., (who was down at the river superintending Pontoon work at the moment when warning was received of the nearness of the Zulus), devised all the rapid arrangements for the defence as well as working like a Trojan himself with the men at the barricades and did much gallant work during the night. All this was gratefully acknowledged by Lieutenant Chard in his report to the Commander-in-Chief after the fight, but neither Dalton nor Smith received any further distinction than promotion. Mr Thomas Atkins is the best judge of gallant deeds, and when he applauds you may be certain that he is right and does so with good reason, and I noticed that directly Mr Smith or Mr Dalton showed themselves they received an ovation from the men, which was unmistakable.

Among the six or seven young soldiers of the 24th who garrisoned the hospital and received the V.C. for defending it against such tremendous odds, and removing most of the sick while absolutely surrounded by Zulus, was one named Hook, who was taken on as servant by Major Black, whose shrill voice with its Scotch accent could be heard above the Fort calling for "H-o-o-k!" many times a day. So the men had their little joke, and whenever Hook was called for they themselves shouted for Hook and then yelled out, "I think he's hooked it, sir!", which always caused great merriment.

The following astounding incident of Colonel Harness's servant's escape from the hands of the Zulus was told me by one of the garrison; Colonel Harness, C.R.A. of the 3rd Column, had been obliged to leave his servant behind sick at Rorke's Drift when the Column crossed into Zululand, and on the night of the attack on the Fort he happened to be outside the barricades at the moment when the Zulus made their sudden rush on the hospital. As he would to a certainty have been shot down by the fire of our own men had he attempted in the darkness to run in and clamber back again, he quickly bolted under a small hand-cart that had accidentally been left propped up outside against the back of the hospital wall and which (luckily for him, but unfortunately for the garrison), was in such a position as to be completely out of the line of fire. Here he remained throughout the night, wrapped up in his blanket, with the Zulus swarming all round him - many of them actually jumping on to the cart to try and get on to the roof of the hospital, which some of them succeeded in doing and setting fire to it. But none of them, curiously enough, made any attempt to move the cart, in which case he would have been done for. In the morning, however, when the Zulus had decamped and all firing had ceased, to the great astonishment of the garrison he walked in safe and sound, after about as terrifying an experience as any man could have gone through.

By another lucky coincidence, too, the whole garrison had escaped a terrible catastrophe as only a very short distance away at the back of the Fort, between it and the Itchiane hill, a large hay rick had been left standing, there being no time to clear it away before the Zulus commenced their attack, which if they had fired it would have smoked everyone out and rendered the Fort enterable; but luckily, in their eagerness to wipe out the garrison with the assegai, it was left untouched. our several ways. It was an adventure, and but for the disgraceful act of one solitary individual, we had got out of the mess all right...

...Occasionally I rode out by myself to take a look round, and one afternoon about a mile from the Fort came across a portmanteau torn in half and empty, but lying by the side of it was a Bible, and a few feet further on a silver watch, which I restored to their rightful owner, the Rev. Mr Smith, when I got back, and very pleased he was to have them in his possession again. The portmanteau itself was far too damaged to be of any further use, so was left where it was.

The same day, I think it was, I came across the body of a very fine specimen of a Zulu in the skeleton stage, which I took Surgeon Reynolds out to have a look at. He too was impressed with the stature and splendid proportions, and brought away one or two bones of scientific interest, and the soles of the feet which had become detached and were just like solid pieces of horn. I also took one of the collar bones and the lesser bones of one of the arms, which I intended some day to give to the Durban Museum...

...In front of the Fort and some 600 or 700 yards down the slope of the hill, a scaffold had been put up by the Commissariat Department on which the carcasses of the cattle were hung up previous to issue, and one morning Major Black and I were sitting outside, warming ourselves in the sun and chatting, when we saw a most extraordinary-looking object suspended on the scaffold, and wondered what on earth it could be. Presently, a Private of the 24th came up from that direction, and Black asked him what the thing was, and he said that it was a Kaffir spy that had been hanged. "Good Heavens!," said Black, "By whose orders was he hung?" "Captain Harford, sir," was the reply, so we went down at once to look into the matter. The poor wretch, who was an old, wizened-up, grey-headed Native, had apparently been dead for some hours, and must have been hung some time during the night, but by whom it was never discovered. Every possible enquiry was made, but not a soul knew anything about it and nothing was known of the Native or where he could have come from...

Lieutenant John Maxwell, Natal Native Contingent

Extract from "Reminiscences of the Zulu War," by John Maxwell, (Edited by Leonie Twentyman Jones), Capetown, 1979

...We were anxious to reach Rorke's Drift not knowing how matters stood there. Firing had been heard distinctly during the night from that direction, and we pushed on with that object, enemy being in sight on each side the road, until we arrived within some five miles of the drift. And then a number were made out on the Shean, the mountain at the back of the missionary's house, the place left occupied by a company of the 2nd 24th Regiment, stores, a few invalids and some of the Commissariat. And what was then of great moment, we expected our breakfast.

Those that had glasses eagerly scanned the place. but I was looking at the river which seemed to be a perfect torrent. The ponts appeared all right, so the Infantry would have no difficulty in crossing. We received orders to march on a spot further up the river, and to cross in the best manner we could. After a very rough time of it in the river, we found ourselves across all right with the exception of a soaking and marched on the house. By this time we could distinguish several soldiers waving their hats and apparently very glad at our appearance. On approaching nearer we saw several dead bodies of the enemy lying about, which at once told us the place had been attacked. It was 8 o'clock when we arrived at the front of the place, scattered over which we saw about 2 hundred of the enemy lying dead. At the back the greatest damage must have been caused to the enemy, as the hill sloped down towards the building or temporary fort. The walls consisted of bags of corn meal flour and boxes of tinned beef. biscuits etc. So our fears with regard to breakfast were set at rest. I took a stroll round, when I learnt from 2 of the 24th all about the attack which had commenced the previous afternoon and only finally ceased on our being seen from the top of the hill at sunrise advancing along the road. The men bared their shoulders and I saw that they were black and blue and swollen, caused by the recoil or kicking of their Martinis, proving to what extent they had been firing. In fact they told me that towards daylight they were unable to place the rifle to the shoulder, but held it out pointing to the front and firing. They had during the night to change shoulder constantly, which caused both being in this state. I heard that a friend of mine had been shot, and that his body was with other dead laid out in the cattle kraal. I proceeded thither but found a sentry placed over these bodies numbering five. They were covered with straw. His orders were to keep everybody off. I failed to ascertain who they might have been. I now sought the house, but perceived no change there, with the exception that it was minus thatch which had been pulled off. The outhouses I saw were burnt down. Of course I was told the story of the attack on these, and the gallant rescue from the fire. This was told me by a corporal of ours we had left behind on account of his having a severely blistered foot. He was a young foreigner who afterwards received the Victoria Cross from Sir Garnet now Lord Wolsey on the market square in Maritzburg. Leaving this I walked to the front again, and to my astonishment perceived a Kethla, or ringed native, hanging to the crossbeam that had been erected some days previously for the butchers. It appeared he had been found under suspicious circumstances in the neighbourhood, and so met his end in rather a summary manner.

Orders were out for the burying of all dead, the Contingent and the 24th to provide the fatigue parties. And it was arranged that the first mentioned should dig the holes, on account of their prejudice against touching the dead, and that the 24th should place them therein. And so the dead were buried at Rorke's Drift, occupying some two to three hours; we digging large holes in various places and the 24th with the assistance of reins, placing the bodies therein. I believe there must have been a number of dead taken away by the enemy on their retiring across the river. I may mention here that at various times for a period of six weeks, bodies were found in the caves and among the stones on this mountain, and two months afterwards two brother officers and myself discovered in a cave near the summit three bodies, which were quite hard and sound. These had been wounded and managed to crawl thus far to die...

An account by a former member of the Natal Native Contingent

"The Natal Witness," January 19th, 1929

A Native Eyewitness

An old Zulu, probably eighty years of age, who works in Maritzburg, has a very vivid recollection of the battle.[Isandlwana] A member of the Native Contingent under Captain Russell, he viewed the fight from about half a mile away while he and his compatriots were guarding children...

...They cleared from here and went over to Rorke's Drift. There the soldiers had built walls of sandbags and made holes for their guns to go through. There were still thousands of Zulus, though many of them had been left behind. But the soldiers killed lots of them. They fired at them all through the night. Their guns grew hot in their hands. They were burned and their faces were black with the powder. Next morning early the Zulus ran off leaving many dead bodies on the ground, though the soldiers had not lost so many...

Here the old man concluded his tale. He had opened with a very vigorous and graphic description and then as he told of the dead, calmed impressively almost to a whisper. For a moment he stood, one arm on his chest fingering his chin, staring vacantly into the past. Then 'Bayete.' He gave the Royal salute. 'Se ngi gedile.'...

Charles L. Norris-Newman, a war correspondent

An unidentified Natal newspaper, c. January 1879

With Head-quarter Column
The Story Of Isandhlwana
(From the Times War Correspondent.)

Pietermaritzburg, Jan. 26th, 1879

Our surprise and delight may be easily imagined when we heard a good English cheer greet us, and upon getting close up we saw that the place was surrounded by a barricade of mealies in sacks, with the bodies of numerous Zulus lying around. We quickly dismounted and when inside, to our great relief, that the little garrison had received warning in time from fugitives from our late camp, and were able to prepare themselves so that they successfully withstood and repulsed, with severe loss to the enemy, a large body of over 4000 kaffirs, which had attacked them at five on Wednesday evening, and had only retired at daylight that morning...

...The gallant defenders had to relate the whole night's experience to us all, and were then much complimented on their splendid resistance. The small garrison consisted of a little over 130 men, under Lieutenant Broomhead, 2-24th. The following officers were also with him at the time, and gave material assistance:-

Dr. Reynolds, 2-24th, Lieutenant Chard, R.E., Lieutenant Adendorff, 1-3rd Natal Native Contingent, and Messrs. Dunne, Dalton, and Byrne, of the Commissariat department. The Reverend Mr. Smith, was also present throughout the attack.

Several bodies of men who had escaped from the scene of the massacre at Insandhlwana passed by Rorke's Drift, but, although some were strong bodies, they would not, much to their discredit, stay to help the little garrison. The fire we had seen was that part of the building used as a hospital, which was detached some distance from the house itself, and, therefore, had to be given up. The loss sustained in this night attack is given in my return...

...C.L.N.N."

Extract from "In Zululand - With the British Throughout the War of 1879," by Charles L. Norris-Newman, London 1880

...We quickly reached the brow of the hill overlooking the Buffalo River and Rorke's Drift, with our previous camping ground on the opposite bank; but the sight of buildings in flames at the station by no means allayed our fears. Before we quite reached the river I carefully examined the house at Rorke's Drift through my field-glasses, and thought I could distinguish the figures of men on parts of the wall and roof of the large building, and one of them seemed to be waving a flag. The attention of the General having been called to this, Colonel Russell, with some of his mounted infantry and myself, at once crossed the river and galloped up to the station at full speed. Much to our delight and relief, we were greeted with a hearty English cheer, showing that here at least no irreparable disaster had befallen. We quickly dismounted, and found the place had been temporarily defended by a barricade of empty biscuit-boxes and mealies in sacks, while outside numerous bodies of dead Zulus were lying all around. The little garrison, it appeared, had received timely warning from the fugitives escaped from the camp at Isandwhlana, and they were thus enabled to make some slight preparations for the anticipated assault, so that they successfully withstood, and repulsed with severe loss to the enemy, a body of over 4,000 Zulus, that had commenced the attack on them at five on the previous (Wednesday) evening, and continued almost unintermittently till daybreak, only retiring upon the approach of our little column. The small garrison consisted of only about 130 men, under Lieutenant Chard, R.E., and Lieutenant Bromhead, 2-24th. Major Spalding, D.A.Q.M.G., had been left in command of the post, but had gone away to Helpmakaar late on Tuesday afternoon preceding. The following officers were also present at the post and rendered material aid in the defence: Dr. Reynolds, 1-24th, Lieutenant Adendorff, 1—3rd N.N.C., Messrs. Dunne, Dalton, and Byrne, of the Commissariat Department, as also the Rev. Mr. Smith, Protestant Chaplain to No. 3 Column...

CHAPTER 6: Other accounts

<u>Field Marshal Sir Garnet J. Wolseley</u>

Extract from "Sir Garnet Wolseley's South African Journal 1879-80," edited by Prof. A. Preston

Wednesday, 16th July 1879
...I presented Major Chard R.E. with his Victoria X: a more uninteresting or more stupid-looking fellow I never saw. Wood tells me he is a most useless officer, fit for nothing. I hear in this camp also that the man who worked hardest in defence of Roorke's Drift Post was the Commissariat officer who has not been rewarded at all. The only one who behaved badly was the Doctor, & reports say that he is a coward. Bromhead of the 24th Regt. who was the 2nd in Command of the post is a very stupid fellow also...

Sunday 3rd August
...I gave away a Victoria X this morning to a private of the 24th Regt. named Hook...

Thursday 21st August
...The Revd. Mr. Smith who was at the defence of Roorke's Drift is reported to have corrected the men for cursing whilst the fight was at it's height. 'Don't swear men, don't swear, but shoot them boys, shoot them.'...

Thursday 11th September
..The troops paraded at 9 a.m. I gave away two Victoria Crosses, one to Major Bromhead 24th & the other to Private Jones 24th Regt. - I have now given away these decorations to both officers who took part in the defence of Roorke's Drift, and two duller, more stupid, more uninteresting even or less like Gentlemen it has not been my luck to meet for a long time...

<u>Surgeon General John A. Woolfryes, M.D., A.M.D.</u>

Extract from "Medical History of the War in Zululand in 1879" , by Surgeon General J.A. Woolfryes, M.D., C.B., C.M.G., Appendix No. iv, Army Medical Department Report for 1879. [courtesy of the Curator, Army Medical Services Museum, Aldershot]

...On sighting the post at Rorke's Drift dense smoke was seen to be rising from the house and Zulus to be retiring from it. All hopes of getting supplies appeared gone, and those at Helpmakaar (distant 12 miles) might have shared the same fate. To the great relief of the force on nearing the Buffalo River the waving of helmets was seen from inside the entrenchment, and it was now found that the brave garrison, consisting of 80 of the 2/24th Regiment, some Volunteers, and Native Contingent, in medical charge of Surgeon-Major Reynolds, had for 12 hours made a most gallant resistance against the attack of 3,000 Zulus.

It would appear that after the massacre at Isandhlwana the reserve of the Zulu force advanced towards Rorke's Drift. Notice of the disaster and that the Zulus were advancing was received at 3.15 p.m. The little garrison at once determined to hold the post at all costs, and set to work to loophole and barricade the store buildings and hospital, and to connect the defence of the two buildings. The hospital was a commodious structure surrounded by a verandah, and capable of accommodating 40 sick. There were in it at the time only 35. It had been selected as the base hospital of the column, and contained all the field equipment and medical and surgical stores left behind by the column. In little more than an hour the sound of firing was heard behind the hill to the south, and in a few minutes 500 or 600 of the enemy came in sight and advanced at a run against the south wall. They were met with a well-sustained fire which checked them. The greater number, however, without stopping made for the hospital, and after a short but desperate struggle were driven back with great loss. The main body of the enemy now came on, and taking advantage of some bush advanced under cover, and soon held one side of the wall while the garrison held the other. A series of desperate assaults were made, but repulsed with the bayonet. All this time the enemy had been attempting to force the hospital, and shortly after set fire to its roof. "The garrison of the hospital defended it room by room, bringing out all the sick that could be moved before they retired." Four privates of the 24th were the last to leave, holding the doors with the bayonet, their ammunition being expended. At this time Surgeon-Major Reynolds with conspicuous gallantry rushed from the hospital to the store building and brought back a supply of ammunition, having been exposed both going and returning to the cross fire of the enemy. From the want of interior communication and the burning of the house, it was impossible to save all; 5 of the sick were therefore massacred through not being able to move. When the building could be held no longer the garrison retired to the store, the roof of which the enemy were trying to fire. As darkness came on the post was completely surrounded, and the garrison was forced to retire to the middle, a position which was retained to the last. Several assaults were made and repulsed, the vigour of the attack continuing until after midnight. About 4 a.m. the firing ceased, and at daybreak the enemy were out of sight.

350 of the enemy were killed.

The total number of the garrison was 8 officers, 96 non-commissioned officers and men, and 35 sick.

The casualties were: killed, 1 officer, 13 non-commissioned officers and men, and 1 native; wounded, 12 - 2 afterwards dying.

There were 3 men of the Army Hospital Corps doing duty in the hospital who all behaved bravely...

...Of the force in the camp, a few mounted men only managed to escape and swim the river. Our loss was, therefore, 30 officers and 500 non-commissioned officers and men of the Imperial troops, 21 officers and 70 non-commissioned officers and men of the Colonial forces, with 300 Native Contingent Amongst the slain were Surgeon-Major Shepherd, Lieut. and Acting Surgeon Boue, of the Native Contingent, and Lieut of orderlies Hall, and 8 men of Army Hospital Corps. A large quantity of hospital equipment, medical and surgical stores, and 6 ambulances were captured...

Colonel, the Hon., Frederick A. Stanley, Secretary of State for War

[WO32/7710, The National Archives, (P.R.O.), London]
(see also Lord Chelmsford's letter forwarding the original recommendations for the Victoria Cross)

Lt. Gen. Lord Chelmsford KCB

My Lord,
I have received with great satisfaction your despatch of the 8th Feb. last, and its Enclosure from Lt Chard R.E. containing a narrative of the heroic defence of the Post at Rorke's Drift on the night of the 22d Jan. last.
Having laid these documents before The Queen, I have received Her Majesty's Commands to express to you Her admiration of the gallantry of all who took part in that brilliant defence. The fertility of resource displayed in improvising defences and the cool & determined courage by which they were guarded and maintained have been especially remarked by Her Majesty and will worthily take a prominent place in the annals of the British Army.
I have conferred with H.R.H. the FM C in C as to the recognition which those officers, N.CO's Privates & others who are officially mentioned should receive, and I shall lose no time in making the necessary recommendations to Her Majesty on the subject
I have &c
Fred Stanley

Brevet-Major Henry Spalding, 104th Foot

"The Times," c. March 1879

To The Editor Of The Times.

Sir, - In *The Times* of to-day a letter appears from your Correspondent at Rorke's Drift, describing the defence by Lieutenants Chard and Bromhead, in which the following passage occurs:-

"The post was under the command of Major Spalding... News having arrived that the enemy were advancing on the post and that they would be there in less than an hour, Major Spalding handed over the command to Lieutenant Chard, R.E., and rode to Helpmakaar to bring up the two companies of infantry from that place."

From this it would be inferred that Major Spalding was in command at Rorke's Drift only, and that he surrendered his command to a subordinate on news arriving of an impending attack. Will you allow me to state that Major Spalding writes by the last mail, - "I left for another part of my command just an hour before intelligence of our disaster arrived." This is consistent with Lieutenant Chard's report, which clearly implies that Major Spalding had left before the news of the defeat reached Rorke's Drift.

I am, Sir, your obedient servant,

J.H.S.

March 23.

Captain Walter Parke Jones, 5th (Field) Company, Royal Engineers

Extract from a letter written to his friend, a Mr Jackson, dated St Pauls, Zululand, August 2nd, 1879. [The Royal Engineers Museum, Chatham]

...Chard got his orders to leave the 5 Compy for good & departed yesterday. He is most amiable fellow & a loss to the mess, but as a company officer he is hopelessly slow & slack. I shall get on much better without him & with Porter as my senior sub. - Chard makes me angry, with such a start as he got, he stuck to the company doing nothing. In his place I should have gone up & asked Lord C. for an appointment, he must have got it & if not, he could have gone home soon after Rorke's Drift, at the height of his popularity & done splendidly at home. - I advised him, but he placidly smokes his pipe & does nothing. Few men get such opportunities...

Lieutenant Charles Ernest Commeline, 5th (Field) Company, Royal Engineers,

Extract from "Marching Over Africa", by Frank Emery, London Hodder & Stoughton, 1986

...In fact the army was saved from utter annihilation by the brilliant defence of the little mission house at Rorke's Drift at which Chard of our Company was the Senior Officer. He had with him Bromhead of the 24th Regt. and his Company of 100 men and Dr. Russell, when at 4 o'clock in the afternoon they saw a great force of Zulus coming down on them. These had been detached from the main army as soon as it was seen our poor fellows were done for, doubtless with the intention of destroying the detachment at the Drift and the pontoons fro crossing the river, thus cutting off the General's retreat. The fighting was most desperate. lasting till 4 o'clock next morning, and the Zulus probably lost over 1,000 men, 367 bodies being counted in the enclosure of the house.

They were twice repelled at the point of the bayonet, their advance being blocked by the dead bodies of their killed. Our fellows only lost 13, most of whom were sick men lying in a hospital close by, which the Zulus fired just as it was growing dark, thus probably saving the remainder by the sacrifice of these few, as the light from the fire enabled our fellows to use their rifles on the masses of the enemy with terrible effect. One gallant old soldier of he 24th probably saved them again. He observed a Zulu on the opposite hill light a torch and rush down to apply it to the thatch of the Mission house at a retired corner. The soldier leant out of the window and fired at the man at 5 yds. distance and missed him, but loaded again and shot him through the head just as the thatch had given signs of taking fire. The Zulu was found afterwards dead with his torch gone out, but raised to the thatch.

Probably no more desperate and brilliant defence of a post has ever been chronicled among the gallant deeds of British soldiers than the defence of Rorke's Drift. It consequences must also be most important, as the General was enabled to bring his little force back over the river, and such a disastrous repulse must in some way have restored our prestige in the eyes of the Zulus...

A.F. Pickard, Private Secretary to H.R.H. Queen Victoria

A letter to Sir Evelyn Wood, dated Balmoral Castle, October 14th, 1879: [Kwa-Zulu Natal Archives, Pietermaritzburg]

...Chard has been here and left this morning. He explained the defence of Rorke's Drift to the Queen, Prince Leopold, the Grand Duke of Hesse, and Princess Beatrice in the Queen's private room, and did it al very clearly and modestly. After dinner he did likewise to us in the billiard room on the table, where store and hospital were books and boxes, and mealie bags and biscuit tins were billiard balls.

I gather from all I hear that Dalton was quite as much (if not more) of the presiding genius there, as himself. He conceived the idea of joining the two buildings with mealie bags, etc., before Chard's arrival on the scene; tho' perhaps Chard would have done so, had he not found it in operation. The inner line, which was their great safeguard, was Chard's own idea, I fancy, and when they were deserted by so many of the defenders (natives, etc.) it was soon found that the first line of defence was too extended.

Bromhead (commanding B Company, 2/24th Regiment) had of course great influence over his own men, and kept them in their places or moved them about, controlled their fire with great judgement. Only one and a half boxes of ammunition was left when morning came, besides what they had in their pouches. Chard made no complaint, but it seemed odd to me that he was not consulted as to the distribution of the Victoria Crosses. He is not a genius and not quick, but a quiet, plodding, dogged sort of fellow who will hold his own in most of the situations in which, as an Engineer officer, his lot may be cast...

An unidentified officer serving with No. 3 Column

"The Cornish and Devon Post," March 8th, 1879

A Letter from Natal

Among the letters received at Aldershot Camp from South Africa, is one from an officer attached to Colonel Glyn's column who, writing on the 27th January, says;-

...We arrived too late to be of service. The sight I witnessed at the Drift exceeds anything I saw during the Mutiny. I could hardly recognise Chard, for he had his tunic off, and was begrimed with powder. Bromhead and his people must have fought like demons. Their only protection against the Zulus consisted of meal bags, and they were so low that anyone who had pluck enough could have jumped over them.

CHAPTER 7: Excerpts of Rorke's Drift

"The Natal Witness," c. January 1879

Lord Chelmsford's Return to Isandhlwana

...The march to Rorke's Drift was made without further incident save some twenty or thirty shots fired by the Native Contingent. There were plenty of Zulus hovering about, seemingly afraid to attack us, and twice we passed columns of them debouching from the Buffalo, while burning kraals on the Natal side showed plainly from whence they were returning. These men had also evidently no wish to come into collision with us; and had it not been for the peculiar position in which we were placed, a successful attack might have, to a certain extent, revenged us for our losses. Those, however, with whom decision lay saw that it would be risking too much to make any avoidable attack. As yet it was unknown whether Helpmakaar with our ammunition, and the depot at Rorke's Drift, had escaped, and should we even have gained a complete victory, we should have been, in common with the whole northern portion of the colony, completely at the mercy of the Zulus, if our reserves of ammunition were no longer intact; while, had we been repulsed, Natal would have been laid open in an irreparable manner. Wiser and truer councils therefore prevailed, and we marched steadily forward to Rorke's Drift, the smoke rising from the missionaries' house on the other side suggesting to us further disaster. As, however we neared the river, men could be seen manning the walls of an old ruin next to the building used as a commissariat store, some of them waving coats, &c., and Colonel Russell, with the Mounted Infantry, was ordered to ford the river, and go straight up to them. Our belief in Zulu cunning had by this time got so strong that it was not until the mounted men reached the building, and were received by true English cheers that we were fully persuaded it was not a trick. The fact that the pont ropes were untouched also proved to us that the Zulus could not have had everything their own way; and it was with anxiety to reach our men, and hear their news, that we watched the Carbineers, who had crossed at the ford, cast of the ropes, and prepare to tug us over. Little time was occupied in so doing, or in reaching the commissariat store, and the cheers which burst forth from our men as the General cantered up and said, "Thank you all very much for your very gallant defence," were pleasant to hear. A gallant defence it indeed had been - eighty men, ten of whom were sick in hospital, had beaten off and thoroughly defeated some 3000 Zulus, flushed with their late victory. They had hardly had half an hour's warning, during which to make what preparations were possible for defending an extremely weak position. Fortunately there were plenty of sacks of mealies, &c., to be had, and temporary fortifications were rapidly constructed with them. From 3 a.m. to 5 a.m. the Zulus came on again and again with undaunted pluck. They succeeded in taking the hospital and burning it, though, in doing so, they lost ten times the number they killed; and they charged up to the very walls, and attempted to unscrew the bayonets which met them. Greater bravery than that displayed on either side could not have been, but the little body of English soldiers behind their frail rampart knew they were fighting to hold a most important post, and never hesitated for an instant; whereas the Zulus, who no doubt thought they could easily cut up a handful of men like those opposed to them, after their recent achievement, were beginning to find out their mistake. The engagement, however, continued the whole live-long night, the Zulus once and again attempting to take the place by storm. At last, fairly discouraged, they retreated just as dawn was breaking. Our loss, as may be imagined, was severe; out of eighty men one fourth had fallen, thirteen killed and nine wounded, of whom some have since died; but if our loss was severe, that of the enemy must have been something enormous. They had come on again and again in broad daylight, and by the light of the burning house, up to the very muzzles of the guns, and their dead were heaped up in scores all round the barricade. Within 300 yards of the spot, our burying parties counted 351 bodies, whilst on the road they had taken in retreat the dead and wounded lay thick. That in this engagement the enemy lost 500 killed and 200 or 300 wounded is, I think, a very moderate calculation, and the lesson taught them by that gallant company of the 24th is one they will not soon forget. I fully believe the loss the Zulus incurred in taking our camp, which I cannot estimate at less than 2000 to 3000 men in killed and wounded, added to their repulse and loss at Rorke's Drift, will have a very great effect on their minds, nor do I anticipate that they will run the risk of incurring such again, unless under circumstances exceptionably favourable to themselves.

So ended the four days during which No. 3 column advanced into Zululand from Rorke's Drift, and returned to it - four days which will be memorable so long as the colony exists, and so long as England takes an interest in the deeds of her little armies in foreign lands

"The Natal Witness," c. 1879

The Splendid Defence of Rorkes Drift.

The *Witness* concludes an article on the Isandhlwana disaster as follows: - It is a relief to turn from the contemplation of this disastrous field - a field which might verily be called the Field of Blood to the world's end - to consider the noble heroism of those who, behind their extempore entrenchments at Rorke's Drift, repeated with greater success some of the glories of Thermopylæ. They knew perfectly well what would follow upon any failure on their part, and they were prepared, if need were, to sacrifice their lives to the last man, in order to gain time for some temporary reparation of Isandhlwana. Unless the gap had been stopped by their heroic resistance, the whole northern portion of the colony would probably by this time have been laid waste. Greytown would have been attacked and the camp at Helpmakaar, with all its reserve of stores and ammunition, would have fallen into the enemy's hands. As it was their resolute defence not only saved Helpmakaar from an attack, but enabled Colonel Glyn's column to retire and take up a formidable defensive position. It is pleasant to think that the heroes of this fight with but few exceptions, still live to receive the thanks not only of the colony, but of the empire at large. They have done a deed which will live for ever in the military history of their country, and which may be placed side by side with any of those achievements of which Englishmen are rightly proud. It is something to be able to know that the prowess of Waterloo and of Inkermann is still present in the race, though we may at the same time excusably hope that but few will be the occasions in the future of South Africa on which it will be called upon to reveal itself.

The following is the official return of the wounded in the engagement with the one company of the 2-24th Regiment at Rorke's Drift: - Dangerously: Sergeant Williams, Corporal Lyons, Privates Hitch and Beckett (latter since dead). Severely: - Corporal Allen, Storekeeper Dalton, and Private Walters. Slightly - Private Jones and E. Schiess, N.N.C. The total number of killed were fourteen.

An unidentified Natal newspaper, c. January 1879

The Repulse at Rorke's Drift

Private accounts that have reached us regarding the defence of the small thatched store at Rorke's Drift more than confirm all that has been said about the gallantry and heroism of the resistance offered by a handful of 70 or 80 men to the determined onslaught of two or three thousand Zulus. The latter came on again and again with torches, hoping to fire the building, but were driven back not only by the fire, but by the bayonets of soldiers thrust over the walls at the masses of the infuriated and elated enemy. The moral effect of this inflexible defence of a feebly fortified little farmhouse, cannot be over-rated. Lieutenant Bromhead, of the 2-24th, and Lieutenant Chard, of the Royal Engineers, with the men under them, deserve as high honour as has ever been accorded anywhere to British soldiers who have distinguished themselves anywhere under corresponding circumstances.

A letter published in "The Times of Natal," February 3rd, 1879

A letter from a private correspondent

"...the entire defeat of an enormous force of Zulus by some 130 troops barricaded in the house. R. Hall, who was in the attack at the camp, rode off as hard as he could to Rorke's drift, after seeing the camp taken by the enemy. He joined the soldiers in Rorke's house, and finding the Kafirs there wanting to bolt, fired a shot over their heads, and told them the next would be into them if they would not remain to assist in barricading the place. He made them fill sacks with earth and block up places where an entrance could be effected. He remained until the Zulus were down upon the place, and made off to Helpmakaar after seeing the soldiers shoot about ten Zulus, and got the people to fortify their position there. I think the reception the Zulus met with at Rorke's Drift is a caution to them against crossing the border. After the fight, the Zulus returned to their own country, after leaving an enormous number killed and wounded. Thirteen soldiers were killed; and it is estimated about 1,000

Zulus fell in this affair; 315 bodies of Zulus were counted all about the house, piled one on the other; as some were killed, others returned to the attack over the dead bodies, and thus added to the pile.

Many wounded must have been too weak to cross the river, and consequently were carried down..."

"The Natal Mercury," February 7th, 1879

The following is an extract of a private letter:-

...I am afraid you will think we have forgotten you up here. It is such a job to get paper, envelopes, or even a pencil; if you get hold of one you may consider yourself lucky, indeed...

...They taught the Zulus a lesson at Rorke's Drift, didn't they? We counted 351 bodies round the camp. One of our spies came in the other day. He says Cetywayo had the induna who led the attack at Rorke's Drift killed, for attacking a place that was barricaded; but he was very angry with all his men for not following up and wiping us all out; but now the beggars are afraid to attack. They did not know we were short of ammunition - lucky for us.

"The Weeks News," Saturday, February 22nd, 1879

Chief Intelligence of the Week...

...The defence of the camp at Rorke's Drift, under Lieuts. Chard, R.E., and Bromehead was a most brilliant episode...

...The Colonists' belief that every man at the Rorke's Drift station has earned the Victoria Cross will be felt by all that read the account of Lieut. Chard and Lieut. Bromehead's gallant defence. They had to meet the savages flushed with excitement by their victory at the camp nine miles from the river. Hastily as the Zulus came on at nightfall, a barrier of corn sacks and biscuit tins was thrown up, and behind these the little company fought till daybreak. All this time it would seem Lord CHELMSFORD was encamped on the scene of the disaster of the previous day amid the dead of the British and of the enemy, but rendered no succour to the gallant band at the Ford - did not, indeed, know of the struggle until the Zulus had decamped. A portion of the men at Isandula fought their way against the Zulus until they reached the river. A few - but very few - escaped to Helpmakaar...

The Zulu War
The Late Defeat

There was a sequel to the disaster of Jan. 22 which is thus mentioned in the Telegraph's despatches:-

In the attack made on Rorke's Drift on Wednesday evening, after the destruction of the camp, Lieut. Bromhead, 2-24th, Adendorff, 1-3rd Natal Contingent, who had escaped from the camp attack, and 100 men, succeeded in keeping off over 4,000 Zulus. They fought that evening from five till daylight on Thursday, when the main column arrived back to them. They only lost Assist.-commy. Byrne, and twelve men, out of whom five were massacred in the hospital through being unable to move...

Extract from an unidentified Natal newspaper, possibly "The Times of Natal," c. 1879

Recognition of the Rorke's Drift Action

A correspondent writes us:-

"I am desirous of getting up a subscription for the men who defended Rorke's Drift, not to exceed a sovereign - less if you like. Of course we cannot give the soldiers money, though I dare say we can, for all that, manage to please them."

We quite fall in with our correspondent's view, and would be very glad indeed to bring home to the gallant fellows who so nobly defended their outpost, the thorough appreciation the colonists entertain of their gallant conduct. We shall be glad to head a subscription list and receive contributions..,

"The Irish Times," March 6th, 1879, page 5

Lieutenant Chard, R.E.
To the Editor of the Irish Times

Sir,

May I ask why you, in conjunction with the editors of other leading journals, record to Lieutenant Bromhead the lion's share of your praise for the ever-to-be-remembered gallant defence of Rorke's Drift?

The officer who, by virtue of his seniority, commanded there was Lieutenant Chard, of the Royal Engineers, as you may fins either by reference to the Army List or to Lord Chelmsford's dispatch and you do not require to be told that the chief credit of a successful military engagement is invariably given to the senior officer, unless it can be shown that he has not acted up to the full requirements of his responsible position, and of this we have no evidence in the case of Lieutenant Chard. Now, the fact that such a handful of men defended themselves against a host throughout a whole night points first of all to the indomitable pluck of all concerned, and secondly to the excellence of the entrenchments hastily improvised and thrown up, without which that pluck must have ended in defeat, as at Isandula. Chard, being an Engineer officer, had in all probability more knowledge of entrenching than any other officer associated with him at Rorke's Drift.

Therefore I shall be surprised if he does not eventually receive the full meed of praise and glory to which his fortunate position of senior officer has entitled him. In justice to the officer about whom I write, whose acquaintance, I regret to say, I have not the honour to enjoy, I trust you will do me the courtesy of publishing this letter. I am, sir, your most obedient servant,

F.E.B.L.

"The Irish Times," March 6th, 1879

General War Items.
(By Telegraph)

The *Cape Argus,* in an account of the defence of Rorke's Drift says:-
"The cheers which burst forth from our men as the General cantered up, and said - 'Thank you all very much for your gallant defence,' were very pleasant to hear. A gallant defence it indeed had been. Eighty men, ten of whom were sick in hospital, had beaten off and thoroughly defeated some 3,000 Zulus flushed with their late victory. They had hardly had half an hour's warning during which to make what preparations were possible for defending an extremely weak position. Fortunately there were plenty of sacks of mealies, &c., to be had, and temporary fortifications were rapidly constructed with them. From 3 p.m. to 5 a.m. the Zulus came on again and again, with undoubted pluck. They succeeded in taking the hospital and burning it, though in doing so they lost ten times the number they killed, and they charged up to the very walls, and attempted to unscrew the bayonets which met them. Greater bravery than that displayed on either side could not have been; but the little body of English soldiers behind their frail rampart knew they were fighting to hold a most important post, and never hesitated for an instant, whereas the Zulus, who no doubt thought they could easily cut up a handful of men like those opposed to them, after their recent achievements, were beginning to find out their mistake. The engagement, however, continued the whole livelong night; the Zulus once and again attempted to take the place by storm. At last, fairly discouraged, they retreated just as dawn was breaking. Our loss, as may be imagined, was severe. Out of eighty men, one-fourth had fallen - thirteen killed and nine wounded, of whom some have since died; but if our loss was severe, that of the enemy must have been something enormous. They had come on again and again in broad daylight, and by the light of the burning house, up to the very muzzles of the guns, and their dead were heaped up in scores all round the barricade. Within 300 yards of the spot our burying parties counted 351 bodies, while on the road they had taken in retreat the dead and wounded lay thick. That in this engagement the enemy lost 500 killed and 200 or 300 wounded is, I think, a very moderate calculation, and the lesson taught them by that gallant company of the 24th is one they will not soon forget."

"The British Medical Association Journal," March 8th, 1879

The gallant conduct of Lieutenant Chard and Lieutenant Bromhead, at Rorke's Drift, has been universally and justly eulogised, and will no doubt be rewarded. It will not be thought unbecoming if we direct attention to the equally gallant services of Surgeon Reynolds, who constantly risked his life during the same defence in attendance upon the wounded.

"The Lancet," March 29th, 1879

We observe with great satisfaction that the *Gazette* of the 21st inst. announces the promotion of 'Surgeon James Henry Reynolds, M.B., to be Surgeon-Major (supernumerary), in recognition of his gallant services in the defence of Rorke's Drift post against the attack of the Zulus on the night of the 22nd January, 1879.' This prompt recognition cannot fail to prove gratifying to his brother officers in the department and to the members of the profession generally. Mr. Reynolds entered the service in 1868, having joined the medical school at Netley on the 31st March in that year. We have no doubt that Surgeon-Major Reynolds will share in any further honorary rewards which may be conferred on the officers concerned in this galant affair.

"The Aldershot News," c. 1879

Pietermaritzburg, Jan. 29 (11.20 p.m.)
The action at Rorke's Drift was a splendid affair. Lieutenant Broomhead, 1-24th, and Lieutenant Chard, R.E., had been left in charge of the Drift, with a company of the 1-24th. Their first intimation of the disaster at Isandula was seeing fugitives making for the Drift, some of whom, including Lieutenant Coghill, who rode away, to communicate with Helpmakaar, were killed by Zulus, in crossing the river. Seeing an attack imminent, they hastily thro up barricades with mealie bags and biscuit tins belonging to the Commissariat, part of the time under fire. They were attacked soon after dark by at least 3,000 Kaffirs, chiefly of the Nilwana Regiment. The fight was kept up the greater part of the night, and the Zulus six times got inside the barricades, and six times were driven out at the point of the bayonet.
Meantime another body passed on the military hospital in the rear and fired it, killing five patients and destroying the medical stores. A servant of Col. Harness had a narrow escape, but got away from the hospital and sat in the bush all night, exposed to the fire from both sides.
At dawn the attacking force withdrew, and Lord Chelmsford's column was seen approaching, being hailed enthusiastically by the gallant defenders, who first mistook them for another force of Zulus.
351 dead Zulus were counted near the entrenchment, but the number killed has since been estimated at 1,000.

An unidentified Natal newspaper, possibly "The Natal Mercury," c. March 1879

Honour to the Brave

Lieutenant Bromhead, of H.M. 24th regiment, is now Major Bromhead, and well he deserves the promotion and the title. But what about the leader of that noble defence at the little thatched farmhouse of Rorke's Drift - Lieutenant Chard, of the Royal Engineers?

Surely technical rules of professional promotion will not interfere with the award of his proper due!

We hear that Lieutenant Chard (would that we could designate him a higher title) is suffering severely from fever - and no wonder. There is no distinction which it is in the power of his Queen or his service to bestow which would exceed the merit of the man 'who held the drift' in that time of dire extremity, and against odds so overwhelming.

"Punch," March 29th, 1879, page 133

The Rorke's Drift Roll-Call
"An Officer" writes to Punch -

"In your Cartoon of March 22, you, as worthy head of the Army, thank Lieutenants CHARD and BROMHEAD for their heroic defence of Rorke's Drift. In the background are seem some men of the 24th Regiment, and scattered about are quantities of Commissariat Supplies. Cannot you find some corner for a memorial to the only officer who was killed that night while gallantly doing his duty, Assistant-Commissary BYRNE? Should you ignore the only officer 'severely wounded,' to whom all were indebted for his advice and skill in turning his supplies of flour and biscuits into parapets - Assistant-Commissary DALTON? Or the young officer who gained the admiration of al by erecting the last line of defence under a heavy fire, Assistant-Commissary DUNNE? Or Surgeon REYNOLDS, who only laid on one side his rifle to attend to the wounded?"

"Punch only wishes his Cartoon was as large as his gratitude, in which case he would certainly have found room not only for these gallant officers - combatant or non-combatant, who assisted in the defence of Rorke's Drift - but for every man who piled a biscuit-box, fisted a mealie-bag, levelled a rifle, or plied a bayonet on that memorable night. But pages have their limits, though gratitude has none, and so Punch and his artist have been fain to lump under the names and presentments of the most prominent leaders of that noble defence all the officers and men who contributed to it, in their several ranks and capacities. He rejoices that 'An Officer's letter, in mentioning many of these names, secures a record of them in his immortal pages.'"

...Although Majors Chard and Bromhead have not been gazetted to the Victoria Cross, there is no doubt that they will shortly receive that much coveted decoration, and that the men specially mentioned in the despatch will be similarly rewarded. It is probable that the medal for distinguished service in the field will be given to the whole of the garrison of Rorke's Drift, and that B Company, 2d Battalion, 24th Foot will be permitted to wear on its appointments the words 'Rorke's Drift' in commemoration of the gallant stand it made on the 22nd January 1879. This will be a lasting honour to the company and the regiment.

It is satisfactory to note that the non-combatant officers have also received a step in rank. Surgeon-Major Reynolds and Messrs. Dalton and Dunne have richly deserved their promotions...

"The Times of Natal", April 23rd, 1879

Rorke's Drift

Having just returned from a short visit to the celebrated but out-of-the-way corner of the world, Rorke's Drift, I venture to think a letter from me may interest some of your numerous readers. I found the 2nd bat. 24th regt. thoroughly 'at home' there, after their sojourn of thirteen weeks. The officers and men look fit and ready for any amount of hard work, and as they turn out for fatigues in their red nightcaps and blue 'jumpers' they give a busy and picturesque look to the laager and its surroundings. They are daily waiting for and expecting an order to move to Dundee, to join General Newdigate's column. Should they be kept at Rourke's Drift they tell me their hearts would break, and certainly most will agree with me that there is no regiment in the country more deserving of being sent to the front. In fact, after all they have done for the General Commanding, I don't see how he can keep them back. For many weeks past, assisted by the men of Major Bengough's Native Contingent, they have been engaged on the new fort, 'Melville,' so called after the late lieutenant and adjutant of the 1-24th regiment. It is now completed, and is an oblong fort, flanked with towers, a broad ditch surrounding the walls, built partly of masonry and partly of dry wall. An obstacle of six rows of aloes round and outside the ditch completes a position which, manned by 300 Europeans, could not be taken by thousands of Zulus.

Lieut. Porter, RE., a most affable young officer, has had the entire responsibility of construction, and a more difficult ground to work could not have been chosen. It is composed of huge boulders, heaped together in wild confusion, evidently the result of ice action in the glacial age, reminding one forcibly of the 'morraines to be found at the foot of modern glaciers, upon which the hardest steel instruments fail to have any effect. The fort commands the ponts and drift, and in the distance, eight miles away, the Isandhlwana height shows in bold relief, a constant reminder of the late heart-sickening disaster.

Amongst my rambles I climbed to the top of the Ascarberg; 680 feet above Rorke's Drift, and had an opportunity of examining the country over which the Zulus passed from Isandhlwana to Rorke's Drift. The wagons are still scattered about the former place as they were left on the 22nd January last. I took with me the description given by that first class imposter and romancer Mr. de Witt to the home papers. He states that the distance between the two places is three miles, and that he could see the place where the camp was pitched, and that he saw the battle and heard the firing from the rifles. The facts are that from the highest point of the Ascarberg to Isandhlwana is in a bee line not less than seven miles, that no part of the camping ground is visible, and that he could not have seen the firing, all for the reason that the hill and ridge hide the camp and battle field. As for his having heard musketry fire at that distance; well, all I can say is, it speaks well for the length of his ears. Verb. sap. I fancy he will get a very hearty reception should he ever return to the colony.

Another place that I visited and found of great interest was the cemetery. It is situated at the back of the old laager, and is surrounded by a wall and ditch. The graves, 25 in number, are neatly and regularly laid out side by side, and rose trees and blue gums just planted will, in due time, bloom over and shade the resting-place of these heroes. In the centre is an obelisk, ten feet high, of white granite, standing on a square pedestal, and the names of the men of the 24th regiment who are there buried and the regimental badge are engraved on the sides.

At night everyone sleeps inside the fort, and you may be sure that I felt very secure, as no less than 28 sentries watch from the walls, and besides these, four non-commissioned officers and one officer keep watch throughout the night being relieved every two hours. The officer in command also, Colonel Degacher, C.B., is ever nervously anxious for the safety of his little garrison, and frequently goes round during the night.

I noticed that all the soldiers of the 24th regiment had pieces of bullock hide neatly fastened round the barrels of their rifles to prevent their hands being burnt by rapid firing. It is laced round the wood-work, and has a hole cut out for the back-sight. I give this as a useful hint for their *confrères*. It is not unsightly, and does not interfere with the firer's aim.

An unidentified Natal newspaper, c. May 1879

Umsinga.
(From a Correspondent)

May 14, 1879

...In one of the papers you sent me, was Lieut. Chard's report of the defence of Rorke's Drift. It reads very well after seeing the place in all its bearings, *Punch's* explanation for not having included more of the defenders in the cartoon is good. There is a little soreness felt, I believe, at all the honours having been heaped upon two men. It is said that Dalton is *the* man, who deserved most praise.

A nice civil spoken little non-com, I was with told me all about it. He told me how he himself had shot 'Mr Johnny Zulu,' who was in the act of lighting the thatch...

"The Natal Mercury," May 13th, 1879

A Visit to Rorke's Drift

A private correspondent writes;- "I was at Rorke's Drift yesterday on duty; I started early, before daylight, and got there about half-past nine. It is very similar to the picture that appeared in the Illustrated News. The hill at the back is not so large, and the trees are cut down now. A high loopholed wall has been built all round it; the hospital has disappeared, a portion of the walls being built into the fort. I spent an hour looking over the place in company with a very intelligent non-commissioned officer - one of the defenders. He showed me the place where he shot the Zulu that was trying to light the thatch with a bundle of burning grass on the end of an assegai. The walls of the building are about 12ft high, which accounts for the difficulty they had in setting it on fire. The front of the building has a verandah, and it was in front of this where the celebrated barricade of mealie bags was, and the Zulus never got properly over it. It was very interesting walking round and seeing things. There is a neat graveyard, with a monument of cut free stone built on the spot where the men that fell are buried. It all looks very peaceful and quiet now, and it is hard to realise what once took place. A new fort has been built close to the drift. It is a very fine piece of work, and will be a permanency. Fort Melville it is called. It commands a fine view of the Isandhlwana Hill. I felt strongly tempted to ride and see the latter place. It looks about eight miles, but is rough country. By the road it is 12 miles.

"The Natal Mercury," c. May 1879

The Rorke's Drift Defence.

We have received the following from Mr. Jameson:-

TO THE EDITOR OF THE NATAL MERCURY.

Durban, May 27,1879.

Sir,-The little brochure containing the account of the Rorke's Drift defence, the M.S. of which I hold, has been received with so much favour in its former limited private circulation, that I am induced to believe very many people will be glad to purchase copies if procurable. I have, therefore, placed it in the hands of the printer for republication, with the intention of handing the entire proceeds of the sale to our Mayor, towards forming the nucleus of a fund to purchase some colonial testimonial, to be presented to the survivors of the night of the 22nd January; feeling confident that not only would it be graceful thus to recognise their services, but that it is widely felt by colonists in all districts to be a duty we owe to those who so gallantly and successfully saved our colony from the horrors of an invasion by a horde of savages, flushed with victory and eager for fresh plunder.

Particulars I send for your advertising columns, - I am, &c.

R. JAMESON.

"The Stroud News and Gloucestershire Advertiser," June 13th, 1879

...The Tamar, troopship, Captain Lidell,.....arrived at Spithead late on Sunday evening, bringing home sick and wounded from Zululand...

...Private Hitch, of the 24th Regiment who comes home dangerously wounded, is one of those who, with four others, when surrounded at Rorke's Drift by the Zulus, held the right front of the position and prevented the enemy from sweeping away the small body of men ensconced behind the barricade of biscuit boxes. Hitch and those who supported him were subjected to a heavy fire from the rear left flank and the front; but they maintained their position until they were incapacitated by reason of their wounds from making further active resistance, and then, after having their wounds dressed, they, with the remaining strength left, continued to serve out ammunition to their comrades during the whole of the time that the gallant resistance lasted. Private Hitch, who still wears his right arm in a sling, was unaware of the honour conferred upon him until his arrival home. On being told he, with much emotion exclaimed 'Have they given me the Cross?' On being assured that Her Majesty had been pleased to confer that distinguished recognition of his services upon him the poor fellow was completely overcome.

Private Waters, another hero of the Rorke's Drift engagement, comes home in the Tamar. He secreted himself in a cupboard in the hospital and shot several Zulus as they came in, but, being at last wounded in the right arm, he covered himself with a black cloak and took refuge in the bush, where he remained all night, at times being passed in dangerous proximity by bands of prowling Zulus. Next morning he got safely into camp to receive the congratulations of his friends. The bullet with which Waters was wounded passed into his shoulder, and made its exit at his elbow, and the missile is now saved and prized by him as a memorable memento of the struggle in which he took part. All agree that the defeat of the Zulus, whose approach in such dense masses against the diminutive garrison is described by eyewitnesses as being really appalling, undoubtedly saved the colony of Natal from utter annihilation. The wounded men arriving home from the affair at Rorke's Drift assert that the Zulus did not throw their assegais, but waited until they had chance of getting within stabbing distance, and then used them with deadly effect...

"The Times," c. October 1879

...The hired transport Egypt, Captain Grogan, belonging to the National Steamship Company of Liverpool, arrived at Spithead at 8 o'clock yesterday morning, with the 1st Battalion 24th Regiment, invalids, and time-expired men from South Africa...

...The individual officers who took passage are Major J.R.M. Chard, R.E., V.C., and Surgeon-Major Reynolds, V.C., the heroes of Rorke's Drift;...

...Among the men of the 1st Battalion of the 24th who disembarked were Sergeant Wilson, Lance-Corporal Roy, and Privates Desmond, Payton and Jenkins, who had been to the rear with prisoners, and who returned in time to join with B Company of the 2nd Battalion in the defence of Rorke's Drift...

"The London Gazette," May 2nd, 1879

War Office, May 2, 1879

The Queen has been graciously pleased to signify Her intention to confer the decoration of the Victoria Cross on the undermentioned Officers and Soldiers of Her Majesty's Army, whose claims have been submitted for Her Majesty's approval, for their gallant conduct in the defence of Rorke's Drift, on the occasion of the attack by the Zulus. as recorded against their names, viz.:-

Royal Engineers. - Lieutenant (now Captain and Brevet Major) J. R. M. Chard. 2nd Battalion, 24th Regiment. - Lieutenant (now Captain and Brevet Major) G. Bromhead. - For their gallant conduct at the defence of Rorke's Drift, on the occasion of the attack by the Zulus, on January 22nd and 23rd, 1879.

The Lieutenant-General commanding the troops reports that, had it not been for the fine example and excellent behaviour of these two officers, under the most trying circumstances, the defence of Rorke's Drift post would not have been conducted with that intelligence and tenacity which so essentially characterised it.

The Lieutenant-General adds that its success must, in a great degree, be attributable to the two young officers who exercised the chief command on the occasion in question.

2nd Battalion, 24th Regiment. - Private John Williams. - Private John Williams was posted, with Private Joseph Williams and Private William Horrigan, 1st Battalion, 24th Regiment, in a distant room of the hospital, which they held for more than an hour, so long as they had a round of ammunition left. As communication was, for the time, cut off, the Zulus were enabled to advance and burst open the door. They dragged out Private Joseph Williams and two of the patients, and assegaied them. Whilst the Zulus were occupied with the slaughter of these men, a lull took place, during which Private John Williams, who, with two patients, were the only men now left alive in this ward, succeeded in knocking a hole in the partition, and in taking the two patients into the next ward, where he found Private Hook.

2nd Battalion, 24th Regiment - Private Henry Hook. - These two men together, one man working whilst the other fought and held the enemy at bay with his bayonet, broke through three more partitions, and were thus enabled to bring eight. patients through a small window into the inner line of defence.

2nd Battalion, 24th Regiment. - Private William Jones and Private Robert Jones. - In another ward, facing the hill, Private William Jones and Private Robert Jones defended the post to the last, until six out of the seven patients it contained had been removed. The seventh, Sergeant Maxfield, 2nd Battalion,. 24th Regiment, was delirious from fever. Although they had previously dressed him, they were unable to induce him to move. When Private Robert Jones returned to endeavour to carry him away, he found him being stabbed by the Zulus as he lay on his bed.**2nd Battalion, 24th Regiment. - Corporal William Allen and Private Frederick Hitch.** - It was chiefly due to the courageous conduct of these men that communication with the hospital was kept up at all. Holding together at all costs a most dangerous post, raked in reverse by the enemy's fire from the hill, they were both severely wounded, but, their determined conduct enabled the patients to be withdrawn from the hospital, and, when incapacitated by their wounds from fighting, they continued, as soon as their wounds had been dressed, to serve out ammunition to their comrades during the night.

"The London Gazette," June 17th, 1879

War Office, June 17
Surgeon-Major James Henry Reynolds, Army Medical Department - For his conspicuous bravery, during the attack at Rorke's Drift, on the 22nd and 23rd January, 1879, which he exhibited in his constant attention to the wounded under fire, and in his voluntarily conveying ammunition from the store to the defenders of the Hospital, whereby he exposed himself to a cross-fire from the enemy both in going and returning.

"The London Gazette," November 17th, 1879

War Office, Nov. 17
Acting-Assistant (now Sub-Assistant) Commissary James Langley Dalton, Commissariat and Transport Department. - For his conspicuous gallantry during the attack on Rorke's Drift Post by the Zulus on the night of the 22nd of January, 1879, when he actively superintended the work of defence, and was among the foremost of those who received the first attack at the corner of the hospital, where the deadliness of his fire did great execution, and the mad rush of the Zulus received its first check and where by his cool courage he saved the life of a man of the Army Hospital Corps by shooting the Zulu, who, having seized the muzzle of the man's rifle was in the act of assegaing him.

This officer, to whose energy much of the defence of the place was due, was severely wounded during the contest, but still continued to give the same example of cool courage.

"The London Gazette," December 2nd, 1879

War Office, November 29, 1879
Natal Native Contingent Corporal Schiess...F.C. - For conspicuous gallantry in the defence of Rorke's Drift Post on the night of the 22nd January, 1879, when, in spite of his having been wounded in the foot a few days previously, he greatly distinguished himself when the Garrison were repulsing, with the bayonet, a series of desperate assaults by the Zulus, and displayed great activity and devoted gallantry throughout the defence. On one occasion when the Garrison had retired to the inner line of defence, and the Zulus occupied the wall of mealie bags which had been abandoned, he crept along the wall, without an order, to dislodge a Zulu who was shooting better than usual and succeeded in killing him, and two others, before he, the Corporal, returned to the inner defence.

Casualty Reports

[WO32/7711, The National Archives, (P.R.O.), London]

Compiled from Returns received from various sources from 22nd Jany. to 24th February 1879

Rorke's Drift, 22nd Jany. as reported by the P.M.O.

1/24th Regt.

Pte. J. Waters	Severely wounded - Gunshot thro' arm & shoulder
Pte. Beckett	Dangerously wounded - Assegai penetrating abdomen
Pte. Desmond	Slightly wounded - Gunshot thro' fleshy part of thumb

2/24th Regt.

Sergt. T. Williams	Dangerously wounded - Gunshot left side of chest fracturing ribs. Bullet not lodged.
Corpl. Lyons	Dangerously wounded: Gunshot neck, fracturing spine of vertebrae, ball lodged
Corpl. Allen	Severely wounded: Gunshot thro' shoulder & arm
Pte. Hitch	Dangerously wounded: Gunshot thro' shoulder joint
Pte. Jones	Slightly wounded: Assegai contusion of abdomen
Pte. Tasker	Slightly wounded: Gunshot splinter of ball breaking skin of forehead

Native Contingent

Corpl. Scammell	Dangerously wounded: Gunshot, ball passing in at upper part of R. Shoulder & making exit at L. Shoulder
Pte. Scheiss	Slightly wounded: Gunshot contusion of ankle

Commissariat Dept.

Storekeeper Dalton	Severely wounded: Gunshot thro' fleshy part of shoulder & making exit behind

[signed]
J North Crealock Lieut. Colonel
Asst. Mily. Secretary

Extract from an unidentified Natal newspaper, c. January 1879

Return of Wounded in Action at Rorke's Drift, January 23, 1879

1-24 Private Beckett	Dangerously wounded - Assegai puncturing abdomen, no exit (since dead)
1-24 Private Waters, J.	Severely wounded - Bullet entered arm, exit shoulder
2-24 Sergt. Williams, T.	Dangerously wounded - Bullet breaking ribs, no serious injury to lung
2-24 Corpl. Lyons, J.	Dangerously wounded - Bullet in neck, still unextracted
2-24 716 Corpl Allon, W.	Severely wounded - Bullet in shoulder, extracted
2-24 Private Hitch	Dangerously wounded - Bullet entered shoulder, exit shoulder-blade
2-24 Private Jones	Slightly wounded - Bullet abrasion of abdomen
N. Contingent, Scammen	Dangerously wounded - Bullet entered neck (left side), exit shoulder-blade
N. Contingent Schiss, F.	Slightly wounded - Bullet contusion of ankle
Storekeeper, Dalton	Severely wounded - Bullet wound through muscular and upper part of arm

W. Bellairs, D.A.G.

"The Lancet," July 5th, 1879

Surgical Notes on the Zulu War.
By D. Blair Brown, F.R.C.S. Ed., A.M.D.

THE following cases and observations, apart from the intense interest shown concerning all appertaining to the Zulu war, will, I think, be found of sufficient interest to find space in THE LANCET.

Assegai Wound of Left Ham, - Private J. H. M - , of the 1st Battalion 3rd Regiment Native Contingent, was present on the 12th January at the attack on Sirayo's Kraal. Several prisoners were taken, and were being disarmed. One of them, being irritated by our friendly Kaffirs, tried to force his escape, and, assegai in hand, stabbed right and left at everyone. The patient in the case now being described was one thus injured. A bandage was applied, and he was conveyed to Rorke's Drift for treatment. While there several outbursts of severe hæmorrhage occurred from the wound, and though the bleeding points were searched for by all the surgeons at that camp, it could not be permanently stopped, breaking out again after a day or more, or whenever the local means of arrestment were withdrawn. On the 26th of January he was sent to Helpmakaar, and I found a wound of a regularly punctured nature in the lower end of the left ham, a little above the popliteal space. As there was no bleeding from it I did nothing but order the limb to be kept as quiet as possible. Next day, however, hæmorrhage - which was found by the two civil surgeons who immediately attended to be almost impossible to stop - took place. When I saw him this time his pulse could scarcely be felt, and he had fainted: No further bleeding took place for two days, when it burst forth again. Assisted by Surgeon McGann and Civil Surgeon Beresford, the patient being under the influence of chloroform, I enlarged the wound, to look for the bleeding vessels. Having made the incisions, I found a large cavity filled with coagulated blood extending up the limb and amongst the muscles; compression over the femoral during this procedure was maintained.

On relaxing this after the clot was cleared out numerous points of bleeding were seen, none of which could be seized for torsion or ligature. The patient was again almost pulseless, and his face very pale. Raising the limb, prolonged digital and instrumental pressure all failing, it was agreed that ligature of the femoral was the only remedy left to us. I proceeded at once to do that. On reaching the sheath of the vessel the profunda was found to have a longer course than usual, and to be lying very close to the superficial femoral, both vessels being plainly felt pulsating. On applying pressure with the point of one finger on the profunda branch, I found not a drop of blood escaped at the wound after the withdrawal of the tourniquet from the groin. I therefore adopted the lesser operation, and tied the profunda. The wound healed rapidly, and after the first two days, when he complained of slight uneasiness in the limb, there was nothing else to note.

On the 15th of February he left Helpmakaar for the Base Hospital at Ladisnuth. He is now at his duty in a mounted corps at the front, none the worse for his wound. This patient was one of those in the hospital at Rorke's Drift on the memorable 22nd of January, and managed to hop out from the one building, under fire, to the other. He therefore had four marvellous escapes within a few days - first, that of the stab at Sirayos's kraal; secondly, the escape under fire from the hospital at Rorke's Drift; thirdly, the frequent profuse hæmorrhages; and fourthly, the operation...

...On the 21st January I reached Helpmakaar in medical charge of three companies of the 1st - 24th Regiment, the only men who remained of that regiment after the massacre. On the afternoon of the 22nd I accompanied these men, augmented by about a hundred more, en route to Rorke's Drift, intending to be at Isandhlwana on the 23rd January. Having got within a few miles thereof, we met numerous fugitives flying from the camp, from whom we learnt the fate of the Isandhlwana one, and were told that the place we were going to - Rorke's Drift - was surrounded by the enemy in thousands. We turned back to Helpmakaar and formed an entrenched camp. There I remained in medical charge. The accommodation for the treatment of sick at Rorke's Drift being *nil*, they were all sent to Helpmakaar, as we had the end of a commissariat shed with extemporised beds made of biscuit boxes covered over with empty flour sacks there. The whole of the medical equipment of the column was lost at Isandhlwana, so that ordinary means of treatment were not to be had.

From the fact that the men at Rorke's Drift fought from behind shelter the wounds were all in the upper portion of the body. Those who were killed were hit on the head. In one case the bullet entered at the posterior margin of the sterno-mastoid, near its shoulder end, and, without penetrating the cavity of the chest, made its exit at middle of base of scapula. Another was hit near the bicipital groove of the right humerus, bevelling the bone along its line of flight, and getting exit at lower angle of scapula. One received a bullet at the insertion of the deltoid; the missile was found lying a few inches lower down the bone, and extracted at Rorke's Drift. Mr. Dalton was shot in the right shoulder while forming the "laager." The bullet entered 1 half an inch above middle of clavicle, escaping all the important vessels, and ran down the back, finding an exit at the lowest border of the origin of the trapezius muscle.

In every instance the wounds when seen by me on Jan. 26th were in a sloughy condition. Large masses of purulent matter could be withdrawn with a little pulling by dressing forceps. The wounds were unmistakably made by ordinary round bullets fired from smooth-bored guns. The ease with which most of the bullets were turned aside from their straight course after penetrating can, I think, be accounted for by the fact that they were fired, for such weapons, at considerable range, and the charges of powder must have been limited, as the enemy individually carry but one bullock's horn, transformed into a powder-flask; this is usually all they have. Their fire is described to be very poor, blazing away and only occasionally hitting. It is with the assegai, however, they can do their deadliest work; but this necessitates very close quarters, what is scarcely likely to occur again. The assegais - a lance-shaped piece of steel or iron, on a comparatively thin but well-balanced round stick as a handle are of two kinds; the "throwing" assegais are longer and broader in the blade than the "stabbing" kind. The handles of both also differ; that of the first kind is exceedingly well-balanced, to allow of its flight through the air, which it traverses like an arrow, the broad blade acting the part the feathers do in the other, only at opposite ends of the instruments. The Zulus hold them in their right hand, their fingers clenched round the handle not far from the blade, and bending their forearm at right angles to their arms, with a backward and forward movement they direct with a sudden jerk the instrument upwards into the air, where it is seen coursing like an arrow, and descending in a similar manner. At thirty yards many of them are very accurate in hitting their object. The "stabbing" assegai has a short and stouter handle, has a much smaller and narrower blade, and is attached to the handle by a continuation of the blade in the form of a steel shaft for about half a foot, and there securely fastened. In stabbing they keep the edge very low, making numerous cuts, stabs, and dashes therewith as they approach; suddenly raising the point, they make a direct stab, and, without withdrawing, a rip. It appears to be a thoroughly methodical operation, requiring considerable skill to acquire. It is an error often made to think that, on nearing an enemy, they all, at a certain signal, bend the handles of their long assegais on their knees, and break them short. I am told this does I not take place except when they have no "stabbing," and all "throwing" instruments with them - a circumstance which rarely occurs, as they always keep close to one of the latter as their chief defence.

The wounds, therefore, received from these different proceedings must also differ in character. My late confrere and friend. Surgeon-Major Shepherd, was killed by a thrown assegai just as he was starting from the side of a wounded Natal Carabineer whom he was examining . Trooper Muirhead, of the Carbineers, who was with him at the time informs me that he saw it coming, bent his head down on his horse's neck, and escaped it. Shepherd was close to him, and received it in his back. He at once fell from his horse with a loud exclamation, and was surrounded by Zulus and finished. The depth a thrown assegai will penetrate is great. In stabbing the abdomen appears to be the target they aim at, if possible. Assegai wounds of the extremities I have met with none - except the case already recorded - of any interest, no important vessel having been injured. One officer of the Contingent received one through the calf of his leg, "pinning him to his saddle"; this healed at once, and he hopped about all the time. I simply kept a bandage upon it.

It will, therefore, be readily conceived that severe an numerous case of gunshot injuries are not likely to occur in Zulu warfare as far as we are concerned.

If we have to retreat rapidly, then a wounded man means a dead one, as the enemy converts the one into the other at once. Assegai wounds of regions not immediately fatal generally require but the simplest treatment.

Without medicines, lint, bandages, or any of the usual equipment at Helpmakaar, I had to make use of what I could find. A considerable amount of well-tarred tow was found in a box where some wine bottles were packed. This I used as the dressing for all the wounds, and no case did badly. Water or watery lotions were not used, except the former to wash the skin in the neighbourhood of the injuries. A few fibres of the tow were used as drains in the wounds, and appeared to serve the purpose as well as anything else.

BIBLIOGRAPHY

Published Sources

Abbot, P.E., Recipients of the Distinguished Conduct Medal, 1855-1909, London 1975

Atkinson, C.T., The South Wales Borderers, 24th Foot 1689-1937, Cambridge 1937

Bancroft, J.W., Rorke's Drift, Tunbridge Wells 1988

——————————————-, The Zulu War V.C.'s, Liverpool 1992

Bennett, I.H.W., Eyewitness in Zululand, London 1989

Blair Brown, Surgeon D., Surgical Experiences in the Zulu and Transvaal Wars, London 1882

Child, D., (Ed.), The Zulu War Journal of Col. H. Harford, Pietermaritzburg 1978

Creagh, Sir G.O'M., & Humphries, E.M., The V.C. & D.S.O. , London 1924

Emery, F., The Red Soldier, London 1977

Gordon-Roe, E. The Bronze Cross, London 1945

Greaves, Dr. A.., Rorke's Drift, London 2002

Holme, N., The Silver Wreath - Being the 24th Regiment at Isandlwana and Rorke's Drift, 1879, London 1979

——————————-., The Noble 24th, London 1999

Johnson, B.C., Rorke's Drift and the British Museum: The Life of Henry Hook V.C., London 1986

Knight, I., (Ed.) There Will Be An Awful Row At Home About This, Shoreham by Sea, 1987

——————————————., Queen Victoria's Enemies, Volume 1: Southern Africa, Osprey Men at Arms Series 1989

——————————————., Nothing Remains But to Fight, London 1993

——————————————., By The Orders of the Great White Queen, London 1992

——————————————., Rorke's Drift 1879, London 1996

——————————————., ZULU; The Battles of Isandlwana and Rorke's Drift, London 1992.

——————————————., The Anatomy of the Zulu Army, London, 1995

Laband, J., Fight Us in the Open, Pietermaritzburg 1991

——————————-., Kingdom in Crisis, Pietermaritzburg 1992

Laband, J., & Matthews, J., Isandlwana, Pietermaritzburg 1991

Laband, J.P.C. & Thompson, P.S., Field Guide to the War in Zululand 1879, Pietermaritzburg 1979

Lock, R., Blood on the Painted Mountain, London 1995

Lock, R & Quantrill, P, The Red Book - Natal Press Reports, Anglo Zulu War 1879, South Africa

——————————————————————-, Zulu Victory, The epic of Isandlwana and the Cover-Up, London 2002

Lloyd, W.G., John Williams, V.C., Cwmbran 1993
Lugg, H.C., A Natal Family Looks Back, South Africa, 1970
Lummis, W.C., Padre George Smith of Rorke's Drift, Norwich 1978
Mackinnon, J.P., & Shadbolt, S., The South African Campaign, London 1880
Moodie, D.C.F., Moodie's Zulu War, 1879 (reprinted Capetown 1988)
Morris, D.R., The Washing of the Spears, London 1966
Norris-Newman, C.L., In Zululand with the British throughout the War of 1879, London 1880 (reprinted 1988)
Paton, G., Glennie F., & Penn Symons W., Historical Records of the 24th Regiment, London 1892
Preston, A., (Ed.), The South African Journal of Sir Garnet Wolseley, 1879-80, London 1973
Reynolds Geoffrey, D.M., (Oxon), The Diary of a Civil Surgeon serving with British Army in South Africa during the Zulu War, Dunstroon, Australia 1997
Stevenson, Lee, The Rorke's Drift Doctor, James Henry Reynolds, V.C., and the Defence of Rorke's Drift, Brighton 2001
War Office, Rothwell, J.S.,(compiler), Narrative of Field Operations connected with the Zulu War of 1879, London 1881 (reprinted 1907 & 1989)
Whitton, Lt. Col., F.E., Rorke's Drift, 1979 (reprinted from Blackwoods Magazine)
Author unknown, The World of Adventure, c. 1900

Official Records

United Kingdom

The Royal Archives, Windsor Castle, Berkshire
1. Handwritten account of the defence of Rorke's Drift by Capt & Bvt. Major JRM Chard, V.C., R.E., dated February 21st, 1880
2. Letter from Captain Liddell of H.M.S. Tamar re. the services of Pte. J. Connolly, 2/24th.

The National Archives (Public Record Office), Ruskin Avenue, Kew, London

WO138/3	Confidential Report on the services of Surgeon Lt. Colonel J.H. Reynolds, V.C., Army Medical Staff
WO32 Series	War Office Correspondence: Reports and Diary of Ops from South Africa 1877-78-79, including;-
WO98/4	The Register of the Victoria Cross 1864-1900
WO146/1	Register of the Distinguished Conduct Medal
WO103/13	Queen's Submission Book for the Distinguished Conduct Medal
WO100/48-9-50	South African Campaign medal roll, 1877-8-9
WO97 Series	Soldier's service & discharge Papers 1855-1913
ZJI Series	London Gazette

South Africa
The Brenthurst Library, Johannesburg
Killie Campbell Africana Library, Campbell Collections, University of Natal, Durban
Natal Museum, Pietermaritzburg
Kwa-Zulu Natal Archives Depot, Pietermaritzburg
Cape Archives Depot, Capetown
Transvaal Archives Depot, Johannesburg
Local History Museum, Durban

Newspapers & Periodicals
Ireland:
The Irish Times, Irish Independent.

Britain:
Daily Mail, Daily Mirror, The Graphic, Illustrated London News, London Gazette, News of the World, Sunday Express, The Times, The Weeks News; Aldershot News, Brecon County Times, Brighton Examiner, Bristol Observer, Cambrian, Cardiff Times, Cornish & Devon Post, Hereford Journal, Hereford Times, Manchester Evening Chronicle, Dorking & Leatherhead County Post, Free Press of Monmouthshire, Manchester Weekly Post, Merthyr Express, Montgomery County Times, Monmouthshire Beacon, Northern Mail, North Devon Herald, Oldham Weekly Chronicle, Pontypool Free Press, Preston Guardian, Somerset Guardian, South Wales Argus, South Wales Daily Star, South Wales Weekly Telegram, Stroud News & Gloucestershire Advertiser,Western Daily Mail, Western Daily Mercury,

South Africa:
Cape Argus, Cape Times, Eastern Province Herald, Natal Mercury, Natal Witness, The Times of Natal, Natal Colonist

Journals & miscellaneous publications
Punch, The Royal Magazine, The Strand Magazine, "V.C." Magazine, Chums. The Listener, The Farmer, The Prompter.
The Lancet, Medical Press and Circular, The British Medical Journal; Army Medical Department Annual Reports, Army Medical Services Magazine, Journal of the Army Medical Corps, Royal Engineers Journal, South Wales Borderers Regtl. Journal;
'Soldiers of the Queen,' the Journal of the Victorian Military Society, Journal of the Anglo-Zulu War Historical Society, Journal of the Anglo-Zulu War Research Society.

INDEX